Immigration and Membership Politics in Western Europe

Why are traditional nation-states newly defining membership and belonging? In the twenty-first century, several Western European states have attached obligatory civic integration requirements as conditions for citizenship and residence, which include language proficiency, country knowledge, and value commitments for immigrants. This book examines this membership policy adoption and adaptation through both medium-N analysis and three paired comparisons to argue that while there is convergence in instruments, there is also significant divergence in policy purpose, design, and outcomes. To explain this variation, this book focuses on the continuing, dynamic interaction of institutional path dependency and party politics. Through paired comparisons of Austria and Denmark, Germany and the United Kingdom, and the Netherlands and France, this book illustrates how variations in these factors – as well as a variety of causal processes – produce divergent civic integration policy strategies that, ultimately, preserve and anchor national understandings of membership.

Sara Wallace Goodman is an assistant professor in the Department of Political Science at the University of California, Irvine. She has previously held a postdoctoral fellowship at Maastricht University, in association with the EUDO Citizenship Observatory. Her work has been published in *World Politics*, *West European Politics*, *Political Studies*, and the *Journal of Ethnic and Migration Studies* and has received awards from the European Politics and Society Section and the Migration and Citizenship Section of the American Political Science Association as well as from the British Politics Group.

Immigration and Membership Politics in Western Europe

SARA WALLACE GOODMAN

CAMBRIDGE
UNIVERSITY PRESS

CAMBRIDGE
UNIVERSITY PRESS

32 Avenue of the Americas, New York NY 10013-2473, USA

Cambridge University Press is part of the University of Cambridge.

It furthers the University's mission by disseminating knowledge in the pursuit of education, learning and research at the highest international levels of excellence.

www.cambridge.org
Information on this title: www.cambridge.org/9781107635852

First published 2014
First paperback edition 2016

A catalogue record for this publication is available from the British Library

Library of Congress Cataloguing in Publication data
Goodman, Sara Wallace, 1979–
Immigration and membership politics in Western Europe / Sara Wallace Goodman.
pages cm
ISBN 978-1-107-06314-3 (hardback)
1. European Union countries – Emigration and immigration – Government policy. 2. Immigrants – Cultural assimilation – European Union countries. 3. Social integration – Government policy – European Union countries. 4. Citizenship – European Union countries. I. Title.
JV7590.G66 2014
325.4–dc23

2014027831

ISBN 978-1-107-06314-3 Hardback
ISBN 978-1-107-63585-2 Paperback

Dedicated to
my parents and husband

Contents

List of figures — *page* viii
List of tables — ix
Acknowledgments — x

Introduction — 1
1 Membership matters: concept precision and state identity — 16
2 Identifying empirical variation in civic integration policies — 37
3 Explaining civic integration diversity: citizenship legacy and government orientation — 65
4 Examining context: Austria and Denmark — 90
5 Examining politics: Germany and the United Kingdom — 118
6 Examining interactions and processes: the Netherlands and France — 161
7 External dimensions of civic integration: requirements for entry — 202
Conclusion: the anchoring of citizenship — 226

Appendix I Common European Framework of Reference (CEFR) on languages — 243
Appendix II Other indices for civic integration policy and calculated correlations — 244
Appendix III Citizenship indicator scores — 247
References — 249
Index — 265

Figures

1.1 Conceptual hierarchy of membership *page* 19
2.1 Distribution of CIVIX scores today 54
2.2 Changes in mandatory integration requirements 55
2.3 Relationship between CIVIX (1997, today) and ICRI (1990, 2008) 58
2.4 Relationship between CIVIX today and MIPEX 2010 60
3.1 Citizenship policy score clustering across and within indices 81
3.2 A disaggregated citizenship policy view using CITLAW 2011 83
3.3 Intersections of citizenship context and government orientation at civic integration policy adoption (t_0) and first adaptation (t_1) 86
4.1 Type of fulfillment of the integration agreement, 2006–June 2009 101
5.1 Acquisition of citizenship in Germany, 2000–2011 138
6.1 Acquisition of citizenship in the Netherlands, 2000–2011 180
6.2 Acquisition of French citizenship by category 199
7.1 Partner choice of Turks and Moroccans, 2007 214

Tables

2.1	Civic Integration Policy Index (CIVIX) scoring in 1997	*page* 49
2.2	Civic Integration Policy Index (CIVIX) scoring today	50
4.1	Fulfillment of Integration Agreement in Austria, 2003–2010	101
4.2	Success rates for naturalization test in 2007, by state	102
4.3	Applications for permanent residence in Denmark, 2003–2009	114
4.4	Refusals of naturalization due to lack of Danish language proficiency, 2001–2008	115
5.1	Pass rates for integration course and language requirement for permanent residence in Germany, 2005–2011	136
5.2	Number of grants of settlement by integration requirement	156
5.3	Integration reasons for refusal of British citizenship, 2002–2011	157
6.1	Pass rates percentages for Dutch naturalization exam by nationality, 2003–2007 average	179
6.2	Full integration exam results, Jan–July 2012	181
6.3	Pass rates for integration exam components, 2007–2009	182
6.4	Participation and success rate of French language evaluation sessions, 2008	198
7.1	Results of civic integration from abroad for first-time takers, Jan.–Jun. 2008	217
7.2	Pass rate of civic integration from abroad for first-time takers by nationality	218
7.3	Change in family-based migration by year	219
7.4	Migration inflow by type, percentage distribution for 2006	220

Acknowledgments

Anyone who knows me is already aware – or could probably guess – that the "Acknowledgments" section is my favorite part of any book. Not merely does it contextualize an academic work among a cast of intellectual influences, it primarily personalizes the author behind the work. And, at my Midwestern core, I am, alas, a "people person." To wit, I can say without qualification that this work would not be what it is, nor would I be who I am, were it not for the brilliant and helpful people with whom I have been fortunate enough to cross paths. I hope this acknowledgment successfully expresses my sincerest appreciation, though I fear mere words may be insufficient to convey the full spectrum of my gratitude.

The first version of this project was as my doctoral dissertation in the Government Department at Georgetown University. My work benefitted from the helpful advice and careful reading provided by Susan Martin and R. Kent Weaver. Kathleen McNamara not only helped me see the greater picture but taught me how to proceed confidently into the next stages of my academic career. The constellations also aligned to place me in a cohort of truly exceptional graduate students. In particular, Ariel Ahram and Gregory Baldi were there to give detailed and insightful comments as well as emotional support from this project's earliest stages to the final revisions and editing. I continue to benefit from their brilliant minds and count myself lucky to have them as lifelong friends. Anthony Martinez is responsible for planting the seed in my mind that it was possible to write a dissertation on this topic in the first place, and connected me to key people that could help me make it happen. Lastly, I struggle whether to include Marc Morjé Howard in the "advisor" category or in the "friend" category. He served as my dissertation advisor and provided invaluable direction, inspiration, much-needed levity, and sometimes unsolicited copyediting in this capacity, but our friendship has long outlasted that temporal relationship.

After graduate school, the book took shape during a postdoctoral fellowship at Maastricht University and was completed at the University of California, Irvine. I thank both of these institutions for their support. At UCI in particular, I owe much gratitude to Daniel Brunstetter and Diana Kapiszewski for their open doors and solidarity. Diana brought clarity to early steps. Daniel was, and is, ever-patient and thoughtful in feedback. Moreover, he knows how I take my coffee. I think that says it all.

In addition to the two anonymous reviewers of Cambridge University Press, whose incisive comments improved the work immeasurably, I would also like to express thanks to the following people for their notes and thoughts – large and small – at various stages of this process: Michael Bacon, Rainer Bauböck, Erik Bleich, Dimitris Christopoulos, Eva Erbøll, Andrew Geddes, Simon Green, Kees Groenendijk, Randall Hansen, Christian Joppke, Willem Maas, Per Mouritsen, Will Somerville, and Ricky Van Oers. Silvia Adamo and Saskia Bonjour provided careful readings and helpful thoughts on case studies. Maarten Vink was instrumental in helping me work through some difficult issues. Turns out all you need to do is trap someone in your car along the Pacific Coast Highway during rush hour traffic to get some real work done. My work also benefitted from feedback at countless conferences and presentations, but in particular at the University of California, San Diego and the University of Oxford.

The multi-country fieldwork required to collect data for this project would not have been possible without the kindness of scholars and friends, including: the late Sir Bernard Crick, Dina Kiwan, Maxwell Keyte, Patrick Weil, as well as the hospitality of Solonge and Ionel Soloman in Paris and Nina Huygen in Amsterdam. Also, thank you to the many civil servants who have chosen to remain nameless but deserve acknowledgment nonetheless.

Thank you to Lew Bateman, my editor at Cambridge University Press, for his equal balance of optimism and insight. In particular, Shaun Vigil suffered through my gentle nudges and incessant questions with earnest patience. Thank you also to Sunita Jayachandran, David Morris, and to the copy-editor, who faced a Sisyphean task and is forever my hero. Here would also be an appropriate space to thank the Cambridge University Press and Routledge for allowing me to adapt, but in some cases, reprint ideas presented in previously published material.

I am sorry if I forgot anyone (but – rest assured – the guilt will haunt me forever . . .). I should also add that any remaining and inevitable errors are entirely my own.

Finally, this book would never have been here without my friends and family. I have accrued a sizable debt by drawing on their love and support, a debt so large I fear I may never be able to pay it down. My big brother, Jacob, generously drove me to the library every day on his way to work and proofread every chapter of my dissertation. He always generated enthusiasm and a smile when I could not. My emotional health would not have been preserved if it were not for my best friends, Missy Newhouse and Saul Kaufman, who exemplify the concepts of empathy and compassion. Thank you to my wonderful in-laws, Howard and Nicole Goodman, who went above and beyond the call of duty. Whether housing me during my field work in London, picking me up from the tube station with alacrity, or driving me from England to the Netherlands – to name but a few examples – I am incredibly grateful and humbled by their love and generosity.

To my parents, Roni and Benjamin Wallace, no words do justice. My mom may have not directly labored on this project but she suffered equally, absorbing my frustrations as her own, celebrating my triumphs, and supporting me at each mile in this marathon. I strive every day to be that kind of mother to my child. My father, Dr. Daddy, not only provided the inspiration, motivation, and occasional positive reinforcement to get this book done, he extended unwavering confidence in my ability. Dad – I think often about the extreme circumstances your parents went through, and the gifts of safety, freedom, and education America extended to the Wallace family. These gifts allowed so many of us to end up in academia, and while it might sound cheesy, I am honored to play but a small role in that new tradition. To my husband, Adam Goodman, I owe the greatest debt of all. "The blood of the covenant is thicker than the water of the womb." In other words, he volunteered to take me on, as it were, and with that choice all the frustration and trials that come with being the spouse of an academic. Adam – I thank you for your steadfast patience, optimism, understanding, support, forgiveness, and energy. You are the current that keeps my boat moving in the right direction. Finally, to my greatest joy – my son Micah – I started this book for many reasons but I finished it for one: you. Now, let's go blow some bubbles . . .

Introduction

What flower is traditionally worn by British people on Remembrance Day? Where do you register the birth of a child in the Netherlands? When can a political party be banned in Germany? These are examples of real questions that have appeared in national integration exams in the respective Western European states. They reflect a range in test content, including cultural knowledge, practical information on day-to-day activity, and an understanding of the rule of law. More than mere trivia, being able to correctly answer these questions in the national language determines whether an immigrant can acquire citizenship or long-term residence. Therefore, preparing for an exam plays a key role in immigrant integration, while successfully passing it is decisive for obtaining political membership.

Assessing language proficiency and knowledge of the country and its values are relatively new strategies for promoting integration and regulating membership inclusion in Western Europe. They represent the cornerstone of a new policy known as "civic integration." This concept is the embodiment of a belief that active and productive participation by immigrants in society and the labor market is possible through their acquiring a set of "citizen-like," or civic, skills that include speaking the language of the host country, having knowledge of the country's history, culture, and rules, and understanding and following the liberal-democratic values that underscore their new home. In other words, civic integration policies uniquely express the idea that successful incorporation into a host society rests not only on employment (economic integration) and civic engagement (political integration), but also on individual commitment to characteristics typifying national citizenship, i.e., full membership in society. Civic integration policy promotes these characteristics through the use of new assessment tools such as integration tests, courses, and contracts. These instruments serve as gatekeepers, where the path of transitioning from an outsider to an insider is marked by these mandatory integration requirements as a condition for obtaining various legal statuses.

This points to a paradoxical dimension of civic integration: immigrants – sometimes both new and old – are *required* to obtain these skills of autonomy. Immigrants enter into a metaphorical (or, in some cases, physical) contract with the state, whereby the former has an obligation to integrate, while the latter sets standards and defines avenues for doing so. Without completion of civic requirements, immigrants are ineligible to obtain citizenship, permanent and long-term residence permits, and in some cases, entry and permits for family reunification. This dimension – promoting positive skills through sanctions – has imbued civic integration with a particularly negative connotation. Scholars have referred to these practices as an instance of "repressive liberalism,"[1] later modified to "illiberal liberalism,"[2] as well as the anchor of a "restrictive backlash" of obligations against the expansion of rights and liberalization typifying citizenship policy change in the 1990s. Setting aside normative implications, however, the tethering of new integration requirements to different legal stages indisputably secures a new, closer role for the state in promoting and, indeed, ensuring integration. Policymakers play a key role in defining the content of (a) new identity, and civil servants ensure adherence to these new norms where assessment is largely facilitated by state institutions or contracted proxies.

Yet civic integration is significant not merely because new requirements impact the immigrant experience of settling in a new society, in which the state plays a closer role, but ultimately because these requirements redefine what it is that immigrants are asked to join. By highlighting shared rules of society and concepts of belonging, states are articulating (some for the very first time) concrete and, in principle, accessible definitions of what it means to "be British" or "Dutch" or "German." In this, civic integration represents the latest iteration of the ongoing project of nation-building. I label this most recent articulate of belonging as "state identity."[3] In contrast to national identity, forged in the heyday of nationalism to justify distinct statehood projects by underlining "sameness" in groups, state identity promotes "togetherness" among different groups, where individuals can join the larger national community through initiative and commitment and not resemblance to inherited or ascriptive attributes. This new functional identity is reflected in the content of integration courses and exams, where immigrants are asked to obtain an understanding of political institutions and learn values of

[1] Christian Joppke, "Beyond national models: Civic integration policies for immigrants in Western Europe," *West European Politics* 30, no. 1 (2007), 2.

[2] Christian Joppke, "Transformation of immigrant integration in Western Europe: Civic integration and antidiscrimination policies in the Netherlands, France, and Germany," *World Politics* 59, no. 2 (2007), 268.

[3] While, in principle, civic integration foments a civic identity, I adopt the term "state identity" to avoid conflation with the civic vs. ethnic paradigm of nationalism in drawing a contrast to national identity. Though there are overlaps (see Chapter 1), temporal differences require conceptual distinction as even national identity created out of civic nationalism (e.g., France) adopts civic integration strategies to define contemporary membership.

political liberalism (from the German test: "What is the function of regular elections in a democracy?"), as well as acquire information for everyday life, such as how to contact a doctor, obtain a prescription, enroll a child at school, volunteer, etc., prominent in both the Dutch and British exams. History is emphasized for the purposes of understanding the origins of political institutions, practices, and contemporary culture, not to establish religious or ethnic criteria for community. Though there are clear overlaps in content of national and state identity, showing that these two identities are not mutually exclusive and are concomitant in time, state identity creates contemporary possibilities of membership for immigrants where national identity does not.

The difference between state identity and national identity is particularly visible in the orientation and audience of civic integration requirements. Specifically, we see the promotion of civic *qua* citizen-like values and skills to decidedly non-citizen stages. The term civic integration is the English translation of the Dutch *inburgering*, which appears at the heart of the primogenitary 1998 *Wet Inburgering Nieuwkomers* (subsequently referred to as WIN), translated as The Newcomers Civic Integration Act. *Inburgering* is a verbal noun, fusing the concept of citizen (*burger*) with the process or performance of becoming (indicated by the suffix *-ing*). Marie-Claire Foblets succinctly interprets *inburgering* as "citizenization."[4] But, importantly, this is distinct from naturalization, the process whereby eligible immigrants become citizens. "Citizenization" is the promotion of participation-enabling skills among a variety of *non-citizen* populations, from persons seeking citizenship to immigrants seeking entry and permanent residence. Achieving civic integration milestones, therefore, establishes state identity among persons both in *and* outside of citizenship.

While it is not unique for traditional countries of immigration to forge identity with the outsider in mind,[5] the introduction of language, society knowledge, and value requirements has been among the most visible if not the most significant of the policy changes for addressing the aggregate impact of mass immigration to Western Europe. States as diverse as Germany, the UK, Denmark, France, the Netherlands, Austria, Greece, Italy, and Luxemburg, are all strong practitioners of civic integration, through tests, courses, interviews, etc. in order to exhibit language skills and knowledge in exchange for legal status acquisition. In their adoption, we witness the fundamental transformation of the European nation-state from passive labor importer (in other words, a country that merely receives immigrants) into a country of immigration, where "the nation" is treated as a form of illiberal particularism and immigrant-related

4 Marie-Claire Foblets, "Legal aspects of the multicultural society. Tensions and challenges for policy making," in *New Citizens, New Policies? Developments in diversity policy in Canada and Flanders*, ed. Leen d'Haenens, et al. (Gent, Belgium: Academia Press, 2006), 89–104.

5 The United States, for example, has practiced assessment of language/literacy and civic knowledge for the better part of a century.

diversity – for better or worse – assists in and serves as the catalyst for defining criteria for national membership and belonging.

This book is not the first examination of civic integration in Western Europe; to describe immigration and citizenship scholars as preoccupied with civic integration would be an understatement. In political theory, there has never been more interest in reconciling multicultural realities with liberalism.[6] Perhaps, as a result, examining the role of the state in managing ethnic diversity vis-à-vis civic integration has largely proceeded in normative not empirical assessment. Among descriptive work, there have been volumes dedicated to detailing, categorizing, and comparing new policies.[7] Surprisingly, however, none have puzzled over the empirical *diversity* of civic integration policy design or have any presented systematic, comparative explanations for policy variation. In fact, in one account, Christian Joppke strangely dismisses this variety altogether, stating in the same breath that "despite obvious national variation in the scope and level of restrictiveness of civic integration policies across Europe, a focus on 'obligation' (and reverse de-emphasis on 'rights') is a shared feature of all of them"[8] and, therefore, "the notion of national models no longer makes sense, if it ever did."[9] As such, an overwhelming academic consensus has settled on identifying the empirical landscape as one of widespread and restrictive convergence, accounting for a uniform,

[6] A small sample includes Rainer Bauböck and Christian Joppke, eds., *How Liberal are Citizenship Tests?*, vol. 2010/41, EUI Working Papers (Florence, Italy: Robert Schuman Centre for Advanced Studies, EUI, 2010); Amitai Etzioni, "Citizenship in a communitarian perspective," *Ethnicities* 11, no. 3 (2011), 336–349; Christian Joppke, *Citizenship and Immigration* (Immigration & Society series) (Cambridge; Malden, MA: Polity, 2010); Dora Kostakopoulou, "The anatomy of civic integration," *Modern Law Review* 73, no. 6 (2010), 933–958; Phil Triadafilopoulos, "Illiberal means to liberal ends? Understanding recent immigrant integration policies in Europe," *Journal of Ethnic and Migration Studies* 37, no. 6 (2011), 861–880; Liav Orgad, "Illiberal liberalism: Cultural restrictions on migration and access to citizenship in Europe," *American Journal of Comparative Law* 58, no. 1 (2010), 53–105; Keith Banting and Will Kymlicka, "Is there really a retreat from multiculturalism policies? New evidence from the multiculturalism policy index," *Comparative European Politics* 11, no. 5 (2013), 577–598; Jeanine Klaver and A. W. M. Odé, *Civic Integration and Modern Citizenship: The Netherlands in perspective* (Groningen: Europa Law Publishing, 2009).

[7] See Anita Böcker and Tineke Strik, "Language and knowledge tests for permanent residence rights: Help or hindrance for integration?," *European Journal of Migration and Law* 13, no. 2(2011), 157–184; Elspeth Guild, Kees Groenendijk, and Sergio Carrera, eds., *Illiberal Liberal States: Immigration, citizenship, and integration in the EU* (Farnham, Surrey; Burlington, VT: Ashgate, 2009); Ricky van Oers, Eva Ersbøll, and Theodora Kostakopoulou, *A Re-definition of Belonging? : Language and integration tests in Europe* (Boston: Martinus Nijhoff Publishers, 2010); Tineke Strik et al., "Synthesis Report," in *The INTEC Project: Integration and naturalisation tests: The new way to European citizenship* (Nijmegen, the Netherlands: Centre for Migration Law, Radboud University, 2010); Ricky van Oers, *Deserving Citizenship: Citizenship tests in Germany, the Netherlands and the United Kingdom* (Martinus Nijhoff Publishers, 2013).

[8] Joppke, "Beyond national models: Civic integration policies for immigrants in Western Europe," 14.

[9] Ibid.: 2.

"civic turn"[10] as a shared response to large-scale demographic change,[11] the general presence of an "integration crisis,"[12] indicators of "integration failure," including unemployment and welfare state dependence,[13] the "rightist turn of the political climate,"[14] elite consensus over the idea of civic integration,[15] and shifts in the welfare state from public to private accountability.[16] These studies provide important insight on the background conditions in which change is likely to take place, but not into why states ultimately design what we see as quite different policy configurations. Civic integration requirements significantly vary in terms of *design* (how requirements are organized), *scope* (which legal categories are targeted), *sequencing* (the ordering of requirements), and, as this book primarily aims to show, purpose.

Building upon this state of the literature, this book seeks to make three central contributions to our existing understanding of the increasingly prolific practice of mandatory integration politics in Europe as a contemporary practice of nation-building. First, it *identifies and examines variation* in civic integration policy in Western Europe. European states face common pressures to articulate a coherent identity in the face of immigrant-related diversity and to define avenues for inclusion for these now-permanent populations. Navigating out of membership problems may involve similar, obligatory instruments, but the case studies in this book show how states design these instruments as part of different strategies to address different problems.

The second significant contribution is in *providing an explanation* for what we see as meaningful empirical diversity. I argue that missing from these aforementioned explanations for integration policy adoption – aside from the mischaracterization of the civic integration phenomenon as convergent – is the existing institutional context that enables actors to interpret significant but ultimately indeterminate variables, like influx, politics, or welfare state realignment. Specifically, existing approaches do not account for inherited citizenship

[10] This phrase first appears in Per Mouritsen, "Political responses to cultural conflict: Reflections on the ambiguities of the civic turn," in *Constituting Communities. Political solutions to cultural conflict*, ed. Per Mouritsen and Knud Erik Jørgensen (London: Palgrave, 2008), 1–30.

[11] Joppke, "Transformation of immigrant integration in Western Europe: Civic integration and antidiscrimination policies in the Netherlands, France, and Germany," 245–46.

[12] Ibid.: 243; Böcker and Strik, "Language and knowledge tests for permanent residence rights: Help or hindrance for integration?," 166.

[13] Joppke, "Beyond national models: Civic integration policies for immigrants in Western Europe," 6.

[14] Ibid.: 7; Ruud Koopmans, Ines Michalowski, and Stine Waibel, "Citizenship rights for immigrants: National political processes and cross-national convergence in Western Europe, 1980–2008," *American Journal of Sociology* 117, no. 4 (2012), 1232.

[15] Joppke, "Transformation of immigrant integration in Western Europe: Civic integration and antidiscrimination policies in the Netherlands, France, and Germany," 244; S.A. Bonjour, "Governing diversity. Dutch political parties' preferences on the role of the state in civic integration policies," *Citizenship Studies* 16, nos. 6-7 (2013), 837–851.

[16] Joppke, *Citizenship and Immigration*, 150–51.

policy (that is, the relative ease or difficulty with which immigrants obtain citizenship) as a politically consequential structure for the politics that seek to alter or reify it. Not only does citizenship give formal "institutional expression to the state's prerogative of inclusion and exclusion,"[17] but it also leads state actors to different understandings of how to perceive and repair membership problems. In other words, new civic requirements in traditionally restrictive (exclusive) citizenship states necessarily address different challenges – and produce different effects – than new civic requirements in traditionally liberal (inclusive) citizenship states. Therefore, a mandatory civics test or language course that may be restrictive in one context could enable integration in another. This institutional setting then provides a meaningful context for a more traditional account of membership policy change that focuses on preferences of the party in power, where right parties pursue restriction and left parties pursue liberalization.[18]

My central argument is that civic integration policies are crafted as part of different policy strategies to address different problems of membership, defined by inherited citizenship policy and extant political preferences of the party in power that seeks to change or fortify these approaches. Existing citizenship policy – interchangeably referred to here as policy legacy or inherited policy – not only reflects formal opportunities for political inclusion and exclusion but also defines the parameters of the debate in which policy actors propose and implement change. The second condition – ideological orientation of government – recognizes that likelihood for continuity or change depends not merely on the context in which policymaking plays out, but also on the preferences of the policymakers.

To examine this more closely, I explain diversity in membership strategies based on the interaction of existing restrictive or liberal citizenship policy starting points and politics, which seek to change or maintain those initial policy positions. This dynamic approach builds upon existing insights on the various means by which politics produce citizenship change, noting the agenda-setting role played by far-right parties, policy gains through campaigns, coalition partnership, opposition pressure, etc., but integrates an institutional perspective to highlight the different contexts in which these politics play out. In states with restrictive (exclusive) citizenship, where opportunities to naturalize are already limited and rightist governments in power identify no interest to break this practice, membership requirements serve to continue and retrench existing citizenship postures. In this scenario, permanent residence may become a durable alternative membership status – a type of ancillary, demi-citizenship. On the other hand, in restrictive states where leftist governments are predicted to have a

[17] Randall Hansen and Patrick Weil, eds., *Towards a European Nationality: Citizenship, immigration and nationality law in the EU* (London: Palgrave-Macmillan, 2001), 1.

[18] On this, see Christian Joppke, "Citizenship between de- and re-ethnicization," *European Journal of Sociology* 44, no. 3 (2003), 429–458; Marc Morjé Howard, *The Politics of Citizenship in Europe* (Cambridge: Cambridge University Press, 2009).

significant interest to liberalize, civic integration policies represent more contained, or limited, change, where government views are modulated to maintain electoral competitiveness or bargains are struck to stay in power in a restrictive policy environment. In sum, this negotiated procedure may soften initial restriction but not to the extent that liberal proponents hope. In both instances, where citizenship remains closed off, a strong focus of integration and immigration occur at both the stages of permanent residence and citizenship, thereby establishing a significant chain of conditionality to full legal incorporation.

In liberal (inclusive) citizenship regimes, however, states pursue fundamentally different objectives in adopting civic integration. Where left governments are not predicted to pursue restriction – and face no political pressure to do so – changes that introduce new membership requirements reify an existing liberal orientation, enriching citizenship by encouraging more participation and incentivizing naturalization of long-term residents. In other words, where citizenship is already accessible, the challenge of membership is primarily one of achieving incorporation and defining an accessible civic identity in multicultural states. Finally, liberal citizenship states in which governments on the right seek to pursue restriction may use integration requirements to constitute that new restriction, but like restrictive regimes with liberalizing governments, the intensity of change will be contained, resulting from self-modulation or negotiation. In both of these scenarios, costly alteration to the fundamental parameters of naturalization establishes instead equivalence between permanent residence and citizenship whereby statuses are, by and large, indistinguishable from one another.

The promotion of membership through civic integration is a discrete phenomenon, limited to advanced democratic systems in Europe and traditional immigrant receiving states (e.g., the United States, Canada, and Australia). However, limiting analysis to Western Europe provides sufficient variation to test convergence claims and other endogenous pressures. In testing existing theories for citizenship policy and providing important modifications to those predictions that take into account the unique nature of membership requirements, the comparative case studies included in the book demonstrate how similar policy instruments can yield different effects where they are bound by different institutional parameters. Thus, while civic integration is largely confined to Europe, this observation is generalizable to cases of citizenship change beyond the continent, and potentially to other policy areas, in that it illustrates the importance of context for assessing convergence claims, while highlighting the value-added of detailed, comparative case study analysis.

Finally, after identifying variation in civic integration policy as well as the factors that produce those outcomes, this book's third major contribution is in *providing important confirmatory evidence for the continued relevance of national citizenship* in contemporary nation-states, against faddish postnational, supranational and transnational predictions that say otherwise. If there is a common theme underlying these policies, it is that of states employing the informal and identity-providing ties of membership to fortify citizenship in a new context of ethnic diversity and fiscal constriction. Moreover, this is achieved through the innovation of state identity, not the reinvigoration of national identity. In the end, new requirements do not change or signal a departure from national citizenship but anchor and strengthen it. Despite predictions that "distinct national models of dealing with immigrants are giving way to convergent politics of civic integration,"[19] this book shows how European states are using new tools to address national membership problems, thereby perpetuating national differences in membership. If anything, new requirements show the truly adaptive and resilient nature of the nation-state in the twenty-first century. Large-scale immigration in the postwar period has disrupted the European myth of the homogenous nation-state, forcing Europeans to rethink what it means to be a member of the core group. Through the innovation of state identity, new civic requirements articulate clear definitions for belonging and lay out arbitrary steps for outsiders to become insiders in principle, if not always in practice, without fundamentally altering the parameters of what the state already possesses.

Methodologically, I approach these three objectives with a research design that uses a medium-N sample to identify patterns and variation in civic integration policy, but employ in-depth case studies and a series of paired comparisons to examine the interacting effects of citizenship policy starting points and politics. I include six case studies in total in order to provide typical, diverse, as well as influential cases of civic integration adoption.[20] Cases are paired in order to illustrate the importance of condition interactions, where citizenship legacy can induce differently oriented governments to pursue similar membership policy design (Chapter 4), where differences in citizenship steer similarly oriented governments to policy divergence (Chapter 5), and where process of causal change can yield differences of outcome despite similarity of conditions (Chapter 6). I use a variety of evidence in these case studies to observe causal processes and elucidate mechanisms for how institutional starting points and politics yield different membership strategies, including primary legislation, government and non-governmental organization (NGO) reports, interviews, as well as the vast secondary literature on civic integration policies by area experts, which provides hefty descriptive content but little analysis. Each case study examines both policy output and outcomes (effects), in order to fully characterize civic integration policy strategy and variation across states.

[19] Joppke, "Transformation of immigrant integration in Western Europe: Civic integration and antidiscrimination policies in the Netherlands, France, and Germany," 243. Klaver and Ode also argue that "countries with very different traditions with regard to immigration and integration issues have resorted to similar policies" in Klaver and Odé, *Civic Integration and Modern Citizenship: The Netherlands in perspective*, 4.

[20] For more on techniques of case selection, see Jason Seawright and John Gerring, "Case selection techniques in case study research: A menu of qualitative and quantitative options," *Political Research Quarterly* 61, no. 2 (2008), 297–98.

The remainder of this introduction looks more closely at existing work on civic integration policies, identifying some problems that require attention and discussion before analysis can proceed. Finally, I present the organization of the book by summarizing individual chapters.

CHARTING A NEW COURSE FOR CIVIC INTEGRATION STUDIES AND ANALYSIS

The study of civic integration tells us much about existing membership problems in citizenship practices and concepts of belonging, and analysis of policy adoption sheds critical light on perceived deficiencies of existing citizenship approaches as well as how states adapt to new conditions to maintain control over nation-building. The importance of studying civic integration is reflected in the many articles, edited volumes, and policy reports comparing these new state practices. Yet while this burgeoning research has unearthed a bevy of important facts on policies, detailing specific nuances of each policy design from price to targeted population to test content, the singular focus on ideational convergence – and consequently, relegation of policy diversity to an afterthought or minor detail of the civic integration phenomenon – has yielded a series of problematic observations that have been concretized as *prima facie* claims. These biases create problems for concept validity, i.e., for defining what is a civic integration policy and what is not, which then creates problems for measurement and comparison. These problems require acknowledgment and discussion before analysis can proceed and include, but are not limited to: (1) interpretation of restriction; (2) a lack of acknowledged policy differentiation; and, (3) differences of interpretation over what civic integration requirements represent. I would argue that these problems largely proceed from the fact that existing work is almost entirely descriptive, identifying patterns and drawing conclusions without attempting comparative analysis of causes or outcomes. Or, what there is in terms of analysis is largely relegated to concerns of effects of civic integration on multiculturalism and other integration models, not citizenship and legal status.[21]

I. *Interpretation of restriction:* The first problem is that because obligations are *required* by definition, they should be interpreted as synonymous with a restrictive change; that is, more requirements equal more barriers.[22] Viewed

[21] For example, see Keith Banting and Will Kymlicka, " Is there really a retreat from multiculturalism policies? New evidence from the multiculturalism policy index," *Comparative European Politics* 11, no. 5 (2013), 577–598; Will Kymlicka, "The rise and fall of multiculturalism? New debates on inclusion and accommodation in diverse societies," *International Social Science Journal* 61, no. 199 (2010), 97–112; Christian Joppke, "The retreat of multiculturalism in the liberal state: theory and policy," *British Journal of Sociology* 55, no. 2 (2004), 237–257.

[22] For examples of this usage, see Howard, *The Politics of Citizenship in Europe*; Joppke, "Beyond national models: Civic integration policies for immigrants in Western Europe."; Ruud Koopmans et al., *Contested Citizenship. Immigration and Cultural Diversity in Europe* (Minneapolis, MN:

from this theoretical vantage point, integration requirements have been interpreted as representing an "illiberal liberalism"[23] that constitutes a "restrictive turn" or "backlash" against the vast liberalization of citizenship policies in the 1990s – policies that included the widening acceptance of dual citizenship and the lowering of residence duration.[24] These perspectives all identify a primary role for far- and center-right parties in introducing this restriction. But these approaches are limiting because: (1) if *any* requirement is considered restrictive, then the bar of acceptable requirements the state *can* ask of a newcomer is essentially set at zero, which betrays the widely accepted notion of citizenship as an exchange of rights from the state for obligations by the citizen; (2) language proficiency and society knowledge tests can actually enable integration and produce inclusion, not exclusion; and (3) policies get introduced by a bevy of actors outside of the right.[25] Overreliance on this blunt characterization tool diverts attention from what is happening on the ground.

II. *Lack of acknowledged policy differentiation:* The second problematic claim stems from taking ideational convergence as the starting point for analysis. Simply put, the belief of ideational convergence produces a type of empirical cherry picking that seeks out only similarities. The view of convergence is predicated on the idea that similar instruments produce similar outcomes, even going so far as to posit that they were adopted for similar macro-reasons. Change is seen as part of a larger, comprehensive strategy of major immigrant-receiving states for addressing the demographic shifts and diversity-related pressures of immigration. But if a mandatory membership strategy is a response to large-scale immigration, why do states make changes at the stage of citizenship if other requirements for naturalization make it so that only a tiny percentage of foreign residents will be able to obtain it? And, in countries where immigrants are more likely to obtain citizenship and have higher rates of naturalization over time, why do policy actors perceive membership problems at this time?

University of Minnesota Press, 2005); Migration Policy Group, "The Migrant Integration Policy Index (MIPEX)," (Migration Policy Group & British Council, 2011); Bernard Ryan, "Integration requirements: a new model in migration law," *Journal of Immigration Asylum and Nationality Law* 22, no. 4 (2008).

23 Guild, Groenendijk, and Carrera, eds., *Illiberal Liberal States: Immigration, citizenship, and integration in the EU*; Orgad, "Illiberal liberalism: Cultural restrictions on migration and access to citizenship in Europe."; Triadafilopoulos, "Illiberal means to liberal ends? Understanding recent immigrant integration policies in Europe."

24 For more on this "backlash" or the return of assimilation, see Rogers Brubaker, "Return of assimilation? Changing perspectives on immigration and its sequels in France, Germany, and the United States," *Ethnic and Racial Studies* 24, no. 4 (2001), 531–548; Christian Joppke and Ewa T. Morawska, *Toward Assimilation and Citizenship: Immigrants in liberal nation-states* (Migration, Minorities, and Citizenship series) (Houndmills, Basingstoke, Hampshire; New York: Palgrave Macmillan, 2003).

25 See Randall Hansen, "A new citizenship bargain for the age of mobility? Citizenship requirements in Europe and North America," (Washington, DC: Migration Policy Institute, 2008).

The "idea" of civic integration is present across these states, manifested in a variety of tests, contracts, courses, and oaths, but there are visible differences both in how difficult requirements are and in how states arrange these requirements. Austria, Denmark, and Germany emphasize civic integration for immigrants seeking permanent residence, in that it is a significant, preceding barrier of admission with integration demands. Additional requirements then exist for citizenship, binding the immigrant to a formidable chain of conditionality. The Netherlands and the UK differ in exempting immigrants from integration for citizenship if they have completed the requirements for permanent residence (effectively removing the distinction between the two). Differences between state practices are also evident in the sequence of policy adoption. Assuming a greater role for policy learning over time, the order in which integration policies are adopted is even more telling. In terms of mandatory integration requirements, the UK and the Netherlands comprehensively focused on citizenship, in 2002 and 2000 respectively, before extending requirements to permanent residence, both in 2007. Austria and Germany are cases of a reverse trend, anchoring integration conditions in permanent residence in 2002 and 2005, before replacing weak integration conditions with robust testing for citizenship in 2006 and 2007 respectively. Denmark is the quintessential case of this latter strategy. An aggregate view of policy obfuscates these important differences; sequencing of mandatory integration clearly indicates populations given top priority.

III. *Interpretation differences:* The final problem seems surprising given the aforementioned ideational and policy consensus. While scholars agree and treat civic integration as the same phenomenon, i.e., as one set of policy ideas sweeping across European states, they strongly disagree about what it means. In fact, the preoccupation with ideational convergence and the resulting diminution of national variation have led to significant scholarly disagreement over the significance of new policy in the absence of a parallel discussion of initial causes. One camp interprets integration requirements as representing a move away from the nation,[26] while the other sees the promotion of language and society knowledge as a return to it.[27] The

[26] Joppke, *Citizenship and Immigration*; Jan-Werner Müller, "Is Europe converging on constitutional patriotism? (And if so: Is it justified?)," *Critical Review of International Social and Political Philosophy* 10, no. 3 (2007), 337–387; Orgad, "Illiberal liberalism: Cultural restrictions on migration and access to citizenship in Europe."; Ines Michalowski, "Required to assimilate? The content of citizenship tests in five countries," *Citizenship Studies* 15, no. 6/7 (2011), 749–768.

[27] Dirk Jacobs and Andrea Rea, "The end of national models? Integration courses and citizenship trajectories in Europe," in *European Union Studies Association Annual Conference* (Montréal, Quebec 2007); Per Mouritsen, "Beyond post-national citizenship: Access, consequence, conditionality," in *European Multiculturalisms*, ed. Anna Triandafyllidou, Tariq Modood, and Nasar Meer (Edinburgh: Edinburgh University Press, 2011), 88–115; Oers, Ersbøll, and Kostakopoulou, *A Re-definition of Belonging? : Language and integration tests in Europe*; Sue Wright, ed. *Citizenship Tests in a Post-national Era, International Journal on Multicultural Societies* 10, no. 1 (UNESCO, 2008); Sergio Carrera, "A typology of different integration programmes in the EU," in T. Balzacq and S. Carrera (eds.), *Security versus Freedom? Security* (Ashgate: Aldershot, 2006).

re-nationalizing position might be summarized by Dora Kostakopoulou's view: "In framing integration as an obligation on the part of the migrant, implicit equivalences – such as indigenous/superior/complete and foreign/inferior/lacking – and ethnocentricity resurface."[28] The de-nationalizing position was summarized by Christian Joppke as: "One is inclined to interpret repressive policies toward them in 'nationalist' or 'racist' terms' . . . Instead, the repressive impulse, at least at the level of state policy, now stems from liberalism itself."[29] I submit that this disjuncture is more of a reflection of differences between civic integration policies than existing studies acknowledge or take seriously.

As evident in this review, the predominant concern in existing studies is the significance and impact of policies, as opposed to *why* new policies are cropping up in the first place. Studies are predominantly focused on the fact of civic integration convergence, not the causes of it nor the possibilities of potential variation. While empirically rich, studies lack both theory development and the generation of testable hypotheses to account for initial civic integration policy change, respective state usage, or timing of policy change.

ORGANIZATION OF THE BOOK

Acknowledging but setting aside these debates, this book takes a fresh and comprehensive view of civic integration by starting at the beginning. The book's seven chapters as well as the conclusion take the reader through an empirical and theoretical study of variation in civic integration requirements and the contemporary promotion of membership in the liberal-democratic nation state. Following this introduction, Chapter 1 establishes civic integration policy as a strategy of membership promotion and provides background on the content of civic integration. To do so, it identifies conceptual differences between membership as a relational identity that an individual shares with the state, i.e., a sense of belonging, while the term "citizenship" reflects a subtype of membership and is reserved for describing formal status. It argues that membership and citizenship are related concepts, but they are not coterminous. In particular, membership contributes unique "goods" to the state that citizenship does not inherently or necessarily provide. Having established the meaning of membership and why it matters to states, the final section examines its most recent form: state identity. I draw contrasts between state identity and national identity as overlapping but distinct theoretical and empirical articulations of national political membership.

Chapter 2 establishes the empirical scope of civic integration policy adoption. It presents membership requirements in two "snapshot" periods in the countries

[28] Dora Kostakopoulou, "Introduction," in *A Re-definition of Belonging? Language and integration tests in Europe*, ed. Ricky van Oers, Eva Ersbøll, and Dora Kostakopoulou (Leiden; Boston: Martinus Nijhoff, 2010), 7.

[29] Joppke, "Beyond national models: Civic integration policies for immigrants in Western Europe," 16.

of the EU-15. The first snapshot captures membership policy before the widespread adoption of civic integration (policy in 1997; "t_0"), while the second snapshot period captures membership policies today (2013; "t_1"). To systematically score and compare integration requirements across time, cases, and statuses of residence, I construct a Civic Integration Policy Index (CIVIX). It employs a coding scheme that records individual requirements, specifically whether a state has language, country knowledge, and/or values requirements for entry, settlement, and citizenship for the average immigrant (in other words, excluding refugees and other minority categories). Scores are reflected in an additive scale, providing an overall score by which we can compare the robustness of civic integration requirements across cases. A detailed discussion of coding rules and results is reported in the chapter. By comparing CIVIX scores across two time periods, we see that remarkable change has taken place in moving from informal to formal membership requirements, and in terms of the expansion of the expectations of state-mandated integration across stages of legal access. We also see a number of patterns in terms of policy instruments, with states employing similar tests and courses in order to promote civic integration. These views would seem to support ideational and policy convergence accounts. However, by looking more closely at the empirical diversity of the degree of civic integration policy adoption (portrayed in CIVIX), as well as design, scope, and sequencing, we see significant variation. This puzzle sets up the research question for the following chapter, as well as the case studies in the remainder of the book.

Chapter 3 presents the central argument of the book, accounting for variation in civic integration policy by looking dynamically at the institutional path-dependency of citizenship and the party politics that seek to either reaffirm or change starting positions. First, I consider what effect existing citizenship policy configurations – namely the rules that make acquisition easier or more difficult – have on producing new membership requirements. The second consideration is how the party in power may have membership preferences that coincide with or differ from the existing start positions. Citizenship and integration prove to be ripe ground for partisanship and populism, particularly around election time. In the absence of opposition (where the government in power's preference aligns with existing orientation), policy can continue unperturbed, in either liberal or restrictive directions through membership requirement reinvestments. By contrast, opposing preferences can have a moderating effect. Membership requirements are sometimes produced as a compromise to opposition voices, sometimes offered as carrots or concessions to much-needed coalition partners, and sometimes crafted in an insulated policy environment absent far-right actors. In other words, The interaction of politics and initial starting position of citizenship orientation, I argue, accounts for what we see as significant variation in membership policy design, and ultimately, different strategies of membership. I develop an explanatory typology to reflect these different settings of interaction. These are not static, however, and a state may easily move from one strategy to another, depending on whether new political leadership is supportive or opposed to existing policy. This argument sets the framework for the case study chapters that follow.

Chapter 4 begins the examination of case studies by looking at Austria and Denmark as two cases of restrictive citizenship retrenchment, where new membership requirements have been adopted by both right and left governments, respectively, and in the absence of significant external pressure for liberalizing change. Chapter 5 examines Germany and the United Kingdom, where citizenship understandings have shaped similarly oriented governments (left-dominated but right-influenced) to identify different parameters of belonging and thus adopt divergent membership policies, namely restriction and citizenship enrichment respectively. Recent restrictions that break from this strategy in the UK are also discussed in light of the theoretical framework, where we see the Conservative party take power and alter a decade-long trajectory. Finally, Chapter 6 contrasts processes of politicization in the Netherlands and France. Despite similar liberal citizenship starting points and similar political trajectories (left government policy adoption followed by right government policy adaptation), different policy outcomes are observed. By focusing on causal mechanisms, or how these conditions interact to produce the outcome of interest, we see politicization in the Netherlands occur in the context of consensus, producing successive restrictions through institutional layering, while politicization in France yielded polarization, which was less entrenched and more easily overturned with an inevitable change in government.

Each case study and paired comparison reveals different strategies of and purposes for civic integration policy, and they are structured in a similar fashion. First, each begins with an examination of the starting position of citizenship, identifying the existing rules for acquisition in order to characterize policy as restrictive or liberal. This not only highlights the extent to which those rules reflect traditional ideas of national belonging, but also the frame of reference in which policymakers operate. Second, initial policy adoption is situated in extant political and immigrant-related circumstances, discussing the impetuses for citizenship debates. Here, I locate left and right party preferences to illustrate how parameters of belonging are reflected in and constrain party position. Third, I trace the policy adoption process for new civic requirements from adoption to adaptation, acknowledging that because political actors and extant conditions change over time so might the purpose of civic integration policy. Finally, I examine not only how membership preferences are articulated in policy over time, but how they are practiced by examining policy effects (i.e., outcomes). Each case shows how citizenship context and distinct political configurations – along with different national political processes – produce divergent membership policy strategies that preserve national citizenship and, ultimately, nation-state differences.

In Chapter 7, I shift the discussion from internal applications of civic integration (for citizenship and permanent residence) to examine the external dimensions of civic integration as they are applied at the first gate of admission: entry. One of the novelties of civic integration is that it lays out expectations of language, knowledge, and/or value competence at multiple points of admissions. However, regulating immigration is an entirely separate policy venue to regulating persons in the process of seeking long-term status, as states have direct interests in seeing that residents are integrate. States also want to prepare potential immigrants for integration, but – given the choice – they have shown a rhetorical preference to limit entry altogether. This chapter examines adoption of mandatory integration for immigration, identifying a shared objective of migration control. The chapter focuses on the role of the EU as a venue for precedent-setting as well as early state practitioners, including a discussion on mechanisms of learning and diffusion.

Finally, the conclusion (titled "The Anchoring of Citizenship") considers the significance of this book's main thesis, that new requirements and articulations of state identity do not signal departures from national approaches to citizenship, but rather fortify them. It not only asserts the renewal of citizenship in the nation-state, but also provides an alternative voice to the growing viewpoint among citizenship scholars that suggests citizenship itself is becoming less national and "thick." Membership is once again "re-imagined" – to reference Benedict Anderson's description of nationhood – through the construction of state identity so that citizenship may persist as a continually relevant and meaningful concept in the increasingly ethnically diverse nation-states of Europe. Short of a "citizenship lite," where dense understandings give way to shared liberal practices,[30] a more appropriate description of this phenomenon is *anchoring* citizenship in new content and rules. Civic requirements represent new tools of addressing national membership problems. To wit, we do not see diminishing national differences, but the maintaining of the nation-state's stronghold to confer unique and meaningful citizenship and identity.

Overall, the book's findings contribute new knowledge to our understanding of citizenship and membership today. They also highlight how European states are innovatively responding to diverse immigration, illustrating an overall adaptability and resilience of the nation-state in the twenty-first century. Just when the dilution of citizenship, interconnectedness of the global economy, and immigrant-related diversity were seen as indicators of the end of national belonging, we see the nation-state rediscovering membership in the form of state identity, albeit through a contorted practice of liberalism. It shows how states – through real innovation – jealously guard their right to confer citizenship, as well as the continued if misplaced hope that membership can mitigate problems of immigrant-related diversity, especially with the rise of radical Islam among immigrant generations in Europe.

30 Joppke, *Citizenship and Immigration*, 145–72; Christian Joppke, "'Rejoinder', review symposium of Christian Joppke's Citizenship and Immigration," *Ethnicities* 12, no. 6 (2012), 859–863.

1

Membership matters: concept precision and state identity

INTRODUCTION

Civic integration policies consist of cultural requirements, namely language and knowledge of society, that empower individuals to act independently in their host society. Alongside this goal of autonomy, they are also designed to foster cohesion and imbue newcomers with a sense of belonging. Belonging is defined as feeling a part of the national political community. It engenders both a sense of acceptance as well as commitment and shared ownership of national rules, norms, and even common resources (both physical and ideational). This sense of membership is typically considered to be part and parcel of citizenship, where an outsider not only obtains rights and status in a formal, legal transformation but also identity through symbolic change. However, empirical realities illustrate that membership is not an automatic by-product of naturalization. We also see citizenship itself no longer remaining the exclusive status for establishing membership, as some states deliberately extend "citizen-like" expectations to persons seeking residence, not citizenship. Membership is clearly related to citizenship – in the traditional nation-state model, national belonging is formally reflected in citizenship – but contemporary change suggests it holds unique and desirable properties.

This chapter looks closely at the concept of membership in order to understand the character, context, and contributions of new civic integration policies. It answers two simple questions: What is membership and why does it matter? Addressing these questions gets to the heart of why civic integration policy is significant, representing a real sea change in political identity. While the case studies provide descriptive content and context for respective civic integration programs, this chapter answers these questions by examining conceptual and theoretical dimensions. Conceptually, civic integration defines membership and belonging in the contemporary nation-state. Theoretically, these new investments in membership are distinguishable from traditional national identity, promoting an alternative understanding of belonging that I label "state identity."

This chapter is organized into three sections. First, I examine the concept of membership in order to establish civic integration as the most recent articulation of belonging in the nation-state. This section defines political membership as a relational sense of belonging distinct from status, formally conveyed through the institution of citizenship. Membership is an umbrella category that captures the way in which an individual identifies, feels a part of, demonstrates an awareness of, or behaves connected to a political community. Citizenship is a formal subtype, consisting of various rules for acquisition and loss. Consequently, there are other statuses that also convey membership. Belonging and status are related but not the same thing; the former can exist without the latter and the latter does not guarantee the presence of the former.

Membership as belonging is also a distinct concept from citizenship as status because we can identify different values that each yields for the state. In this second section, I look to the existing literature on belonging to identify the unique attributes of membership. Most works consider how status and belonging empower or alienate an individual, but in this section I turn the lens around to examine why membership is desirable to the conferring political entity, i.e., the state. Where citizenship is a formal instrument for effectively allocating resources, achieving democratic legitimacy, and even surveilling a population, belonging and membership serve to establish and strengthen social cohesion, foster common group goals, and build loyalty.

Having established civic integration as an articulation of membership and examined how it uniquely matters to the state, the third section contemplates the theoretical significance of this new membership iteration. In examining the content of civic integration and contrasting it to existing understandings of membership derived from national identity, we see the emergence of an alternative script of belonging: state identity. The heading for this section, "Civic integration content: The new and the old," is borrowed from the title of a 2003 British Home Office paper advocating new and clear citizenship content to replace older and vague tropes of belonging. Where national identity provides a traditional understanding of membership, drawing on the historical experience of nationalism in which rules of belonging are based on a similarity of attributes ("logic of sameness"), the latter and newer notion of state identity draws on contemporary realities of diversity to define rules of belonging to hold together otherwise disparate groups and interests ("logic of togetherness"). And, in conclusion, without the conceptual distinction between citizenship as status and membership as belonging, the unique benefits of promoting membership and the novelty of state identity itself would be lost.

WHAT IS MEMBERSHIP? CONCEPTUAL PRECISION

Civic integration articulates new expectations for belonging in the contemporary nation-state. This phenomenon – that European states *require* immigrants to integrate *civically* – is novel, but it is only the most recent iteration of a long-standing state concern with nation-building and the promotion of membership. I define political membership here as belonging to an arbitrary community that has the ability to self-perpetuate. It is arbitrary because the relationship is defined by concrete rules (formal) or norms of understanding (informal), where membership versus non-membership is unambiguous. Its ability to endure – whether by the mechanisms of state sovereignty or by the organized, shared traditions and narratives of a nation – allows generations, removed from the moment of creation, also to be a part of the political community.[1] Membership requirements, therefore, are mechanisms to formally promote attributes or features of belonging that constitute the membership group.

Membership is traditionally conferred through and recognized in the holding of national citizenship; Rogers Smith even defines the "oldest, most basic, and most prevalent meaning [of citizenship as] a certain sort of membership in a political community."[2] This overlap is further concretized in attaching "the nation" to "the state" vis-à-vis citizenship (also referred to as "nationality") and, academically, by the heavy influence of the nationalism literature on citizenship studies. If one were to examine only native-born citizenship-holders, citizenship and membership appear indistinguishable. However, we see less of an overlap if we examine immigrants and naturalization. New citizens may not feel connected to the national group or, as is also the case, long-term migrants remain in the polity and establish enduring social and economic linkages to the host society but remain outside the formal political community of citizenship. This exclusion may be self-selected, where an immigrant does not perceive a substantial difference between permanent residency and citizenship, or institutional, where rules prohibit inclusion. Citizenship can and often does designate belonging by ascribing formal membership to individuals, establishing what others have referred to as the identity or symbolic (as against formal, legal) dimension of citizenship,[3] though this is not inevitable. To wit, recent investments in civic integration strategically bolster state membership precisely because existing citizenship practices are found wanting in this regard.

[1] This emphasis on the *formalized and enduring relationship* between an individual and a political community is similar to Soysal's conception of membership models, which she defines as "institutionalized scripts and understandings of the relationship between individuals, the state, and the polity, as well as the organization structures and practices that maintain this relationship." Yasemin Nuhoglu Soysal, *Limits of Citizenship: Migrants and postnational membership in Europe* (Chicago: University of Chicago Press, 1994), 36. For membership in other contexts, see Michael Walzer, *Spheres of Justice: A defense of pluralism and equality* (New York: Basic Books, 1983).

[2] Rogers M. Smith, "Citizenship: Political," in *International Encyclopedia of the Social & Behavioral Sciences*, ed. Neil J. Smelser and Paul Baltes (New York: Pergamon, 2001), 1857.

[3] Christian Joppke, *Citizenship and Immigration* (Immigration & Society series) (Cambridge; Malden, MA: Polity, 2010); Ruud Koopmans et al., *Contested Citizenship. Immigration and cultural diversity in Europe* (Minneapolis, MN: University of Minnesota Press, 2005).

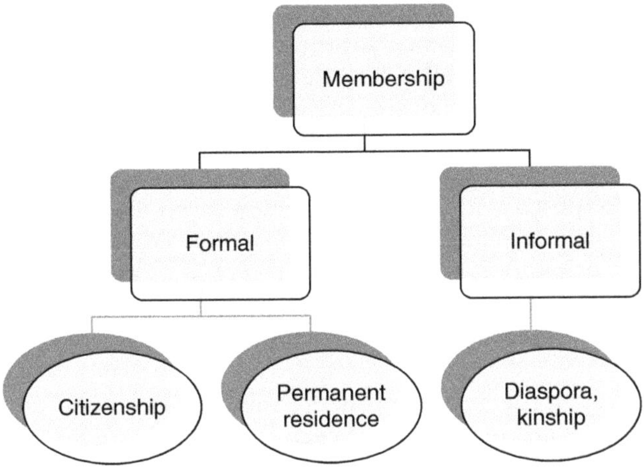

1.1 Conceptual hierarchy of membership

Therefore, conceptual precision is needed to examine membership change. Using "citizenship" as a catch-all phrase for describing rights, status, and identity – as Christian Joppke demonstrates in his formidable treatment, *Citizenship and Immigration* – increases the concept's extension but decreases its intension,[4] which is a problem for identifying and examining dimensional change. In principle, if each aspect of this tripartite description is distinct, then they can move independently and changes to the identity dimension of citizenship can occur while the rights dimension remains untouched. Citizenship is one place where "states seek to impute [normative beliefs] on people,"[5] but it is not the only place. Figure 1.1 maps a precise hierarchy of concepts. Political membership is a reference category for identity and belonging, and citizenship is a subtype designating formal legal status, conveying protection and access to rights under state rules. But there are other ways to belong to a political community, both formally (permanent residence) and informally (co-ethnics living abroad, e.g., Jews in the diaspora who do not hold Israeli citizenship but maintain an affinity – even a fidelity – to the Jewish state). This figure is illustrative, not exhaustive.

This conceptual map enables the examination of membership changes through civic integration and how it affects both categories of formal belonging: citizenship and permanent/long-term residence. Examining citizenship as a legal category remains consistent with usage employed by political scientists and legal

[4] For more, see Giovanni Sartori, "Concept misformation in comparative politics," *American Political Science Review* 64, no. 4 (1970), 1041. Sartori employs the terms "stretching" and "straining" to capture the same idea.

[5] Joppke, *Citizenship and Immigration*, 30.

scholars.[6] It is defined by a series of rules that enable or inhibit acquisition of status, including but not limited to: residence duration, dual citizenship allowance, criminal record requirements, as well as language and country knowledge requirements.[7] Citizenship for outsiders can sometimes be acquired at birth (*jus soli* confers citizenship by birth in a territory to non-citizen parents or *jus sanguinis* to citizen parents), while after birth typically requires a process of naturalization.[8] This is juxtaposed with the usage of citizenship in sociology, which tends to take a wider view as that of a status enabling or prohibiting access to rights of equality and participation, much like gender or class.[9] Finally, it is a distinct usage to that employed in normative theory,[10] as the use of citizenship here evaluates rules as they are, considering the impact – not justness – of these arrangements.

Membership certainly plays a role in conferring or inhibiting the acquisition of citizenship. These concepts are not mutually exclusive by any means. As

6 There is also a strain of citizenship studies in political science that examines the concept in a non-legal context, referring to practices and virtues of individuals oriented toward the common good (i.e., "good citizenship") and active participation in civil society and political institutions. See, e.g., Russell J. Dalton, *The Good Citizen: How a younger generation is reshaping American politics* (Washington, DC: CQ Press, 2008). However, this behavioral interpretation of citizenship is not the scope in which this study operates.

7 High correlations between the many indices of citizenship suggest that picking a few key indicators is sufficiently representative. On correlations, see Marc Helbling, "Validating integration and citizenship policy indices," *Comparative European Politics* 11, no. 5 (2013), 555–576. For an in-depth comparison of the full scope of material and administrative requirements for naturalization in thirty-three European countries, see Sara Wallace Goodman, "Naturalisation policies in Europe: Exploring patterns of inclusion and exclusion," in *EUDO Citizenship Comparative Reports* (Florence: EUDO Citizenship, Robert Schuman Centre for Advanced Studies, EUI, 2010). For a detailed comparison of *jus soli* policy, see Maarten P. Vink and Gerard-Rene de Groot, "Birthright citizenship: Trends and regulations in Europe," in *EUDO Citizenship Comparative Reports* (Florence: EUDO Citizenship, Robert Schuman Centre for Advanced Studies, EUI, 2010).

8 Declaration and registration are also processes for acquiring citizenship after birth. For a more detailed discussion on different modes of citizenship acquisition, see the twenty-seven different modes of acquisition presented at eudo-citizenship.eu.

9 This tradition begins with T. H. Marshall's understanding of social citizenship as a series of unfolding and teleological rights that produce full inclusion (from civil to political to social rights), and runs up to the work of contemporary sociologists who look at "citizenship rights" as inclusive of policies as broad as access to nationality to anti-discrimination law (T.H. Marshall, *Citizenship and Social Class and Other Essays*. Cambridge: Cambridge University Press, 1950). For an example of this usage, see Koopmans et al., *Contested Citizenship. Immigration and cultural diversity in Europe*; Ruud Koopmans, Ines Michalowski, and Stine Waibel, "Citizenship rights for immigrants: National political processes and cross-national convergence in Western Europe, 1980–2008," *American Journal of Sociology* 117, no. 4 (2012), 1202–45.

10 The list is too numerous to be exhaustive, but some examples include: Ronald Beiner, *Theorizing Citizenship* (Albany: State University of New York Press, 1995); Rainer Bauböck and Christian Joppke, eds., *How Liberal are Citizenship Tests?*, vol. 2010/41, EUI Working Papers (Florence, Italy: Robert Schuman Centre for Advanced Studies, EUI, 2010); Ayelet Shachar, *The Birthright Lottery: Citizenship and global inequality* (Cambridge, MA: Harvard University Press, 2009).

Charles Tilly outlines in his contract definition of citizenship, "If citizenship is a tie entailing mutual obligations between categorically-defined persons and a state, the identity 'citizen' describes the experience and public representation of that tie."[11] However, deconstructing and conceptually locating the concept of citizenship as a membership subtype not only offers clarity but also enables a more careful view of membership policy change and impact.

WHY DOES MEMBERSHIP MATTER? IDENTIFYING UNIQUE ATTRIBUTES

Why is it important to distinguish membership from citizenship? In short, membership conveys unique and desirable properties and citizenship is not always sufficient for delivering them. These include establishing and strengthening social cohesion, fostering common group goals, and building loyalty. Historically, these goods were conveyed through citizenship as an institutional lever for recognizing and regulating national identity. However, in a globalized age of migration, this scenario is narrow at best. The promotion of new membership requirements illustrates that it is clearly not enough that people *are* citizens, and formally interact with the state through mutual agreement, but also that people are integrated into the state, *identifying* with that state in some meaningful capacity, whether by feeling or by behavior. If citizenship were sufficient to foster this kind of identity, we would not see the kind of massive, wholesale repairs to belonging through civic integration in which states are "rediscover[ing citizenship] as a tool for integration."[12] This integration imperative exists both inside but also beyond the status of citizenship. In particular, membership matters where citizenship is insufficient in facilitating identity, and especially where it is inaccessible to deserving and eligible persons in a democratic state.[13] Citizenship is still relevant, of course, but it is not without its problems.

In contrast to political behavior studies that question the impact of identity and belonging on immigrant participation or preference formation, this study turns the lens of analysis around to look at the membership-conferring entity

[11] Charles Tilly, "The emergence of citizenship in France and elsewhere," in *Citizenship, Identity and Social History*, ed. Charles Tilly (Cambridge: Cambridge University Press, 1996), 227. Tilly goes on to detail a multidimensional view of citizenship policy, differentiating between formal access criteria ("definitions of ties") and cultural obligation ("conceptions of those ties"), as well as to note that membership is typically born out of ethnicity, but acknowledges that there are many bases of membership, including primordial (e.g., Israel, Ottoman Empire) and learned (in the cases of assimilationist France or the United States).

[12] Joppke, *Citizenship and Immigration*, 22.

[13] See for example Jens Hainmueller and Dominik Hangartner, "Who gets a Swiss passport? A natural experiment in immigrant discrimination," *American Political Science Review* 107, no. 1 (2013), 159–87. One can debate the extent to which "eligible" and "deserving" is interpreted. For an expansive view, see Joseph H. Carens, "Aliens and citizens: The case for open borders," *The Review of Politics* 49, no. 2 (1987), 251–73.

itself. Why do *states* care about membership? How do they benefit by promoting belonging to newcomers? There has been considerable research that examines the tangible benefits of national citizenship to states, while there is comparatively little that examines membership, particularly from a perspective that disaggregates these benefits from citizenship. Both citizenship and membership matter to the state, but they matter in different ways.

Beginning with citizenship, a large number of studies have delved into how citizenship affects immigrants in terms of inclusion and access. In this framework, national citizenship still matters as the "sole basis for certain rights" and a "predictor of ... other forms of political participation."[14] But what do states get out of ascribing citizenship? Particularly, why do they jealously guard their right to confer and withhold citizenship in an ever-integrated if lackluster European Union? First, citizenship is the most effective instrument for allocating resources. Brubaker's definition of citizenship is along these lines in describing it as an "international filing system."[15] This function dates all the way back to Aristotle's examination of the city, noting that an ideal regime is one with a population size with "the greatest excess of number with a view to self-sufficiency of life that is readily surveyable."[16] In other words, a precise understanding of the number of citizens enables the state to effectively identify and allocate resources. A city is deemed too large when "it is easy for aliens and foreigners ... to escape notice on account of the excess of number."[17] Citizens participate in decision-making and governance, while members are ruled but do not have the right to rule. This relates to a unique, more elemental second value of citizenship: it is a foundation to democratic legitimacy. As democracy is government accountable to and run by citizens, the rules for how states create those citizens is significant to determining democratic quality.[18]

[14] Randall T. Hansen, "The poverty of postnationalism: Citizenship, immigration, and the new Europe," *Theory and Society* 38, no. 1 (2009), 1–24.

[15] Rogers Brubaker, *Citizenship and Nationhood in France and Germany* (Cambridge, MA: Harvard University Press, 1992), 31.

[16] Aristotle and Carnes Lord, *The Politics* (Chicago: University of Chicago Press, 1984), 205 (1326b23–25).

[17] Ibid., 205 (1326b20–22). This, of course, is the basis for a more contemporary function of citizenship: an instrument of surveillance. John Torpey even suggests that a state's right to distinguish between citizens and outsiders, and its ability to control movement inside and outside its territory is the very core of "state-ness." John Torpey, *The Invention of the Passport: Surveillance, citizenship and the state* (Cambridge: Cambridge University Press, 2000), 1–2.

[18] Robert Dahl even defines inclusive citizenship as an institutional minimum for good governance, where "no adult permanently residing in the country and subject to its laws can be denied the rights that are available to others ... [including liberties and opportunities that may be necessary to the effective operation of the political institutions of large-scale democracy." Dahl does not appear to be making a claim one way or the other about immigrant inclusion in this community, but he is unambiguous about the importance of inclusionary citizenship (specifically by gender, religion, and race) to high performing, consolidated democratic regimes. Robert A. Dahl, "What political institutions does large-scale democracy require?," *Political Science Quarterly* 120, no. 2 (2005), 189.

Citizenship as a membership category continues to convey group feeling and attachment to a majority of its holders. But membership and belonging is also promoted outside this status.[19] Existing research on membership is primarily concerned with the nature of state attachment (namely, that it is liberal and universal[20]) and not with what state attachment achieves or why it matters. This is a critical oversight in the literature. If we desire to know why states promote and preserve membership, we need to establish what membership and attachment produce in terms of state goods. By examining a wide range of literatures, these can be identified as strengthening social cohesion, fostering common group goals, and – potentially – building loyalty.

First, membership produces social cohesion by imbuing individuals with a set of values and skills that – in their absence – would lead to anomic living.[21] In one of the earliest definitions of social cohesion, Moreno and Jennings establish it as "the forces holding the individuals within the groupings in which they are."[22] Looking at the policies of civic integration – the stated goal of which, in the language of the original law implementing civic integration in the Netherlands, is to "increase the self-sufficiency of newcomers"[23] – it does not seem obvious how it produces social cohesion, or togetherness; the promotion of autonomy might even imply the direct opposite of social cohesion. Yet, in liberal democratic settings, it is the very idea that individuals are self-sufficient – able to enter the labor market, politically participate, and interact in a variety of spaces – that pulls otherwise isolated individuals together in society. Immigrants who possess autonomy in these societies have the potential to experience the full extent of individualism and pluralism, for where there is social cohesion, liberal democratic societies can "handle conflict and remain stable."[24]

Some of the specific values that social cohesion relies on include trust, engagement, and organizational membership. None of these is possible if an individual lacks the skills or incentives to participate. The idea of social cohesion – and specifically of civic integration – is that individuals begin to participate in different kinds of interactions – not just "bonding" forms of social capital within one's family or ethnic community but "bridging" networks of cross-cutting, interpersonal relationships between ethnic, economic,

[19] In fact, even the allocation of resources is no longer exclusive to citizenship. In the UK, for example, access to non-contributory welfare is contingent on settlement and not citizenship.

[20] See, for example, Joppke, *Citizenship and Immigration*, ch. 5.

[21] Of course, membership necessarily produces both social cohesion and social exclusion, where some people must necessarily be excluded to have a coherent whole. On this, see Linda Bosniak, *The Citizen and the Alien: Dilemmas of contemporary membership* (Princeton, N.J: Princeton University Press, 2006).

[22] Cited in Noah E. Friedkin, "Social cohesion," *Annual Review of Sociology* 30 (2004), 411.

[23] Ministry of Justice (the Netherlands), "Wet Inburgering Nieuwkomers (Newcomers Integration Act)," ed. Ministry of Justice (The Hague, 1998).

[24] Michael Mann, "The social cohesion of liberal democracy," *American Sociological Review* 35, no. 3 (1970), 423.

or familial lines.[25] Sociologists and psychologists explain this phenomenon through the "contact hypothesis," which suggests that contact through cross-cutting networks, across inter-ethnic, racial, ideational, and interest-based groups, reduces intergroup biases, and therefore conflict.[26] Within political science, research shows that the absence of cross-cutting networks in the context of ethnic and religious diversity erodes social capital.[27] Low levels of social capital reflect low levels of trust and participation, and thus impact the quality of democratic governance. Inversely, a robust civic society and high levels of participation from a cross-section of society directly contribute to democratic health and good governance. Therefore, states directly benefit from promoting skills and state-imputed values associated with membership at all stages of permanent status, as they yield democratic goods among legally included insiders.

The second benefit of membership is that it establishes common group culture. Smith notes that force alone is not enough for leaders to keep society together: "Most aspirants to power wish to govern people who are genuinely persuaded that ... they are one people."[28] Common culture is distinct from social cohesion, where society "hangs together" through participation and trust. The promotion of common culture establishes a point of orientation for society to rally around. This, in turn, becomes a baseline of shared norms and goals that enable representative and legitimate democratic decision-making. As a result, it is not simply in the interest of those who hold citizenship; residents and newcomers are also affected by government decisions. Moreover, social psychologists tell us that privileging superordinate identity (as opposed to subgroup identity) not only leads individuals to value societal authorities rather than narrower instrumental interests,[29] it can also contribute to the reduction of intergroup bias.[30]

[25] This notion of social capital as social networks and the associated norms of reciprocity and trustworthiness comes from Robert D. Putnam, *Bowling Alone: The collapse and revival of American community* (New York: Simon & Schuster, 2000).

[26] Thomas F. Pettigrew, "Intergroup contact theory," *Annual Review of Psychology* 49, no. 1 (1998), 65–85.

[27] Robert D. Putnam and David E. Campbell, *American Grace: How religion divides and unites us* (New York: Simon & Schuster, 2010); Christel Kesler and Irene Bloemraad, "Does immigration erode social capital? The conditional effects of immigration-generated diversity on trust, membership, and participation across 19 countries, 1981–2000," *Canadian Journal of Political Science* 43, no. 2 (2010), 319–47.

[28] Smith goes on to articulate that the scripts used to bind people together are myths, in other words constructs indicating "how a political community originated, who is eligible for membership, who is not and why, and what the community's values and aims are." Rogers M. Smith, *Civic Ideals: Conflicting visions of citizenship in U.S. history* (Yale University Press, 1999), 32–33.

[29] Yuen J. Huo et al., "Superordinate identification, subgroup identification, and justice concerns: Is separatism the problem; is assimilation the answer?," *Psychological Science* 7, no. 1 (1996), 40–45.

[30] Samuel L. Gaertner and John F. Dovidio, *Reducing Intergroup Bias: The Common Ingroup Identity model* (Psychology Press, 2000).

The notion of the liberal-democratic state promoting common goals and culture has been problematized by a number of political theorists who take umbrage with the "ethnoculturally neutral" liberal state prioritizing some values/goals/cultures over others.[31] However, Will Kymlicka rejects this act as a violation of liberalism, noting that the liberal democratic state is quintessentially a "nation-building" state into which outsiders must minimally integrate. In contrast to perceptions that societal culture must be a "thick, ethnographic sense, referring to the sharing of specific folk-customs, habits, and rituals," Kymlicka points out that just as the "lack of a common thick ethnographic culture is part of the very definition of a liberal society . . . it is equally essential to modern liberal forms of governance that citizens share a common culture in a very different, and thinner, sense, focusing on a common language and societal institutions."[32] Accordingly, thin nation-building that promotes common language, culture, and public institutions serves a number of goals, including creating an "equal opportunity to work," "equal access to mainstream institutions," and "the sort of solidarity required by a welfare state," as well as proving "essential to democracy." He asks, for example, "How can 'the people' govern together if they cannot understand one another?"[33]

A final contribution of membership is the establishment of loyalty. The benefits of membership most directly intersect and overlap with the benefits of citizenship here. Non-birth based citizenship was traditionally obtained by, among other criteria, demonstrating fidelity and swearing an oath to the state and its laws. In this coordinated concept, citizenship *as* nationhood was understood not only as giving an individual rights and protections, but also in playing a role in "fostering solidarity."[34] Today we understand these connections to be more contingent. The idea of loyalty, according to David Miller, is not necessarily that a citizen would take up arms, but is more "subterranean" in nature: "even those who profess their indifference to nationality under ordinary circumstances are very likely to find that, at those exceptional moments when the fate of the whole nation is determined collectively, their sense of identity is such that they see their own well-being as closely bound up with that of the community."[35]

[31] Any acts that violate this neutrality are seen as illiberal. See Christian Joppke, "Transformation of immigrant integration in Western Europe: Civic integration and antidiscrimination policies in the Netherlands, France, and Germany," *World Politics* 59, no. 2 (2007), 243–73. For the quintessential practice of state neutrality, see Michael Walzer, *What it Means to Be an American* (New York: Marsilio, 1992).

[32] Will Kymlicka, *Politics in the Vernacular: Nationalism, Multiculturalism, and Citizenship* (Oxford, UK; New York: Oxford University Press, 2001), 25, fn. 18. While immigrants integrate into receiving societal culture, they also need a societal culture as a resource to access freedom and equality. This cultural membership – that they bring with them to the host society – is protected by multicultural citizenship.

[33] Ibid., 26.

[34] Hansen, "The poverty of postnationalism: Citizenship, immigration, and the new Europe," 13.

[35] David Miller, *On Nationality* (Oxford: Oxford University Press, 1997), 14–15.

In fact, one of the most strident defenses against dual citizenship today is the notion that multiple citizenships create multiple loyalties, therefore undermining a singular state solidarity.[36] While a number of states have moved to allow dual citizenship for immigrants (Finland, Italy, Luxembourg, Sweden), others have been moderate (Germany, the Netherlands) or have resisted change altogether (Austria). States formally limit the multiplication of loyalty when they do not allow for dual citizenship, but do states *get* loyalty by extending citizenship? This is the wager – not the foregone conclusion – of naturalization. The very purpose of citizenship ceremonies, introduced in the UK and the Netherlands and modeled on the American experience, is to actively foster loyalty to the state and particular conceptions of national identity.[37] Individuals are more likely to feel loyalty if they perceive their citizenship represents more than merely a passport. There is also evidence to suggest that where migrants earn citizenship and feel a sense of accomplishment in achieving citizenship, they have a higher value of it.[38]

In conclusion, membership provides important "goods" to the state. While traditionally these were formally conveyed through citizenship, new membership requirements at any number of status venues suggest that this picture of exclusivity is long gone. Yet, as both the concept formation and theoretical discussion sections show, membership does not replace citizenship. On the one hand, membership "reinvigorates"[39] citizenship by introducing new content and obligations in a mutually reinforcing – not zero-sum – relationship. On the other hand, while strengthening citizenship with these new investments in identity, membership also invigorates other statuses, namely long-term residence. In the next and final section of the chapter, I characterize this new, instrumental membership directly by contrasting contemporary articulations of belonging – which I term "state identity" – to that of its historical antecedent, national identity.

CIVIC INTEGRATION CONTENT: "THE NEW AND THE OLD"

Given that membership matters, and matters as a category of belonging in ways unique to citizenship as a legal status, what sort of membership does civic integration create? How similar or different is membership defined through civic integration from that of traditional national identity? In answering these

36 For evidence testing this claim, see Irene Bloemraad, "Who claims dual citizenship? The limits of postnationalism, the possibilities of transnationalism, and the persistence of traditional citizenship," *The International Migration Review* 38, no. 2 (2004), 389.

37 Susan M. Gordon, "Integrating immigrants: Morality and loyalty in US naturalization practice," *Citizenship Studies* 11, no. 4 (2007), 367–382.

38 See the interviews with immigrants undergoing integration in the case studies of the INTEC Project (Integration and Naturalisation Tests: the new way to European Citizenship), funded by the European Integration Fund. Available at http://www.ru.nl/law/cmr/projects/intec.

39 Hansen, "The poverty of postnationalism: Citizenship, immigration, and the new Europe," 14.

questions, this final section identifies civic integration policies as producing not only a new type of membership – state identity – but an identity in clear contrast to traditional national identity. Both define types of political belonging, but vary in logic and design. I argue they represent an overlapping continuum, in which state identity is only the latest iteration of belonging in the ongoing project of peoplehood-building.[40] This section begins by examining the essence of belonging *before* civic integration, i.e., the contents of national identity, and then considers differences as a result of new membership requirements. I argue that each identity is supported by a different logic of inclusion: the logic of sameness versus togetherness, respectively. These identities can and, indeed, do coexist; state identity (logic of togetherness) does not replace national identity (logic of sameness) but exists alongside it as different people become citizens for different reasons. Concepts of national belonging also, in part,[41] continue to account for the contours of citizenship law. But while citizenship continues to be the focal point for promoting membership, new iterations of belonging in state identity represent significant transformation of the meaning of citizenship and the nation-state in the long run.

National identity is a well-known concept. Political in nature, it contains distinctly ethnic origins. Anthony Smith argues in his formative definition that a nation takes on the attributes of an *ethnie* or ethnic community, wherein a national identity consists of the following features: (1) historic territory or homeland; (2) common myths and memories; (3) common, mass culture; (4) common legal rights and duties for all members; and (5) common economy with territorial mobility.[42] Its political dimension distinguishes national identity from mere ethnic identity. Furthermore, the nation is a political phenomenon independent of the state, which, as mentioned earlier in this chapter, is seminally defined by Max Weber as an entity that successfully claims a "monopoly on the legitimate use of violence." Others have extended this monopoly to include resource extraction,

40 This alternative word to "nationalism" comes from Rogers M. Smith, *Stories of Peoplehood: The politics and morals of political membership* (Cambridge: Cambridge University Press, 2003).

41 While Rogers Brubaker's initial claim of the impact of nationhood on citizenship policy was quite strong, he later distanced himself from this stark view, arguing with Jaeeun Kim that the explanatory power of ethnic nationalism (in reference to Germany and South Korea) is actually quite weak and that membership politics are "more crucially framed and constituted by geopolitical contexts, state categorization practices, and political struggles." He does not examine this claim in civic nationalism contexts. See Rogers Brubaker and Jaeeun Kim, "Transborder Membership Politics in Germany and Korea," *European Journal of Sociology* 52, no. 1 (2011), 25.

42 Anthony D. Smith, *National Identity* (Reno: University of Nevada Press, 1991), 14. In later work, Smith revises his definition of nation to exclude the emphasis on the *mass* character of public culture, the reference to a "common economy," and the replacement of "common legal rights and duties" with "common laws and customs." One assumes that these revisions extend to the definition of national identity as well. For an analysis of this shift, see Montserrat Guibernau, "Anthony D. Smith on nations and national identity: A critical assessment," *Nations and Nationalism* 10, no. 1–2 (2004), 125–41.

allocation, and organization of people.[43] There is variation in terms of nations existing *before* and thus justifying statehood (e.g., Israel) or political projects for recognition (e.g., Catalans) versus nations created in *response* to the challenge of statehood consolidation (e.g., France). However, once nations and states become "nation-states," the definitive linkage between the two in practice is forged in citizenship. This is the central argument to Rogers Brubaker's *Citizenship and Nationhood in France and Germany*, where he posits that citizenship – defined as an "instrument and object of social closure"[44] – perpetuates notions of national belonging, with the rules conferring citizenship based on cultural idioms of nationhood. Insiders are those with access to rights and membership, and that is – in turn – determined by understandings of nationhood.[45] In citing Brubaker elsewhere, Joppke summarizes that citizenship is not just state membership but "national membership," in which "[t]he political community should be simultaneously a cultural community, a community of language, mores, or belief."[46] Formal membership of the state is initially ascribed to co-nationals, while those who are not co-nationals at birth or by descent have to "naturalize" to the national political community. It is therefore appropriate that citizenship and nationality are colloquially synonymous, and rules that convey citizenship are often labeled or translated as nationality laws and acts. One who holds citizenship is a national; therefore, becoming a citizen is the process of taking on national membership and its attendant identity and culture.

How does an immigrant become a member in the nation-state? Belonging is conveyed through the acquisition of status, where rules for becoming a citizen – *jus soli* provisions, residency requirements, etc. – regulate the width or narrowness of the aperture for membership. These rules carry implied expectations for belonging over time. For example, long durations of residence (e.g., Germany used to require fifteen years, Austria ten years) in theory ensures language proficiency and social connections for the applicant at the end of that period. The key difference between these mechanisms and civic integration is, of course, the rigor of objective assessment versus the implicit assumption that integration naturally occurs over time. Instead of integration through performance and proactive behavior, the latter represents integration through what Peter Spiro describes as merely "being there."[47]

The extent to which the content of national identity is not implied but articulated is captured in what can be called generalized integration clauses. In

[43] Charles Tilly, *The Formation of National States in Western Europe* (Princeton, NJ: Princeton University Press, 1975); Michael Mann, *The Rise and Decline of the Nation State* (Cambridge, MA: Blackwell, 1990); Torpey, *The Invention of the Passport: Surveillance, citizenship, and the state*.

[44] Brubaker, *Citizenship and Nationhood in France and Germany* (Cambridge, MA: Harvard University Press, 1992), 31.

[45] Ibid., 1–3. [46] Joppke, *Citizenship and Immigration*, 111.

[47] Peter J. Spiro, *Beyond Citizenship: American identity after globalization* (Oxford [England]; New York: Oxford University Press, 2008).

1977, for example, Germany first required that naturalizing foreigners demonstrate a "voluntary and lasting orientation towards Germany" without consistent measures of assessment.[48] France has maintained an assimilation requirement since 1927 that it primarily evaluates through language ability.[49] And Greece has long-maintained a "lasting orientation" requirement, which was satisfied through a subjective interview assessing lifestyle and social connections. While technically an integration requirement, they all illustrate an enduring logic of sameness. The intention is that of circumscribing, not transforming, an eligible population for citizenship. In fact, evidence considered to support sufficient integration can easily be changed; once an historical marker for cultural ties, today it is a proxy for policymakers to enforce opposition to polygamy, among other values.

But perhaps the oldest form of national membership promotion practiced by European nation-states is the oath. This, too, is primarily an historical handprint of the nation-state as it emerged from the nineteenth century and not an adjustment of national citizenship law to large-scale immigration today. France has had an oath since the eighteenth century,[50] Finland between 1920 and 1941, and Greece since 1955. Even as far back as medieval Italian city-states, citizens were "required to take an oath, for example, to obey the laws, attend meetings, to pay taxes, to undertake military service."[51] Oaths taken today are not all that dissimilar: immigrants in Germany are required to uphold the democratic values and Constitution of the federal republic, and in the UK to "bear true allegiance to Her Majesty Queen Elizabeth the Second . . ." as well as give "loyalty to the United Kingdom and respect its rights and freedoms." The longevity of oath practices indicates that fidelity to the state has long been a valuable component

48 Simon Green, *The Politics of Exclusion: Institutions and immigration policy in contemporary Germany* (Manchester; New York: Manchester University Press, 2004), 40.

49 Christophe Bertossi and Abdellali Hajjat, "France," in *EUDO Citizenship Observatory Country Reports* (Florence: EUDO Citizenship, Robert Schuman Centre for Advanced Studies, EUI, 2013), 18. Assimilation into the French community has been recently defined in the Civil Code (21–4) in more specific terms to include "a sufficient knowledge of the French language, history, culture, and society," a knowledge of "rights and duties conferred by French nationality" (since 2003), as well as "adherence to the principles and values essential to the Republic" (since 2010).

50 According to the French Constitution of 1791, a foreign-born person could naturalize "after five years of continuous residence in the kingdom if, in addition, they have acquired real estate, married a French woman, or founded an agricultural or commercial establishment, and if they have taken the civic oath (*serment civique*)." The oath was as follows: "I swear to be faithful to the nation, to the law, and to the King, and to maintain with all my power the Constitution of the kingdom, decreed by the National Constituent Assembly in the years 1789, 1790, and 1791." Available at the Conseil Constitutionnel website (http://www.conseil-constitutionnel.fr) (accessed June 4, 2014). Note that the Americans quickly followed suit, adopting an oath in the Naturalization Act of 1795.

51 Derek Benjamin Heater, *Citizenship: The civic cdeal in world history, politics, and education* (Manchester, New York: Manchester University Press; distributed in the USA by Palgrave, 2004), 51. Of course, non-citizens are not "foreigners" as we understand the term today, but typically persons from outside the city-state or persons just coming into property.

of gaining citizenship, but we see in the expansion of requirements that it is no longer sufficient.

In these practices, national identity is preserved and citizenship conferred based on the logic of sameness. Inclusion in national identity is based on resemblance and recognition. For outsiders to become insiders, they must be absorbed into the host society. It might seem surprising that more formal membership articulations were not attached to acquisition sooner, especially as some European countries are regarded as quintessential "ethnic states." In a general sense, it reveals a previous "taken for granted" quality of membership, defined in national citizenship for primarily monocultural nation-states. It also indicates a belated reaction to large-scale demographic change in receiving states to formally articulate what was once implicit, bringing European receiving-states more closely in line to traditional countries of immigration, like the United States and Canada.

State identity is quite distinct from national identity. First, we see states actively defining the essence of belonging, instead of implying norms of belonging. Parliaments and policymakers are having debates about what it means to write a single definition of "Germanness" or "Britishness." In late 2009, for example, Nicolas Sarkozy's government launched a series of town hall meetings and online forums to debate what it means to be French in the twenty-first century. Second, it maintains inclusion through achievement, instead of recognition. Inclusion is not an amorphous transformation through a permeable skin of membership; it is a step-system where an individual fulfills certain criteria and "climbs the ladder" to inclusion. Third, inclusion and membership can be achieved in a non-citizenship status. While an immigrant becomes a member of the national community only through the acquisition of citizenship, state membership can be obtained by passing integration hurdles to become a permanent resident. And, finally, while the ultimate goal of state identity might be characterized as individual independence underscored by common values, we might ascribe national identity as more limited with just an interest in group solidarity. In a post-immigration reality, state identity reflects recognition by policymakers that there are unique "goods" unto membership, but that national membership is declining as a desirable or even meaningful category of belonging.

To sample the content of civic integration, one can peer into any number of course syllabi, exam preparation booklets, instructional videos, etc. made available to prepare an immigrant for requirements for settlement or citizenship and obtain a similar impression. The first pages of the British handbook read as follows: "The fundamental principles of British life include: democracy, the rule of law, individual liberty, tolerance of those with different faiths and beliefs, participation in community life."[52] The first value articulated in the French Welcome and Integration contract is "France, a democracy," followed directly

[52] Home Office, "Life in the United Kingdom: A guide for new residents," ed. Home Office (London: Home Office, 2013), 7–8.

thereafter by "France, a country of rights and duties." Similarly, the first line on the Danish declaration on integration and active citizenship commits an applicant for permanent residence to "comply with Danish legislation and respect the Danish democratic principles in every respect."[53] In the Danish study guide for citizenship – "Denmark: Past and Present" – the first pages are preoccupied with understanding history, like the origins of Denmark's Constitution, not for its own sake but as the "starting point for the development toward the existing parliamentary democracy," as well as a means for understanding the monarchical system, the welfare society, and everyday life.[54] In Germany, the citizenship test primarily assesses knowledge in three areas: life in a democracy, history and responsibility, and man and society.[55] And for immigrants integrating in the Netherlands, a compulsory exam for settlement primarily focuses on Dutch language proficiency, assessing reading, listening, and writing. Immigrants also take a "knowledge of Dutch society" exam, which requires the test-taker to listen to scenarios and answer questions that vary from "What do you do during the moment of silence [on Dutch Remembrance Day]?" to "Who can give you a prescription?"

These examples suffice to illustrate that the common sinew across different devices and strategies is content emphasizing liberal values, including democracy, freedom of speech, toleration, autonomy, and equality. This includes content covering the rule of law, government, freedom and rights, as well as holidays and national customs. While nationally specific cultural references and customs are interspersed throughout, the emphasis on values and institutions is unequivocal. The overarching theme reflects what Jürgen Habermas describes as "constitutional patriotism," in other words, to promote a loyalty to common values (codified in a Constitution or body of law). Specifically, it embraces the idea that "political attachment ought to center on the norms, the values, and more indirectly, the procedures of a liberal democratic constitution."[56] Liav Orgad redirects this loyalty away from Habermas' amorphous, universal "just constitutional regime" by emphasizing national constitutionalism, which manifests in the state's interest of "protect[ing] core constitutional principles because they are *ours*."[57] In

53 Ministry of Refugee Immigration and Integration Affairs (Denmark), "New to Denmark." Available at http://www.nyidanmark.dk/en-us/frontpage.htm (accessed June 18, 2013).

54 Ministry of Refugee Immigration and Integration Affairs (Denmark), "Denmark past and present," ed. Ministry of Refugee Immigration and Integration Affairs (Denmark) (2007), 10–11. Note: A new Danish test will be in place by June 2014 and will contain new content that "emphasizes everyday life" that confronts "citizens in a modern society." See http://statsborgerskabsprove.com (accessed June 21, 2013).

55 Questions from these three areas constitute 30 out of 33 questions. The remaining three questions are on the applicant's *Länder* of residence.

56 Also see Jan-Werner Müller and Kim Lane Scheppele, "Constitutional patriotism: An introduction," *International Journal of Constitutional Law* 6, no. 1 (2008): 67.

57 Liav Orgad, "Illiberal liberalism: Cultural restrictions on migration and access to citizenship in Europe," *American Journal of Comparative Law* 58, no. 1 (2010), 100.

other words, it is important to understand not only the institutions of democracy but a country's unique path to democracy.

An ancillary theme is individualism, where it is incumbent upon immigrants *as individuals* to understand their rights, the rights of others, and how to function with autonomy – and not as a member of a subgroup – in their adoptive home. This is in contrast to integration approaches like multiculturalism, where the idea is that immigrants participate in a host society through maintaining group attributes, such as offering language translation for state services. This repertoire is designed to empower individuals to participate in their new society, from finding a job and obtaining education for their children to participating in democratic institutions, and even availing themselves of welfare services. Language is not a marker of culture or ethnicity in this regard but rather a functional tool for participation and labor mobility.

Through the acquisition of skills and enablement of individual autonomy, membership under state identity is *achieved*, not merely bequeathed. The membership community is shaped through proactive behavior, not an acknowledgment of pre-existing attributes. In theory, the type of belonging promoted through civic integration creates an accessible, common bond uniting otherwise "most-different" people. And, regardless of ethnicity or religious background, a commitment to liberal values safeguards plurality in membership. Therefore, I refer to the type of identity promoted through civic integration as defined by a "logic of togetherness." It promotes a minimally transformative process, advocating common values and skills for autonomy without sacrificing home culture. State identity can be shown to be distinct from historical projects of national identity, in which common traits were identified to bind most-similar people together for the purposes of self-determination, recognition, and legitimacy. In principle, state identity and liberalism provides enough of a common bond to glue native and immigrant communities together, but not so much that one needs to forego home culture or traditions.[58] It is a horizontal bond that can achieve group solidarity without sacrificing vertical, multicultural affinities. Obtaining membership through state identity may be just as difficult as obtaining it through national identity, but it is at least possible and, if achieved, is due to a migrant's own efforts. In sum, state identity – operating under the logic of togetherness – pulls individuals together. It does not transform them to be similar, as traditional assimilation and the logic of sameness under national identity would direct.

This question of balance between shared state values (liberalism) and toleration of religious or ethnic values (ostensibly illiberal), as well as the idea of promoting autonomy and liberal values through mandatory and potential illiberal means, raises a question as to how liberal these tests and requirements really are. Assessments of test illiberality are different than assertions that they are hard. Tests can legitimately measure knowledge of institutions and culture with varying degrees of difficulty. Accusations of illiberality are based on a perceived

[58] Unless, of course, they violate tenets of liberalism, such as free choice (e.g., honor killing).

crossing-of-the-line from assessing knowledge to assessing morality.[59] The morality line can theoretically be breached in terms of content, the availability of preparation materials,[60] as well as whether it is reasonably possible that citizenship applicants can pass over integration hurdles (what Randall Hansen calls a "reasonableness standard"[61]). But this raises an even further and more elusive proposition: Is a test that asks an immigrant to learn country values (e.g., freedom of speech, choice, etc.) still illiberal if it does not measure one's cognitive commitment? Knowing national values and believing in them are two different things. Even raising one's hand to take an oath stating beliefs in certain values is a behavioral commitment, not a measure of one's actual cognitive commitment and thus, theoretically, does not violate one's personal or conscience-related choices. The state can mandate knowledge and the professing of loyalty, but not morality or belief. In this, an oath of fidelity or value commitment to a set of values can be nothing more than theater, where an individual publically expresses one view (the appropriate, state-sponsored view), but privately holds another.

This proposition is slightly murkier when it comes to religion, but, again, the majority of civic integration requirements do not prize Christian values or Christian practices.[62] An exception is found in the Dutch case, where religious (read: Muslim) leaders are required to watch a video in which they see homosexuals kissing, and this video is required viewing to prepare for the integration-from-abroad exam. Viewing does not constitute an assessment of understanding liberal freedoms; one can respect another's rights in the abstract without being made to exercise that respect in practice, potentially assaulting one's own sensibilities and rights. Just as an individual has the right to love whom they wish and to display affection publically, religious freedom dictates an individual has the right to morally object and look away. In an analogous event, the tenets of a liberal democracy empower the Ku Klux Klan to march through a predominately Jewish neighborhood of Skokie, Illinois, but Jewish residents do not have to sit and watch them march. Overall, however, immigrants do not have to undergo deep moral change to complete integration requirements. It is certainly the hope that they do where they differ from state imputations of belonging through liberalism, but this is not enforceable. Instead, the state ensures that immigrants – at the very least – have an understanding of those rules. I raise these

59 For example of both Kantian and Rawlsian versions, see Bauböck and Joppke, eds., *How Liberal are Citizenship Tests?*

60 For more, see Amitai Etzioni, "Citizenship tests: A comparative, communitarian perspective," *The Political Quarterly* 78, no. 3 (2007), 353–63.

61 Bauböck and Joppke, eds., *How Liberal are Citizenship Tests?*, 25.

62 Yes, Christmas is a "Christian holiday," but when it is defined in the UK handbook as potential test material, it informs the reader that celebrating in the "traditional way" includes "spend[ing] the day at home and eat[ing] a special meal, which often includes roast turkey, Christmas pudding and mince pies," not Church attendance for non-Christians. Home Office, "Life in the United Kingdom: A guide for new residents," 79.

points to highlight that this new state identity has not gone uncontested or unexamined.[63] Of course, it should be said that in these studies, European practices deemed illiberal are always compared to what is deemed the most liberal case: the United States as the ideal-type. However, as Smith painstakingly points out, even the United States is a diminished example by design, describing how it has "always expressed illiberal, undemocratic ascriptive myths of U.S. civic identity, along with various types of liberal and republican ones, in logically inconsistent but politically effective combinations."[64]

The politics of civic integration are not only defined by academic concerns over compliance with or violations of liberalism, there is also significant debate within practicing states over content. Civic integration projects hang together by a common thread of liberal values and the "logic of togetherness," but this does not negate the very substantial discussions that occur over what the content of membership should be. Certain states experience more muted dialogues – for example, Dutch policymakers primarily debated who would pay for integration and not the substance of integration itself[65] – while debates in other states were more heated. As a result, there has been some significant rewriting of citizenship tests in the past decade or so. Two examples suffice as they illustrate exact opposite trajectories. The original format of the "Life in the UK" citizenship test under New Labour focused on knowledge deemed necessary for what its creator Bernard Crick called "active citizenship," which excluded questions on history. The Conservative–Liberal Democrat coalition government, however, introduced a new citizenship test in 2013 which is almost entirely comprised of history and culture. For example, the new study guide covers topics from Oliver Cromwell to the Beatles. The Danish test has also changed, but in the opposite direction by moving from trivia to assessment on practical knowledge. This is reflected in the name change of the test itself, from the "Indfødsretsprøve" – where "Indfødsret" is an historical designation of a citizenship-like legal status acquired by foreigners – to the "Statsborgerskabsprøve," or citizenship test.[66]

State identity remains contested from any number of perspectives; some may decry the content as too minimal, while others identify the succession of integration barriers as an unnecessarily arduous chain of conditionality. Identity is

63 Scholars have been preoccupied with this question of liberality. See for example: Phil Triadafilopoulos, "Illiberal means to liberal ends? Understanding recent immigrant integration policies in Europe," *Journal of Ethnic and Migration Studies* 37, no. 6 (2011), 861–80; Bauböck and Joppke, eds., *How Liberal are Citizenship Tests*; Elspeth Guild, Kees Groenendijk, and Sergio Carrera, eds., *Illiberal Liberal States: Immigration, citizenship, and integration in the EU* (Farnham, Surrey; Burlington, VT: Ashgate, 2009).

64 Smith, *Civic Ideals: Conflicting visions of citizenship in US history*, 470.

65 S. A. Bonjour, "Governing diversity. Dutch political parties' preferences on the role of the state in civic integration policies," *Citizenship Studies* 17, no.6/7 (2013), 837–851.

66 These two statuses used to be distinct categories in Danish law and were not merged until the twentieth century. See Eva Ersbøll, "Denmark," in *EUDO Citizenship Observatory Country Reports* (Florence: EUDO Citizenship, Robert Schuman Centre for Advanced Studies, EUI, 2013), 1.

an inherently contested concept because it is intersubjective. Still, it remains quite distinct from national identity and represents the most current iteration of membership and, for lack of a more differentiated vocabulary, nation-building. It is nation-building in the least "national" way imaginable. Compared to national identity, in which the logic of sameness acknowledges membership based on shared ascriptive attributes, recognizing inclusion of outsiders as a contingent process, the starting point of state identity is a set of value commitments, including individualism and toleration, to which any interested person regardless of ethnic background can ostensibly commit. While, in practice, this minimal articulation of entry criteria may be quite substantial for an immigrant to achieve, particularly language proficiency, the principle is that with acquisition they achieve membership – ironically – through their own autonomy. State identity pulls people together, establishing solidarity among different groups by creating a baseline of values and skills and without requiring individuals to sacrifice their differences.

CONCLUSION

This chapter has illustrated not only how belonging has continuously served as an important and unique component to the contemporary nation-state, but also that the substance of and logic behind membership has altered quite significantly. State identity is the most current iteration of membership, promoting a sense of belonging that is distinct from traditional national identity. The two identities continue to exist alongside one another, and both rely on citizenship as a reference point for membership. However, while national identity continues the tradition of maintaining a perfect overlap of membership with citizenship, state identity challenges the seamlessness of the membership–citizenship nexus.

Moreover, by comparing the closely related but distinct concepts of citizenship and membership in this chapter, we see that they are both integral to establishing lasting connections between states and newcomers, but integral for different reasons. The payoff of distinguishing the concepts of citizenship from membership is to get hold of contemporary states' astonishing investments in immigrant integration into mainstream institutions and values both in and short of citizenship acquisition. It allows the identification of civic integration as a unique set of policies that does not alter existing citizenship configurations, but rather is layered on top of them. And in isolating membership, we can contrast civic requirements to earlier imputations of belonging that are derived from nationhood and encapsulated in citizenship as a policy legacy. Civic integration requirements, in other words, provide an explicit framework for understanding membership in now-multiethnic nation-states. What it leaves, however, is a very legalistic and anodyne citizenship stripped of its symbolic dimension and meaning. This is the very heart of what we might call the contemporary citizenship problem: citizenship – born under the nation-state system – is designed to be both a status and a membership category. That it is deemed insufficient to circumscribe and support a national community by contemporary policy-makers (as evidenced in the adoption of *new* parameters for and expectations of belonging) is the starting point for understanding the significance of civic integration contributions, not a consequence of it. Reinvestments in citizenship through membership indicate that states still care about national discretion to designate insiders and outsiders, but also that citizenship by itself is (no longer) enough.

2

Identifying empirical variation in civic integration policies

INTRODUCTION

This chapter develops and presents systematic comparisons of civic integration policies in Western Europe in a Civic Integration Policy Index (CIVIX).[1] Civic integration requirements are distinguished by both their *content* (articulated expectations for belonging, including society rules) and innovative *commitments*, including language and civic orientation courses, knowledge tests, naturalization ceremonies, integration contracts, etc. In developing a comparative index for capturing this variety of commitment across three legal statuses (entry, settlement, and citizenship), we see confirming evidence of a convergent "civic turn," consistent with a number of existing studies. However, we also see distinct variation in the degree to which states adopt civic integration. Indeed, developing an index to represent new membership requirements enables systematic comparison across cases, providing evidence both of cross-national change and of continued variation.

This aggregate, index-level view reflects significant variation in policy. But, beyond CIVIX scores, variation is also visible by looking more closely at (1) policy design (i.e., what instruments are used); (2) scope of requirements (i.e., how many categories of status are targeted); and, (3) sequencing of policy adoption across legal stages (specifically, whether requirements are unveiled first at permanent residence versus citizenship). This diversity has not gone entirely undetected in existing studies of civic integration policy. In fact, many have taken up the task to descriptively map policy patterns, identifying differences not only across states but also across legal statuses that paint very

[1] This chapter modifies and updates earlier publications of CIVIX scores, in Sara Wallace Goodman, "Integration requirements for integration's sake? Identifying, categorising and comparing civic integration policies," *Journal of Ethnic and Migration Studies* 36, no. 5 (2010), 753–772. Also see Sara Wallace Goodman, "Measurement and interpretation issues in civic integration studies: A rejoinder," *Journal of Ethnic and Migration Studies* 38, no. 1 (2012), 173–186.

different civic integration portraits across Europe.[2] However, this diversity is either not accurately reflected in existing policy coding schemes or scholars have not deemed this evidence of variation significant enough to counterweigh convergence arguments. While ideational convergence, through diffusion and policy learning across states, is undoubtedly present, particularly over time, the robust variation in civic integration policy design not only suggests different applications but also different objectives. Chapter 3 looks more closely at these objectives and argues that this diversity is a product of unique rationales behind civic integration policy adoption (what I term a state's "membership policy strategy"), shaped by national citizenship policy context and politics. But, for our purposes here, this chapter maps the empirical plane and establishes the extent of variation in civic integration policies.

DEVELOPING A CIVIC INTEGRATION POLICY INDEX (CIVIX)

A number of studies have been conducted on integration requirements in Europe, providing rich, within-country detail by making use of country experts as part of collaborative projects. However, to gain the most analytical leverage out of these descriptions of policy and establish a baseline for comparison, there remains a need to translate this rich content into systematic scores. In order to categorize and compare empirical variation, this section identifies and scores existing integration requirements for citizenship, permanent residence, and entry in two snapshot periods: before the introduction of civic integration (1997) and today.[3] By examining two points in time, we observe not only the expansive practice of civic integration across Europe but also the degree of within-case

[2] Some examples include Ricky van Oers, Eva Ersbøll, and Theodora Kostakopoulou, *A Re-definition of Belonging? : Language and integration tests in Europe* (Boston: Martinus Nijhoff Publishers, 2010); Tineke Strik et al., "Synthesis report," in *The INTEC Project: Integration and naturalisation tests: The new way to European citizenship* (Nijmegen, the Netherlands: Centre for Migration Law, Radboud University, 2010); Migration Policy Group, "The Migrant Integration Policy Index (MIPEX)," (Migration Policy Group & British Council, 2011); Ruud Koopmans, Ines Michalowski, and Stine Waibel, "Citizenship rights for immigrants: National political processes and cross-national convergence in Western Europe, 1980–2008," *American Journal of Sociology* 117, no. 4 (2012), 1202–1245; Elspeth Guild, Kees Groenendijk, and Sergio Carrera, eds., *Illiberal Liberal States: Immigration, citizenship, and integration in the EU* (Farnham, Surrey; Burlington, VT: Ashgate, 2009). There have also been countless projects that examine only one or two cases; they provide crucial in-depth understanding of cases but not across-national perspective.

[3] "Today" is an arbitrary cut-point to represent policies as of August 2013. It only includes policies that are implemented and not merely passed. Thus, for example, I exclude a Spanish draft bill to introduce "formal review" through language and integration tests. See Vera Guitiérrez Calvo, "Los extranjeros que pidan la nacionalidad pasarán un test de españole 'integración'," *El Pais* 2013. Additionally, French policy is still moving, where the Socialist government announced intentions to make naturalization easier, including the easing of language and integration requirements. See http://www.lemonde.fr/societe/article/2013/08/28/le-gouvernement-veut-faciliter-les-demarches-des-candidats-a-la-naturalisation_3467493_3224.html (accessed August 28, 2013).

change over a relatively short period of time. In this diachronic and comparative view, requirements have only become more rigorous and there have not been significant reversals of policy that challenge the representativeness of these snapshot years. This is a modified and updated coding scheme of the Civic Integration Policy Index (CIVIX) that first appeared in a 2010 article in the *Journal of Ethnic and Migration Studies*. I update the coding to include changes since publication and, with the space afforded here, revise the coding for easier classification. Specifically, I equalize all requirements across legal statuses.[4] I also simplify the coding rules (e.g., re-categorized requirements previously classified under the "additional integration requirements" category) and focus it strictly on assessment instruments (also removing the family member requirement, which is "built in" to the entry test component). Related to this, I distinguish language certification from civic testing at the stage of settlement. This enables a more accurate snapshot of variation and nuance in policy design, and replicates the categories of other statuses. Finally, I distinguish between mandatory and preparatory courses – bridging the gap between *de jure* and *de facto* requirements, and remove coding for regional variation, like mandatory integration in Flanders, or voluntary schemes, such as voluntary language in Finland and Portugal. In principle, a migrant can volunteer to learn the national language in any country without state assistance. In removing these variations, the index more accurately captures national requirements of integration.[5]

Civic integration is innovative in both the cultural requirements it promotes and the mechanisms used to promote it. The coding is structured around new and traditional instruments to assess knowledge, language, skills and values for entry, permanent residence and citizenship. By using an additive scale, without normative or categorical coding rules, relational assessments can follow from the scoring of each country, where final scores indicate states with more requirements versus less.[6] Scoring is for the "most-difficult" scenario for an ordinary, third-country national migrant completing all three stages.[7] In reality, migrants might earn financial reductions in paying for courses, exemptions from language requirements because of the linguistic or historical characteristics of their sending country or education level, or not seek citizenship. After all, there is nothing teleological or inevitable about status acquisition. However, depicting the most-

[4] In allowing for each requirement to be scored equally, a result of unpegging the CIVIX scale from Howard's Citizenship Policy Index where the maximum score was limited to six, CIVIX scores are boundless and can climb as high as the number of requirements adopted.

[5] CIVIX 2009 scores under the revised coding scheme significantly correlate to CIVIX 2009 scores made with the original coding scheme at r =0.93. On file with the author.

[6] For a deeper discussion on methodological issues of coding civic integration policies, see Goodman, "Measurement and interpretation issues in civic integration studies: A rejoinder."

[7] Minors and spouses experience different permutations of requirements, such as shorter residence durations, lower education or language requirements, and exemptions. For example, family members in Austria must meet a lower language level (A2) for permanent residence than ordinary migrants.

difficult scenario indicates the full force of new policy in theory, if not always in practice.

The coding rules are as follows. First, obligatory civic requirements at entry, settlement and citizenship receive one point per criterion. Examples include and range from the "civic integration test from abroad" in the Netherlands, through civic orientation courses in Germany, to the Austrian citizenship test.[8] Requirements can take different forms in the same category: language proficiency at citizenship can be demonstrated through certification, testing, obtaining a waiver based on education, or completing an interview. Each of these mechanisms of assessment is given equal weight. Likewise, declarations of value commitments take multiple forms (e.g., oral oaths, written statements, signing charters, naturalization ceremonies). All these instruments are coded equally, avoiding the interjection of subjectivity, for what is easy for one migrant, say, certification of language, might be impossible for another.

Second, there are *compounding* factors – particularly in regard to requirements for establishing permanent residence – which increase a requirement's difficulty. An additional half point is added for each of these factors, such as if the migrant has to pay fees to participate in an integration course or if tests are assessed at a high language level.[9] Language level assessment for all stages corresponds to a common scale: the Common European Framework of Reference for Languages (CEFR). The CEFR provides a standardized instrument to comparatively assess the difficulty of national language levels. The CEFR divides learning levels into three broad divisions (A: basic speaker; B: independent speaker; C: proficient speaker), which are further subdivided into six levels (in escalating difficulty: A1: breakthrough; A2: waystage; B1: threshold; B2: vantage; C1: effective operational proficiency; C2: mastery).[10] In translating

[8] This is different from the 2009 coding, where citizenship barriers were only given half a point because "language fluency and country knowledge increase over time, therefore a final citizenship test is less arduous than a settlement test," in Goodman, "Integration requirements for integration's sake? Identifying, categorising and comparing civic integration policies," 760. Removing this assumption frees the index of bias.

[9] I exclude fees for tests and language certification at all stages. All states that require tests charge administrative fees, rendering a potential penalty weight redundant and its exclusion yields little effect on the overall representativeness of scoring. For example, the "Life in the UK" test costs £50 (≈ €60), Denmark at DKK 704 (≈ €95), and the Netherlands at €250. Unlike language, there is no external standard for determining cut points between acceptable and onerous fees. Moreover, these prices can pale in comparison to the total cost of naturalization, which is £874 (≈ €1013), DKK 1000 (≈ €135), and €810, respectively. Regarding certification, proficiency can be assessed through any number of means and at any number of private institutions. As is the case in Austria and Germany, prices for language training are determined by the providing vendor (i.e., set by the market) and not the state. Additionally, immigrants may pay for preparatory classes to successfully obtain certification, but are not under an obligation required by the state. CIVIX avoids potential distortion by excluding fees for tests and certification.

[10] For more, see Council of Europe, *The Common European Framework of Reference for Language: Learning, teaching, assessment* (Cambridge: Cambridge University Press, 2001). The CEFR levels are also reproduced in Appendix I.

these stages to the index in the form of compounding weights, entry level (A1) serves as the baseline and receives no additional points, while escalating levels receive incrementally escalating requirement "weights": A2 adds a quarter of a point; B1 adds half of a point; and, B2 adds three-quarters of a point. Finally, if a course is not required but recommended for the average migrant to adequately prepare for mandatory language certification and testing (Austria, the UK, the Netherlands), then this preparatory course is ascribed half a point.[11] This is distinct from voluntary language learning, in which immigrants are encouraged to obtain language skills to improve integration and labor market mobility but are not assessed on proficiency as a condition for status (e.g., Sweden).

Third, and finally, there is an *ameliorating* factor in terms of design that can make the chain of requirements less arduous. If a requirement completed for permanent residence "double counts" for citizenship, a deduction of 1 is given for each requirement (either language proficiency or knowledge testing). In the case that a language requirement for citizenship is fulfilled at permanent residence, any weight for language level added at citizenship is also deducted in this column.

These simple scoring rules yield a representative and parsimonious policy snapshot that portrays both scale and variety. I recognize that by treating all requirements as equal time commitments, I lose variation that could emerge from scaling potential number of course hours or test fees. This may yield a more detailed picture of requirements, but the slippery slope to infinite regress would sacrifice the parsimony necessary for sustained comparison. A number of edited works and projects already bring to bear sufficient, detailed descriptions to satisfy the former, but one of the foundational goals of this research project is to provide comparisons to enable medium-N comparisons. Moreover, as I discuss further later in this chapter, high levels of correlation between CIVIX and indices with more indicators suggest that more measures are not necessary for depicting the general landscape and differences between policies.

Before turning to the actual CIVIX scores across the EU-15, the different integration requirements across the three legal status-acquiring processes require further explanation. Each process – immigration (acquiring the right to enter or settle temporarily), settlement (acquiring permanent residence), and naturalization (acquiring citizenship) – can be punctuated with integration assessment, but a rear-view look at fifteen years of policy development has shown distinct norms for practice at each legal barrier.

11 To fulfill the language obligation, an immigrant must obtain certification. To do so, they may either self-prepare or take preparatory classes. Therefore, the state may not obligate an immigrant to take a class *de jure*, but it may be the only means of possible preparation, rendering it a requirement *de facto* under the "most difficult" scenario. Each state offers the opportunity of waiving out of coursework or a test with high language proficiency in the host language. For example, in the Netherlands a migrant that passes the NT2 exam ("Dutch as a second language exam") earns exemption from the integration test and, therefore, would also not take the preparatory course. However, this exemption would not apply to the average immigrant.

Entry

Immigration tests are a new component to the entry process in the major immigrant-receiving states of Western Europe. States have traditionally required language proficiency for highly skilled migrants, but the extension of this language requirement to a more generalized population, namely to family-based migration and religious leaders, is entirely new. While a number of states require assessment for immigration, there is significant variation in design. The first point of difference is content. The Dutch "Integration from Abroad" is alone in assessing knowledge of society in addition to basic-level language proficiency (speaking, reading, and listening comprehension).[12] All other practicing countries exclusively assess language. France is alone in conducting an interview-based evaluation on language and values, but also in setting no minimum level of language requirement. Immigrants undergo an assessment of language and values of French society in their home country. If an immigrant does not pass the evaluation, he/she is required to take language sessions and orientation courses ("formation sessions") in France, but is not barred from entry. In other words, unlike the Dutch, German, British, and Austrian permutations, passing a test is not a condition for entry or family unification. (N.B. For this reason, the French test receives only half a point for entry.)

Alongside the mechanism of evalution, a second difference in assessment is the point or location of evaluation. In the Dutch case, the computer-based exam is administered at the embassy or consulate in the applicant's home country and an entry visa cannot be granted without first passing the exam. In Denmark, the exam is administered after immigration to Denmark. The family-based migrant has six months from the date of entry to take and pass the Danish as a second language exam at the A1 level or higher. Language assessments for Germany and the UK can be taken either in the receiving state or abroad, both relying on private institutions for training and examination. For third-country nationals to temporarily settle and join family members in Germany, language assessment is largely conducted by the Goethe Institute, a private cultural organization. In the UK, spouses, partners or adult dependents seeking temporary settlement can demonstrate they understand everyday English by undergoing assessment at any number of organizations in the UK (including universities, colleges, and councils) and abroad (including private organizations, such as Educational Testing Service and Pearson).[13] More empirical variation is discussed in Chapter 5.

Still, despite these differences, we can measure three common dimensions of pre-entry requirement to compare relative difficulty. The first component

[12] Between 2011 and March 2013, Denmark also had an immigration test that assessed knowledge of Denmark and Danish society.

[13] The latest list of approved English language tests and centers was released in January 2012 and is available at http://www.ukba.homeoffice.gov.uk/sitecontent/applicationforms/new-approved-english-tests.pdf (accessed July 4, 2012).

measures whether states require language certification for the granting of family reunification and temporary residence. The mechanisms of assessment are variable, including tests at privatized institutions, interviews, tests at embassies, or prior education. A second component is the use of knowledge tests. While a number of states conduct language assessment at this first stage, only the Netherlands (introduced in 2006) maintains a state-designed test to assess both knowledge and language. Certification and tests are each scored at one point. The third component – a compounding factor recorded as a restrictive penalty – reflects the relative difficulty of the language level assessed. Each state assesses language at the A1 entry level, and therefore receives no weight at this stage.

Settlement

Requirements for obtaining permanent residence are similar to those of entry, with the addition of a possible obligation to attend a course in order to prepare for language certification and/or a country knowledge exam. Here, despite variation in design, we can identify a number of common structures that enable cross-national coding. The first component measures whether states require or recommend courses as a preparation for or in lieu of formal assessment. The second and third components reflect these formal assessments, including language certification/testing and a civic knowledge exam. Tests are ubiquitous across all three legal processes, but courses are unique to long-term/permanent residence. This follows the logic that sustained learning and socialization at the earliest stages of settlement are most likely to improve skills and, thus, mobility of new immigrants.

Of course, like pre-entry requirements, not all settlement courses or tests are created equal. In Germany, immigrants who do not possess language ability at the B1 level for obtaining a permanent settlement permit participate in integration courses, combining language and civic orientation (introduced in 2005). A standardized language and integration test is the culmination of this course, and only after this can a certificate of successful participation be issued. An immigrant can gain exemption from the language component if they present a certificate of skill, but proof of societal knowledge for exemption from the integration test can only be demonstrated if a migrant has "finished German secondary school."[14] Thus, Germany is scored with one point for its mandatory integration course, and two additional points for language certification and the civic test. A half-point weight each is also added for language

[14] Marina Seveker and Anne Walter, "Country Report Germany," in *The INTEC project: Integration and Naturalisation Tests: The new way to European Citizenship* (Nijmegen, the Netherlands: Centre for Migration Law, Radboud University, 2010).

level (B1) and course fee (€792 for 660 hours of integration coursework[15]). Greece maintains a similar design. Denmark exhibits a variation of this approach, where an immigrant must meet the B1 language level by attending an obligatory language course that includes skills training and culminates in both language certification and an "active citizenship exam" (or evidence of active community involvement under the new points system). In contrast to Germany, this mandatory course is provided free by the state. Italy maintains a similar practice in its new credit-based approach; any migrant who resides in Italy for one year or longer signs a contract in which they commit to "learn spoken Italian and achieve at least the level A2 ... [and] acquire adequate knowledge of the fundamental principles of the Italian Constitution."A test or participation in social activities is not, therefore, mandatory but it can earn the migrant points toward settlement.[16]

Austria represents a second approach to civic integration for settlement in that there is no obligation to attend any integration course. Rather there is only an obligation to demonstrate knowledge of German by obtaining a certificate from a recognized language institution. Austrian scholar Bernhard Perchinig writes that in assessing language, not country knowledge for settlement, "Austria does not follow a model including cultural assimilation or the provision of knowledge about the political system, but a model strictly confined to language competency testing."[17] In this instance, an applicant is required to demonstrate language certification by any means convenient; they can self-prepare or attend a language course.

In a final model, the UK and the Netherlands have both recently abandoned more nuanced assessment tools in favor of a single-exam approach.[18] Both maintain a laissez-faire, market-oriented approach to preparation in which immigrants may self-prepare or voluntarily attend and pay for language classes. In both cases, the requirement of language proficiency and country knowledge

15 Special courses with more hours cost more (up to €1152). Exemptions can also be obtained for those who receive unemployment benefit or social assistance. See the Federal Office for Migration and Refugees (BAMF) website at http://www.bamf.de/EN/Willkommen/DeutschLernen/Integrationskurse/TeilnahmeKosten/Aufenthaltstitel_nach/aufenthaltstitel_nach-node.html (accessed August 28, 2013).

16 Additionally, obtaining language proficiency at levels above A1 or attending more hours of social integration courses can earn the migrant more points. For specific credits, see the agreement at http://www.welcomeoffice.fvg.it/media/16457/integration%20agreement_en.pdf (accessed September 3, 2013).

17 Bernhard Perchinig, "Country Report Austria," in *The INTEC Project: Integration and naturalisation tests: The new way to European citizenship* (Nijmegen, the Netherlands: Centre for Migration Law, Radboud University, 2010), 25.

18 In 2013, the UK abandoned the "two-path" approach to settlement and citizenship, where an immigrant could take the "Life in the UK" exam at the B1 level to satisfy both language and knowledge requirements, or attend an English language with civic content course and improve one language level. In the same year, the Netherlands dropped the practical exam component from the integration exam.

is assessed through exams (the "Life in the UK" test and the Dutch "integration exam," respectively), not course attendance.

Despite these variations in design, we can systematically record whether states require courses and tests (broadly defined to include certification). Regarding courses, the comparative table delineates between obligatory and preparatory courses. To restate the distinction: obligatory courses require proof of attendance for status acquisition; preparatory courses do not have required attendance but language is assessed for status and are, therefore, recommended for learners. Both are distinct to voluntary courses, in which language acquisition is promoted as a key to integration but there is no formal assessment for status acquisition. In addition to scoring the course requirement itself, I also include a weight for course fees. A unique pattern emerges in this respect; states that *require* course attendance provide them at no cost (Denmark, Greece, Italy), while states that do not require but *encourage* course participation place the financial obligation on the individual (Austria, the Netherlands, the UK). This latter practice is consistent with the individual-oriented, liberal model of preparation in which the migrant can choose his/her means of preparation. An exception to this pattern is Germany, as previously mentioned.

I should note an important caveat to the conceptualization of requirements for permanent residence in CIVIX: the exclusion of contracts. Austria, Denmark, France, Italy, Luxembourg, and the Netherlands all make use of an integration contract to bind an applicant to integration commitments within a certain period of time in exchange for assistance and rights. The integration contract is a significant innovation that can be seen as the hallmark of the "civic turn": transforming the metaphorical contract relationship between the individual and the state into an actual one. In this contract, the immigrant formally commits to participation in language training and education, including respecting the state's laws and values, while the state commits to providing language and civic instruction, which in theory enables mobility and opportunity equal to natives. In these cases, the contract *enables* participation and *activates* the requirement of integration, but does not constitute nor is evidence of integration itself. So while the membership obligations of the contract are reflected in CIVIX, the commitment mechanism itself (as well as other dimensions of the contract, such as a clean criminal record) is excluded.

Citizenship

The final set of measures addresses integration at the stage of citizenship. I assign one point for each requirement: language certification, civic knowledge testing, and proactive value commitments. With regard to language, a majority of states require certification of language proficiency, assessed through formal certification (e.g., France), testing (e.g., the UK), education (e.g., Austria), or through a personal interview (e.g., Spain). This is the most popular practice, and is carried out in a number of states that do not require civic integration at earlier stages.

The only exceptions are Ireland, Italy, and Sweden. Belgium was a former exception, but re-introduced a language and integration requirement in 2012 after having jettisoned it in 2000. And – as an unambiguous indicator of the population of concern – Italy introduced comprehensive integration and language requirements for permanent residence with the Security Act of 2009 (in force in 2012), but without similar changes to citizenship. As in the earlier stages, I include a weight to capture difficulty of language.

In terms of civic assessment, we see variation in terms of how knowledge is evaluated: France and Greece appraise knowledge of society and values through an interview; Luxembourg requires attendance at citizenship classes; Austria, Denmark, Germany, the Netherlands, and the UK use citizenship tests. Importantly, however, points assigned for language and civic evaluation (including any added weight for language difficulty) are subtracted from the total score if requirements are fulfilled at permanent residence. So while an immigrant is required to pass the "Life in the UK" and English language test for permanent settlement in the UK *and* for citizenship, fulfilling the requirement for permanent residence exempts the applicant from having to repeat it should they seek naturalization. In the case of France, a migrant is only exempt from the language requirement for citizenship if they obtained a B1 level diploma for permanent residence. As there is no set language level for permanent settlement, however, I do not "double count" this requirement under the most-difficult scenario. For civic assessment, France also receives one point for its assimilation interview. This is separate from the language certification at the B1 level, in which a candidate for citizenship participates in an interview to assess his/her knowledge of rights and duties and culminates in the signing of a charter of rights and duties of French citizens.[19]

A final component of citizenship is the assessment of value commitments. Unlike entry and permanent residence, naturalization still represents the formal joining of a national political community. As with historical oaths, this status still denotes a set of values and commitments to the nation-state. Contemporary values may more accurately resemble "constitutional patriotism"[20] than cultural nationalism, but civic integration is notable for interjecting formal measures of individual commitment to liberal-democratic values. Any mandatory commitment made to the state, the Constitution, the government, rules, etc., is assigned one point, whether it is sworn publically in a naturalization

19 Not signing the charter renders the applicant "inadmissible for 'lack of assimilation'," according to Abdellali Hajjat, "Naturalisation procedures for immigrants: France," in *EUDO Citizenship Observatory Naturalisation Procedures Reports* (Florence: EUDO Citizenship, Robert Schuman Centre for Advanced Studies, EUI, 2013), 4. For this reason, I include the charter as part of the interview, where signature takes place, and do not record an additional point for value commitments made at the naturalization ceremony, which is optional to attend.

20 Jan-Werner Müller, "Is Europe converging on constitutional patriotism? (And if so: Is it justified?)," *Critical Review of International Social and Political Philosophy* 10, no. 3 (2007): 377–387.

ceremony, privately in an oath in front of a judge, or as a written declaration. Unlike integration contracts, fulfillment of this criterion is the act itself. Integration contracts also require an understanding and commitment to values, but this is measured through behavior, such as participation in language courses or independence from social assistance. In the case of citizenship, there are no measures for this commitment outside the commitment itself.

Here I mention a second caveat, similar to that for integration contracts: I have omitted a separate score for what I term generalized integration requirements. Nationality law in several states includes language that an immigrant demonstrate "sustainable" (Austria) or "sufficient" (Luxembourg, the Netherlands, Spain) integration. Much of this language was in place before civic integration policies were introduced, and a number of the language and oath requirements recorded in the 1997 CIVIX score come from these general integration clauses. One could even argue that their initial ambiguity impelled the explicit articulation of requirements through mandatory integration policies.

Measuring these vague clauses separately, however, is problematic primarily because much of this language has been made redundant by more recent articulations and specifications of integration over time through civic integration.[21] These integration clauses are still meaningful as a proxy for evaluating desired behavior traits; in Austria, France, the Netherlands, and Spain, integration is not only language acquisition but also commitment to liberal-democratic values, demonstrated in behavior (such as monogamous marriage and repudiation of female circumcision) and general adaptation to culture. While polygamous marriage is also illegal in the UK, it is a rule maintained entirely separate from integration. The same can be said for economic considerations; Austria includes secure employment as a condition of integration, while other states maintain it as a requirement outside the integration context. This type of inconsistency makes it difficult to evaluate systematically.

Data for coding is drawn primarily from state policy, derived from relevant ministry websites, as well as from country reports by national legal experts for the EUDO Citizenship Observatory.[22] This project, hosted at the Robert Schuman Centre of the European University Institute in Florence, Italy, represents a consortium of legal experts and country specialists from across Europe, whose task is to present comparable data on citizenship law and policy. Country reports were published in 2010, and updated in 2012–2013, continuing the detailed work of original reports published as part of the NATAC project.[23]

[21] The only state to maintain a general integration requirement without introducing formal policies of integration is Spain, subjectively assessing "adaptation to the Spanish culture and Spanish life style." Since this ambiguous requirement is patently outside the scope of civic integration, reflecting instead a requirement of national identity attachment, I omit it from coding.

[22] See country reports under "country profiles" at www.eudo-citizenship.eu.

[23] Rainer Bauböck et al., eds., *Acquisition and Loss of Nationality in Fifteen EU States. Volume 2: Country analyses. Policies and trends in 15 European countries* (Amsterdam: Amsterdam University Press, 2006b). EUDO Citizenship also expands the number of cases, from 15 to 33

When country reports did not provide necessary or updated information, I corresponded directly with country experts. Evidence was also drawn from newspaper reports, especially for more recent legal changes, journal articles, interviews, and edited volumes, particularly for capturing the intricacies of requirements at entry and settlement.

CIVIX SCORES

In order to identify both policy and change, Tables 2.1 and 2.2 reflect membership requirements by scoring for entry, settlement, and citizenship before change (1997) and today, respectively. Though I use the rules of CIVIX scoring to measure policy at both times, I recognize that it is anachronistic to label integration requirements that precede the Dutch WIN Act (the first civic integration policy in Europe) under a *civic* integration policy rubric. In fact, one of the most significant differences between pre-civic integration policy and today is that, in the turn toward promoting common values and autonomy, dimensions of general integration requirements – namely sufficient knowledge of a national language – have been separated out and shored up with objective measures.[24] Another difference, of course, is the entirely new component of assessing country knowledge. However, for the purposes of consistency across two points in time, I maintain the CIVIX nomenclature.

Starting with 1997 and consistent with the significance of the "objective turn" of civic integration, we see very little in terms of formal integration requirements at any stage of membership. There is no common standard for defining "sufficient" or "adequate" as levels of language acquisition (which prohibits adding point weights). There are also almost no integration requirements at entry or residence. This paucity of formal requirements reflects a different way of thinking about integration, largely to do with the degree to which newcomers had access to citizenship. As previously mentioned, where migrants were subject to long and continuous durations of residence it was *assumed* that residence would result in sufficient integration. A second way to interpret these requirements is not from the perspective of when and under what conditions the state acknowledges the outsider as eligible for naturalization, but how it defines citizenship that is oriented toward insiders. The most robust practices of integration are in Greece and Spain, two traditional émigré societies that organize citizenship around special treatment of co-ethnics. Both recognize language as a key facet of membership – in the Greek phrasing, it is evidence

and beyond (some countries added after the initial round of 33 include Albania, Armenia, Belarus, Bosnia-Herzegovina, Ukraine, Kosovo, Macedonia, Montenegro, and Serbia).

24 For example, a number of states assessed language in 1997 but did not use formal certification to do so. Therefore, despite the column heading, the "certification" was primarily informal, conducted through interviews and without standardized assessment or benchmarks, such as the CEFR.

TABLE 2.1. *Civic Integration Policy Index (CIVIX) scoring in 1997*

	1: Immigration				2: Permanent residence				3: Citizenship					SCORE
	Language certification	Civic test	Language level	Course	Language certification	Civic test	Language level	Course fee	Language certification*	Civic test	Language level	Ceremony/ oath	PR double count?	
Points	*1*	*1*	*.25 at A2* *.5 at B1* *.75 at B2*	*1* *.5 if preparatory*	*1*	*1*	*.25 at A2* *.5 at B1* *.75 at B2*	*0.5*	*1*	*1*	*.25 at A2* *.5 at B1* *.75 at B2*	*1*	*-1 for C* *-1 for L* *-L weight*	
AUT	N (0)	N (0)	–	N (0)	N (0)	N (0)	–	–	Y (1)	N (0)	"sustainable"	N (0)	–	1
BEL	N (0)	N (0)	–	N (0)	N (0)	N (0)	–	–	Y (1)	N (0)	"evidence"	N (0)	–	1
DEN	N (0)	N (0)	–	N (0)	N (0)	N (0)	–	–	Y (1)	N (0)	"speaking"	N (0)	–	1
FIN	N (0)	N (0)	–	N (0)	N (0)	N (0)	–	–	Y (1)	N (0)	"sufficient"	N (0)	–	1
FRA	N (0)	N (0)	–	N (0)	N (0)	N (0)	–	–	Y (1)	N (0)	"sufficient"	N (0)	–	1
GER	Y (0)†	N (0)	speaking	N (0)	interview (1)	N (0)	basic	–	Y (1)	N (0)	"sufficient"	N (0)	–	2
GRE	N (0)	N (0)	–	N (0)	N (0)	N (0)	–	–	Y (1)	N (0)	"adequate"	Y (1)	–	2
IRE	N (0)	N (0)	–	N (0)	N (0)	N (0)	–	–	N (0)	N (0)	–	Y (1)	–	1
ITA	N (0)	N (0)	–	N (0)	N (0)	N (0)	–	–	N (0)	N (0)	–	Y (1)	–	1
LUX	N (0)	N (0)	–	N (0)	N (0)	N (0)	–	–	Y (1)‡	N (0)	"sufficient"	N (0)	–	1
NET	N (0)	N (0)	–	N (0)	N (0)	N (0)	–	–	Y (1)	N (0)	"reasonable"	N (0)	–	1
POR	N (0)	N (0)	–	N (0)	N (0)	N (0)	–	–	Y (1)	N (0)	"sufficient"	N (0)	–	1
SPA	N (0)	N (0)	–	N (0)	N (0)	N (0)	–	–	Y (1)	N (0)	–	Y (1)	–	2
SWE	N (0)	N (0)	–	N (0)	N (0)	N (0)	–	–	N (0)	N (0)	–	N (0)	–	0
UK	N (0)	N (0)	–	N (0)	N (0)	N (0)	–	–	Y (1)	N (0)	"sufficient"	N (1)	–	2

* See note 24.

† This requirement applied only to *Aussiedler* (ethnic German) immigrants, where assessment of German dialect qualified immigrants for a right of entry. Because it was narrow to a specific population, it does not count as a general integration requirement.

‡ While a language requirement was not officially or explicitly stipulated in nationality law until 2001, Luxembourg has maintained a "sufficient assimilation" clause since 1940, which involved the "foregrounding of applicants' proficiency to varying degrees."

TABLE 2.2. *Civic Integration Policy Index (CIVIX) scoring today*

	1: Immigration				2: Permanent residence				3: Citizenship					SCORE
	Language certification	Civic test	Language level	Course	Language certification	Civic test	Language level	Course fee	Language certification	Civic test	Language level	Ceremony/ oath	PR double count?	
Points	*1*	*1*	*.25 at A2* *.5 at B1* *.75 at B2*	*1* *.5 if preparatory*	*1*	*1*	*.25 at A2* *.5 at B1* *.75 at B2*	*0.5*	*1*	*1*	*.25 at A2* *.5 at B1* *.75 at B2*	*1*	*-1 for C* *-1 for L* *-L weight*	
AUT	Y (1)	N (0)	A1 (0)	Preparatory (.5)	Y (1)	N (0)	B1 (.5)	Y (.5)	Y (1)	Y (1)	B1 (.5)*	ceremony (1)	L (-1.5)	5.5
BEL	N (0)	N (0)	–	N (0)†	N (0)	N (0)	–	–	Y (1)	N (0)	A2 (.25)	N (0)‡	–	1.25
DEN	Y (1)	N (0)	A1 (0)	Y (1)	Y (1)	Y (1)	B1 (.5)	N (0)	Y (1)	Y (1)	B2 (.75)	written (1)	N (0)	8.25
FIN	N (0)	N (0)	–	N (0)	N (0)	N (0)	–	–	Y (1)	N (0)	B1 (.5)	written (1)	–	2.5
FRA	Y (.5)	N (0)	A1 (0)	Y (1)	Y (1)§	N (0)	A1 (0)	N (0)	Y (1)	interview (1)	B1 (.5)	voluntary (0)	N (0)	5
GER	Y (1)	N (0)	A1 (0)	Y (1)	Y (1)	Y (1)	B1 (.5)	Y (.5)	Y (1)	Y (1)	B1 (.5)	oral (1)	L (-1.5)**	7
GRE	N (0)	N (0)	–	Y (1)	Y (1)	Y (1)	A2 (.25)	N (0)	Y (1)	interview (1)	A2 (.25)	oral (1)	L (-1.25)	5.25
IRE	N (0)	N (0)	–	N (0)	N (0)	N (0)	–	–	N (0)	N (0)	–	oral (1)	–	1

ITA	N (0)	N (0)	–	Y (1)	Y (1)	Y (1)	A2 (.25)	N (0)	N (0)	N (0)	–	oral (1)	N (0)	4.25
LUX	N (0)	N (0)	–	N (0)	N (0)	N (0)	–	–	Y (1)	class (1)	B1 (.5)	N (0)	–	2.5
NET	Y (1)	Y (1)	A1 (0)	Preparatory (.5)	Y (1)	Y (1)	A2 (.25)[††]	Y (.5)	Y (1)	Y (1)	A2 (.25)	ceremony (1)	B (-2.25)	6.25
POR	N (0)	N (0)	–	N (0)	N (0)	N (0)	–	–	Y (1)	N (0)	A2 (.25)	N (0)	–	1.25
SPA	N (0)	N (0)	–	N (0)	N (0)	N (0)	–	–	Y (1)	N (0)	B1 (.5)	Y (1)	–	2.5
SWE	N (0)	N (0)	–	N (0)	N (0)	N (0)	–	–	N (0)	N (0)	–	N (0)	–	0
UK	Y (1)	N (0)	A1 (0)	Preparatory (.5)	Y (1)	Y (1)	B1 (.5)	Y (.5)	Y (1)	Y (1)	B1 (.5)	ceremony (1)	B (-2.5)	5.5

* For permanent residence and citizenship, a migrant must achieve the B1 level with "sustainable personal integration," which may include volunteering, professional work or general welfare work as stipulated by the integration agreement. For citizenship, if the immigrant does not complete the integration contract and instead is "exceptionally well-integrated," the required level is B2.

† Integration courses are required in Flanders only, not Wallonia or Brussels-region.

‡ A written declaration is required for the naturalization procedure, but this is an exceptional route as most immigrants use the declaration procedure, which requires no statement.

§ Test only required if level of proficiency is below A1.1.

** Plans to count the civic education test for residence as proof of knowledge for citizenship have not yet been implemented. Zweite Verordnung zur Änderung der Integrationskursverordnung, February 2012, §13d.

†† New immigrants have a higher required level of Dutch (A2) than settled migrants (A1).

of "genuine Greek consciousness"[25] – and require both language as a component of integration and value commitments in the form of oaths.

A second pattern visible in this early snapshot is that where there are requirements of integration, they predominantly exist at the stage of citizenship. In contrast to contemporary policy, these provisions required that immigrants had either a working knowledge of the country's language, or social connections to the host country, or both. Again, this was often achieved through prolonged residence (if not by marital connection). In other words, the state did not provide nor facilitate this integration directly. Language assessment was also subjective; two immigration officers in one office might have strikingly divergent interview procedures, not to mention the confounding discrepancy that takes place across regions and cities in the same state. Generalized integration requirements are prevalent, but the linguistic components have since been "filled in" with formalized assessment procedures in a number of receiving states. There is a notable absence of society knowledge in this early snapshot, though the practice was already well-entrenched across the Atlantic in the United States and Canada. Finally, we see that a number of states use oaths. This is perhaps the most historical remnant of the golden age of nationalism, where persons (from new citizens to soldiers) swore fidelity to the state, monarch, constitution, etc.

It is important to address the representativeness of 1997 as a snapshot or historical watermark of integration in citizenship. While the decade or so afterward can be characterized by large amounts of change, including expansion of integration to non-traditional membership statuses, the preceding decade can be characterized instead by continuity.[26] In fact, many of the sample states have maintained language requirements for decades (Denmark's requirement dates back to 1849; the UK's since 1911; France's since 1927).

In looking at 1997, Germany stands out as an exceptional case. Since the 1977 Naturalization Guidelines, it required citizenship applicants to demonstrate a "voluntary and lasting orientation towards Germany" and its culture.[27] This cultural assimilation test informally assessed attitude and language, with different *Länder* responsible for implementation. Since 1978, an unrestricted permanent residence permit could be conferred for many reasons, among which

[25] Bruno Nascimbene, *Nationality laws in the European Union = Le droit de la nationalité dans l'Union européenne* (Milano; [London]: A. Giuffrè; Butterworths, 1996).

[26] Koopmans et al. find "the predictive power of the 1980s level" for policy continuity in the 1990s, supporting a national path dependence argument for policy outcomes. Koopmans, Michalowski, and Waibel, "Citizenship rights for immigrants: National political processes and cross-national convergence in Western Europe, 1980–2008," 1227. Looking just at their data collected on cultural requirements (see Appendix II), the 1980 and 1990 scores correlate at $r = 0.89$.

[27] Simon Green, *The Politics of Exclusion: Institutions and immigration policy in contemporary Germany* (Manchester; New York: Manchester University Press, 2004), 40.

was German language proficiency.[28] Ethnic Germans were exempt from language for citizenship (because they were already considered to have German nationality).[29] In 1990, the Aliens Act introduced basic oral language ability as a requirement for persons seeking permanent residence. In 1997, a language test was introduced to serve as a "filtering" device of ethnic Germans immigrating to Germany.[30] The language test, according to Seveker and Walter, assessed "use of a German dialect . . . as an indication of their German ethnicity."[31] Each of these policies resembles contemporary practices, but differs on important grounds. For the immigration test, it was never billed as an instrument to assess or promote integration. In the case of citizenship, like other vague integration requirements, language and country knowledge was subjectively measured through the application process, and not through state-designed courses or examinations. This type of integration requirement is prolific across the EU-15 in this first snapshot year. The *content* might be similar to civic integration today, but the instruments and objectives are plainly different.

The story in 2013 – portrayed in Table 2.2 – reveals a dramatically altered picture. Consistent with convergence views, the use of integration requirements is widespread across major immigrant-receiving states. States assess not only language but also society knowledge in the form of citizenship tests. Among similar practices, Austria, Denmark, Germany, the Netherlands, and the UK have each introduced a citizenship test to assess knowledge of society for the first time. France and Greece assess knowledge through interviews, and Luxembourg requires citizenship class attendance. Cultural requirements have also expanded from naturalization to settlement and entry, indicating that the expectation of "citizenization" has likewise expanded to non-citizen populations. Civic testing for permanent residence is conducted by Denmark, Germany, Greece, Italy, the Netherlands, and the UK, with Denmark, France, Germany, Greece, and Italy requiring civic-oriented coursework.

Not only do CIVIX scores portray a general proliferation of new requirements and new content across the policy landscape, they also portray how old and vague requirements have been transformed into standardized measures of integration. Germany, Austria, and the Netherlands stand out in this regard by replacing vague pronouncements for integration with state-provided courses and benchmarks for measurement. Overall, CIVIX presents a coding approach that best portrays the landscape of requirements, across both country and legal status. This macro-view provides taxonomical evidence of variation for scholars who would otherwise only look unsystematically or anecdotally at major cases.

28 Koopmans, Michalowski, and Waibel, "Citizenship rights for immigrants: National political processes and cross-national convergence in Western Europe, 1980–2008." Note comes from data tables.

29 I thank Simon Green for this point.

30 Kees Groenendijk, "Pre-departure integration strategies in the European Union: Integration or immigration policy?," *European Journal of Migration and Law* 13, no. 1 (2011): 4.

31 Seveker and Walter, "Country Report Germany."

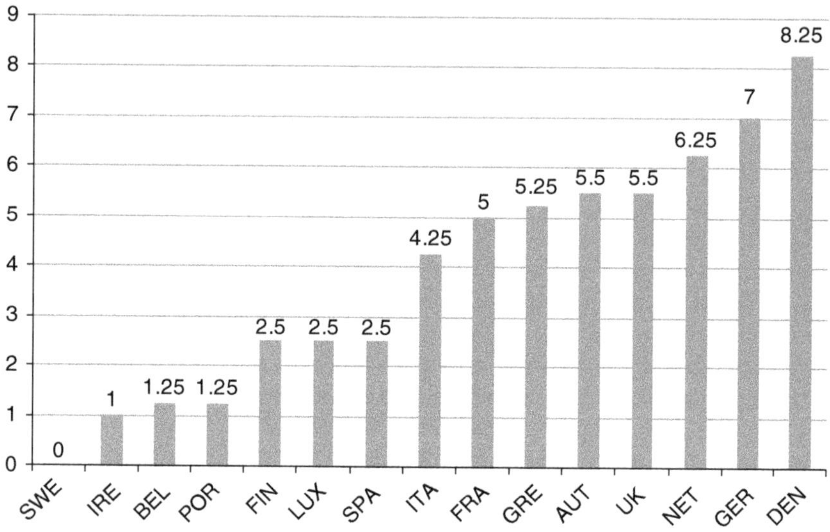

2.1 Distribution of CIVIX scores today

The CIVIX rubric yields scores that not only characterize state membership policy but also enable researchers to compare and identify patterns of similarity and difference between states. A dichotomous response to a dichotomous question – Is there a civic integration trend or not? – would support a bifurcation of practices, where some states have made the "civic turn," while others have not. Figure 2.1 rank orders states by their current CIVIX scores. Here, we see support for the "civic turn" hypothesis, as some states clearly maintain robust practices in contrast to others. However, in the same figure, the variegated distribution of scores reveals a full spectrum of practices. The empirical story is not merely one of civic integration or not, but one of variety and differentiation.

This aggregate view of variation underlines a number of interesting findings. First, there is significant difference even between the maximal practitioners (Denmark, Germany) and the still-rigorous but slightly less robust practitioners (UK, Austria). This is meaningful variation, wherein we identify not only difference between practitioners and non-practitioners, but between gradations of practice. Second, this distribution contains a number of curious outcomes that suggest different motivations for policy adoption. France and Greece are two "most different" immigrant-receiving systems, yet boast similar CIVIX scores: the former because it is a major, immigrant-receiving state that, unlike the others, has resisted the robust and rigorous adoption of tests and courses[32];

[32] The French exception may not be so exceptional, considering Joppke's characterization of civic integration as "only an inch (but still an inch!) away from the cultural assimilation that had once been attributed to the French." Christian Joppke, "Beyond national models: Civic integration policies for immigrants in Western Europe," *West European Politics* 30, no. 1 (2007): 2.

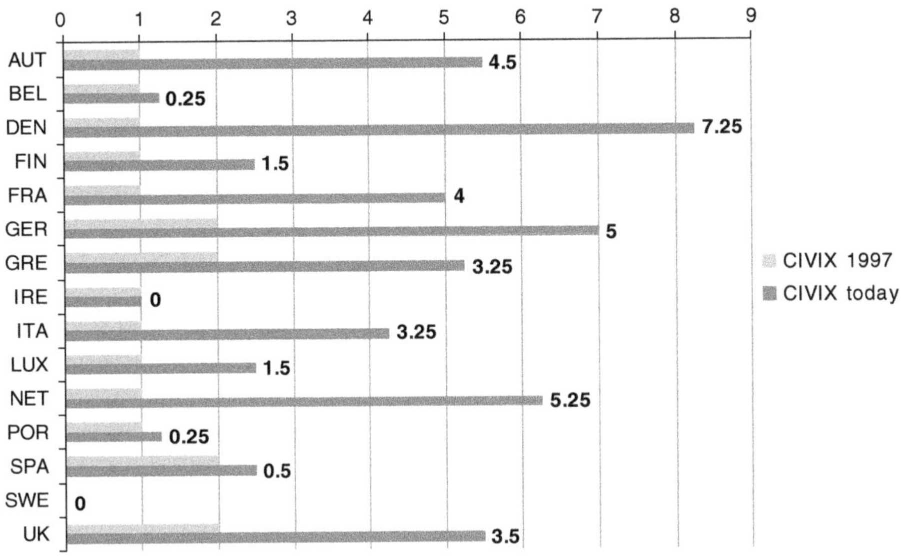

2.2 Changes in mandatory integration requirements

the latter because it is a recent immigrant-receiving state that, unlike the others, has adopted comprehensive testing for permanent residence despite demand.

Variation in the "civic turn" is evident not only in aggregate scores but also in differences of change between 1997 and today. Figure 2.2 displays CIVIX scores from 1997 alongside CIVIX scores today, the bold number at the end of each bar denoting the difference between the two scores. While one would rightly argue that change in CIVIX scores indicates broad, unidirectional change, some states have changed more than others. The most robust practitioners of civic integration experienced the most change: Denmark 7.25, the Netherlands 5.25, Germany 5. Other changes have been more modest: France 4, UK 3.5, Greece 3.25, Luxembourg 1.5, owing to a context of previous practice.[33] Spain (.5) and Portugal (.25) show even less change, while Ireland (0) and Sweden (0) post no change at all. Civic integration is a new phenomenon whereby all adopters experience change, but the extent to which new policy measures redefine existing requirements adds variety to the amount of change taking place.

VALIDITY TESTING

Before proceeding to causal analysis, this section establishes CIVIX as a reliable and externally valid indicator of mandatory integration requirements. CIVIX is a set of scores that indicates the number of requirements as a proxy for relative

[33] Recall that Belgium removed the requirement of language and integration in 2000 and reintroduced it in 2012. The selected snapshot years of CIVIX do not depict this change.

difficulty (at the high end) or ease (at the low end) of membership requirements under the "most difficult" scenario for the average, third-country national migrant. The index is ordinal in that it depicts increasing levels of difficulty, and is not scaled, where the difference between values is equal. In other words, a score of 7 is "more difficult" than a 3, assuming the average immigrant has no prior linguistic knowledge or educational advantage, but the distance between 3 and 4 or 6 and 7 may not be equal.

There are a number of projects that examine policy and capture civic integration in indices. Crucially different, however, is what these indices aim to represent and the scoring rules they use to do it. Two major projects that translate descriptive data on civic integration policies into comprehensive and comparable indicators are Koopmans et al.'s "Indicators for Citizenship Rights of Immigrants" (ICRI) and the Migrant Integration Policy Index (MIPEX).[34] Beginning with Koopmans et al.'s study, the analysis examines policies of citizenship that either promote individual equality or emphasize cultural difference.[35] Mandatory integration requirements are categorized as policies that promote cultural difference, labeled as "cultural requirements" for residence, naturalization, and family reunification. Entry and permanent residence make use of a trichotomous (−1, 0, 1) scale where the presence of civic and language requirements are scored as −1, the presence of one requirement (civic or language) as 0, and the absence of requirements receives a score of 1. Coding for naturalization employs a five-score system (−1. −.5, 0, .5, 1) to capture language assessment, civic knowledge, oath/declarations of loyalty, as well as general assimilation/integration. In each case, higher scores equate to more liberal or inclusive policy. This coding scheme is, in principle, indifferent to the instrument of assessment (courses versus tests, or cases that use both) and the diversity of those instruments themselves (fees, language level), yet the subjective nature of a traditional assimilation requirement is so central to their coding of citizenship that it earns a score of −1, the maximally negative score a country can

[34] There are others still. The following, however, only code for requirements for naturalization. First, Howard's 2009 study includes civic requirements as a restrictive "correction" to his linear measure of the relative inclusiveness of citizenship policy, but coding is not comprehensive. The only scoring rule is whether the extent of civic integration policy is very restrictive (− 0.5) or partially restrictive (− 0.25). Second, Janoski's 2010 study includes language requirements and willingness to integrate (including oaths) as two out of twelve components of his "barriers to nationality" index, but does not provide these sub-scores for testing or the rules for replication Thomas Janoski, *The Ironies of Citizenship. Naturalization and integration in industrialized countries* (Cambridge: Cambridge University Press, 2010), 38. Finally, the EUDO Citizenship Observatory CITLAW indicator scores language (ANAT06c) and civic and cultural requirements (ANAT06d) for ordinary naturalization based on policy in 2011 across 35 countries. This index is compressed to yield scores of between 0 (most restrictive) and 1 (most inclusive). Correlating an average of these variables with only the citizenship scores of CIVIX 2013 for the EU-15 sample shows a strong inverse correlation at $r = -0.817$.

[35] It is a continuation and updating of Ruud Koopmans et al., *Contested Citizenship. Immigration and cultural diversity in Europe* (Minneapolis, MN: University of Minnesota Press, 2005).

earn. The categorical and non-additive nature of coding obfuscates other policies that might be in place for a respective state's citizenship policy. Austria, for example, has an integration requirement ("orientation towards social, economic and cultural life in Austria") for citizenship *and* a formal citizenship test assessing language and country knowledge, but it only earns a score of –1. This is the same score that France earns for cultural requirements for citizenship, which by contrast – in 2008 – only practiced an informal language assessment (assessed through interview) in addition to an assimilation requirement.

Despite these issues, the number of cases (with seven overlapping countries[36]), coverage of policy across all three legal stages, and measurement across multiple years makes this a useful comparative reference for CIVIX.[37] ICRI 1990 and CIVIX 1997 both capture a time period before civic integration adoption (t_0), while ICRI 2008 and CIVIX 2013 represent an "after" period (t_1). Examining scores at t_0 show a generally weak inverse relationship at $r = -0.66$. This largely reflects the decision to exclude Germany's language testing for immigrating co-ethnics as a general immigrant integration policy in CIVIX.[38] It may also reflect general disagreement over how to code generalized integration requirements, where language may or may not be articulated separately. The correlation of indices at t_1 is considerably stronger at $r = -0.93$. This is powerful external validation for the reliability of CIVIX across cases. Figure 2.3 plots these scores alongside each other to portray fit.

A second study to examine mandatory integration requirements and translate them into comparative scores is the MIPEX project. Coordinated by the Migration Policy Group in partnership with the British Council, it uses country experts to collect and score data on immigrant integration policy. The 2010 index provides data for 33 countries (the EU-27, Norway, Switzerland, Canada, the United States, Australia, and Japan) and across 148 policy indicators.[39] These indicators span a number of immigrant integration policies and practices, including labor market mobility, family reunion for third-country nationals, education, political participation, long-term residence, access to nationality, and anti-discrimination. Integration requirements are included as a condition for acquisition of status for family reunification, long-term residence, and

[36] Koopmans et al. include Belgium. However, the regions of Wallonia and Flanders have different practices, where integration for settlement is required in the latter and not the former. Koopmans et al. code these regional practices separately, and aggregation for the purposes of national comparison would distort these differences.

[37] I calculate the sum of relevant indicators for correlational testing. While Koopmans et al. report their indicator scores in the form of averages, individual scores for each barrier of legal status are reported in their raw data (on file with the author). From this I calculated an aggregate score using an additive scale for the purposes of comparability to CIVIX, recognizing that averages distort policy representation. Calculated aggregate scores are reported in Appendix II.

[38] See Table 2.1. If CIVIX 1997 ascribed a point to this *Aussiedler* policy, the correlation would change to $r = -0.83$.

[39] Previous iterations were conducted in 2004 (as the "European Civic Citizenship and Inclusion Index") and 2007.

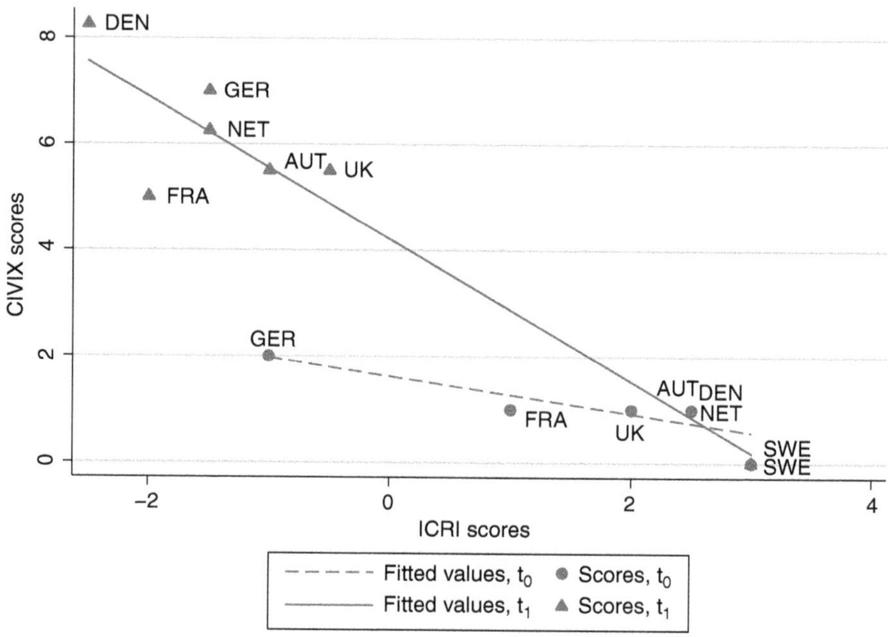

2.3 Relationship between CIVIX (1997, today) and ICRI (1990, 2008)

nationality, and cover facets as diverse as cost, institution/conductor of exam, and exemptions from language or integration requirements. Scores are assigned to policy based on whether it is in compliance with a normative framework of best practices to "promote societal integration in practice," which depends on whether requirements "facilitate or hinder participation" and the "extent to which all residents are legally entitled to equal rights and responsibilities."[40] This translates to, for example, the scoring in MIPEX 2010 of an integration test for citizenship as a 1 ("furthest from highest standards"), an integration course for citizenship as a 2 ("halfway to the highest standards"), and no requirement or a voluntary requirement as a 3 ("highest standards for equal treatment"). In practice, this coding is converted to a scale out of 100: 1 = 0, 2 = 50, 3 = 100. Where any given policy dimension has multiple indicators (e.g., target populations, cost of preparation material, institution in charge of running integration programs, and penalties associated with non-compliance), an average is taken.

As evident in these scoring rules, the objective is not measuring policy *per se* but immigrant opportunity. This renders MIPEX a very different type of index

[40] MPG, "The Migrant Integration Policy Index (MIPEX)," (Migration Policy Group). British Council (2011), 6. Standards that define benchmarks of equal treatment and societal integration are derived from a diversity of sources that include "Council of Europe Conventions or European Union Directives." Moreover, "where there are only minimum standards, European-wide policy recommendations are used," p. 7.

from CIVIX. In fact, MIPEX coding can produce some counterintuitive results if a researcher is strictly interested in comparing policy. For example, France and Spain both receive surprisingly "restrictive" scores for a citizenship requirement (both 17/100), in contrast to states that actually have citizenship tests (Austria 75, Denmark 42, Germany 83, the Netherlands 42). This stems from the position that the use of interviews in France and Spain reflects an ambiguity of administrative discretion that is more unequal and unfair than testing. Of course, making an assumption that an interview is more exclusionary than a test, when there is no evidence – like high rejection rates – associated with this scoring rule, is a problem. Aggregate MIPEX 2010 scores do not represent whether policies are restrictive or not; rather, they indicate supranational and civil society perceptions about what is conducive toward migrant inclusion.[41]

Despite the manifold differences between MIPEX 2010 and CIVIX today, including the former's use of normative coding, they significantly and negatively correlate with one another at $r = -0.87$.[42] This second test of external validity affirms the reliability of CIVIX scores across a larger sample of countries (fifteen in total). It also suggests that a more parsimonious model with fewer indicators is just as useful for capturing policy and identifying patterns. Figure 2.4 plots these scores alongside each other to illustrate both similarities and differences.

EMPIRICAL VARIATION BEYOND CIVIX

CIVIX offers a fitting and valid proxy for different magnitudes of policy output, but it only skims the surface as to the depths of empirical variation. First, it is important to consider that there may be a mismatch between how a policy is designed and scored to how it is practiced. For example, France may be scored as more restrictive than it is in reality. The mandatory civic orientation course is only one day long and the interview assessing assimilation and values at citizenship is not restrictive for most applicants (there were only 20 refusals of citizenship in 2009 to spouses for failure to assimilate[43]). In a second example, Greece's restrictive practice is actually unreported by CIVIX. Pass rates for the integration exam for long-term residence are high (93.4 percent for April 27, 2013), but the

41 For a more in-depth discussion of MIPEX coding, see Goodman, "Measurement and interpretation issues in civic integration studies: A rejoinder."

42 A single measure for MIPEX was computed by taking an average of the following indicators: the average of pre-departure conditions (indicator 22), the average of upon arrival conditions (indicator 23), the average of long-term residence integration conditions (indicator 79), the average of language requirements and exemptions for citizenship (indicator 99), and the average of citizenship/integration requirements and exemptions (indicator 100). Scores are available in Appendix II. I present a correlation between CIVIX and a MIPEX average, instead of a sum score, because entry and citizenship both contain sub-averages. However, both average and sums correlate to CIVIX at $r = -0.87$.

43 "Le refus de nationalité pour 'Défaut d'assimilation'," *Le Nouvel Observateur* 2011 (June 10). Available at http://tempsreel.nouvelobs.com/societe/20110610.OBS4903/le-refus-de-nationalite-pour-defaut-d-assimilation.html (accessed September 4, 2013).

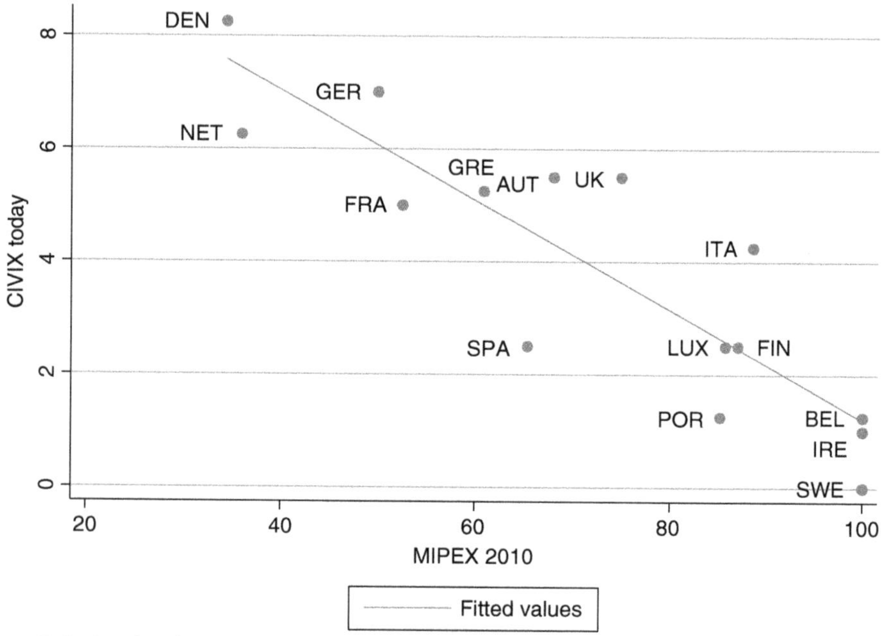

2.4 Relationship between CIVIX today and MIPEX 2010

numbers that take the exam are extraordinarily low (only 634 across the whole country for the April test[44] – and the test is only offered twice a year!). Moreover, while Greek language classes are free, the number of slots is limited (3,000 for the entire country[45]), which significantly increases wait time. These discrepancies do not reflect a weakness in scoring rules or measurement error; instead they illustrate the potential gap between policy and its effects. The case studies in the following chapters attend to this gap by examining both policy (output) and practice (outcome).

Moreover, this attention to qualitative evidence reveals further layers of variation. In addition to practice, there are significant empirical differences in terms of *design* (how requirements are organized), *scope* (which legal categories are targeted), and *sequencing* (the ordering of requirements) that contribute to overall difficulty and impact. These additional differences do not call into question the utility of CIVIX, or the degree to which it can "travel" to other cases, but suggest the importance of qualitative casework for descriptive leverage. While the case studies examine each of these themes in greater detail, I briefly discuss them here.

[44] See http://www.gsae.edu.gr/el/geniki-ekpaidefsi-enilikon/ellinomatheia/eksetaseis-kai-pistopoiisi/apotelesmata-eksetaseon-apriliou-2013 (accessed September 4, 2013).

[45] See http://livingingreece.gr/2007/05/13/free-greek-language-lessons (accessed August 28, 2013).

Design: Much has already been said regarding differences in design, particularly the discussion on design diversity as a potential impediment to systematic coding across legal barriers. While a large degree of this difference can be chalked up to institutional legacy and opportunity, as well as the embedded, historical relationship between state and society,[46] variation highlights major differences between civic integration *ideas* and civic integration *practices*.

Austria, Denmark, and Germany focus civic integration requirements on immigrants seeking permanent residence, in addition to maintaining exams for citizenship. In Germany and Denmark, migrants without language proficiency are required to attend integration courses that include language and civic orientation (and, in the case of Denmark, skills training). Exams are at the culmination of the course and serve as evidence of completion. In Austria, no integration course or test is required, but language courses may be taken as a means for reaching the B1 level, as specified by the Integration Agreement. Each of these states maintains a chain of conditionality regarding integration; a citizenship-seeking immigrant must complete not only requirements for permanent residence but also additional requirements at the stage of citizenship. Integration requirements strengthen permanent residence as a new barrier to status. By contrast, while the UK and the Netherlands also test language and country knowledge and the stage of settlement, there are no further integration requirements for citizenship outside of the naturalization ceremony. This functionally equates citizenship and permanent residence as membership categories.

We also see variation in how the state interprets its role in facilitating integration. In some states, providing and promoting integration is defined as a state obligation, wherein the state cements its commitment in the form of a contract (Austria, Denmark, France, and Italy). Sometimes this obligation manifests in the form of free courses on language and country knowledge (Denmark, France, and Greece). States that use a points-based approach (Denmark, Italy) offer greater flexibility to the individual to chart his/her own route to integration. There is also variation in terms of the role of the state across legal statuses. A potential permanent resident necessarily involves a different type of integration investment than a potential immigrant. Until 2013, Dutch municipalities were financially responsible for an individual's integration. Today, migrants are financially responsible for their own integration, with "soft" loans available for assistance. This notion of state facilitation is entirely – if purposefully – absent when it comes to the civic integration test for newcomers (the immigration test). In fact, while today a potential immigrant can order the self-study pack, *Naar Nederland*, online, in the past one was only able to obtain the pack if

46 On immigrant integration approaches, for example, see Yasemin Soysal, *Limits of Citizenship: Migrants and postnational membership in Europe* (Chicago: University of Chicago, 1994).

it was mailed by a spouse living in the Netherlands. This was a way to encourage learning Dutch through communications in the absence of organized language classes abroad.[47] And, unlike Germany and Austria, which avail themselves of widespread yet private market-run institutions to offer language courses, there is no Dutch equivalent abroad.

France is a case that illustrates variation not only in instruments but also in difficulty. A lack of beginners-level French (A1) does not bar an immigrant from admission, but instead commits him/her to a language course upon arrival.[48] Moreover, the integration contract that mandates civic orientation and language for permanent residence does not have the "teeth" other state requirements have; for example, there is no target of language proficiency. French authorities have also maintained the interview as the mechanism for evaluating the "assimilation" and a knowledge of "rights and duties of French citizenship" for citizenship despite proposals for formal testing.[49]

Scope: The second dimension in which we see significant variation is scope, or the number of legal statuses affected by civic integration measures. The most robust practitioners of civic integration are those states that extend requirements to all three legal barriers (Austria, Denmark, France, Germany, the Netherlands, and the UK). Of these, Denmark represents the most expansive practice of integration requirements, where entry, settlement, and citizenship barriers are individual and non-overlapping. In Germany and Austria, language certification fulfilled at permanent residence exempts aspiring citizens from a similar requirement at citizenship; they are only responsible for completing the citizenship test that assesses knowledge of society. In the Netherlands and the UK, persons are exempt from integration for citizenship if they complete the integration contract as part of their permanent residence acquisition.

By way of contrast, Luxembourg has attached cultural requirements to citizenship but not to permanent residence, while Italy has focused integration on long-term residence and not citizenship. Still other states have made no change at all (Finland, Portugal, Spain), maintaining a correlation between membership and citizenship. Greece has recently introduced rigorous integration requirements for long-term residence (including mandatory courses, a country knowledge test, and A2 language proficiency), while shoring up the existing interview for citizenship and despite attempts to introduce a formal test. In contrast to other European practices, this requirement for permanent

47 The degree of distance between the exam and the provisions provided by the state to prepare for it are criticized by Human Rights Watch as one dimension, among many, rendering this test "discriminatory." See Human Rights Watch, "The Netherlands: Discrimination in the name of integration" (Human Rights Watch, 2008).

48 This is also reflected in fees; while other countries charge for entry assessment, the evaluation by the Immigration and Integration Office (*Office Français de l'immigration et de l'intégration*) is free.

49 Hajjat, "Naturalisation procedures for immigrants: France," 3.

residence does not extend to spouses or other family members on the application. Greece has also not extended these requirements to entry.

Sequencing: Finally, differences between state practices are evident in looking at differences not only in aggregate state practices, but in the sequence of policy adoption. Despite the added advantage of CIVIX in identifying patterns of policy and degrees of change, the sequencing of policy is not evident in this or any other index, though it remains one of the most critical elements in distinguishing priorities for policy adoption. Assuming a greater role for policy learning over time, the order in which integration policies are first adopted is telling. In terms of mandatory integration requirements, the UK and the Netherlands focused on citizenship, in 2002 and 2000 respectively, before extending requirements to permanent residence, both in 2007. Austria and Germany are evidence of a reverse trend, anchoring integration conditions in permanent residence, in 2002 and 2005, before replacing weak integration conditions for robust testing at citizenship, in 2006 and 2007 respectively. Denmark is a further example of this latter strategy.

There are also patterns among states that have adopted membership requirements at only one legal barrier. New-receivers demonstrate a preoccupation with long-term residence. Italy has implemented a rigorous credit-based program for any immigrant residing for over a year, amidst failed proposals to promote integration at citizenship. Likewise, in Greece, change to permanent residence succeeded where proposals for citizenship tests and other changes have been stymied by a shift in government and eclipsed by the Eurozone debt crisis. In older receiving states (Belgium, Luxembourg), proposals for language requirements have all been at the stage of citizenship exclusively. An aggregate view of policy obfuscates these important differences, where sequencing of mandatory integration policies clearly indicates which populations are of first-priority and concern.[50]

CONCLUSION

The development and comparison of integration polices through CIVIX scores reveals a reality teeming with variation underneath a superficial veneer of convergence. This comprehensive and externally valid measure enables comparison across states, stages of legal status acquisition, and time, and provided some analytical leverage to this widespread and intensely scrutinized policy phenomenon. It also improves upon existing studies by presenting a set of parsimonious measures that both identify and differentiate policy, transforming detail-rich description into comparable scores.

CIVIX offers a valid baseline for identifying diversity in membership policy outcomes. But, beyond these scores (or any index), there are further depths of

[50] The adoption of pre-entry requirements happened independent of these aforementioned sequences, justifying separate treatment of immigration requirements in Chapter 7.

variation to be found in the practice, design, scope, and sequencing of new civic integration requirements. In other words, CIVIX scores convey the size or volume of change, while in-depth case-study comparisons can speak to the quality or nature of that change. Moreover, comparing CIVIX scores across states only speaks to the degree of robustness – not difficulty – of membership requirements. The impact of civic integration policy can only be derived by examining the specific contexts for which they were designed. These observations raise a number of new questions: What accounts for empirical variation? Why do states interpret civic integration differently? Do states use civic integration for the same reason? The next chapter takes up the task of examining some of these new questions by accounting for variegated policy outcomes.

3

Explaining civic integration diversity: citizenship legacy and government orientation

INTRODUCTION

Having established significant empirical variation in size of civic integration policy change through CIVIX scores in Chapter 2, as well as pointing to diversity in the scope, intensity, and sequencing of requirements, the objective of this chapter is to account for this variety. Why do states exhibit different civic integration policies? Existing studies are preoccupied with convergence, attributing the widespread adoption of civic integration policies to domestic problems ranging from a general demographic shift to failures or "crises" of immigrant integration policy and the rightist turn, including far-right politicization. But these functionalist explanations do not account for variation. They also suffer from under-specification and indeterminacy; in other words, they do not stipulate how and why states define these general trends as problematic.

Missing from prevailing accounts is the existing institutional context that enables policymakers to interpret and act on these ultimately indeterminate pressures. Specifically, convergence accounts do not consider existing citizenship conditions – i.e., policy starting points of being comparatively liberal (inclusive) or restrictive (exclusive) – as a politically consequential context in which respective political processes play out. It is perhaps not surprising then that the consensus of immigration scholars defines civic integration as a convergent trend. Namely, that observing similar policy adoption without systematic examination of the context in which it is created can lead to issues of omitted variable bias. Endogenous variables are significant, but whether they overturn otherwise enduring traditions is a matter of analysis, not assumption. Overlooking citizenship context also reflects the primary bias in civic integration studies that exclusively considers how new requirements challenge integration philosophies and models, such as multiculturalism. Here, the omission of citizenship in the literature is more surprising. Requirements *may* impact integration policy by challenging state policies of accommodation for newcomers. But they *definitely* affect the acquisition of secure legal status.

In light of these problems, I draw on generalized theories of policy outcomes from the related literature on citizenship to lay out a framework for understanding empirical *variation* in new membership requirements. I point to two key variables: (1) existing citizenship policy (the context and starting point) and (2) ideological orientation of government. Existing citizenship policy – interchangeably referred to here as policy legacy or inherited policy – not only reflects formal opportunities for political inclusion and exclusion but also defines the parameters of the debate in which policy actors propose and implement change. In states with restrictive (exclusive) citizenship, where opportunities to naturalize are already limited and parties in power identify no interest to break this practice, membership requirements serve to *retrench* existing citizenship postures, deepening exclusivity in citizenship and further disincentivizing naturalization. In this scenario, permanent residence may become a durable precondition and alternative membership status – a type of ancillary, demi-citizenship. In liberal (inclusive) citizenship regimes, however, where governments identify no interest or face no pressure for policy change, new membership requirements reify an existing liberal orientation, *enriching* citizenship by encouraging more participation and incentivizing naturalization of long-term residents. In other words, where citizenship is already accessible, the challenge of membership is primarily one of achieving incorporation and defining an accessible civic identity in multicultural states.

However, policy is not made in a vacuum. The second variable – ideological orientation of government – draws on existing accounts to recognize the likelihood for continuity or change and depends not merely on the context in which policymaking takes place, but also on the preferences of policymakers. Left governments are traditionally predicted to produce inclusive policies, while right governments produce exclusive ones. Therefore, leftist governments seeking to open restrictive settings and rightist governments seeking to close liberal settings can achieve incremental change to existing orientations. It is initially incremental, or contained, because governments modulate more drastic views (like wholesale change) to obtain electoral competitiveness or strike bargains to stay in power. Over time, however, incremental change can be successfully layered to yield real differences in membership.

As such, many have suggested that the "restrictive turn" of civic requirements is a reflection and by-product of the conservative shift in national governments in the 2000s. However, modifications are needed to a politics-based approach to gain more explanatory leverage. The first modification is empirically driven. Left governments do not always pursue or produce inclusive policy, especially when they operate in an entrenched, restrictive policy framework in which change is difficult. This is where the dynamic, context-based approach proposed here is helpful. The second modification is conceptual and addresses problems of under-specification. Governments are not merely defined by the position of the majority party in power, but by composition. Single party systems differ from coalition systems, as coalitions are often comprised of political actors with different ideological orientations. As a result, establishing and maintaining a majority government requires costs, whereby a ruling left party may be a filter for heavy-handed policy to appease coalition partners. To summarize the problem of underspecification, a politics-based approach to membership focuses on party position but not the context in which those positions are expressed, i.e., the nature of government composition. It leaves a host of questions unanswered. Are policies designed by the organizing party? By the kingmaker? By active participants on politically salient issue areas?

By drawing on and modifying existing theoretical accounts, this chapter puts forward a dynamic understanding for membership policy variation shaped by past experiences and the current political context in which membership debates play out. This requires removing the assumption that more requirements is equivalent to more restriction, and looking to the rich contexts in which policy gets adopted *and* adapted in major immigrant-receiving states. With this view, we see states take several, unique routes to robust civic integration outcomes. These different paths are significant. They not only illustrate the presence of equifinality (the idea that multiple, distinct casual paths may lead to the same outcome) but also suggest, in fact, that civic integration is a policy area defined by conjunctural causation (where those paths may be made up of combinations of more than one causal condition). While such complexity may be described as "messy" among those that prize grand theorizing or "unsatisfying" among those that prize parsimony, these different pathways to robust civic integration policy only serve to underscore the presence of continued national differences in defining both problems of and solutions for contemporary membership. As such, states may come out of the "civic turn" looking similar, but differences in context, as well as policy sequencing, design, content, and effect perpetuate nation-state differences.

This chapter is structured as follows. First, I examine and identify limitations of existing accounts of civic integration. I argue that these approaches identify important background conditions for what they define as a convergent trend, but do not offer analytical leverage to provide satisfying explanations for diversity. For these endogenous claims, problems of causal asymmetry and indeterminacy are widespread. Given these limitations, I then look to the broader literature on citizenship for explanations that account for policy outcome, focusing on theories of institutional inheritance (path dependence) and citizenship preferences of the governing party or parties. In drawing insight from these works, I identify two key variables to account for variety in civic integration policy strategy: citizenship policy legacy and political orientation of government. Finally, I provide specific theoretical predictions for membership policy strategies, recognizing that politics is a dynamic process in which relevant conditions for policy adoption may be different from those of policy adaptation. This discussion sets up the comparative case studies in Chapters 4–6, which examine the distinct strategies of civic integration policy that result from interactions of citizenship starting points and political party orientation.

EXISTING ACCOUNTS AND THEIR LIMITATIONS

Existing explanations for membership change shed critical light on why civic integration becomes desirable, but do little to account for differences in outcome. In methodological terms, these approaches are valuable for their generality, identifying large-scale endogenous pressures that coincide with civic integration policy adoption. However, they do not supply satisfying explanations for observed empirical diversity, and they do not provide sufficient parameters for testing. While there are a limited number of explanations in the field of civic integration studies and none that account for diversity, this section reviews three explanations for civic integration adoption (a theoretical prior to the question of variation examined here): integration model failure, immigration and welfare state strain, and the "rightist turn" of political parties in power. It concludes by suggesting that instead of trying to develop a general explanation for membership requirements, an understanding of policy variety can be achieved by examining policy in context.

Policy failure

The first explanation for civic integration policy – the integration failure hypothesis – identifies convergence as a result of a shared experience of integration policy failure, namely the "inadequacy of existing models to cope with main immigration and integration challenges."[1] In other words, the state has created institutions to accommodate and promote inclusion, but these have failed to produce their desired effect (owing to institutional design, system misuse/abuse, volition on behalf of the immigrant, etc.). New cultural requirements, therefore, are reported to replace existing integration approaches as part of the "retreat of multiculturalism."[2] In citing a Dutch parliamentary report, for example, Christian Joppke notes the "devastating conclusion" that if "migrants in the Netherlands succeeded, then they did so in spite of, rather than thanks to, government policy."[3] Not only is this the most prevalent explanation among scholars for discussing civic integration in the

[1] Jeanine Klaver and A. W. M. Odé, *Civic Integration and Modern Citizenship: The Netherlands in Perspective* (Groningen: Europa Law Publishing, 2009), 25.

[2] Christian Joppke, "The retreat of multiculturalism in the liberal state: Theory and policy," *British Journal of Sociology* 55, no. 2 (2004): 237–257. For an argument that challenges the zero-sum perspective of civic integration rise in inverse proportion to multiculturalism descent, see Will Kymlicka, "Multiculturalism: Success, failure, and the future," (Washington, DC: Migration Policy Institute, 2012). Moreover, McGhee nicely qualifies this debate by pointing out that the retreat is in "avoiding the term *multiculturalism* rather than moving away from the principles of multiculturalism altogether in Derek McGhee, *The End of Multiculturalism? Terrorism, integration and human rights* (Milton Keynes: Open University Press, 2008), 85.

[3] Christian Joppke, "Beyond national models: Civic integration policies for immigrants in Western Europe," *West European Politics* 30, no. 1 (2007): 1.

Netherlands[4] and the UK[5], but it has also been rhetorically popular in states with no multicultural policies, such as Germany.[6] In this view, where we observe a closer role for the state in facilitating integration through mandatory tests and courses, we see a purposeful departure from more laissez-faire or group-oriented procedures of incorporation.

In evaluating this hypothesis, however, studies have shown that civic integration coexists alongside – instead of replacing – policies of multiculturalism.[7] For example, the adoption of language requirements does not negate classic multicultural policies, such as ethnic representation, affirmative action, or even mother-tongue instruction. Additionally, this hypothesis does not draw on a greater theory of policy failure. Therefore, the type of outcomes we expect to find for a given diversity of systems remains underspecified. Is it integration policy *in general* that fails and requires civic integration solutions? Is it a particular *type* of integration policy that injures an immigrant more than others? Are there theoretical expectations that multiculturalism produces one type of failure while assimilation produces another, or is the prediction merely one of model failure? Lack of specification on these matters makes testing, case selection, and controlled comparisons in particular, a challenge.

A third limitation to this explanation is that the mechanism by which policy shows to be unsuccessful in its objective remains undefined. How does integration policy produce integration failure? Is it through policy drift, where outcomes of policy are different from what was anticipated because the policy was not adapted to new circumstances?[8] In this case, is the transforming "new

[4] Han Entzinger, "The rise and fall of multiculturalism: The case of the Netherlands," in *Toward Assimilation and Citizenship: Immigrants in liberal nation-states*, ed. Christian Joppke and Ewa T. Morawska (Houndmills, Basingstoke, Hampshire; New York: Palgrave Macmillan, 2003): 59–86.

[5] Randall Hansen, "Diversity, integration and the turn from multiculturalism in the United Kingdom," in *Belonging? Diversity, recognition and shared citizenship in Canada*, ed. Keith G. Banting, Thomas J. Courchene, and F. Leslie Seidle (Montreal: Institute for Research on Public Policy, 2007): 351–386; Steven Vertovec, "Towards post-multiculturalism? Changing communities, conditions and contexts of diversity," *International Social Science Journal* 61, no. 199 (2010): 83–95; Christian Joppke, "Limits of integration policy: Britain and her Muslims," *Journal of Ethnic and Migration Studies* 35, no. 3 (2009): 453–472.

[6] France is also an example of where other integration models – in this case, assimilation – fails. In a high-profile 2009 speech, where Sarkozy proposed the burqu ban, he asked "Who doesn't see that our integration model isn't working anymore?" He continued: "Instead of producing equality, it produces inequality. Instead of producing cohesion, it creates resentment."

[7] Keith Banting and Will Kymlicka, "Is there really a retreat from multiculturalism policies? New evidence from the Multiculturalism Policy Index," *Comparative European Politics* 11, no. 5 (2013): 577–598; Matthew Wright and Irene Bloemraad, "Is there a trade-off between multiculturalism and socio-political integration? Policy regimes and immigrant incorporation in comparative perspective," *Perspectives on Politics* 10, no. 1 (2012): 77–95.

[8] Ellie Vasta makes this kind of claim by arguing that Dutch integration policy actually produces "pervasive institutional discrimination," in Ellie Vasta, "From ethnic minorities to ethnic majority policy: Multiculturalism and the shift to assimilationism in the Netherlands," *Ethnic and Racial Studies* 30, no. 5 (2007): 713–740.

circumstance" the nature of immigration (a cultural claim) or the expansion of rights (an institutional claim)? This lack of specification creates further problems for testing. Moreover, there is an issue of timing. Why is integration policy deemed to have suddenly failed? Why are immigrants worse off in a given year instead of the preceding year? In sum, failure may be an accurate rhetorical cue for a handful of countries, but it does not fit as a generalizable explanation where several states do not have a comprehensive integration policy but still adopt civic integration. It also does not resolve the timing problem.

Intake and resource competition

A second explanation for membership requirements attributes widespread integration requirements to the impact of large-scale migration. This immigration hypothesis focuses on the extent to which new requirements serve as a "tool to control the level and composition of immigration."[9] The volume and characteristics of new immigrants are the implied cause, as scholars really offer an interpretation *of* and not an explanation *for* requirements. Integration is an extension of the immigration process and, according to Anita Böcker and Tineke Strike, mandatory requirements help "to make the integration process 'administrable' – or at least help to create the impression that it is a manageable process."[10] Judicial constraints have played a role in defining the limits within which this instrument can be used.[11] Work within this approach also sets up a false choice between promoting integration and controlling immigration, arguing that policies are very much preoccupied with the latter goal.[12]

A subset to this argument goes beyond the effects of intake on policy to identify an intervening effect: welfare state strain. As with the the "civic turn," Western Europe is identified as undergoing a "social downturn," in which welfare state arrangements reflect an emphasis on neo-liberalism and values of self-reliance for newcomers,[13] as certain social policies – including pensions and

[9] Amitai Etzioni, "Citizenship tests: A comparative, communitarian perspective," *The Political Quarterly* 78, no. 3 (2007): 353. Also see Oded Löwenheim and Orit Gazit, "Power and examination: A critique of citizenship tests," *Security Dialogue* 40, no. 2 (2009): 145–167; Sue Wright, ed. *Citizenship Tests in a Post-national Era, International Journal on Multicultural Societies* 10, no. 1 (UNESCO, 2008); Ricky van Oers, Eva Ersbøll, and Theodora Kostakopoulou, *A Re-definition of Belonging?: Language and integration tests in Europe* (Boston: Martinus Nijhoff Publishers, 2010), 312.

[10] Anita Böcker and Tineke Strik, "Language and knowledge tests for permanent residence rights: Help or hindrance for integration?," *European Journal of Migration and Law* 13, no. 2 (2011): 182.

[11] Saskia Bonjour, "Between integration provision and selection mechanism. Party politics, judicial constrains, and the making of French and Dutch policies of civic integration abroad," *European Journal of Migration* 12, no. 3 (2010): 299–318.

[12] Ricky van Oers, *Deserving Citizenship: Citizenship tests in Germany, the Netherlands and the United Kingdom* (Leiden; Boston: Nijhoff Publishers, 2013).

[13] Carl-Ulrik Schierup, Peo Hansen, and Stephen Castles, *Migration, Citizenship, and the European Welfare Stat : A European dilemma* (Oxford: Oxford University Press, 2006); Sergio Carrera,

unemployment assistance – have contracted under conditions of continued migration and economic austerity. This downward shift exacerbates the notion that instruments of the welfare states have long been "internal" mechanisms for regulating migration,[14] predominantly through the conditionality of access to entitlements. This is especially the case where rights contraction has an observed, disproportional effect on newcomers and visible minorities.[15] In this argument, integration obligations are among the costs for benefit receipt. As such, economic self-sufficiency and non-utilization of public assistance and other benefits appear as requirements alongside integration conditions to obtain settlement, family unification, and citizenship. And in the context of the cash-strapped declining welfare state, those who favor welfare benefits are most likely to place restrictions on provisions to immigrants, i.e., welfare chauvinism.[16]

In evaluating these hypotheses, changes in the empirical landscape over the past two decades have provided abundant evidence in support of each of these arguments. The 1990s and early 2000s are largely defined by the expansion of rights, benefits, and security of residence for an increasing number of immigrants in the context of a general easing of citizenship laws. By contrast, the years that follow have been defined as a perceived "backlash" against this liberalization through restrictive immigration and citizenship policy,[17] austerity measures, and – as these explanations maintain – the promotion of mandatory and restrictive membership obligations. These explanations provide a general and parsimonious account for the recent shift toward civic integration, but they are lacking in a number of similar respects to account for the diversity of outcomes.

Among the most prominent problem is that they do not specify what it means to have "excess" –immigrants, benefits, rights, etc. If we understand excess as an imbalance between obligations and rights – a reflection of Charles Tilly's definition of citizenship as a "continuing series of transactions between persons and agents of a given state in which each has enforceable

"Nationality, immigration and 'the republican integration' in France: Normativisation, expansionism and externalisation," in *Illiberal Liberal States: Immigration, citizenship and integration in the EU*, ed. Elspeth Guild, Kees Groenendijk, and Sergio Carrera (Farnham, Surrey; Burlington, VT: Ashgate, 2009): 315–336.

14 Andrew Geddes, "Migration and the welfare state in Europe," in *The Politics of Migration: Managing opportunities, conflict and change*, ed. Sarah Spencer (Oxford: Blackwell, 2003); *The Politics of Migration and Immigration in Europe* (London; Thousand Oaks, CA: Sage Publications, 2003): 153.

15 Diane Sainsbury, *Welfare States and Immigrant Rights: The politics of inclusion and exclusion* (Oxford: Oxford University Press, 2012).

16 Tim Reeskens and Wim van Oorschot, "Disentangling the 'new liberal dilemma': On the relation between general welfare redistribution preferences and welfare chauvinism," *International Journal of Comparative Sociology* 53, no. 2 (2012): 120–139.

17 However, see Sara Wallace Goodman and Marc Morjé Howard, "Evaluating and explaining the restrictive backlash in citizenship policy in Europe," *Studies in Law, Politics, and Society* 60 (2013): 111–139.

rights and obligation uniquely"[18] – then under what conditions do states perceive a paucity of obligations and excess of rights? Why do some states have an imbalance of rights to obligations while others do not? Why do some *perceive* an imbalance where others do not? When is a deficit or imbalance in social rights, immigrant quotas, etc., a problem, and when is it characteristic of an acceptable status quo? This also raises a host of other questions: Does the inverse also hold, that an excess of obligations comes at the expense of rights? Overall, is it really a zero-sum relationship defined by trade-offs? Is there a point of rest for the pendulum, or state of equilibrium, where states have a sufficient rights-to-obligations ratio? Replication and testing is stymied by the undefined nature of "costs" and tipping points. Moreover, while a shorthand test might be to see if there are patterns between recent CIVIX scores and various indicators of immigration intake, integration failure, or welfare state adjustment and strain, these correlational tests assume that explanatory conditions are actual and proportional, instead of rhetorical or symbolic. In other words, the *perception* of immigration threat or integration failure can be a direct cause for policymaker action, but is, by nature, hard to measure. This is where the qualitative case study approach is particularly beneficial.

Ideological orientation of government

Political orientation of government (i.e., orientation of political party in power) is among the most prevalent explanations for policy change in the citizenship literature, in which inclusive change is attributed to the presence of left parties in power and restrictive change to the presence of right parties in power (especially in cases where the far-right gains popularity). Specifically, as Joppke describes, the "political left, true to its universalist vocation, generally supports de-ethnicized citizenship rules, which lower the threshold of citizenship acquisition for immigrants. By contrast, the political right [. . .] generally supports re-ethnicized citizenship rules, strengthening the ties with members abroad even across foreign-born generations."[19] In other words, right governments are predicted to support co-ethnic immigration and limited citizenship for outsiders, while the political left governments support "de-ethnicizing" policy. This should not be interpreted to imply broadly *favorable* immigration and citizenship rules in Europe, just equitable ones.

[18] Charles Tilly, "Introduction," in *Citizenship, Identity and Social History*, ed. Charles Tilly (Cambridge: Cambridge University Press, 1996), 8.

[19] Christian Joppke, "Citizenship between de- and re-ethnicization," *European Journal of Sociology* 44, no. 3 (2003): 431–32. Also see Tim Bale, "Turning round the telescope. Centre-right parties and immigration and integration policy in Europe 1," *Journal of European Public Policy* 15, no. 3 (2008): 315–330.

This approach draws on the basic notion that certain political parties have membership preferences and, when in power, those preferences are either compatible or not compatible with existing citizenship conditions. Simply put, who governs shapes the direction and detail of state policy. Party preferences are shaped by a myriad of factors: political opportunism, exogenous shock, endogenous change (such as austerity), polarization at election time, even "ideological residue" from class cleavages.[20] Thus, when a left or right party is in power we anticipate positions on new policies to be consistent with existing ideological orientations and preferences.[21] In the field of immigration, however, parties on the right and the left both appear to be skewed toward more restriction during periods of issue salience,[22] in which the left faces a unique challenge of courting immigrant voters without losing core constituents.[23] In fact, many studies have shown where native-born working-class voters jump in support from the left all the way to parties of the far right, particularly under conditions of perceived economic competition.[24] However, if political elites manage not to politicize immigrant-related policies, studies predict mainstream parties will exhibit "broadly expansionist and inclusive" immigration proclivities, where employers and civic rights groups play an influential role outside of the public eye.[25] This, of course, would require counterfactual testing, as electoral competition has kept immigrant-related politics front and center.[26] It is also unclear how successfully this prediction maps onto citizenship or membership, whereby the aforementioned groups might hold different views on the expansion or contraction of a

[20] Gary Marks and Marco Steenbergen, "Understanding political contestation in the European Union," *Comparative Political Studies* 35, no. 8 (2002): 880.

[21] As Lipset and Rokkan establish, political actors have incentives to interpret new issues in light of existing left–right ideological alignments. Seymour Martin Lipset and Stein Rokkan, *Party Systems and Voter Alignments: Cross-national perspectives*, vol. 7 (Free press, 1967).

[22] Terri Givens and Adam Luedtke, "European immigration policies in comparative perspective: Issue salience, partisanship and immigrant rights," *Comparative European Politics* 3, no. 1 (2005): 1–22; Ruud Koopmans, Ines Michalowski, and Stine Waibel, "Citizenship rights for immigrants: National political processes and cross-national convergence in Western Europe, 1980–2008," *American Journal of Sociology* 117, no. 4 (2012): 1202–1245.

[23] Jeannette Money, *Fences and Neighbors: The political geography of immigration control* (Cornell University Press, 1999).

[24] Hans-Georg Betz, *Radical Right-wing Populism in Western Europe* (Macmillan Basingstoke, 1994); Herbert Kitschelt, *The Radical Right in Western Europe: A comparative analysis* (University of Michigan Press, 1997); Terri E. Givens, *Voting Radical Right in Western Europe* (Cambridge: Cambridge University Press, 2005).

[25] Gary P. Freeman, "Modes of immigration politics in liberal democratic states," *International Migration Review* 29, no. 4 (1995): 881. Also see Virginie Guiraudon, "Policy change behind gilded doors: Explaining the evolution of aliens' rights in contemporary Western Europe (1974–1994)" (PhD. Dissertation, Harvard University, 1997).

[26] Marc Morjé Howard, *The politics of citizenship in Europe* (Cambridge: Cambridge University Press, 2009); Anthony M. Messina, *The logics and politics of post-WWII migration to Western Europe* (Cambridge: Cambridge University Press, 2007); Martin A. Schain, "The extreme-right and immigration policy-making: Measuring direct and indirect effects," *West European Politics* 29, no. 2 (2006): 270–289.

labor workforce than they would on the expansion or contraction of a political electorate or national political community.[27]

Unlike immigration where the left and right broadly support restriction and increased security, citizenship policy elicits a lesser narcissism of small differences.[28] Janoski focuses on the role of left and green parties in shaping liberal citizenship policy and, specifically, higher naturalization rates.[29] Howard also notes the likelihood of liberalization when a left party is in power, but acknowledges the blocking role that restrictive proponents can have when anti-immigrant public opinion is "activated," either by a strong, far-right party or by public mobilization (e.g., referenda, petition campaigns).[30] Elsewhere, Goodman and Howard examine the other side of this argument: prospects for restrictive policy as a product of right governments.[31] These treatments not only ascribe causal significance to the ideological orientation of governments, but also expand causality to increase agency of opposing political actors.

Surprisingly, however, the civic integration literature has tended to focus less on ideological diversity of governments and more on the role of the right, and the far-right in particular. Perhaps because of its preoccupation with requirements as a form of restriction, scholars have interpreted the "restrictive turn" in citizenship and membership as a by-product of a "conservative turn" in the 2000s. This view is not only predicated on a problematic assumption (that requirements are inherently restrictions) but reflects a truncated view of policy change, in which requirements only "count" when they become forceful. A quick, back-of-the-envelope test shows adoption of policy by both left and right governments. A truncated view of only rightist governments would miss the necessary groundwork laid by the left in earlier periods of policy craft, just as aggregate policy indices that count requirements would miss the importance of this sequencing. Moreover, when the restriction assumption is relaxed to allow for variation in purpose, the proposition that civic integration policies are adopted by different governments for different reasons becomes testable. In other words, without assuming all requirements are synonymous with restrictive

[27] This divergence in preferences – where parties may pursue inclusive immigration policy but exclusive citizenship policy – aptly reflects Herb Kitschelt's observation that party systems are structured on two dimensions: economic and authoritarian-liberal (i.e., sociocultural). See Kitschelt, *The Radical Right in Western Europe: A comparative analysis*.

[28] Terri Givens and Adam Luedtke highlight how partisanship plays a significant role in shaping differences when it comes to integration policy, in contrast to immigration policy. See Givens and Luedtke, "European immigration policies in comparative perspective: Issue salience, partisanship and immigrant rights."

[29] Thomas Janoski, *The Ironies of citizenship. Naturalization and integration in industrialized countries* (Cambridge: Cambridge University Press, 2010), especially 187–220.

[30] Howard, *The politics of Citizenship in Europe*, 61. For a thorough examination of organized nativist backlashes, but by anti-immigrant parties, see Messina, *The Logics and Politics of Post-WWII Migration to Western Europe*, ch. 3

[31] Goodman and Howard, "Evaluating and explaining the restrictive backlash in citizenship policy in Europe."

change, we see governments on the left initially adopt generally inclusive or minimal requirements (France, the Netherlands, the UK, Denmark), while governments on the right are largely responsible for restrictive adaptation in these very same cases.

Finally, in addition to relaxing this assumption, further specifications need to be made before proceeding to case-study analysis, namely how to interpret coalitions and mixed preferences, how to interpret federal behavior and multilevel balancing, and how to interpret the behavior of influential actors in opposition. Governments are not unobstructed in pursuing preferences. There are several mitigating factors, ranging from costs of coalition to opposition politics and exogenous events. It is certainly the case that the party position of government plays a determinative role in setting the tone and direction of new policy, but it may not be because they are in power *per se*. First, governments operate in different institutional settings. Parties ruling in single party systems operate with different cost structures to parties in coalition governments (either majority or minority). Specifically, coalition governments may produce policy out of the need to compromise, as policymaking often requires consensus and coalition-building among actors with diverse interests and ideas. As such, coalitions are often defined by ideological heterogeneity, in which the coalition-former may hold different values from the coalition-joiner. For example, the Dutch purple coalition that resulted from the 1994 election was comprised of both social democrat (red) and liberal (blue) components, in which the Labour Party (PvdA), the progressive D66, and the conservative VVD forced the Christian Democrats into opposition. While the Labour party was technically the first party – and formed a coalition government under Wim Kok – the VVD's conservative agenda significantly influenced the tenor of policy. Second, governments are also incumbents; they may espouse certain views to compete for votes or bargain to stay in power. For example, in the UK we see New Labour propose significant restriction in 2005, in the shadow of an upcoming election and in the context of diminished popularity over immigration issues.[32] Third, an exclusive focus on the ideological orientation of government can overlook who the real actors are behind membership policy. Aside from coalition partners, which can alter the direction of policy through kingmaker roles, governments are also part of political processes in which other branches (especially under federal systems) can check executive power. In Germany, for example, the right-of-center initially operates *from opposition* to effectively broker the first iteration of civic integration policy.

Studies that focus too much on government preferences can miss the greater context in which policy is made, while studies that focus too much on players on

[32] This election started voter defection from Labour over the issue of immigration. See Geoffrey Evans and Kat Chzhen, "Explaining voters' defection from Labour over the 2005–10 electoral cycle: Leadership, economics and the rising importance of immigration," *Political Studies* 61, no. S1 (2013): 138–157.

the margins, like far-right parties, can minimize the work that governments undertake to stay in power and stave off populist threats. In fact, Tim Bale describes explanations that primarily focus on the far right to understand immigration and integration policy outcomes as both "misleading" and "patronizing," in that they presume center-right parties are "incapable of coming to their own conclusions on the seriousness of the issues and the policy direction they should take on them."[33] He continues by noting that we should expect center-right parties to take hard lines on these issues, where "part of their *raison d'etre*, after all, is to defend the socio-economic and cultural status quo to which the entry of large (or at least highly visible) numbers of migrants would appear to present something of a challenge."[34] In other words, far-right parties may set electoral tones, but some of their issues resonate with Europe's economically liberal, socially conservative, and Christian Democratic parties irrespective of elections. Tjitske Akkerman also illustrates through regression analysis that "although parties matter, radical right parties do not matter in particular."[35]

In sum, governments do not operate in a vacuum, but – at the same time – governments are not entirely victims of circumstance. They are comprised of parties continually seeking a mandate. Therefore, I argue the left–right explanation requires some modification, whereby civic integration is properly characterized as something more than a tool of restriction and greater attention is paid to other actors in the political process. Government is not always the source, but it is always the filter. In more methodological terms, a government ideology explanation conveys the nature of a membership policy outcome but not the mechanism, in which any number of political processes or actors may prove relevant.

Stepping back, we see the government ideology hypothesis as offering analytical leverage on the question of civic integration policy diversity, with the caveat of relaxing assumptions of restriction and government independence and omnipotence. However, hypotheses about integration policy failure, demographic change, and welfare state strain offer less to account for what we have already defined as a significant range in policy outcomes. These purposefully general explanations are problematically vague, overlooking in particular the possibilities of multiple paths (equifinality) and conjunctural causation in

[33] Bale, "Turning round the telescope. Centre-right parties and immigration and integration policy in Europe," 320.

[34] Ibid., 318–19.

[35] Tjitske Akkerman, "Comparing radical right parties in government: Immigration and integration policies in nine countries (1996–2010)," *West European Politics* 35, no. 3 (2012): 511–529. Also see "Immigration policy and electoral competition in Western Europe. A fine-grained analysis of party positions over the past two decades," *Party Politics* (2012), DOI: 10.1177/1354068812462928; Sjoerdje van Heerden et al., "The immigration and integration debate in the Netherlands: Discursive and programmatic reactions to the rise of anti-immigration parties," *Journal of Ethnic and Migration Studies* (2013): 1–18.

producing civic integration outcomes. Second, just because a series of factors are present does not mean they are causal, and if they are causal they may not necessarily be equally impactful across cases. Finally, one cannot assume *a priori* that the presence of shared pressures is responsible for policy results, particularly when a closer look reveals that these outcomes are non-uniform. A discrete policy phenomenon taking place in a geographically circumscribed set of cases can certainly yield more analytical precision. To conclude, these background conditions are *conducive* to but not *determinative* of civic integration policy. They constitute what James Mahoney describes as "trivial necessary causes," in that they are "always present, irrespective of the presence/absence of the outcome."[36]

The next section presents the book's central argument: it is not merely *distinct political configurations* (left–right government in power, institutional checks, etc.) but the *context* in which these decisions are made – specifically existing understandings of membership as defined by citizenship policy – that produce *divergent membership policy strategies*. For example, leftist governments in an exclusive citizenship setting are not only limited in terms of what they can achieve through policy, but fundamentally produce something different than a similarly oriented government in an inclusive citizenship setting. Membership policy does not merely produce change or continuity, but a specific kind of change or continuity that ultimately preserves nation-state differences.

CITIZENSHIP POLICY AS A CONTEXT FOR POLITICAL PROCESSES

The argument that citizenship matters for understanding membership policy choices seems obvious. Yet it is a surprising omission from existing studies, which claim (1) that all civic integration adoption is for the purposes of restriction and (2) that national models and differences are giving way to a common, postnational identity defined by liberal democratic values that have no national specificity. Yet a more considered examination of conditions for policy adoption – as well as degrees of adaptation – reveals a significant role for existing citizenship policy in defining parameters of debate and, in several cases, the problem itself.

What does it mean to consider citizenship policy as an inherited legacy or starting position? Citizenship as a starting point refers to the rules that define acquisition affecting ordinary (i.e., without pre-defined "ethnic ties") migrants. It entails an aggregate examination of formal rules, including birth-based and naturalization procedures, which I refer to as the overall orientation of

[36] James Mahoney, "After KKV: The new methodology of qualitative research," *World Politics* 62, no. 1 (2009): 135. This also raises the issue of causal asymmetry, or the idea that a set of causal conditions that lead to the presence of an outcome may be different from the set of conditions that lead to the absence of an outcome. If these are ever-present conditions, the question of what accounts for policy adoption in certain cases and non-adoption in others remains unanswered.

citizenship, as an institutional reflection of understanding of national membership, and argues that it is the general tenor of policy configurations as overall inclusive (liberal) or exclusive (restrictive) toward immigrants that define parameters of debate for membership policy. I employ the terms "policy legacy" and "inherited policy" to denote citizenship at the point of membership policy adoption (i.e., the starting point; t_0) and to distinguish it from later iterations of adaptation (t_1, t_2, etc.). Many studies of citizenship policy have identified the causal role that previous rules have on subsequent rules in an approach known as path dependence. For example, Randall Hansen traces costs militating change in British citizenship law in the postwar period, while other studies have illustrated the strength of policy traditions and continuity in areas such as dual citizenship,[37] liberal citizenship policy generally,[38] and immigrant rights.[39] All of these support the view that citizenship policy as a starting point is a meaningful framework for future policy by setting costs for change or, in a softer version, by setting parameters of debate and constraints on discourse.

Citizenship orientations not only reflect state priorities for inclusion or exclusion through formal rules, but also implicit understandings of nationhood and other scripts of belonging. These ideas serve as a necessary backbone to justify the settings of formal policy, and a number of studies have already identified historical origins of belonging and the trajectories that lead these understandings to contemporary policy.[40] The comparative work on Britain and France by Erik Bleich and Adrian Favell, as well as Rogers Brubaker's study on France and Germany,[41] stand out as particularly influential for understanding how national philosophies and ideas of belonging inform contemporary policy. They paint a useful portrait of antecedent processes that produce contemporary membership preferences as expressed through citizenship and related polices, like integration. In particular, it is interesting and useful to note when these prior processes deposit salient scripts for belonging (German *Leitkultur*) and where they do

[37] Thomas Faist, Jürgen Gerdes, and Beate Rieple, "Dual citizenship as a path-dependent process," *International Migration Review* 38, no. 3 (2004): 913–944.

[38] Howard, *The Politics of Citizenship in Europe*, Ch. 2; Janoski, *The Ironies of Citizenship. Naturalization and integration in industrialized countries.*

[39] Koopmans, Michalowski, and Waibel, "Citizenship rights for immigrants: National political processes and cross-national convergence in Western Europe, 1980–2008." While this is one of the central findings of the piece, the article does not argue that costs prevent change, but merely illustrates that policies at t_0 strongly predict policies at t_1.

[40] Many have told path-dependent stories about how these ideas and other critical antecedent conditions and processes shape contemporary policy. The current study recognizes the importance of this history, but is agnostic about the specific sequence by which this contemporary understanding came about.

[41] Erik Bleich, *Race Politics in Britain and France: ideas and policymaking since the 1960's* (Cambridge: Cambridge University Press, 2003); Adrian Favell, *Philosophies of Integration: immigration and the idea of citizenship in France and Britain* (New York: St. Martin's Press); Rogers Brubaker, *Citizenship and Nationhood in France and Germany* (Cambridge, MA: Harvard University Press, 1992).

not (the perpetually ill-defined concept of "Britishness"). The case studies in Chapter 4–6 are serviceable to this end by providing a fuller background on what membership connotations are captured in contemporary policy. As contemporary policy is considered a formal institutional reflection of more informal understandings of belonging, these can both be methodologically reflected in a single indicator: citizenship policy orientation.[42]

Having established the concept of citizenship policy orientation as both a formal set of rules and a proxy for national belonging, a more direct question can be raised: How does citizenship matter for interpreting civic integration policy? This question has both an empirical and a theoretical answer. Empirically, citizenship is the policy venue in which membership expectations are historically derived and contemporarily applied. In other words, citizenship defines the standard of inclusion that *civic* integration strives to promote, including the ability to participate socially and politically, even if it is promoted outside of citizenship itself. To wit, citizenship also determines the relative possibility of obtaining legal status (and, through delimitation, the value of permanent residence, where we also see membership requirements). Therefore, citizenship starting points not only dictate opportunity of acquisition for citizenship, but indirectly define the value and necessity of obtaining permanent residence. Interpretations of this extension traditionally point toward the diminution of citizenship as a membership category, but these views overlook the role citizenship actually plays in defining the meaningfulness of these other categories. In other words, permanent residence can become a location for integration and a desirable alternative to citizenship status *by design*. In the context of large-scale migrant populations, permanent residence matters precisely where citizenship is unobtainable, because of renunciation requirements prohibiting dual citizenship (Austria, Denmark, the Netherlands, Germany) or non-granting for second- or third-generation migrants born in the country (Austria, Denmark, Finland, Greece, Italy, Luxembourg). In these cases, immigrant-related integration policies are strongly tied to settlement procedures. Moreover, where permanent residence is a precondition for citizenship (Austria, Denmark, the Netherlands), early requirements serve as indirect citizenship policies. On the other hand, where citizenship is comparatively easy to obtain (France, the Netherlands, the UK), permanent residence is of lesser importance. Or, in these liberal contexts, the concern for citizenship is even starker if migrants show a preference for permanent residence instead of citizenship.

Turning to its theoretical importance, citizenship policy orientations express preferences for belonging, which in turn define the parameters in which conjunctural political processes play out. In other words, citizenship starting points

[42] John Gerring notes that the purpose of an indicator is to "help to locate the concept in empirical space." Therefore, citizenship policy as a variable can be a suitable empirical proxy for more abstract concepts like national belonging. In John Gerring, *Social Science Methodology*, 2nd edn. (Cambridge: Cambridge University Press, 2012), 116.

define the parameters of debate. Where membership is historically inclusive and where inclusion is maintained in liberal citizenship policy, policymakers on the left and the right operate within different parameters of acceptable reform compared to states in which the concept of belonging and its attenuated policies are more restrictive. This understanding of citizenship policy as a starting point tests the role of inherited policies in shaping politics, whereby "organization factors affect both the degree of pressure an actor can bring to bear on policy and the likely direction of that pressure."[43] I argue here that inherited citizenship policy or "starting points" set the parameters of the political debate on membership as – in the words of John Zysman – "the definition of interests and objectives is created in institutional contexts and is not separable from them."[44] Evidence of these parameters can be seen in mapping left/ right party positions and observing degrees of similarity and difference, as well as which policy proposals are viable and under what conditions.

Given citizenship's empirical and theoretical importance as a context for examining membership requirements, how can we identify and categorize these orientations cross-nationally? The comparative study of citizenship policy is robust.[45] One of the more recent trends in this field has been to develop comparative indices for scoring policy.[46] These indices range in terms of the

[43] Peter A. Hall, *Governing the Economy: The politics of state intervention in Britain and France* (Cambridge, UK; Oxford, UK; Polity Press, 1986), 19.

[44] John Zysman, "How institutions create historically rooted trajectories of growth," *Industrial and Corporate Change* 3, no. 1 (1994): 244. Kathleen Thelen and Sven Steinmo refer to this context as a type of endogenous preference formation in Kathleen Ann Thelen and Sven Steinmo, "Historical institutionalism in comparative politics," in *Structuring Politics: Historical institutionalism in comparative analysis*, ed. Sven Steinmo, Kathleen Ann Thelen, and Frank Longstreth (Cambridge: Cambridge University Press, 1992), 9.

[45] Randall Hansen and Patrick Weil, eds., *Towards a European Nationality: Citizenship, immigration and nationality law in the EU* (London: Palgrave-Macmillan, 2001); Rainer Bauböck et al., eds., *Acquisition and Loss of Nationality in Fifteen EU States. Volume 2: Country analyses. Policies and trends in 15 European countries* (Amsterdam: Amsterdam University Press, 2006b); Thomas Alexander Aleinikoff and Douglas B. Klusmeyer, *Citizenship Policies for an Age of Migration* (Washington, DC: Carnegie Endowment for International Peace: Migration Policy Institute: Brookings Institution Press, distributor, 2002); Sara Wallace Goodman, "Naturalisation policies in Europe: Exploring patterns of inclusion and exclusion," in *EUDO Citizenship Comparative Reports* (Florence: EUDO Citizenship, Robert Schuman Centre for Advanced Studies, EUI, 2010); Maarten P. Vink and Gerard-Rene de Groot, "Birthright citizenship: Trends and regulations in Europe," in *EUDO Citizenship Comparative Reports* (Florence: EUDO Citizenship, Robert Schuman Centre for Advanced Studies, EUI, 2010).

[46] Harald Waldrauch and Christoph Hofinger, "An index to measure the legal obstacles to the integration of migrants," *New Community* 23, no. 2 (1997): 271–285; Edward A. Koning, "Ethnic and civic dealings with newcomers: Naturalization policies and practices in twenty-six immigration countries," *Ethnic and Racial Studies* 34, no. 11 (2011): 1974–1994; Howard, *The Politics of Citizenship in Europe*; Janoski, *The Ironies of Citizenship. Naturalization and integration in industrialized countries*. There are also a handful of studies that examine citizenship in the context of other policies, namely immigrant rights, integration strategies, and immigration policy. These include Ruud Koopmans et al., *Contested Citizenship. Immigration and cultural*

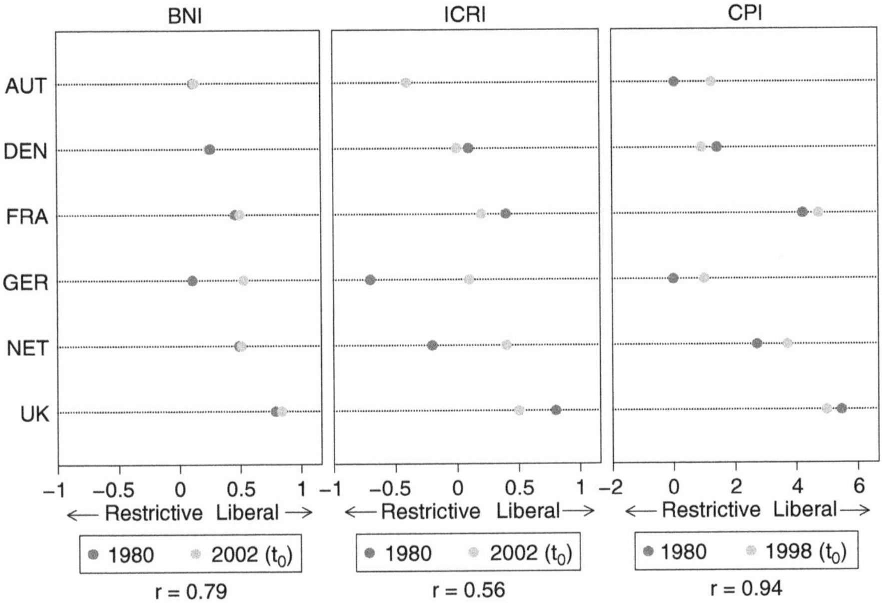

3.1 Citizenship policy score clustering across and within indices

number of policies that are scored, which policies are scored, and what categories of immigrants are included (e.g., spouses, minors, and refugees). Yet, despite variation in the number of indicators, policies included versus excluded, and the intricacies of scoring instruments, these unique indices prove to be highly correlated with one another.[47] Figure 3.1 maps citizenship policy values at times proximate to civic integration policy adoption (t_o) in six civic integration-practicing states from three major citizenship policy indices – Janoski's Barriers to Naturalization Index (BNI), Koopmans' Indicators for Citizenship Rights of Immigrants (ICRI), and Howard's Citizenship Policy Index (CPI).[48] Figure 3.1 also includes a snapshot of policy before t_o, to calculate correlations

diversity in Europe (Minneapolis, MN: University of Minnesota Press, 2005); Koopmans, Michalowski, and Waibel, "Citizenship rights for immigrants: National political processes and cross-national convergence in Western Europe, 1980–2008;" Migration Policy Group, "The Migrant Integration Policy Index (MIPEX)," (Migration Policy Group & British Council, 2011).

47 Sara Wallace Goodman, "Concluding remarks: What can we learn from citizenship policy indices?," *Migration and Citizenship. Newsletter of the American Political Science Association. Organized Section on Migration and Citizenship* 1, no. 2 (2013): 48–54.

48 This figure adjusts for scoring directionality (inverting Janoski's measure to make high scores equate with more inclusive policy). The comparison here also takes into account measurement differences (i.e., number of indicators, years of policy scoring, scoring techniques) to present scoring in similar years for the purposes of index comparison. Raw and adjusted scores are available in Appendix III.

and illustrate continuity in policy before major politicization and change.[49] As it shows, states cluster similarly across indices. States also cluster similarly within indices over time, revealing natural contrasts between inclusive/liberal and exclusive/restrictive policy orientations and patterns of continuity over time. Policies certainly change over time (ICRI, for example, shows low correlation because Germany and the Netherlands experienced major policy liberalization), but the relationship *between* states remains generally similar. This establishes a useful and reliable heuristic for classifying states. And while these scores suggest the direction of classification in the field is away from bi-modal classification, comparative analysis typically and unsurprisingly reverts back to abstract classifications of restrictive versus liberal policy. As Figure 3.1 illustrates, the UK, France, and the Netherlands group near the right as liberal states at t_0, while Austria, Denmark, and Germany are situated to the left of the figure as restrictive states.

Generally speaking, restrictive citizenship orientations are defined in states with comparatively high residency requirements (7 years or more, where the average among EU Member States is 5 years[50]), a renunciation requirement against holding dual or multiple citizenships, and rules against extending citizenship to children based on birth in the territory (i.e., *jus soli*). Restrictive states may also have low naturalization rates in comparison to other countries. In contrast, liberal citizenship is considered more inclusive because requirements are seen as more easily achievable. These would include lower periods of residence, allowance for dual citizenship, and acquisition for children on the principle of *jus soli*. Naturalization rates may also be comparatively higher than in states with more restrictive policies.

Moving from a snapshot of citizenship policy at civic integration adoption to adaptation, EUDO-Citizenship's Citizenship Law Indicators (CITLAW) in Figure 3.2 offers more recent figures, disaggregating dimensions of policy as they apply to ordinary immigrants in 2011. This view provides confirmatory data for classifications, where the UK, France, and the Netherlands maintain inclusive policy, Germany sits in the middle (with a score of 0.48 out of 1 for *jus soli* and 0.57 for naturalization), while Austria and Denmark remain strongly concentrated at the left for both *jus soli* and naturalization. By taking the average of these three scores (ASAN, ASOL, and ANAT), CITLAW 2011 correlates with Howard's 2008 CPI scores at $r = 0.97$. This gives a strong, valid impression of citizenship orientations for t_1 (adaptation). CITLAW data also reveal particulars of policy, where restrictive countries have exclusive *jus soli* and naturalization provisions and liberal countries are comparatively inclusive on these fronts.[51] Notably, it also shows that while states have widely

[49] Many have argued that past policies often serve as useful predictors for future policy. For example, there is high correlation in Janoski's Barriers to Naturalization Index between the years 1970 and 1980 (at $r = 0.99$), between 1980 and 1990 (at $r = 0.95$), and between 1970 and 1990 at $r = 0.948$.

[50] Goodman, "Naturalisation policies in Europe: Exploring patterns of inclusion and exclusion."

[51] A score of 1 indicates "maximum inclusion or individual choice" while a score of 0 indicates "maximum exclusion or state power." Note: I exclude (CITLAW) from Figure 3.1's comparison of single indicators, as the authors make convincing conceptual and empirical claims why maximal

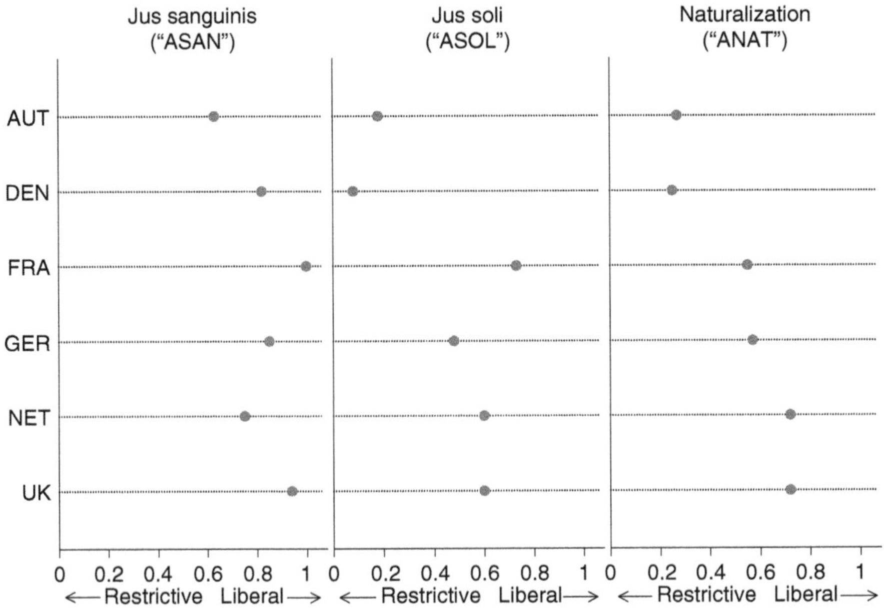

3.2 A disaggregated citizenship policy view using CITLAW 2011

different policy arrangements regarding *jus soli* and naturalization, *jus sanguinis* policies are more grouped and unsurprisingly skewed toward inclusion.

In both of these figures, Germany appears as a more ambiguous case. Its citizenship starting point (policy at t_o) for civic integration adoption is restrictive and consistent with coding across indices. However, the 2000 Citizenship Act introduced significant liberalization, which gets reflected especially in ICRI's second policy snapshot as well as 2011 CITLAW measures for both naturalization and *jus soli.* A look at implementation through qualitative analysis as well as naturalization rates (see Chapter 5) supports the view that liberalization was in name only.[52] Germany's score on Howard's CPI score also shows minimal change, moving from a restrictive score of 1.00 out of 6 in 1998 to a score of 2.04 in 2008, which just crosses the threshold to be categorized on the low end of "medium." Assessing the tone of citizenship policy, and re-examining some of these scores in light of practice, is an additional strength of comparative case study analysis.[53]

aggregation in a single indicator is problematic. See Kristen Jeffers, Iseult Honohan, and Rainer Bauböck, "CITLAW indicators: How to measure the purposes of citizenship laws," in *Comparing Citizenship Across Europe: Laws, implementation and impact* (EUI and University College Dublin 2012), 7–8.

52 Simon Green, "Much ado about not-very-much? Assessing ten years of German citizenship reform," *Citizenship Studies* 16, no. 2 (2012): 173–188.

53 One could also conceive of the labels of "liberal" and "restrictive" as being subjective terminology irrespective of other state practices; two migrants in the same state may experience widely different naturalization processes, with immigrants that begin from a position of employment or having knowledge of the national language experiencing fewer barriers. This presents major challenges to

Finally, having categorized the major civic integration-adopting states as liberal (France, UK, and the Netherlands but just barely) or restrictive (Austria, Denmark, and Germany) at point of civic integration adoption, and without much alteration to these classifications between adoption and adaptation[54] (with the possible exception of Germany), we can make specific predictions about the effect of respective orientations on government actors and, summarily, on civic integration policy choices. To be clear, citizenship policy orientation does not make civic integration more or less likely (a theoretically prior research question); it sets the parameter of debate for political actors interested in altering or preserving membership policy.

In a pure application of an institutional legacy argument, where high costs militate against change, continuity would be predicted for both liberal and restrictive contexts in the absence of intervening or conjunctural processes. In other words, if a state has a restrictive citizenship policy orientation as a starting point for discussions on membership requirements, then we would predict a restrictive orientation to continue through and after such debates. The inherited restrictive orientation is shaped by a past of exclusion and traditional ethnocultural preferences, and defines the set of restrictive parameters in which new and potential policies can be implemented. Likewise, we expect similar continuity for liberal citizenship policy, where the inherited inclusive orientation is shaped by a past of inclusive preferences.[55] Evidence that either citizenship starting point constrains the parameters of a debate on membership would be seen in party position at t_o, where both left and right are constrained against radical change and policies that maintain a continuity of membership orientation have more traction than marginalized alternatives.

While membership policies in each setting produce a type of continuity, they may pursue this goal through several different means. Restriction can be perpetuated by making citizenship more difficult to obtain directly, or as we see through the intricate relationship shared between citizenship and permanent

measurement, and can only be ameliorated with in-depth population analysis. It is true that policies are not evenly applied across a population, because there are numerous elements outside the control of the policy implementers, but for the purposes of understanding national policy, one has to treat it as a coherent whole.

54 Case studies are best suited to identify the dynamics and nature of change, where policy indicators might dilute the impact of change by scoring every policy equally. Still, Koopmans et al. find evidence of recent continuity between 1980 and 2008 in Koopmans, Michalowski, and Waibel, "*Citizenship Rights for Immigrants: National political processes and cross-national convergence in Western Europe, 1980–2008*," 1236.

55 See, for example, Howard, *The Politics of Citizenship in Europe*, Ch. 2; Janoski, *The Ironies of Citizenship. Naturalization and integration in industrialized countries*, Chs. 3–4. But, also Erik Bleich, "The legacies of history? Colonization and immigrant integration in Britain and France," *Theory and Society* 34, no. 2 (2005): 171–195.

residence, by making permanent residence more rigorous, thereby leaving citizenship relatively untouched in its continued restrictive tone or making it even more difficult to obtain by establishing an even denser chain of conditionality. Inclusion can be perpetuated by making citizenship either easier to obtain or more meaningful. Where lowered requirements may make the status of acquisition easier, there is a balancing point at which obtaining something without effort diminishes its value. Therefore, inclusivity can be promoted through liberalization but also through value investment and enrichment.[56] Finally, the perpetuation of a liberal citizenship orientation would also be borne out in permanent residence, as a device to facilitate rather than block full political incorporation.

These predictions are guided by a logic of continuity, but the recent empirical landscape reveals that citizenship is defined by anything but that. Governments may operate within a set of membership parameters, but ultimately they maintain agency in deciding what direction citizenship reform should take – informed by ideological disposition – and whether the costs of change are worth incurring. This is where the predictions about the effects of the ideological orientation of government interact with context. A right government in a liberal citizenship context may adopt the same civic integration policy as a left government in a liberal citizenship context, but to address entirely different problems. Parameters of membership can also change, where large-scale change to citizenship policy creates different conditions for civic integration adaptation than those existing at policy adoption. Governments change too, where a left government can undo policy created under a right government and vice versa. Finally, where some changes may be easy to reverse, others may be more entrenched through successive amendments over time, making it more difficult to peel away layers of change with a change in government.

As such, two general predictions about policy can be made by looking at interactions of context and government orientation. If the ideological orientation and preference of government is *consistent* with an existing citizenship orientation – e.g., restrictive-oriented actors in a restrictive citizenship context or liberal-oriented actors in a liberal citizenship context – then new membership policy will seek to *perpetuate the status quo*. The content of this policy will differ, where continuity can be achieved by increasing barriers (in restrictive policy contexts) or incentivizing acquisition (in liberal policy contexts). If the ideological orientation and preference of government is *opposed* to an existing citizenship orientation – e.g., restrictive-oriented actors in a liberal citizenship context or liberal-oriented actors in a restrictive citizenship context – then new membership policy will seek to *leverage change*, affecting policy instrument settings or the instruments themselves. Totalizing change is

[56] Restrictive citizenship regimes also infuse citizenship with value, which likewise contributes to retrenchment. To maintain conceptual differentiation, I reserve the word "enrichment" – with its positive connotation – for instances of liberal continuity.

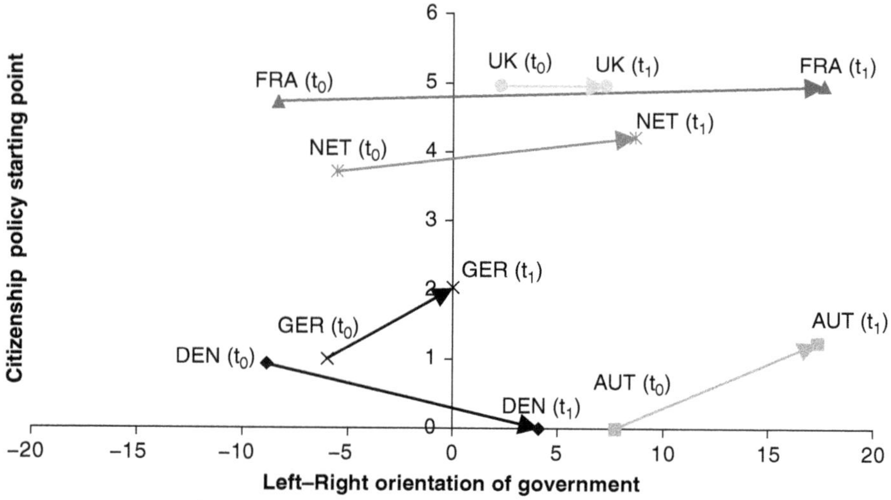

3.3 Intersections of citizenship context and government orientation at civic integration policy adoption (t_0) and first adaptation (t_1)

possible but unlikely as paradigmatic change is only possible, as Peter Hall argues, through "simultaneous changes in all three components of policy: the instrument settings, the instruments themselves, and the hierarchy of goals behind policy."[57] As a result, most changes produced by a contrasting interaction aim to leverage incremental change to existing understandings and practices of belonging.

The interaction between context and government ideological orientation could be mapped in a 2 × 2 explanatory typology.[58] However, such an exercise would constitute only one static snapshot of the policy process, missing dynamic interactions, multiple contexts, and iterations of change that invariably produce a variety of policy output. Therefore, instead, Figure 3.3 illustrates the different configurations of government preferences in a citizenship policy context for two time periods: the adoption (t_0) and first adaptation (t_1) of robust civic integration policy. The horizontal x-axis depicts party position of government, i.e., the left-right orientation of governments based on manifesto data, and the vertical y-axis depicts citizenship context, i.e., policy starting point.[59]

[57] Peter A. Hall, "Policy paradigms, social learning, and the state: The case of economic policy-making in Britain," *Comparative Politics* 25, no. 3 (1993): 279.

[58] See Sara Wallace Goodman, "Fortifying citizenship: Policy strategies for civic integration in Western Europe," *World Politics* 64, no. 4 (2012): 674.

[59] Government right–left ("Rile") orientation scores are taken from the "Positions and salience in European Union politics dataset," reported in Tim Veen, "Positions and salience in European Union politics: Estimation and validation of a new dataset," *European Union Politics* 12, no. 2 (2011): 267–288. This dataset simultaneously accounts for both party position (how conservative

This figure conveys a number of important observations. First, states vary in terms of conditions under which they start the civic integration process and conditions under which they first adapt it. They also do not start either of these processes at the same place as each other. As seen in the graph, policy context and government ideology in the Netherlands not only varied significantly between adoption and initial adaptation, but both of these locations are distinct in value compared to conditions in Austria or Germany. Even if one considered civic integration policy outcomes to be broadly similar, this would show that states overcame distinctly different hurdles in achieving them. Second, even a short, impressionist glance comparing these condition intersections suggests that membership polices in UK, France, and the Netherlands – grouped near the top of the figure as liberal citizenship countries – have a different effect from membership policies in Germany, Denmark, and Austria – grouped near the bottom of the figure as restrictive citizenship countries.

Third, despite its starting position, each state gravitates to the political right, reflecting the cross-national "conservative turn" in governments in Europe. One might deduce from this unidirectional shift evidence in support of the convergence hypothesis, much like aggregate CIVIX scores show some countries as robust practitioners and others as not. However, we know that these policy outcomes differ in terms of design, sequencing, and difficulty. By expanding the scope of analysis to time before the shift toward the political right, we also observe how the majority of states *adopt* mild civic integration policies with left governments in power (with the exception of Austria), after which right actors co-opted and transformed policies in phases of adaptation. Or, we know that left governments may be filters for right-wing preferences, leveraged through institutional design (Germany) or coalition membership (the Netherlands). These transformations and nuances suggest that it is not simply the end that counts, but the pathway to it and the sequencing of policies therein. As such, it is a testable proposition that, where states have adopted distinct policies of civic integration and have taken distinct paths in doing so, they are in fact addressing distinct problems of membership. Civic instruments may appear similar across the board, but strategies for their usage are divergent given extant policy legacies and the ideological orientation of the party in power.

or liberal a government is) and government composition (whether single party or coalition). Orientation is calculated based on manifesto positions on a range of issues, including military, peace, democracy, market regulation, nationalization, welfare state, labor, and education. See Michael Laver and Ian Budge, *Party Policy and Government Coalitions* (St. Martin's Press, 1992). Citizenship policy starting point scores are taken from the Citizenship Policy Index (CPI) in Howard, *The Politics of Citizenship in Europe*. Data points for t_0 (adoption) and t_1 (first adaptation) are measured to proximate conditions around the following legislative junctures: Austria 2003, 2006; Denmark 1999, 2002; France 1998, 2003; Germany 1999, 2005; the Netherlands 1998, 2003; UK 2002, 2005. Arrows connecting t_0 and t_1 are lines of best fit; they indicate the direction of change but do not capture iterative change in citizenship policy or government orientation.

Mapping further iterations of policy would tell an even more diverse story. France, for example, first adapts a previously inclusive civic integration policy by introducing the integration contract in 2003 (t_1) under the right-led Sarkozy government. This contract became obligatory in 2007 with the Second Sarkozy law (t_2). However, a new Socialist government in 2012 saw the rollback of a number of interim restrictions (t_3). The Netherlands also had a change in government but – as Chapter 6 will show – causal mechanisms play an important role in explanation, as the Dutch found rollback more difficult and less desirable than their French counterparts. Therefore, it is not merely the action of governments in context that matters for accounting for policy paths, but also the mechanisms through which these conditions interact to shape policy paths. In fact, as Tulia Falleti and Julia Lynch argue, the "interaction between mechanism and context is what determines the outcome."[60] This highlights an additional value to comparative case study analysis and process-tracing in particular.

CONCLUSION

The argument presented in this chapter about the role of citizenship starting points and government preferences takes a dynamic view of policy adoption and change. It acknowledges a significant role for the party in power, recognizing also that change in governments produces change in civic integration policy strategy as one party has different preferences to another. Still, these preferences are constrained by pre-existing parameters of belonging, defined by national citizenship policy. The insertion of existing policy as a significant context for understanding cross-national policy adoption is a novel contribution to the study of immigrant integration and citizenship. Parameters of debate can move, sliding up and down the scale between inclusive and exclusive concepts of belonging through citizenship. In other words, institutions are not staid, inert relics. Change is real and possible, but it is difficult. The interaction of context and government preferences provides a dynamic and parsimonious explanation for the high degree of empirical variation of civic integration policies.

This argument sets up the next three chapters of paired, case study comparisons, which focus in particular on the effects of citizenship policy orientations on political decision-making and processes. Chapter 4 examines Austria and Denmark, where a similarly restrictive citizenship orientation conditions both right and left governments, respectively, to design dense civic integration policies. Both cases also demonstrate a prominent, agenda-setting role for far-right parties. Chapter 5 presents the inverse example, in recognition that differences in citizenship policy orientation suggest that similarly ideologically

60 Tulia G. Falleti and Julia F. Lynch, "Context and causal mechanisms in political analysis," *Comparative Political Studies* 42, no. 9 (2009): 1143–1166. Causal mechanism identification and analysis has not been explicit in citizenship research.

oriented governments can produce divergent outcomes. It examines this scenario by pairing Germany and the UK. In both cases, we see left-dominated but right-influenced governments adopt and adapt civic integration policy. And while both saw eventual restrictive membership policy adaptation under subsequent rightist government, we can observe different policy outcomes and effects given their initial, respective restrictive and liberal policy contexts. Finally, Chapter 6 suggests that it is not merely the setting of conditions (i.e., liberal or restrictive citizenship, left or right governments), but, crucially, the process that connects these conditions to policy outcomes that can significant impact both design and effect. As such, the Netherlands and France are two cases that boast similar causal *conditions* (liberal citizenship, left-then-right government configurations) but different causal *processes*. As such, successive policy layering in the Netherlands produced more entrenched restriction (where politicization by the far-right accelerated a pre-existing consensus), while in France change was more easily rolled back with a change in government (where politicization by the far-right only exacerbated existing polarization). In sum, a distinct logic lies behind each of these paired comparisons, to highlight the role of both context and process to produce ultimately distinct membership policies.

Each case study illustrates the importance of context and political configurations. They also allow for a careful examination of causal mechanisms.[61] Looking at conditions, causal mechanisms and effects not only engenders the fullest description of policy, it also provides the richest account of causality. Importantly, mechanisms do not have to be the same across cases. In fact, evidence that points to the presence of different mechanisms suggests even greater diversity in outcomes, where what matters is not only differences in citizenship policy orientations, but also how those orientations operate. This is a distinct advantage of examining civic integration policy adoption through comparative case study analysis. And while I anticipate further change to membership policies long after the publication of this book, these detailed cases sufficiently illustrate the central argument: context and distinct political configurations – along with different processes identified through in-depth case study analysis – produce divergent membership policy strategies that ultimately preserve nation-state differences.

61 Following George and Bennett, "Adequate causal explanations require empirically substantiated assertions about both the causal effects of independent variables and causal mechanisms or the observed processes that lead to outcomes." In Alexander L. George and Andrew Bennett, *Case Studies and Theory Development in the Social Sciences* (Cambridge, MA.: MIT Press, 2005), 208.

4

Examining context: Austria and Denmark

INTRODUCTION

This chapter presents two cases that exemplify the use of civic integration policies to maintain existing restrictive citizenship orientations. In the 2000s, both Austria and Denmark introduced new language and country knowledge courses and tests, as well as integration contracts for permanent residence and citizenship. The evolution of Austria's civic integration policy was defined entirely by rightist governments in a restrictive citizenship context and therefore represents a type of control case. In Denmark, on the other hand, civic integration policy was first introduced by a left-wing government. Given this difference in ideological orientation at the point of adoption (t_0), we can observe the significant role of policy context in shaping the parameters of debate and party preferences, and, therefore, policy itself. In Denmark, the left-initiated civic integration policy was focused not on liberalization but on conditionality. While this conditionality was originally aimed at the "improvement" of immigrants, this element would soon be abandoned as civic integration became more forceful when a center-right government – with significant influence from the far-right – came into power.

A competitive party politics-based analysis would be satisfied with examining the effect of far-right actors, in which correlation between restrictive-oriented actors and restrictive outcomes is high. However, including the context of existing citizenship policy underscores how new requirements – even those offered by left governments – were not perceived as controversial, path-changing, or particularly surprising. New integration requirements made already restrictive processes of settlement and naturalization even more restrictive. This did not alter existing membership preferences or policy arrangements but preserved the status quo. In this sense, Austria and Denmark represent typical cases for scholars who interpret new integration requirements as part of a shared, restrictive turn.

To illustrate the strategic use of civic requirements to reinforce existing restrictive citizenship orientations, I begin each case study by examining the content of said restrictive orientation – in other words the policy's starting point. I examine both the concept of belonging behind citizenship and the formal institutional reflection of this preference in policy. Second, I examine extant conditions and relevant political actors who played a role in the introduction of civic integration. In this context, I compare left- and right-wing party preferences to illustrate how concepts of belonging define the parameters of debate. And since both countries experienced nearly decade-long center-right coalitions, this exercise also allows us to imagine the counterfactual outcomes under a leftist, liberal-oriented leadership. The discussion of policy development focuses specifically on integration preferences revealed through design and sequencing (permanent residence versus citizenship). Each case study illustrates, in the absence of left-oriented governments or liberalizing pressure generally, how civic integration policies continue restrictive citizenship practices. I term this "retrenchment," as this process not only maintains existing policies but layers new requirements on top of them, establishing dense conditionality for status. I also examine party position over time – once civic integration is entrenched in practice – to see if positions change. The absence of norms of discourse or shifted parameters of debate suggests that significant change to citizenship orientation as a proxy for belonging has taken place in these cases.

Finally, each case study concludes with evidence to examine the degree to which restrictive retrenchment is achieved through not just civic integration policy but also its implementation – in other words, by shifting the analysis from output to outcome. While it is difficult to map direct causality of integration requirements on citizenship naturalization or permanent residence acquisition, as integration requirements are often introduced alongside other strict conditions such as income thresholds or lengthened residency requirements, we can draw comparisons between rhetorical and actual objectives as well as speculate on possibilities for future policy change. Requirements may even yield the opposite of their intended effect on the individual level by promoting integration, and they may prove popular among immigrants for providing the skills to improve their social and economic integration. However, by building up the chain of conditionality through new requirements for both permanent residence and citizenship, permanent residence becomes the new fulcrum of integration and the "prize" for immigrants. Achieving integration at permanent residence establishes a sense of belonging through state identity. Immigrants are then disincentivized to pass through additional barriers for citizenship, where inclusion is still defined by national belonging. In this, citizenship retains a monopoly on creating full insiders and may even be a deliberate strategy for delaying liberalization in these reluctant immigrant-settling states.

Austria

Austria is a quintessential case of restrictive retrenchment, introducing civic requirements to buttress an existing restrictive orientation in citizenship. Unlike states that sought to positively infuse a value in citizenship to incentivize naturalization (such as the UK) or introduce requirements to reach consensus with political opposition (such as Germany), the process and politics surrounding the adoption of civic integration policy in Austria aimed not only to prohibit naturalization but also to promote integration and membership outside of citizenship at the earlier status of permanent residence. We see retrenchment take shape in a political landscape already oriented toward restriction against new immigration and naturalization, in which anti-immigrant parties – first Jörg Haider's Freedom Party (*Freiheitliche Partei Österreichs*; FPÖ) and then the FPÖ-offspring party, Alliance for the Future of Austria (*Bündnis Zukunft Österreich*; BZÖ) – successfully joined the pro-restriction, conservative People's Party (*Osterreichische Volkspartei*; ÖVP) in government coalitions between 2000 and 2006. While the 1990s were punctuated by intense debate and increasing political pressure by the Freedom Party to limit naturalization and curb migration, it was because of the Freedom Party's position in government and the competition between them and the ÖVP to be the leading party in calling for immigration control that successive rightist governments were able to push through integration requirements for permanent residence and citizenship that narrowed opportunities for acquisition. This right-oriented political consensus pushed through new layers of restriction for almost a decade, despite opposition from parties outside of government, including the Social Democratic Party (*Sozialdemokratische Partei Österreichs*; SPÖ) and Greens, as well as non-governmental and provincial-level actors.

In Austria, we also see how the politics of citizenship neatly dovetails the politics of immigration, where a restrictive naturalization policy is not only a means of limiting access to citizenship but also a mechanism for migration control, for example by stemming family unification. The initial objectives of the far-right, virulently anti-immigrant Freedom Party in the 1990s echoed in the legislative agenda of the ÖVP–Freedom Party coalition, which was oriented toward limiting new immigration not only through strict yearly quotas and circumscribing access to permanent residence, but also through citizenship. It soon became apparent that citizenship acquisition was an alternative route to immigration in enabling family-based sponsorship. Although the rightist coalition government could not deny a migrant's right to family life based on the European Convention of Human Rights, they could limit a migrant's opportunity to gain citizenship, which would legally empower him or her to bring family members to Austria. Therefore, changes to both citizenship and permanent residence policy took on the contours and restrictive tones of an anti-immigrant political agenda. Legislative changes to both Citizenship (2006) and Residence Acts (2002, 2005) transformed permanent residence into a formidable barrier and an alternative to citizenship status in the long term. This increases difficulty not only for citizenship, but also for immigrant families abroad. In the end, new requirements may be useful devices to promote integration, in that individuals obtain skills and training; but they also function as a barrier of restriction, both symbolically (in signaling "control") and in practice.

Austria's restrictive citizenship starting point

Austrian citizenship policy is consistently scored as one of the most restrictive in Europe.[1] This is based on the principle of *jus sanguinis*, a strident ban on dual citizenship, and the requirement of a high residence duration (at 10 years). Citizenship in Austria has historically not been a mechanism to bring outsiders into the national political community, but rather an instrument of recognition that a transition has already been made and earned. As Dilek Çinar notes, rules reflect a "belief that naturalization has to be the last step of 'successful integration.' "[2] This closure has withstood the pressure of postwar immigration. Rainer Bauböck and Çinar point out that, despite the frequent amendments to citizenship policy, "neither the successive admission of refugees from communist regimes in eastern Europe nor the guestworker policy and subsequent family immigration from the 1960s caused major changes to the rules of admission to Austrian citizenship."[3] In fact, the majority of changes to citizenship policy have either been to maintain restriction or, as was the case with revisions in 1998, to harmonize practices at the provincial level, where the federal structure maintains legislative capacity for the national government but relegates adminstrative capacity – and therefore considerable leeway of practice – to the provinces or states.

Traditional, nation-based interpretations of citizenship policy would ascribe this closure as symptomatic of and consistent with Austria's ethnocultural concept of nationhood. However, we can set aside Brubakerian claims about cultural determinism and look at a more instrumental, recent account of ethnocultural preference reinforcement. In the immediate postwar period, Austria constructed a citizenship by defining itself as "a nation apart from Germany and the discredited traditions of German nationalism ... This, however, did not lead to Austria embracing the multiethnic heritage of the Habsburg Empire as an alternative source of identity."[4] Bauböck and Çinar continue by noting that,

1 Howard gives it a maximally restrictive score, at 0 out of 6, and its MIPEX 2010 score is a low 22/100. For these scores, see Marc Morjé Howard, *The Politics of Citizenship in Europe* (Cambridge: Cambridge University Press, 2009), 28; Migration Policy Group, "The Migrant Integration Policy Index (MIPEX)," (Migration Policy Group & British Council, 2011).

2 Dilek Çinar, "Austria," in *EUDO Citizenship Observatory Country Reports* (Florence: EUDO Citizenship, Robert Schuman Centre for Advanced Studies, EUI, 2010), 1.

3 Rainer Bauböck and Dilek Çinar, "Nationality law and naturalisation in Austria," in *Towards a European Nationality: Citizenship, immigration and nationality law in the EU*, ed. Randall Hansen and Patrick Weil (Houndsmills, Basingstoke, Hampshire: Palgrave, 2001), 259.

4 Ibid., 267.

flowing from this ambiguity, Austrian citizenship policies "have been generally seen as instruments for regulating certain aspects of immigration, but not for defining or affirming a positive conception of Austrian identity."[5] Elsewhere, Çinar makes this point more explicit: "A restrictive naturalisation policy is not necessarily the expression of an assimilationist approach. Rather, it can be argued that restrictions in citizenship legislations have more to do with the wish to restrain immigrants' access to social benefits, political rights, and in particular, the right to family reunion and less with an ethnic conception of national identity."[6] Altogether, Austria's "self-image as not being an immigration country"[7] is maintained both rhetorically and in practice through restrictive citizenship policy rules.

Policy adoption: Restrictive integration requirements through political consensus

How did this restrictive orientation set the parameters for a debate on membership? There are two major factors that reveal the effects of a restrictive citizenship orientation starting point: the grand coalition between the leftist SPÖ and the rightist ÖVP (from 1986 to 1999), which established a consensus on immigrant-related issues, and the growing power of the Freedom Party, which became a significant voice of opposition in response to this consensus and effectively set an agenda of retrenchment.

The Grand Coalition came about during a period of stunning demographic change. While, on the one hand, there were policies in place explicitly prohibiting admittance, for example the 1992 introduction of an annual quota for new immigrants, we also see an increase in foreign population that corresponds to a doubling in the number of foreigners as a percentage of the total population, from 4.5 percent in 1988 to 9.1 percent in 1997.[8] This significant shift came particularly from the traditional guest-worker recruitment countries of Turkey and the former Yugoslav republics. We also see related changes in naturalization, as guest-worker migrants started to meet conditions of residence over time and immigration rule changes affected the demand for naturalization among long-term residents. Not only are there more naturalizations in this period as a whole (with a near-doubling of the foreign population, from 2.2 percent in 1992 to 4.2 percent in 2001),[9] we also see stark changes in terms of *who* is naturalizing: "In 1997 EU citizens accounted for only 1.7 percent of all naturalizations compared with about 26 percent in 1986."[10]

In this changing climate, there was an "implicit, cross-party consensus between the Social Democrats and the Conservatives not to politicize nationality

[5] Ibid., 268. [6] Çınar, "Austria," 24. [7] Ibid., 1.
[8] OECD, *International migration outlook: SOPEMI 1999* (Paris: OECD Publishing),264.
[9] OECD, *International migration outlook: SOPEMI 2003* (Paris: OECD Publishing), 309.
[10] Bauböck and Çinar, "Nationality law and naturalisation in Austria," 260.

law."[11] In fact, the coalition originally formed because the Social Democrats did not want to stay in coalition with the Freedom Party once Jörg Haider, the latter's ignominious leader, took the helm and started turning the party toward right-wing populism after the 1986 parliamentary election. This consensus in government against politicization, however, does not imply that there was not a sense among parties that restriction was necessary, not only to stem the tide of immigration but to stave off competition from the Freedom Party. As a result, parties on both sides of the ideological divide began to stress the need for strengthening citizenship rules in order "to preserve the exclusive nature of Austrian citizenship."[12] The Social Democrats, as Karin König and Bernhard Perchinig describe, in their capacity as regularly nominating the Minister of the Interior, were "on the forefront of restricting immigration and proliferating a harsh legal division between citizens and 'foreigners' during most of the nineties, thereby establishing the sharp social exclusion of third country immigrants."[13] In supporting restriction, the Social Democrats (Austria's largest party on the left) proved to be the "hard test" that illustrates the restrictive parameters of debate. Despite the restrictive agendas of both major parties, the consensus against politicization created a political vacuum that the Freedom Party was keen and ready to fill. They began to campaign heavily in the 1990s on immigrant-related issues. In fact, even the conservative ÖVP – as a more direct competitor for Freedom Party votes – came out in support of the Freedom Party's mid-90s' campaign against "premature naturalisation," pointing out "that Austrian citizenship was a 'valuable asset' not to be granted to immigrants 'lacking the will to integrate'."[14]

It was in this political setting of rising naturalization rates and anti-immigrant politics that the consensus among government parties "gradually eroded,"[15] and amendments to change citizenship were first introduced. The ÖVP supported existing restrictions and sought to add the requirements of sufficient knowledge of German and knowledge of Austrian society. The Freedom Party, still from outside government, advocated stridently restrictive changes, surpassing the conservative position to include "*inter alia*, a constitutional amendment to the effect that Austria is not a country of immigration and an 'integration certificate' as a naturalization requirement."[16] The Greens and Liberal Forum pushed against this tide for liberal change, including reduction of residence to five years and introduction of dual citizenship. Once the SPÖ – "who had previously

[11] Ibid., 259. [12] Ibid., 260.

[13] Karin König and Bernhard Perchinig, "Austria," in *EU and US Approaches to the Management of Immigration*, ed. Jan Niessen, Yongmi Schibel, and Raphaele Magoni (Brussels: Migration Policy Group, 2003), 8.

[14] Bernhard Perchinig, "All you need to know to become an Austrian: Naturalisation policy and citizenship testing in Austria," in *A Re-definition of Belonging? Language and integration tests in Europe*, ed. Ricky van Oers, Eva Ersbøll, and Dora Kostakopoulou (Leiden; Boston: Martinus Nijhoff, 2010), 29.

[15] Bauböck and Çinar, "Nationality law and naturalisation in Austria," 259. [16] Ibid., 261.

been reluctant to address the issue" – stepped in, they recognized the "necessity of reforming Austria's nationality law but rejected the introduction of comprehensive assimilation requirements and, contradictorily, toleration of dual nationality."[17] What resulted was a watered-down series of changes with the main aim of standardizing naturalization practices at the provincial level.[18] While the 1998 amendment introduced a formal requirement of "basic of minimum knowledge of German to master everyday life,"[19] it did not specify a required level of proficiency or standard means of assessment. Bauböck and Çinar conclude that "The changes were the result of a compromise between the two leading parties ... [and in general] the existing framework of citizenship policy in Austria was maintained."[20]

This lukewarm change did not produce the decline in naturalizations that the government or the Freedom Party was hoping for. Thus, the tightening of conditions for naturalization became a central issue for the Freedom Party platform. And by entering into coalition with the conservative People's Party after a highly successful second-place finish in the 1999 election (capturing 26.9 percent of the national vote), the Freedom Party "gave notice of a planned amendment to the exiting Nationality Law" that included knowledge of language and society.[21] Yet, in spite of this central preoccupation with limiting access to citizenship, the first major legislative measure on immigration issues proposed by the right-wing ÖVP-FPÖ government was, importantly, directed at the stage of permanent residence (targeting new immigrants and immigrants settled after 1998) and not citizenship.

The idea of restricting access to permanent residence through integration was first laid out by the Freedom Party in April 2001; it suggested an "integration contract."[22] This would include mandatory language training as well as integration courses on the labor market and society. There were some mixed messages about the purpose of the new Integration Agreement (IA); "Whereas the FPÖ stressed the need to improve 'the immigrant's willingness to integrate,' the ÖVP-led Ministry of Interior referred to the success of the Dutch model," pointing to the positive effects of integration courses rather than testing

[17] Ibid.

[18] As Perchinig notes, "Until the 1998 amendment, the regional authorities were relatively free to make use of facilitated naturalisation after four years instead of the regular ten years residence, for 'special reasons'." In Perchinig, "All you need to know to become an Austrian: Naturalisation policy and citizenship testing in Austria," 30. For example, as Çinar notes, some provinces – namely Tyrol and Vorarlberg – assessed language as a practice before 1998, though no formal rule existed. See Çınar, "Austria," 23.

[19] Çınar, "Austria," 8.

[20] Bauböck and Çinar, "Nationality law and naturalisation in Austria," 261.

[21] Perchinig, "All you need to know to become an Austrian: Naturalisation policy and citizenship testing in Austria," 30.

[22] Bernhard Perchinig, "Country report Austria," in *The INTEC project: Integration and Naturalisation tests: the new way to European Citizenship* (Nijmegen, the Netherlands: Centre for Migration Law, Radboud University, 2010), 11.

mechanisms.[23] When the legislation came to the floor of Parliament for debate on July 9, 2002, then-Freedom Party parliamentarian Peter Westenthaler made its primary objective unambiguous: "With this law we make one thing clear: Austria is not an immigration country and it will never be one. We will make sure of that."[24] In fact, despite its earnest intent, the ÖVP would "frequently invoke 'integration' as the main buzzword in order (a) to introduce stricter polices on immigration (in a variety of areas) and (b) to legitimize those policies," as Michal Krzyzanowski and Ruth Wodak point out in their discourse analysis of debate.[25] To illustrate this with one ÖVP parliamentarian:

> One has a one-and-a-half year period during which to attend a German language course. There is the possibility of extensions, and part of the cost of the course is refunded by the state. And only if someone says after four years: 'I want to stay here, but I don't want to learn German', then, I believe, it is in accordance with what the great majority in this country believes that we should say to the person concerned, 'it's one or the other: if you want to stay here, then learn German; if you do not want to learn German, then please go back where you came from![26]

Krzyzanowski and Wodak continue by noting that the ÖVP discourse "clearly becomes similar to that of its new coalition partner, the Freedom Party" where it was "mainly preoccupied with (a) legitimizing the new laws introduced by the FPÖ-ÖVP government and (b) criticizing the SPÖ (its former coalition partner!) for its too-liberal immigration policy and laws."[27] And as Julia Mourão Permoser summarizes, "The primary aim of this policy as portrayed by its initiator was not to empower migrants and improve their opportunities. Rather, the new policy was meant to reinforce the image that the Austrian government was tough on migration and restrictive with regards to migrants' access to rights."[28]

The IA was adopted as part of the 2002 revision to the Residence Law (in force January 1, 2003), and introduced one hundred units of compulsory language training at the A1 level as a condition of remaining in Austria and having access to long-term residence (i.e., applicable to all new residents since 1998).[29] Immigrants were also responsible for incurring up to fifty percent of course fees, with delays in compliance increasing out-of-pocket fees, and non-compliance potentially leading to fines, denial of permanent residence, and expulsion.

[23] Perchinig, "All you need to know to become an Austrian: Naturalisation policy and citizenship testing in Austria," 31.

[24] Julia Mourão Permoser, "Redefining membership: European Union policy on the rights of third-country nationals" (Ph.D. Dissertation, University of Vienna, 2010), 200.

[25] Michal Krzyzanowski and Ruth Wodak, *The Politics of Exclusion: Debating migration in Austria* (New Brunswick, NJ: Transaction Publishers, 2009), 93.

[26] Ibid., 94. [27] Ibid., 99.

[28] Permoser, "Redefining membership: European Union policy on the rights of third-country nationals," 200.

[29] Exemptions were reserved for EU/EEA migrants, children, the elderly, and immigrants with suitable knowledge of German.

Taking a moment to consider the significance of this first major adoption of civic integration policy, we see it as emblematic of restrictive retrenchment. First, quick restriction was produced from a restrictive consensus government. Second, the focus of legislation was on bolstering the significant consequentiality of residence as a status requiring integration. Passage was relatively unimpeded, as those parties outside government pushing pro-immigrant agendas were moving perpendicular to the zeitgeist of public opinion. Opposition and humanitarian NGOs "pointed out that [IA] merely serves as a threat to immigrants and thus does not at all aim at providing a better knowledge of German, which can hardly be acquired in 100 hours,"[30] but gained little traction with this softer approach.[31] And, against predictions that "the crucial opposition-to-government 'switch' " of the Freedom Party would moderate its anti-immigrant tone, the coalition partnership was instead "of particular importance for the further radicalization of FPÖ discourse."[32] Indeed, future reforms of successive rightist governments only built upon this initial restrictive achievement. As we will see, the 2005 Settlement and Residence Act adds more conditions to the integration agreement, while the 2006 Citizenship Act, in addition to adding a citizenship test, established a formidable chain of conditionality by making permanent residence a condition for citizenship.

Policy adaptation: Furthering restriction through integration

As subsequent policy shows, the ÖVP–FPÖ slogan of "Integration before new immigration" would ring true throughout their tenure in government, even after its first coalition failed and was reconstituted with the Freedom Party-breakoff party, BZÖ. And, in a continued departure from far-right talking points, as well as other membership strategies that invest directly in citizenship, we see that integration changes that directly affect citizenship acquisition were, in fact, the last of their major immigrant-related legislation, as the bulk of subsequent membership requirements is directed squarely at permanent residence.

The 2005 Settlement and Residence Act (*Niederlassungs und Aufenthaltsgesetz*; NAG), along with implementing European Union directives on long-term residence and family reunification, widened the integration agreement in a number of respects and without significant contestation.[33] Among the many new changes, including increased categories of exemptions, NAG 2005 restructured the "basic knowledge of German" requirement into two modules: (1) literacy and (2) a language course that promotes knowledge of German and, in the language of the

[30] König and Perchinig, "Austria," 5.

[31] For example, the SPÖ suggested that instead of tying German classes to the threat of losing residence permits, it should instead be linked to the right to vote in local elections. "Citizenship classes: the Austrian way," *BBC News Online*, October 26, 2001.

[32] Krzyzanowski and Wodak, *The Politics of Exclusion: Debating migration in Austria*, 101.

[33] Perchinig notes that "While there was a vigorous public debate on the imposition of the integration agreement in 2003, the reform of 2005 received only scant attention in the public. Perchinig, "Country report Austria," 14.

legislation, the ability to "participate in social, economic and cultural life in Austria." To complete the first module, an immigrant must complete 75 course units of literacy if they are illiterate. The federal government pays the entire cost of this module. To complete the second module, the length of the initial course was extended to 300 course units and the immigrant is refunded 50 percent of the cost of the course. The required level of German proficiency was also raised to the A2 level. And, finally, to assess this new level, a test was introduced at the culmination of the course that is "strictly confined to language competency testing."[34] Unlike other state practices (e.g., in Germany), the test does not assess country knowledge, history, or values. The obligation according to the IA is only to demonstrate knowledge of German and not learn facts on Austria, which does not require a migrant to attend the course or take an exam if it is not necessary. The target population of the IA is regular labor migrants from non-EU/EEA countries and family migrants, for whom this inclusive nuance would not necessarily apply.

Only once comprehensive integration was in place for residence did policy-makers finally attach integration to citizenship with the adoption of a knowledge test with the 2006 Citizenship Act. Against the backdrop of the Freedom Party's rhetoric of tackling "premature naturalization," we see this as the last piece of significant legislation to retrench restriction. Drafting began in 2005 by the Freedom Party and BZÖ, submitting citizenship changes that, among other proposals such as income thresholds, raised the residency requirement,[35] increased the German language requirement from A1 to A2, and introduced a naturalization test. Perhaps as the first indicator of a fraying coalition, with lost confidence in the ÖVP and flagging popularity of the Freedom Party – having already suffered electoral defeats in 2002 and splintering from party-infighting in 2005 – these proposals faced significant political resistance. The bill could not pass the Federal Council (second chamber of the Austrian Parliament), where the SPÖ and Greens held a majority, but the National Council (first chamber) successfully overrode this veto and the bill came into force in March 2006.

In the end, a number of the initial restrictions were achieved, including the raised language level and naturalization test, which assessed knowledge of German as well as basic knowledge both of the democratic order and history of Austria and of the relevant federal province of the applicant's residence. This is an 18-question, multiple-choice test, consisting of six questions on Austrian democracy, six on Austrian history, and six on the province of residence. This

[34] Ibid., 25.

[35] Proposals of residency duration changes could be described as a "race to the restrictive bottom." Perchinig describes two different proposals, each made in a bid to outmaneuver the other as the anti-immigration party. On the one hand, "the Mayor of Innsbruck, Mr. van Staa (ÖVP) ... suggested extending the waiting period for naturalization for third-country nationals to 15 years and for European Union citizens to 13 years." On the other hand, "In July 2005 the newly-installed Minister of Justice of the BZO, Karin Miklautsch, demanded the introduction of harsher naturalization requirements, such as minimum waiting period of 12 years." Perchinig, "All you need to know to become an Austrian: Naturalisation policy and citizenship testing in Austria," 32.

test was clearly to restrict access to citizenship, and as it was produced out of a series of restrictive bargains reached by the Freedom Party in coalition with Conservatives. It was also deemed "in principle unsuitable for fostering integration and developing civic awareness."[36] Additionally, unlike the IA, German speakers and EEA applicants are not exempt from the test, though they are exempt from demonstrating knowledge of German.

But perhaps the most significant change to citizenship is the new requirement of permanent residence. Of the 10 years of residence required for eligibility for Austrian citizenship, 5 years of settlement must be as a permanent resident according to NAG 2005, which includes the requirement of fulfilling the IA. By making permanent residence a condition for citizenship, the differences between the two legal stages are simultaneously diminished in that permanent residence is a way station for those seeking citizenship. Thus, the integration completed for permanent residence is insufficient for citizenship and represents only half the journey to full membership. And citizenship is even further out of reach because of new integration, income, and residency conditions.

Since these major pieces of legislation, and despite changes in the coalition – namely the reintroduction of SPÖ into government – restrictions have continued. A 2010 reform equalized the income requirement for permanent residence and citizenship, while 2011 changes to legislation raised language levels for both permanent residence (from A2 to B1) and citizenship (from B1 to B2 for "exceptionally well-integrated" foreigners). These changes, and the absence of a significant discourse to reverse restriction despite new SPÖ–ÖVP governments, indicate the continued strength of a restrictive understanding of belonging on defining parameters of discourse and the enduring preference for exclusion. And while a 2011 "Integration Report" mentioned the importance of "rais[ing] the interest of those persons complying with all the significant prerequisites for Austrian citizenship to actually obtain such citizenship," no measures had been taken as of 2013.[37]

FROM DESIGN TO IMPLEMENTATION: RESTRICTION IN PRACTICE?

Restriction is the clear, primary objective of new membership policy, but to what extent are these goals born out in practice? There is limited data to answer this question. The Ministry of Interior does not make available information on the success or failure rates of long-term residence applicants in completing the Integration Agreement.[38] Additionally, by looking at sheer acquisition rates of permanent residence or naturalization, it is impossible to separate out the effect of

[36] Hauer et al., cited by Perchinig, "Country report Austria," 54.

[37] Joachim Stern and Gerd Valchars, "Naturalisation procedures for immigrants: Austria," in *EUDO Citizenship Observatory Naturalisation Procedures Reports* (Florence: EUDO Citizenship, Robert Schuman Centre for Advanced Studies, EUI, 2013), 4.

[38] Julia Mourão Permoser, "Civic integration as symbolic politics: Insights from Austria," *European Journal of Migration and Law* 14, no. 2 (2012), 194.

integration requirements from other requirements, including the high-income requirement, raised fees for naturalization, etc. Still, there is some data to consider.

According to Table 4.1, a mere fraction of those required to complete the IA for permanent residence actually do within a given year. And, as we see in Figure 4.1, between thirty-seven percent (for 2008) and fifty-one percent (for 2006) of all fulfillments of the integration agreement are based on participation in integration courses. A majority of candidates complete the agreement by completing education in Austria, vocational education, or being classified as "key personnel." Only a fraction (approximately two percent in 2007) of candidates complete the IA by

TABLE 4.1. *Fulfillment of Integration Agreement in Austria, 2003–2010*[39]

	Required	Fulfilled	Percentage Fulfilled
2003	9,114	951	10.43
2004	5,540	1,568	28.3
2005	3,758	1,683	44.78
2006	22,958	5,795	25.24
2007	16,690	5,485	32.86
2008	15,147	4,655	30.73
2009	13,911	5,219	37.51
2010	12,695	6,841	53.89

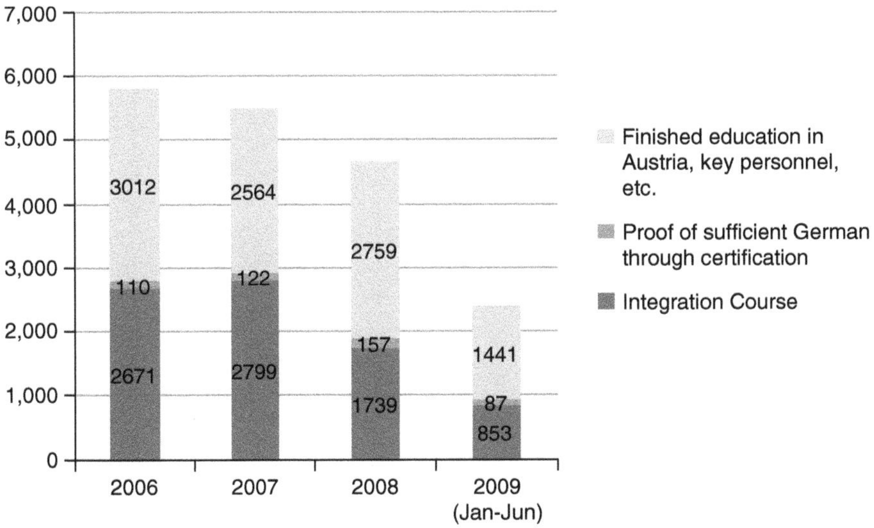

4.1 Type of fulfillment of the integration agreement, 2006–June 2009

[39] Permoser, "Civic Integration as Symbolic Politics: Insights from Austria," 193.

obtaining certification. This does not mean that the majority of persons who do not complete the integration agreement will never do so, nor does it imply that these large percentages proceed to deportation. These data mainly illustrate the large pool of family-based applicants from outside Europe. Family-based migrants constitute a diverse group; some complete the integration course, some complete schooling in Austria (since 2006), and, like other migrants, some are classified as key personnel and therefore exempt from the course or test altogether. This is not conclusive information, but family-based migrants seeking first residence or settlement permits clearly emerge as the most-targeted group of immigrants. This is not an overall control on immigration, but a specific targeting of non-EU migrants who enjoy entry outside the quota system. Even if they do not incur deportation – between 2003 and 2009 only three persons were ever reported to authorities as being non-compliant[40] – they incur delays, fines, and other barriers toward political incorporation and security of status. It is difficult to measure the true impact of the agreement on the acquisition of residence, but this snapshot clearly points to family as a vulnerable category.

Turning to citizenship, the naturalization test is clearly not a barrier. This is not surprising. Immigrants need to complete so much to reach the point of eligibility for citizenship – including long residence, the integration agreement, etc. – that a short, knowledge-based exam with preparation material and sample questions should not be particularly difficult. In looking at naturalization rates for 2007, nearly every province recorded pass rates in the 90th percentile (see Table 4.2). In terms of actual numbers, in Vienna, where the majority of tests are taken, an SPÖ city councilor announced that only 56 out of 1,678 candidates failed the test in 2007.[41]

TABLE 4.2. *Success rates for naturalization test in 2007, by state*[42]

State	Success Rate%
Burgenland	96.0
Carinthia	n/a
Lower Austria	88.6
Upper Austria	91.9
Salzburg	97.5
Styria	95.3
Tyrol	95.2
Vienna	96.7
Vorarlberg	93.3

40 Christina Hollomey, Alfred Wöger, and Albert Kraler, "The national policy frame for the integration of newcomers in Austria," in *Promoting Sustainable Policies for Integration (PROSINT)* (Vienna: ICMPD, 2011), 16.

41 Çınar, "Austria," 21. 42 Perchinig, "Country Report Austria," 56.

CONCLUSION

As the design of policy and these outcome results show, the real barrier to inclusion – and thus the focal point of integration – is long-term residence. Not only does it require significant obligations in terms of integration, as well as delay the benefits that come with secure legal status, it also is a prerequisite for citizenship. And with the right to family reunification for settled third-country nationals, long-term residence is a desirable alternative to citizenship, which offers little in the way of extra rights, is more costly, and requires another five years of residence. While residence requirements are decisive in delaying status, changes to citizenship have been more symbolic, in that "the actual goal of the policy does not coincide with its stated goal because what counts is the message that the policy sends out."[43] In other words, successive rightist governments have introduced integration requirements to reassure a predominantly anti-immigrant population that they are "doing something" to protect citizenship. These restrictions have not been reversed with the center-left re-entering power. In fact, 2011 saw the lowest naturalization rate in recent years, at .71 percent (compared to a 2003 peak of 5.96 percent).[44] And while both long-term residence and citizenship have become more difficult, the former is clearly the more consequential of the two statuses.

By promoting integration at permanent residence and by increasing it as a formidable barrier and delaying acquisition of citizenship in a context of a restrictive political consensus, Austria is emblematic of restrictive retrenchment. New membership requirements – in policy and practice – fortify an existing orientation of exclusion. New requirements serve to buttress other criteria to make permanent residence a significant second barrier of admission, insulating citizenship from liberalizing change and making it an even farther distant prize for newcomers. Not only does this restrict access to citizenship, it also restricts access to long-term residence and, therefore, the ability to bring family members into Austria. Integration requirements certainly yield positive individual effects, like teaching German to newcomers and educating migrants about their host society, thus empowering individuals to access its labor market. They may even be popular among immigrants for these reasons. However, as Perchinig notes, if integration was the real goal of state policymakers, "we would expect to find an elaborate curriculum leading from the integration contract to naturalization. In reality, virtually no connection exists between these elements."[45] This only reaffirms the stated objective of new membership requirements – reducing migration and naturalization – and highlights the purposeful distinction between permanent residence and citizenship to meet that end, particularly the strategic use of the former as an early gate and alternative to full inclusion in citizenship.

[43] Permoser, "Civic integration as symbolic politics: Insights from Austria," 197.
[44] Stern and Valchars, "Naturalisation procedures for immigrants: Austria," 1.
[45] Perchinig, "Country report Austria," 62.

Denmark

Denmark tells a remarkably similar story to Austria. In it, we see a far-right party exert significant influence on a center-right government to increase restriction. The Danish People's Party (*Dansk Folkeparti*) was especially effective in setting this agenda, as they did not even serve in coalition but instead provided supporting votes in parliament. They were successful in adding barriers to status acquisition not only because a rightist government was in power but also, I argue, because membership requirements were crafted and added in the context of an already restrictive citizenship orientation. The impact of this policy context can be observed not only in later, restrictive iterations of policy but particularly in initial adoption, in which a left government first introduced civic integration. On this final point, we note a major point of difference between these two cases; recall Figure 3.3, which illustrates distinct differences in government orientation at the point of policy adoption.

The concept of belonging in Denmark is defined by coinciding and seemingly contrasting narratives. On the one hand, it is "known as a liberal Scandinavian country, tolerant towards alternative lifestyles"[46] where "equality and individual autonomy are often interpreted as valuable ways of life ... [and] the welfare state is the institutional carrier of this modern project of liberation."[47] On the other hand, it "remains ethnocultural in terms of membership and an instrumental pursuit of cohesion-as-homogeneity."[48] In other words, it is internally inclusive while also externally exclusive. This is true for citizenship generally, and comports with Brubaker's fundamental definition of citizenship.[49] However, in the case of Denmark, one might argue we see heightened values on both dimensions: extreme internal liberalism and extreme external exclusion.

This delicate contrast is maintained in both citizenship and permanent residence policy. As citizenship has moved from "moderately restrictive to very restrictive,"[50] the focus on the content and utility of permanent residence has grown exponentially. Indeed, dense integration requirements for permanent residence have front-loaded integration expectations so that Danish citizenship became, as in Austria, a reward for integration. It was "something to strive for,

[46] Per Mouritsen and Tore Vincents Olsen, "Denmark between liberalism and nationalism," *Ethnic and Racial Studies* 36, no. 4 (2013), 691.

[47] Per Mouritsen, "The particular universalism of a Nordic civic nation: common values, state religion and Islam in Danish political culture," in *Multiculturalism, Muslims and Citizenship: A European approach*, ed. Tariq Modood, Anna Triandafyllidou, and Ricard Zapata-Barrero (London: Routledge, 2006), 86.

[48] Mouritsen and Olsen, "Denmark between liberalism and nationalism," 693.

[49] Rogers Brubaker, *Citizenship and Nationhood in France and Germany* (Cambridge, MA: Harvard University Press, 1992).

[50] Eva Ersbøll, "On trial in Denmark," in *A Re-definition of Belonging? Language and integration tests in Europe*, ed. Ricky van Oers, Eva Ersbøll, and Dora Kostakopoulou (Leiden; Boston: Martinus Nijhoff, 2010), 107.

an incentive for foreigners to adapt to Danish society."[51] At the same time, integration requirements "serve as civic-screening and exclusion devices," particularly for family-based migrants, in which "some people just cannot and should not become members."[52]

This case study examines the adoption and adaptation of membership requirements in Denmark as a strategy of restrictive retrenchment. First appearing at the stage of permanent residence and then at citizenship, this sequence establishes significant barriers to inclusion. Each incremental adaptation of restriction was also made by a center-right government that enjoyed support (but also polarizing influence) from the People's Party. After examining existing citizenship policy and the concept of belonging before the adoption of civic integration, I look at the politics of citizenship and the background conditions of migration in the mid- to late-1990s. This view establishes the xenoskeptic political climate in which the left – against theoretical predictions and as a result of context – pursued the first iteration of restrictive integration, which only grew over time, alongside the influence of the far-right People's Party. I then look at the steps taken to adapt civic integration to show the retention of restriction through policy evolution. New restrictions were quickly adopted, relatively uncontested, and summarily popular, and opposition parties were therefore at a disadvantage to block or counterbalance deepening restriction. Finally, I examine pass rates and other outcome evidence, to illustrate the extent to which restrictively designed policies yield restrictive outcomes.

DENMARK'S RESTRICTIVE CITIZENSHIP STARTING POINT

Denmark sits right alongside Austria as boasting one of the most restrictive citizenship policies in Europe, reflecting monocultural roots by denying acquisition through *jus soli* and requiring nine years of residence for acquisition via naturalization (raised from seven years in 2002).[53] Denmark is restrictive not only compared to other European countries, but also in contrast to Nordic countries, in which citizenship was historically characterized by similarity, even degrees of cross-country harmonization. Denmark stands out in this regard by maintaining the highest barriers of admission, including a conduct requirement that permanently excludes persons from naturalization if they have been sentenced to prison for eighteen months or more,[54] as well as the stringent language and country knowledge requirements examined here. This restriction is not only the standard for citizenship, but also the object of recent change. In Eva Ersbøll's description of the 2000s, "There has not been a general perception of *the right to a citizenship* as

[51] Ibid., 133. [52] Mouritsen and Olsen, "Denmark between liberalism and nationalism," 698.

[53] Howard scores Denmark as maximally restrictive on the CPI (at a 0 out of 6), while its MIPEX 2010 "access to nationality" score is 33/100.

[54] Eva Ersbøll, "Denmark," in *EUDO Citizenship Observatory Country Reports* (Florence: EUDO Citizenship, Robert Schuman Centre for Advanced Studies, EUI, 2013), 1.

a means of integrating foreigners into the social and political life of Denmark or as a desirable goal in itself. Instead, *the strengthening of the criteria* for acquisition of citizenship has been seen as a means to fulfill the visions and strategies of the government regarding the integration of foreigners."[55] This commitment to restriction was particularly visible in the early upholding of the ban on dual citizenship. With unsuccessful liberalizing proposals in 2009 and 2011, the government finally committed to dual citizenship in 2014, with even the conservative Liberal (*Venstre*) party expressing support. However, there are two important facets of this change that limit the spirit of liberalization. First, it is primarily discussed as a vehicle to allow Danes living abroad to obtain a second citizenship and not as an instrument to integrate immigrants in Denmark.[56] Expatriate organizations played a significant lobbying role to deliver reform. Second, while parliamentarians support change, "over half of voters ... said they were against it ... [as] it would dilute the definition [of] what it meant to be Danish."[57]

This overall restrictive orientation reflects a highly ethnically homogenous population, so that "even though the country has now, like other European countries, become a country of immigration, it has not identified itself as such.[58] This gets to the inherently contrasting nature of Danish identity as simultaneously externally exclusive in its ethno-nationalism but internally inclusive in its commitment to liberalism. As Per Mouritsen and Tore Vincents Olsen note: "The liberal-convergence thesis is only partly right: there is a movement towards perfectionism, but in the Danish case, this takes place *within the national tradition*"[59] (emphasis added). They continue by noting that while the external contours of nationalism are ethnic, the internal content is "predominantly civic, for example tied to pride in a particular form of small-scale democracy, egalitarianism and welfare society."[60] Maintaining an ethnic or exclusive concept of belonging alongside inclusive rhetoric is a difficult balance. For third-country nationals in Denmark, we see a high degree of rights with status, but the barriers to that status are significantly restrictive.

POLICY ADOPTION: RESTRICTIVE INTEGRATION REQUIREMENTS IN AN ANTI-IMMIGRANT CONTEXT

Immigration to Denmark was not an accidental phenomenon. The 1983 Aliens Act, in particular, secured legal rights for refugees and resident immigrants. However, the inevitable outcome of this inclusive policy – the influx of

[55] Eva Ersbøll, "Denmark," 35.

[56] See, for example, the rationale exhibited by petitioners at http://statsborger.dk (accessed September 11, 2013).

[57] "Dual citizenship ban likely to be overturned." *The Copenhagen Post*. July 23, 2013.

[58] Ersbøll, "Denmark," 3.

[59] Mouritsen and Olsen, "Denmark between liberalism and nationalism," 707.

[60] Ibid.

immigrants – led to rising hostility and restrictive policy counterbalancing. We also see in this cause-and-effect the inherent contrast in Danish belonging: a moral commitment to inclusion but a rhetorical – and later practical – commitment to closure. By 1997, 4.7 percent of the population of Denmark, or approximately a quarter of a million people, were foreign nationals or stateless.[61] This is almost double the figures of only a decade prior (2.8 percent in 1988).[62] As in many European countries, this significant shift is partly accounted for by an influx of family members of guest workers who migrated until the early 1970s, but it also reflects a steep increase in asylum seekers and a general shift from labor migration to refugee-based migration.

While immigration started to gain in momentum after the adoption of the Aliens Act, "it was not until the 1990s that the issue of immigration became the dominant topic in newspapers and, indeed, in political discourse and public debate generally."[63] In addition to debates over restricting immigration, parliamentarians were also preoccupied with the conditionality of citizenship. To wit, Mouritsen and Olsen characterize this period as dominated by the notion "that immigrants must be induced to acquire the 'fundamental values' of Danish society."[64] And, as Erbøll notes, in each year of the 1990s there were "proposals to tighten the requirements of naturalisation, impose more rigorous criteria for the conferment of citizenship, introduce a quota system ... and impose good conduct requirements,"[65] even suggesting that the "periodic discussions on naturalization in parliament encourage[d] populist statements from certain political parties, thus damaging the general public attitude towards foreign residents."[66] These proposals originated from opposition parties on the right, including the Liberals *(Venstre)*, Conservatives (*Konservative)*, and the Danish People's Party (formerly the Danish Progress Party). Another proposal also floated the suggestion of testing an applicant's Danish reading and writing skills. However, most of these proposals failed to gain traction as the Social Democratic-led coalition remained split in terms of its position on immigration. As Jens Rydgren describes: "Originally a defender of refugee immigration and (some sort of) multiculturalism, the SWG party drifted towards a more unsympathetic view of these matters as the Danish People's Party gained ground in the opinion polls – to a large extent at the expense of the Social Democrats – and as the party was attacked by not only the Danish People's Party but also the Liberal Party for being too generous on immigration."[67] In 1997, for

[61] Eva Ersbøll, "Nationality law in Denmark, Finland and Sweden," in *Towards a European Nationality: Citizenship, immigration and nationality law in the EU*, ed. Randall Hansen and Patrick Weil (Houndmills, Basingstoke, Hampshire: Palgrave, 2001), 245.

[62] OECD 1999, p. 264

[63] Jens Rydgren, "Explaining the emergence of radical right-wing populist parties: The case of Denmark," *West European Politics* 27, no. 3 (2004), 493.

[64] Mouritsen and Olsen, "Denmark between liberalism and nationalism," 693.

[65] Ersbøll, "Nationality law in Denmark, Finland and Sweden," 249. [66] Ibid.

[67] Rydgren, "Explaining the emergence of radical right-wing populist parties: The case of Denmark," 494.

example, the government appointed a new, restrictive-oriented Minister of the Interior (Torkild Simonsen). This was an unambiguous sign of the increased competition from the People's Party to the Social Democrats, particularly over working-class votes.[68] As a result, "the party had a hard time providing a coherent response."[69] And, as the People's Party grew in popularity, the Conservatives and Liberals sought their support as "the most attractive strategy to get back into government."[70]

Having moved to the right along with other parties, in 1999 the Social Democrat-led government introduced the first Integration Act. Claiming to be the "the first country in the world" to do so,[71] the state began to provide a free introductory program comprised of societal knowledge and the Danish language, as well as "employment-promoting options" including qualification improvement and work experience for permanent residence.[72] The explicit aim of obligatory participation and especially of individualized contracts was to move immigrants into employment or education. This precursor to more restrictive integration programs differed in that there was no test or level of language to obtain, but merely a requirement of active participation (similar to early Dutch and French platforms). Designed to be completed in the first three years of residence, non-participation could lead to the refusal of a permanent residence application, or result in the suspension of introductory aid – which even so was "intentionally set at a level below the minimum amount of living expenses so as to push immigrants into employment and make them independent from social security payments."[73] And, of course, where failure to participate blocked opportunities to acquire permanent residence, it also prohibited family-sponsored migration, which is a prerogative of permanent residents and citizens.

The significance of this act being introduced by a left government is indicative of the restrictive parameters of membership discourse. This is not tantamount to consensus; there is a significant difference between the left and the right, as evidenced by a decade of policy proposals and failures (particularly on the issue of dual citizenship). However, both the left and right supported varying degrees of immigrant-related restriction, the Integration Act being the mildest. The Act also established a baseline for further retrenchment. It could accurately

68 Ibid.

69 Christoffer Green-Pedersen and Jesper Krogstrup, "Immigration as a political issue in Denmark and Sweden," *European Journal of Political Research* 47, no. 5 (2008), 623.

70 Ibid.: 622.

71 Ministry of Refugee Immigration and Integration Affairs (Denmark), "New to Denmark," website.

72 Ersbøll, "On Trial in Denmark," 113.

73 Anja Wiesbrock, "Discrimination instead of integration? Integration requirements for immigrants in Denmark and Germany," in *Illiberal Liberal States: Immigration, citizenship and integration in the EU*, ed. Elspeth Guild, Kees Groenendijk, and Sergio Carrera (Farnham, Surrey; Burlington, VT: Ashgate, 2009), 302.

be characterized as modulating existing restriction, where the goal of new requirements was not to liberalize membership but condition it. In a political climate where the Social Democratic-led government ceased to be immune to political competition from the People's Party, we still see the moderating effect a leftist party can have on a restrictive citizenship orientation. Counterfactually, this first Act would have been significantly more restrictive had a rightist government been in power (as would happen only two years later). In fact, several of the restrictive contours of the Act were the result of bargains with rightist parties. The opposition Liberal and Conservative parties secured " 'substantial negotiated achievements', including the introduction of non-automatic permanent residence (after three years of residence) and the abolition of the entitlement to family reunification."[74] The People's Party saw the tone of restriction in the new Act as a direct reflection of their rising popularity and achievements.[75] In the end, the Act laid the groundwork for increasingly restrictive and generally uncontested series of new requirements to restrict new immigrants and potential citizens whereby a strategy of membership retrenchment would come to dwarf any moderation achieved early on.

POLICY ADAPTATION: A CHANGE OF THE GUARD AND UNIMPEDED RESTRICTIVE CONTINUITY

Where the Integration Act laid the foundation for strict requirements for permanent residence, the 2001 parliamentary election created an unparalleled political opportunity for center and far-right parties to build on this initial change. Namely, the far-right People's Party, which was "hostile towards cultural pluralism ... [and wishing] to preserve the nation as vessel of majority belonging,"[76] was able to spearhead new restrictions on top of existing ones from their newfound strength in parliament, bolstered by their successful, third-place finish (with twelve percent of the national vote) behind a Liberal–Conservative minority government. While not formally in the coalition, the Danish People's Party proved vital to the right minority government through voting support. In exchange, the People's Party was given significant ministerial posts and advantageous agenda-setting power. And, importantly, because the People's Party gained significant positions "without giving up its xenophobic, neo-racist rhetoric, the effect was increased legitimacy not only for the party per se, but also for this kind of political rhetoric."[77] For example, in their party manifesto for the 2001 election, they state that "Denmark is not a country of immigration, and has never been one. We cannot therefore accept a multiethnic transformation of the

74 Ersbøll, "On Trial in Denmark," 111. 75 Ibid.

76 Mouritsen, "The particular universalism of a Nordic civic nation: common values, state religion and Islam in Danish political culture," 71–72.

77 Rydgren, "Explaining the emergence of radical right-wing populist parties: The case of Denmark," 496.

country."[78] This pithy statement aptly sums up their attitude toward naturalization, integration, and overall legislative agenda. With the success of the People's Party, "Denmark segued from its old humanitarian reputation" and "successfully adopted a fear of immigration platform that foreign commentators found difficult to distinguish from that of the far right, and which followed tough measures already put in place under the previous centre coalition."[79] These results also reflect the general change in salience of the issue of immigration over time, as Rydgren notes: "In 2001, twenty percent of the voters mentioned 'immigration' when asked which problems of the day they considered to be most important when deciding how to vote. In 1990, it was only four percent."[80]

In its newfound role as coalition-supporting agenda setter, the People's Party's goal was to strengthen requirements for family reunification, and, in particular, to restrict naturalization. Therefore, shortly after the formation of a new government, one of the government's first initiatives was to amend the Integration Act. Notably, we again see here that while far-right parties gain a lot of traction on the rhetoric of limiting *citizenship*, we see integration policies primarily targeting permanent residence. The Bill to amend the Integration Act, targeting permanent-resident-seeking immigrants, transformed the 1999 Act in a number of respects, including increasing the residency duration from three to seven years and obliging foreigners to enter individual contracts that enforced a duty to integrate, adding a language test at the culmination of the integration course, and articulating specific sanctions for non-compliance. Importantly, entitlement to family reunification was also repealed, and replaced with several new restrictions, including the "24-year rule" which raised the age requirement of spouses and sponsors of family-based migrants.[81]

This strong link between residence and civic integration serves two purposes: functional integration and effective closure. There are real benefits reaped by immigrants in completing integration during settlement, specifically in terms of obtaining skills for accessing the labor market.[82] However, alongside this function, the exclusionary objectives are palpable. On the one hand, promoting dense membership criteria for settlement is only further confirmation that "the government does not consider citizenship a 'must' for immigrants."[83] On the

78 Cited in Ibid.: 484.

79 Mouritsen, "The particular universalism of a Nordic civic nation: common values, state religion and Islam in Danish political culture," 74.

80 Rydgren, "Explaining the emergence of radical right-wing populist parties: The case of Denmark," 494.

81 Silvia Adamo, "The legal position of migrants in Denmark: Assessing the context around the 'cartoon crisis'," *European Journal of Migration and Law* 9 (2007), 15–16.

82 See participant interviews in Eva Ersbøll and Laura Katrine Gravesen, "Country Report Denmark," in *The INTEC project: Integration and Naturalisation tests: The new way to European Citizenship* (Nijmegen, the Netherlands: Centre for Migration Law, Radboud University, 2010).

83 Ersbøll, "On trial in Denmark," 139.

other hand, it also makes it "more difficult for immigrants who are 'not well integrated' to obtain permanent residence."[84] This sort of dual logic is evident in the Liberal party's manifesto from the 2001 election, where they note that it was "imperative to limit the influx of foreigners coming to Denmark, which would release resources for better integration."[85] In other words, new changes are not only about restriction; restriction can also fund and therefore (perhaps ironically) foster integration. Permanent residence is effectively instrumentalized through membership requirements to be a significant barrier and deliberate alternative to citizenship. As Mouritsen and Olsen strikingly note, "the key immigration-related policy contribution of the Liberal–Conservative government – pushed by the DPP – is its citizenship policies. These are designed to pressure or motivate immigrants into becoming model citizens *before* they achieve actual citizen status (naturalization), and even before they can earn the right to permanent residence."[86] The incongruity should not be missed: immigrants are asked to adapt to Danish society and be "model citizens" without actually becoming citizens. To wit, the distinct advantages of citizenship are diminished.

Only after significant integration rules were introduced to make permanent residence more difficult to obtain (an indirect citizenship policy as permanent residence is a required status for naturalization) did the government turn its attention to citizenship directly. Here we see the second component of restrictive retrenchment: on top of making permanent residence more arduous, citizenship is made more exclusive through membership criteria. The 2002 Government Agreement on Citizenship (which would become the Circular on Naturalization, No. 55 of 12 June 2002) introduced a number of changes, including: a new requirement that immigrants document their language ability for citizenship with either a test or schooling (at the CEFR B1 level); a declaration on faithfulness and loyalty to Denmark; raising the duration of residence (from seven to nine years); maintaining renunciation of dual citizenship; and tightening the conduct requirement.[87]

While the People's Party was not given *carte blanche*, their political sway was undeniable. For example, Erbøll describes the Minister of Integration at the time (2002) not entirely agreeing with the People's Party on new naturalization restrictions, which opened dialogue with other parties, namely the Social Democrats and Social Liberals. However, the succeeding Minister (Rikke

84 Anita Böcker and Tineke Strik, "Language and knowledge tests for permanent residence rights: Help or hindrance for integration?," *European Journal of Migration and Law* 13, no. 2 (2011), 167.

85 Ersbøll, "On trial in Denmark," 110.

86 Mouritsen and Olsen, "Denmark between liberalism and nationalism," 698.

87 Notably, the Circular also repealed the exemption from language testing for applicants aged 65+. This is just one of many examples of Denmark's unique omission of exemptions, rendering permanent residence and citizenship acquisition comparatively difficult for at-risk or vulnerable populations. Ersbøll and Gravesen, "Country Report Denmark," 58–59.

Hvilshøj, Liberal) invariably reached agreement with the People's Party, where "the acquisition of nationality presumes that the applicant is already integrated in Danish society."[88] Erbøll interprets this concession as a "consequence of the government's wish to accomplish its promises to voters which presupposes an agreement with the Danish People's Party."[89]

After the 2005 election renewed the mandate of the Liberal–Conservative government, the People's Party continued using its government-supporting position to restrict citizenship. Strengthened by the election (in which they received 13.3 percent of the total vote), they reached a new agreement with the government, driven by the view that "it was time for a second round of the aliens policy, including more stringent naturalization requirements."[90] New restrictions for citizenship included: raising the level of language proficiency (from B1 to B2); introducing a citizenship test on Danish culture, history, and society (implemented in May 2007); and, later, raising the standards and difficulty of the citizenship test.

This trend of People's Party-led restriction would also continue for settlement. In 2006, another amendment to the Integration Act introduced a comprehensive integration contract that parsed the integration process into two modules: a language/integration course and activation measures "aimed at a better labour-market integration of immigrants," which included improving skills, job training, etc.[91] It also required that an immigrant sign a declaration on integration (for family-based migrants) or an "active citizenship in Danish society" commitment (for persons seeking permanent residence). And, to reaffirm the notion that permanent residence had become an alternative to – not a way station for – citizenship, Erbøll and Laura Gravesen note how "in principle, this declaration is not legally binding; its purpose is to render Danish values visible and indicate that society expects foreigners to make an effort to integrate as participating and contributing citizens, equal to other citizens."[92] In 2007, an integration test was added to culminate the integration process at permanent residence, and in 2010, the entire process was overhauled with a new points system, which rewarded migrants for residence, full-time employment, declarations of integration, active citizenship (including community involvement), and language at the B2 level. Silvia Adamo discusses the list of conditions for permanent residence as so similar to that of citizenship, that it "impinges on the very notion of citizenship, and reduces the latter to a very thin conception that only refers to electoral rights, military duty, and other few exclusive rights of citizenship such as diplomatic protection abroad, or derived supranational citizenship (EU citizenship)."[93] In sum, these changes make acquisition of

[88] Ersbøll, "Denmark," 32. [89] Ibid. [90] Ersbøll, "On trial in Denmark," 135.

[91] Wiesbrock, "Discrimination instead of integration? Integration requirements for immigrants in Denmark and Germany," 303.

[92] Ersbøll and Gravesen, "Country Report Denmark," 11.

[93] Silvia Adamo, "What is the point? Policies on immigration and the language issue in Denmark," in *RECODE Working Paper Series* (2012), 9.

permanent residence easier for well-integrated migrants, more difficult for those that are not integrated, and positions both further away from citizenship.

Only with a new government in 2011 did restrictive retrenchment begin to slow. The new, Social Democratic-led, center-left government lowered the language requirement for citizenship from B2 back to B1. It also repealed the points system just months after it came into force (its being in force from July 2011 to May 2012), replacing it with other rules for permanent residence. And, in a symbolic gesture, it also closed the Ministry for Integration, created by the Liberals with backing from the People's Party in 2001. Still, it would be premature to characterize these changes as liberalization. A more accurate description might be that of softening some of the harsher edges of conditionality. For example, new permanent residence rules to "motivate and ensure better integration in Denmark" include raising the residence requirement from four to five years, maintaining the language and declaration of integration and active citizenship requirement, while also placing the full-time employment and education requirements on an "equal footing."[94] With these changes, Denmark still maintains one of the most arduous series of membership requirements in Europe. Furthermore, despite the change in government, citizenship remains a reward – not a process – of integration.[95] The process of integration remains reserved for permanent residence.

FROM DESIGN TO IMPLEMENTATION: EVIDENCE FOR RESTRICTION IN PRACTICE

In comparing policy output to their effects, a distinct decline in both acquisition of permanent residence and citizenship can be observed.[96] Table 4.3 shows the total number of applications for permanent residence granted and denied between 2003 and 2009. While it is difficult to disentangle the specific effects of integration requirements from others, namely the twenty-four-year rule, lengthened residence, employment requirements, and welfare independence, there is a significant downward trend. At the same time as this increase in refusals, there is also a decline in the number of applications made in the first

[94] See Justice Minister's Written Proposal (April 26, 2012), Bill No. L180. Available at https://www.retsinformation.dk (accessed November 18, 2013).

[95] That citizenship is rewarded to successful integration is articulated in a 2011 government paper, titled "A Denmark that stands together." See Ersbøll, "Denmark," 26.

[96] There are data limitations in examining integration requirements directly, as Ersbøll and Gravesen note: "No general statistical information is available about the number of applicants for permanent residence who have taken part in the language test, etc., how many failed/passed and how many times they have taken the test," (35) not to mention that "due to the general residence requirement of 7 years (introduced in 2002), the full effects of the integration examination had not been seen (or evaluted) before the new and even more restrictive requirements were introduced in 2010" in Ersbøll and Gravesen, "Country Report Denmark," 32–35. For this reason, I examine application trends for this legal stage.

TABLE 4.3. *Applications for permanent residence in Denmark, 2003–2009*[97]

	2003	2004	2005	2006	2007	2008	2009
Total number of permits issued	9360	10738	9161	3641	1788	3058	2726
Total of refusals	2276	2316	2260	2238	966	2349	1786
Total of decisions	11636	13054	11431	5879	2754	5407	4512
Percentage of refusals	19.6	17.7	19.8	38.1	35.1	43.4	39.6

place (evident in the number of total decisions). In this, new requirements are not only an exclusionary barrier but also a disincentivizing selection mechanism for immigrant applications. This precipitates from earlier barriers such as entry and reunification. The controversial points system for family reunification, for example, consisting of language skills, work requirement, community service, and other criteria, was so strict that the number of resident permit approvals had fallen by seventy percent.[98]

One additional effect of integration requirements on the acquisition of permanent residence is how programs can simultaneously produce integration and segregation. Third-country nationals (TCNs) seeking permanent residence commit a significant amount of their time to the integration contract: "TCNs are engaged in a number of activities (language courses and activation activities) for at least 37 hours per week and the entire programme might extend to a period of up to three years. The overall number of hours that immigrants spent in language training depends on their previous knowledge with an average of about 2,000 hours."[99] Just as in the Austrian case, immigrants may certainly benefit from these commitments to integration – namely job and language training. Integration policy also facilitates employment and education opportunities. But this can also yield what Anja Wiesbrock describes as a "lock-in" effect: "If immigrants are forced to participate in integration measures, they will be prevented from using this time more efficiently in seeking work or taking part in the every-day life of the host society in other ways. In that way, the courses could actually increase segregation rather than promoting the integration of TCNs."[100] Therefore, in spite of Denmark's comprehensive integration scheme, she concludes that it does not "score better in terms of integration results,"[101] as it focuses on tying integration to sanctions, such as loss of residence or financial entitlements, instead of positive privileges.

97 Ersbøll and Gravesen, "Country Report Denmark," 33.

98 Jennifer Buley, "Government proposes end to 'points system'," *The Copenhagen Post*, January 9,2012.

99 Wiesbrock, "Discrimination instead of integration? Integration requirements for immigrants in Denmark and Germany," 308–09.

100 Ibid., 310. 101 Ibid., 313–14.

TABLE 4.4. *Refusals of naturalization due to lack of Danish language proficiency, 2001–2008*[102]

	2001	2002	2003	2004	2005	2006	2007	2008
Number of persons	778	503	2507	1632	1185	961	1498	3446
Percentage	41	19.8	59	50	55.3	52.5	28	40

Unlike data for permanent residence, we can observe a direct impact of integration requirements at the stage of citizenship. The language proficiency requirement has proved to be a decisive mechanism of exclusion. Table 4.4 presents percentages of applicants refused citizenship on the grounds of language improficiency between 2001 and 2008. While figures vary across the year, we see language as a significant barrier to acquisition; as high as half of all rejections result from the language requirement. This is one of many factors driving down naturalization, from 6.5 percent of the foreign population in 2002 to 1.1 percent in 2011 (tantamount to only 3,900 people!).[103]

The citizenship test has also been shown to be effective in closure. The requirement of passing this forty-question test about Danish society and history produced 1,016 refusals in 2008, or twelve percent of total refusals.[104] By the time you get to the stage of applying for citizenship, an applicant would have already completed hefty language and integration requirements for permanent residence, including a lengthy period of residence. As Adamo notes, "the test does not further enhance the competences of applicants who want to naturalise and who, fulfilling all the other requirements that Danish legislation lays down, have already proven that they are in effect citizens of the country, even if under another legal status."[105]

Both the language requirement and the citizenship test are meant to be instruments to drive down naturalization rates. A report by the Ministry of Social Affairs, Children and Integration cites the Infødsretskontor (the Naturalization Office in the Ministry of Justice) as partly attributing a decrease in the number of naturalizations to these new requirements. In particular, it highlights successive government agreements tying requirements to this exclusionary goal.[106] As such, the consistent decline in naturalizations since policy adoption can only be interpreted as a policy success story for governments across the political spectrum, from the left to the Danish People's Party.

[102] Ersbøll and Gravesen, "Country Report Denmark," 66.

[103] OECD, *International Migration Outlook: SOPEMI2013*." [104] Ibid., 65.

[105] Silvia Adamo, "Northern exposure: The new Danish model of citizenship tests," *International Journal on Multicultural Societies* 10, no. 1 (2008), 23.

[106] Ministry of Social Affairs Children and Integration (Denmark), *Fakta Om Integration: Status og udvikling* (Copenhagen: Schultzboghandel, 2011), 32.

At the end of 2012, a new citizenship test (*statsborgerskabsprøven*) was announced to replace the old test (*indfødsretsprøven*).[107] Put into place in 2014, the biannually administered, thirty-question test focuses more on daily life and politics and less on history. This new test should only improve pass rates, which, based on the December 2009 test pass rate of 54.5 percent,[108] should not be a difficult task.

CONCLUSION

Denmark exhibits the use of civic integration requirements to maintain a restrictive citizenship orientation, both by reducing access to citizenship directly and by building up permanent residence as both a status and identity alternative. Policy adoption took place under a left government but in a context of restrictive understandings – and therefore parameters – of belonging. These changes were made to maintain political competitiveness where the far-right was gaining in popularity, but also in a policy environment orientated toward closure. A politics-based argument might stop here, concluding that this is an outlier quickly subsumed by a new government and increasing far-right influence. However, the dynamic approach taken here illustrates how the left was initially restrained by policy context, where possibilities for liberalization were already heavily circumscribed. In this setting, the left proposed the mildest restriction tenable both to other policy actors and to public opinion. The subsequent change in government allowed for a predominant membership policy strategy of retrenchment to take root, producing a series of policy changes that would make citizenship and permanent residence more and more difficult. Indeed, the successive restrictive reforms to Danish citizenship and permanent residence acquisition represents a "seismic shift in the overall Danish integration and immigration policy – from a 'soft' liberal equality-of-rights and (modest) room-for-diversity towards a stricter civic integrationism," which is "visible especially in official civic integration and citizenship acquisition programmes."[109]

Overall, Austria and Denmark are exemplary cases where civic integration policies are adopted and adapted to maintain the status quo of restriction. If the analysis stopped here, we might also conclude that they present evidence in support of the restrictive hypothesis (where new requirements are designed to produce/maintain restriction, and cross-national adoption signals a "restrictive backlash" to citizenship liberalization in the late 1900s/early 2000s). This argument could also be made through the comparison of political conditions in these two countries, where both left and right governments pursued restriction. Crucially, however, Austria and Denmark did not liberalize beforehand in a

[107] A new circular on naturalization came into force in June 2013 – CIS nr. 9253 of 06/06/2013 which contained provisions for the new citizenship test.

[108] Ersbøll and Gravesen, "Country Report Denmark," 67.

[109] Mouritsen and Olsen, "Denmark between liberalism and nationalism," 695.

way that would impel a "restrictive backlash." If anything, policies were continually restrictive, but increased demand and perceived threat created a sense of newly established inclusion.

We also see that it is not merely a matter of a left government setting into motion a restrictive policy because it identifies a shared purpose with other right governments. Rather, left governments in restrictive policy settings are initially constrained in terms of what policies they can pursue and what is possible in terms of change. In other words, citizenship policy orientation can be shown to be a meaningful context in defining the parameters of both debate and policy itself. It also shows that right government is not a necessary condition for civic integration policy. Chapter 5 moves from comparing different governments in similar citizenship contexts to similar governments in different citizenship contexts, to further illustrate the full effect of citizenship contextualization on membership policies.

5

Examining politics: Germany and the United Kingdom

INTRODUCTION

Just as similar citizenship orientations can constrain ideologically diverse governments into pursuing similarly restrictive membership policies, so divergent citizenship orientations can produce the opposite effect, where similarly oriented governments pursue different membership goals. To illustrate the enabling effects of the context of citizenship, it is useful to compare Germany and the United Kingdom. Both began the "civic turn" with prior experience in membership policy, where both practiced degrees of language assessment, and both replaced these practices with more rigorous assessment through civic integration instruments. Both expanded expectations of membership to all three stages of status. Both experienced similar political processes, where left governments formally adopted and first adapted civic integration. Moreover, these governments, while organized by parties on the left, were both significantly influenced by the right. Recall Figure 3.3, in which the German Social Democratic-led coalition with the Greens appeared decisively on the left but eventually moved to the center of the ideological spectrum by the point of first adaptation (t_1).[1] In this same figure, we also see the UK's New Labour begin from a position on the center-right. (This is not surprising given the role of self-modulation in a single-actor majoritarian system.) Finally, in this context, both stand out as among the more robust practitioners of civic integration today. But while they are both promoting state identity through civic integration, are they promoting the same identity?

This chapter illustrates the importance of the context of citizenship. Where a politics-centered, government-in-power hypothesis would predict a convergence

[1] Debate began over adapting integration requirements in earnest in 2002. With every year until the 2005 election, where the left-led coalition was replaced (by the narrowest of margins) by a Christian Democrats-led government, which included the SPD, "rile" scores show the government moving more and more to the right. Thus, 2002's score represents a conservative figure.

of policy preferences given similarly oriented governments, we observe in these two cases that citizenship orientations as policy starting points define distinct parameters of policy change, which result in differences of membership policy. Chapter 4 illustrated the effects of similar citizenship policy orientation on differently oriented governments at the point of adoption, and then convergence of government preferences and policy over time. This chapter illustrates the opposite. Additionally, both cases in this chapter are critical for assessing the restriction hypothesis. Germany stands as a "most-likely" case, where a restrictive citizenship policy starting point and a reputation of ethnocultural differentialism would suggest continuity of membership understandings, while the UK is a "hard" or "least-likely" case, where a traditionally liberal and ill-defined conception of national belonging is maintained.

To illustrate the strategic use of civic requirements to reinforce existing and divergent citizenship orientations, I begin each study by examining the content of citizenship policy as a formal institutional reflection of national belonging. The cases then move to an examination of political context and relevant actors at the point of initial policy adoption (t_0). I subsequently trace each case down the causal path from adoption to adaptation, drawing attention in particular to gaps between government preferences and opposition pressures. Germany, for example, is especially illustrative of the effects of opposition actors – at both the federal and sub-state levels – on altering government policies and preferences. In identifying divergence between Germany and the UK, I point not only to policy output (where the former maintains a far denser series of requirements) but also to outcome, where implementation reveals significant differences in both state-coordination/paternalism and difficulty.

GERMANY

Germany is an interesting and challenging case for analyzing both the adoption and adaptation of civic integration requirements. It bears a number of similarities to the cases of restrictive retrenchment discussed in Chapter 4, in that right-of-center parties have strengthened the content of a comparatively restrictive citizenship orientation through new requirements and investment in permanent residence. As such, integration requirements at permanent residence, including lengthy language and civic education courses and a culminating test at a high level of German (B1), effectively begin the process of community admission much earlier and insulate citizenship from large-scale demand. Thus, a one-dimensional view of outcomes, such as comparing aggregate CIVIX scores, would equate German membership policy formations as similarly restrictive to states characterized by retrenchment strategies.

While the end might look the same, Germany took a distinctive route to get there. As such, its path is indicative of more complexity and nuance than mere restriction. Several factors shaped this unique journey. First, in contrast to other restrictive citizenship cases, Germany experienced significant citizenship liberalization in tandem with the process of defining membership through civic integration. This liberalization is an important backdrop to the conditions for the adoption of civic integration, as well as a pretext for later restriction at permanent residence. Second, and related, Germany also exhibited a strong role for the left in government, first when the SPD (Social Democratic Party) formed a government with the Greens in 1998 and then later in joining successive CDU-led (Christian Democratic Union) coalitions under Angela Merkel. In this, we are able to observe a sustained effect of leftist governments (and, therefore, liberalizing preferences) in the context of a restrictive policy starting point.

Third, Germany boasted a unique political consensus for change. Even before the SPD formed a coalition government with the Greens in 1998 – with citizenship liberalization at the top of its agenda – there was agreement across all major political parties in recognizing that Germany's historically restrictive citizenship required a certain degree of updating to address the permanence of non-ethnic German immigrants. This sort of cross-party consensus for citizenship change – of the idea but not the process – manifested in a number of policy proposals throughout the 1990s and did not exist in the cases of restrictive retrenchment.

Finally, and most crucial for analyzing adoption of membership requirements in Germany, requirements came not from the government in power *per se*, but were leveraged by a forceful and calculated opposition. In each stage of Germany's civic integration sequence – first symbolic changes to citizenship in 1999, followed by comprehensive programming for permanent residence through the 2004 Immigration Act, and capped off with procedural changes to citizenship again in 2007 – the impetus for membership policy was outside the government. Integration requirements for citizenship and permanent residence were not "concessions" given to a needed coalition partner in a political climate leaning toward restrictions, but instead a set of domestic policies "won" through careful politics and leveraged through bicameralism and the use of Germany's federal system, where right-leaning states are legally empowered to develop their own policies independent of the federal government. Therefore, while a general party-in-power approach rightly accounts for the policy strategy outcome, the German case illustrates how it can incorrectly specify the initiating actor. This careful look reveals the government as the filter – not the source – of membership requirement adoption.

Civic integration in Germany may ultimately resemble that of Denmark and Austria in aggregate CIVIX scoring, but qualitative analysis reveals a much milder practice as a reflection of the compromises and concessions produced by both leftist and rightist governments, as well as the multiple tiers and venues for effective political action. And, as a further point of contrast, while appearing milder alongside more restrictive counterparts, it appears far more restrictive alongside the British model. This highlights not only the importance of periodization and conjunctural causation in tracing the evolution of policy, but also the importance of perspective for characterization. The outcome of civic integration for immigrants in Germany, in the end, simultaneously achieves the government's 2002 coalition agreement goal to "promote and also demand the integration of immigrants."[2]

The quintessential restrictive citizenship starting point

The introduction of membership requirements for citizenship in Germany immediately signals the "taken for granted" nature of citizenship as a membership category. With little in formal articulations on the parameters of membership in citizenship, Germany has still been considered by scholars to be one of the most internally coherent and historically enduring models of "ethnic" or "differentialist"[3] citizenship in Europe, based on a "near total reliance"[4] on the principle of *jus sanguinis*, or citizenship by parentage and descent. Until the 1999 reforms, Germany had maintained the same citizenship laws since 1913, a fact that Simon Green notes "epitomized the then ethnocultural nature of German citizenship," enacted in the Wilhelmine era, and surviving the Weimar Republic, National Socialism, the Cold War division of East and West Germany, and reunification.[5] Moreover, the federal state successfully maintained this restrictive posture through reunification and large-scale immigration. In the 1977 Naturalization Guidelines, where Germany first recognized its responsibility to foster avenues of naturalization for non-ethnic German immigrants, it also maintained that "the federal Republic of Germany is not a land of immigration. It does not aspire to increase the number of its citizens through naturalization."[6] To wit, Brubaker describes Germany as lacking a political culture that is "supportive of naturalization" where the process involves "not only a change in legal status, but a change in nature, a change

[2] Marina Seveker and Anne Walter, "Country Report Germany," in *The INTEC Project: Integration and naturalisation tests: The new way to European Citizenship* (Nijmegen, the Netherlands: Centre for Migration Law, Radboud University, 2010), fn. 2.

[3] Many scholars have since challenged many of Brubaker's characterizations, including Heike Hagedorn, "Republicanism and the politics of citizenship in Germany and France: Convergence or divergence?," *German Policy Studies* 1, no. 3 (2001), 243–272. Of course, it should be noted that Brubaker does not argue that German citizenship was *first* organic and *Volk*-centered; German citizenship was created in response to the need to coordinate admission and expulsion rules among states in a compact and economically integrated state-system" (p. 27). Ethnicization and nationalization only occurred later on, during Wilhelmine Germany, to foment what is understood today as an "ethnocultural understanding of nation-state membership" (p. 51).

[4] Karen Schönwälder and Triadafilos Triadafilopoulos, "A bridge or barrier to incorporation? Germany's 1999 citizenship reform in critical perspective," *German Politics & Society* 30, no. 1 (2012), 53.

[5] Simon Green, "Much ado about not-very-much? Assessing ten years of German citizenship reform," *Citizenship Studies* 16, no. 2 (2012), 174. Also see Andreas Fahrmeir, "Coming to terms with a misinterpreted past? Rethinking the historical antecedents of Germany's 1999 citizenship reform" *German Politics & Society* 30, no. 1 (2012), 17–38.

[6] Douglas B. Klusmeyer, *Immigration Policy in the Federal Republic of Germany: Negotiating membership and remaking the nation* (Berghahn Books, 2009), 99.

in political and cultural identity, a social transubstantiation that immigrants have difficulty imagining, let alone desiring."[7]

The 1999 Citizenship Act (implemented in 2000) was interpreted at the time as the first, significant break from this restrictive past. In short, this new law lowered the residency duration from fifteen to eight years and introduced a type of *jus soli* for children that created the opportunity to obtain citizenship for a child of foreign parents on the condition that one parent is a long-term resident (legal resident for eight years or in possession of a residence permit for three years). It also brought about a more facilitated naturalization process.[8] However, alongside these liberalizing features, Germany retained a formal ban against the holding of dual citizenship and introduced the *Optionsmodell*, which obligates a child – upon reaching the age of majority (18) – either to pick German citizenship or to retain their foreign citizenship. If no declaration is made, the person loses German citizenship.[9] This "option" certainly limits the inclusionary thrust of *jus soli*, and while the residence requirement was sliced in half, eight years of residence is still among the higher durations of residence in Europe.[10] Some scholars have also since questioned the extent to which this liberalization is anything more than lip service, pointing to low naturalization rates and administrative barriers in the decade since passage.[11]

A second question is whether this liberalizing change altered or opened up the concept of belonging that German citizenship conveys. Thomas Diez and Vicki Squire, for example, argue that despite these changes, "the notion of community linked 'by blood' remains the predominant concept both in legislation and … public discourse."[12] But if the facilitation of integration at permanent residence and citizenship reveals anything, it shows an important adjustment, that of

[7] Rogers Brubaker, *Citizenship and Nationhood in France and Germany* (Cambridge, MA: Harvard University Press, 1992), 77–78.

[8] For extensive and detailed discussions on the 1999 Citizenship Act, see Simon Green, *The Politics of Exclusion: Institutions and immigration policy in contemporary Germany* (Manchester; New York: Manchester University Press, 2004); Kay Hailbronner, "Germany," in *EUDO Citizenship Observatory Observatory Country Reports* (Florence: EUDO Citizenship, Robert Schuman Centre for Advanced Studies, EUI, 2012); Marc Morjé Howard, *The Politics of Citizenship in Europe* (Cambridge: Cambridge University Press, 2009). Howard, for example, as a result of this change, records Germany's Citizenship Policy Index score as significantly liberalizing from 0 to 2.04 out of 6 (p. 27).

[9] Exceptions to allow for retention of other citizenships are given only if renunciation is not possible or if it creates economic disadvantages, to name only a couple of reasons. Swiss and EU children also are exempt.

[10] Sara Wallace Goodman, "Naturalisation policies in Europe: Exploring patterns of inclusion and exclusion," in *EUDO Citizenship Comparative Reports* (Florence: EUDO Citizenship, Robert Schuman Centre for Advanced Studies, EUI, 2010).

[11] See Green, "Much ado about not-very-much? Assessing ten years of German citizenship reform;" Schönwälder and Triadafilopoulos, "A bridge or barrier to incorporation? Germany's 1999 citizenship reform in critical perspective"; Hailbronner, "Germany," 21.

[12] Thomas Diez and Vicki Squire, "Traditions of citizenship and the securitisation of migration in Germany and Britain," *Citizenship Studies* 12, no. 6 (2008), 568.

opening up the promotion of belonging from among co-ethnics to, in principle, defining distinct parameters of belonging that are accessible to third-country nationals, i.e., immigrants without German ethnicity and heritage.

This opening of citizenship, whereby it is feasible to think of outsiders becoming insiders to German membership – at least on a theoretical level, is particularly evident when contrasting today's membership requirements with previous practices. Germany stands in contrast to its European neighbors as the only early practitioner of formal membership requirements. Long before the "civic turn," Germany had language "tests" and value commitments for citizenship and immigration. However, these requirements bore a number of differences to their contemporary counterparts. Beginning with citizenship, Germany introduced in 1977 a requirement for immigrants to demonstrate a "voluntary and lasting orientation toward Germany." Ethnic German returnees were excluded from this provision, as they were already viewed to have German nationality and there was no standardized measurement of this orientation, in either language or knowledge, and it remained open to interpretation of practice by respective *Länder*. While directed toward non-German immigrants, the number of persons eligible for citizenship in this category was relatively insignificant. It was a nominal recognition that persons acquiring German citizenship should be connected to the community, but it was neutral in regard to individual skills or the nature of that connection. And because of the low number of applicants, it was more symbolic than anything else. It echoed the conflicting nature of the naturalization guidelines, maintaining principles of both inclusion through naturalization and exclusion through immigration.

In looking at historical membership conditions for residence and entry, Germany stands distinct from both other states and contemporary practice. Since 1978, administrative guidelines stipulate that basic knowledge of German and integration could be a condition under which permanent residence conditions could be issued. Basic oral German became a requirement with the Aliens Act of 1990. And, since 1997, ethnic German immigrants (predominantly from East and Central Europe) were tested on dialect/language to determine "Germanness" for the purposes of establishing eligibility to settle with access to citizenship. This policy came on the coattails of a near decade of immigration, with over two million German repatriates (*Aussiedler)* coming to a newly unified Germany, "many of whom did not speak German well (if at all) and could integrate into German society only with great difficulty."[13] As a "confirming feature" of eligibility, it invariably served as an important "filtering function," proving to be an "insurmountable obstacle" for a majority of "ethnic German" immigrants.[14] It was a policy for filtering "insiders," not promoting integration for "outsiders." In other words, it tested compatibility and was not concerned

[13] Howard, *The Politics of Citizenship in Europe*, 122.

[14] Independent Commission on Migration to Germany (Süssmuth Commission), *Structuring Immigration, Fostering Integration* (Berlin: Druckerei Conrad GmbH, 2001), 177.

with getting immigrant newcomers off on the right foot. In passing this test, "ethnicity provides an edge that mere residence and payment of taxes does not."[15] These policies are distinct from contemporary practices of civic integration requirements, but they serve as legal precedent for the eventual extension of integration for immigrants.[16]

This discussion of Germany's citizenship policy and concept of belonging highlights the restrictive orientation of membership as a starting point for the adoption of civic integration policy. The line, however, is arguably moved with regards to analyzing policy adaptation, in which the 1999 Act increased access in principle. In fact, this periodization not only establishes temporal bookends, it also enables policy output from the first period to serve as policy input in the second.[17] Despite strong indicators to suggest that liberalization did little to loosen German identity as an intransigent sense of belonging,[18] the expansion of membership requirements to permanent residence shows how initial changes at citizenship created a new context for counterbalancing and restriction.

Membership policy adoption as a trade-off

Examining the context for citizenship policy liberalization – and when civic integration policy adoption first took shape – requires taking a brief view at immigration to Germany. For a country that before 2004 adamantly described itself as "*not* a country of immigration," Germany has experienced perhaps the most voluminous waves of migration in Western Europe. Germany's new demographic reality was shaped by a number of tributaries: *Aussiedler* who acquired German citizenship as expellees or refugees of German descent; "late-comer" (*Spätaussiedler*) immigrants of German descent from former Soviet countries after 1993 (subjects of the German "dialect test"); and, perhaps most notable as a background factor, migrant workers and their descendants. In brief, once the ebb of German expellees and refugees subsided in the immediate postwar period, the West German government initiated a series of bilateral agreements with

15 Brubaker, *Citizenship and Nationhood in France and Germany*, 170.

16 Ines Michalowski, "Integration tests in Germany: A communitarian approach?," in *A Re-Definition of Belonging? Language and integration tests in Europe*, ed. Ricky van Oers, Eva Ersbøll, and Dora Kostakopoulou (Leiden; Boston: Martinus Nijhoff, 2010), 185–210.

17 For example, Paul Pierson argues that policies are "not only outputs of but important inputs into the political process, often dramatically reshaping social, economic, and political conditions." Paul Pierson, "When effect becomes cause: Policy feedback and political change," *World Politics* 45, no. 4 (1993), 595.

18 Cf. fn. 8. In addition to these discussions about policy, there is also evidence to show that immigrant citizens, particularly those of Turkish descent, experience continued problems of exclusion. Ayse S. Cağlar, "German Turks in Berlin: Social exclusion and strategies for social mobility," *Journal of Ethnic and Migration Studies* 21, no. 3 (1995), 309–323; Evelyn Ersanilli and Ruud Koopmans, "Rewarding integration? Citizenship regulations and the socio-cultural integration of immigrants in the Netherlands, France and Germany," *Journal of Ethnic and Migration Studies* 36, no. 5 (2010), 773–791.

countries, including Turkey (1961) and Yugoslavia (1968), to bring (mostly male) foreign workers into the domestic labor market. The idea behind guest-worker schemes was that laborers would be rotational, i.e., they would be mobile to fit the emerging and changing needs of various economic sectors – namely industrial to agricultural, and temporary. The failure of both of these assumptions underscores what is now known as the "guest-worker" myth.[19] When economic migration ceased with the 1973–1974 oil shock, there were already approximately 2.6 million foreigner workers in Germany. And while labor migration ceased, other forms of migration became more popular, namely family reunification and asylum seekers (who might have otherwise come as guest workers). In other words, not only did immigrants not return voluntarily to their country of origin once the need for cheap labor subsided, but they brought their families for settlement. It was assumed that guest-worker schemes would yield a minimal social and political impact, as Germans largely considered immigration to be an economic issue.[20] Alas, these families started to raise children – speaking German, socialized in German culture, and professionalized in the German economy – as second- and third-generation *immigrants* (i.e., children of foreigners) in Germany; they gained permanent residence but were blocked from access to citizenship.

The naturalization of non-national immigrants remained extremely low throughout the 1980s, resulting in an average naturalization rate of below 0.5 percent.[21] By the end of the 1990s, with over 7 million foreign nationals living in Germany, naturalization rose incrementally from 1.02 percent in 1995 to almost 2 percent in 1999.[22] This did not signal increased opportunities for citizenship as much as it did increased demand, where more migrants were completing the necessary duration of residence. In this diversifying picture, Green observes that "the notion of a prevailing elite consensus, especially over the symbolism of German citizenship, is difficult to sustain from the late 1970s onward" and, moreover, that "this lack of consensus means that the policy-making process, far from determining simply 'fine details,' actually plays a critical role in explaining policy output."[23] In this context Germany finally overhauls long-standing

[19] Göktürk et al. describe some of the reasons that the guest worker scheme proved to be incorrect. When industrial concerns realized that the rotational design was too expensive (p. 10), new foreign workers were quietly brought in to meet needs outside city centers. Relatedly, where the costs of finding and retraining workers also were expensive and residency conditions of temporary workers were unclear, the inflow of guest workers subsided (and began to reverse) only with the 1966–1967 recession. In Deniz Göktürk, David Gramling, and Anton Kaes, *Germany in Transit: Nation and migration, 1955–2005* (Berkeley: University of California Press, 2007).

[20] Anthony M. Messina, *The Logics and Politics of Post-WWII Migration to Western Europe* (Cambridge: Cambridge University Press, 2007), 28–29.

[21] Green, "Much ado about not-very-much? Assessing ten years of German citizenship reform," 174.

[22] OECD, *International migration outlook: SOPEMI 2003* (Paris: OECD Publishing).

[23] Green, *The Politics of Exclusion: Institutions and immigration policy in contemporary Germany*, 10.

citizenship laws, through a process defined by significant contestation and bargaining. In recognizing the need to adapt citizenship, existing citizenship rules serve as a baseline in defining parameters of acceptable and possible change. Kay Hailbronner notes regarding debate preceding citizenship change that "There is in principle no dispute about the need to integrate large parts of the foreign population into Germany by inducing them to become German citizens ... There is no consensus, however, on the ways and conditions under which German citizenship should be acquired."[24] In other words, the goal of general opening was shared across political lines; the path to that goal was not.

Amidst broad agreement that something needed to be done, a significant liberalization of citizenship was passed as one of the first priorities of the newly elected SPD–Green coalition, which replaced the longtime conservative presence after the 1998 election. There were two clear objectives to the liberalization of citizenship: (1) to increase the number of naturalizations of permanent residents; and (2) to improve the integration of immigrants and their German-born children through citizenship.[25] Politically, the new citizenship law not only reflected the ideological transitioning of governments, replacing a center-right coalition with a left one; it also culminated a protracted political process stretching over the past two decades. For example, as recently as the mid-1990s, and as evidence of the broad consensus behind citizenship change, the CDU/CSU (Christian Social Union in Bavaria) proposed a number of liberalizations to citizenship, including a reduction in residence and facilitating citizenship for children. This initiative was eventually abandoned because of disagreement among coalition parliamentarians, who held a slim majority in the *Bundestag*, as well as divisions within the CDU itself.[26] However, in the meantime, both the SPD and the Greens had "developed broadly similar positions during their time in opposition."[27] This consensus made rapid citizenship reform possible once they were in power. Many have already written thorough accounts of the 1999 citizenship act; in particular, Green and Howard have provided a careful and lengthy account of the politics involved in this landmark policy change.[28] Without repeating their description or insight, this section will focus on the way in which integration requirements factored into negotiations and, ultimately, policy outcomes.

[24] Hailbronner, "Germany," 3.

[25] These distinctions are made by Ricky van Oers, "Citizenship tests in the Netherlands, Germany and the UK," in *A Re-Definition of Belonging? Language and integration tests in Europe*, ed. Ricky van Oers, Eva Ersbøll, and Theodora Kostakopoulou (Leiden; Boston: Martinus Nijhoff, 2010), 71.

[26] Green, *The Politics of Exclusion: Institutions and immigration policy in contemporary Germany*, 91.

[27] Ibid., 96.

[28] See Ibid.; Green, "Much ado about not-very-much? Assessing ten years of German citizenship reform"; Howard, *The Politics of Citizenship in Europe*.

As context, Green points out that disputes over citizenship liberalization in the 1990s focused not on "finding the most rational policy solution in order to achieve an aim on which all parties in fact agreed" but were instead "dominated by largely symbolic issues such as national identity and integration, as well as by the perennial question of whether Germany was a country of immigration."[29] Therefore, while in principle both parties supported degrees of citizenship liberalization, they differed in terms of how integration was woven into that process. According to Ulrike Davy, the conservative position saw that "Naturalization was (and is) a final and formal step at the end of the process of integration: integrate first, then apply for naturalization." By contrast, for liberals and others on the left, "naturalization should not be withheld until immigrants prove worthy of it; naturalization might considerably facilitate integration: naturalize, then integrate. Hence, immigrants should be able to obtain German citizenship at the earliest convenience."[30]

Yet the fulcrum of disagreement between government and opposition was over dual citizenship as a proxy for integration and loyalty, and not integration requirements *per se*. The liberalizing agenda of the left government stretched beyond previous proposals by the center right and created anxiety. Through an unprecedented petition campaign and regional elections in Hesse that shifted the balance in the *Bundesrat*, these center-right actors were able to block the introduction of dual citizenship.[31] But blocking dual citizenship was the smaller prize. By mobilizing the population on an explicitly anti-foreigner agenda and winning the state of Hesse, the SPD–Green absolute majority in the *Bundesrat* was lost. And, as Green notes, "without this absolute majority, the new citizenship bill could not be passed, and a compromise with opposition parties would have to be sought."[32] One compromise was dual citizenship, and the adoption of the *Optionsmodell* brought in necessary support from the Free Democratic Party (*Freie Demokratische Partei*; FDP) in order to pass legislation.

A second compromise was integration requirements. The citizenship bill carried with it the first round of what Helen Hartnell describes as an "integration price tag," namely introduction of language and loyalty.[33] The new law required proof of integration to be *assessed* through "sufficient oral and written German language skills," instead of *inferred* by demonstrating a "voluntary and lasting orientation." These additions are described by Green as "small print," added

[29] Green, *The Politics of Exclusion: Institutions and immigration policy in contemporary Germany*, 83.

[30] Ulrike Davy, "Integration of immigrants in Germany: A slowly evolving concept.," *European Journal of Migration and Law* 7, no. 2 (2005). 141.

[31] In the end, the government created a type of temporary dual citizenship, where a person holds dual citizenship automatically at birth but is required to give one of the two up by age twenty-three.

[32] Green, *The Politics of Exclusion: Institutions and immigration policy in contemporary Germany*, 98.

[33] Helen Elizabeth Hartnell, "Belonging: Citizenship and migration in the European Union and in Germany," *Berkeley Journal of International Law* 24, no. 1 (2006), 391.

alongside other conservative markers to the new bill.[34] He says that "while the Greens were certainly annoyed at this, their attention was quickly diverted" to the petition campaign in Hesse.[35] In the end, the CDU/CSU ultimately opposed the citizenship bill in the *Bundestag* for not requiring *enough* integration, wanting to require knowledge of constitutional order alongside language in exchange for other concessions of liberalization.[36] During parliamentary debate over the bill, CDU/CSU politicians decried the liberalizing reforms as giving away "naturalization for free."[37]

As the federal government did not articulate a standardized assessment level or instrument for German proficiency, the *Länder* authorities had substantial discretion. This led to varying practices across Germany, ranging from oral interviews to written exams. In addition to language, the 1999 reform also implemented a requirement of a declaration of loyalty – specifically a "commitment to democratic order and constitution." However, this was not an amendment concerned with attachment to values and immigrant integration so much as it was strategically included to have legal grounds to exclude "those applicants from citizenship in which concrete suspicions [...] cast doubt on their willingness to conform to Germany's constitutional order [...] – a provision targeted at applicants with extremist political tendencies."[38]

As a consequence, though integration was the sticking point for CDU/CSU support, they created a political situation in which the left governing coalition was both compromised into accepting integration conditions and penalized because they were not strong enough. Aside from the linguistic changes to the law itself, the integration requirements that were added in the 1999 Act made little difference to the acquisition of citizenship or to efforts to promulgate citizenship as a membership category. This weakness was ironically first created and then politically exploited by the CDU in the following years to politically position the SPD as weak on immigration and to bring about more restriction, specifically at the stage of permanent residence. In the end, a left government adopted integration requirements as part of the bargain to deliver more consequential policy liberalization. Thus, while this was a restrictive concession in and of itself, it was embedded as part of an overall, contained liberalizing strategy. A closer look at the process, however, shows that it was not produced merely because they were left *per se* and wanted to promote inclusion (as predicted by a government ideology approach), but rather because greater liberalizations for access came at a cost. This lends an

[34] Green, *The Politics of Exclusion: Institutions and immigration policy in contemporary Germany*, 99.

[35] Ibid., 101.

[36] van Oers, "Citizenship tests in the Netherlands, Germany and the UK," 72–73.

[37] Ibid., 72.

[38] Green, "Much ado about not-very-much? Assessing ten years of German citizenship reform," 176.

important nuance to a party-in-power approach, looking at the government not only as agenda-setters and preference pursuers, but also as bargainers and concession-makers.

Germany's first Immigration Act and robust integration adaptation

In extending membership requirements to permanent residence, we see more restrictive aims behind policy adaptation. New requirements erect formidable barriers of admission that effectively supersede naturalization. Indeed, this is where the heart of civic integration lies in the German case. And, unlike citizenship reform, new requirements for residence, including the mandatory language and civic orientation courses, were not foisted onto unwilling governing parties. In fact, these restrictions were developed and produced by the same left government that delivered citizenship liberalization. These divergent policy directions are not surprising. In fact, they are consistent with theoretical expectations discussed in Chapter 3; left governments pursue inclusive citizenship but exclusive immigration in a context of issue salience and, in particular, where institutional design strengthens opposition voices. Immigration and citizenship are related policy venue, of course, but are guided by distinct logics as they bear different associative costs.

After citizenship reform, "there was a discernible shift in emphasis onto integration in a broader sense."[39] Both the SPD–Green coalition and the CDU-led opposition showed keen interest in promoting integration for immigrants but, just as with citizenship, they differed over how to promote it. Manifesting in labor-market-resembling logics, the SPD and Greens believed "governments should take the lead in inclusion," while the CDU/CSU believed "it was to be left to the individual foreigner alone."[40] As such, debate over how to "promote and also demand the integration of immigrants" began in earnest in 2000, defined by consensus of goal but not approach. Parties invariably reached broad agreement over integration courses, as subjects like labor migration and asylum grew in importance.

The Independent Commission on Migration to Germany, popularly known as the Süssmuth Commission, proposed in its 2001 report the creation of integration programs for immigrants. The commission's purpose in setting integration requirements was to target poor language skills as an impediment to accessing the labor market and political participation. Drawing on the Dutch model, the Commission advocated adopting obligatory language training and integration courses, but not Dutch-style sanctions, recognizing that "due to the fact that different legal conditions apply in different cases, sanctions for failure to

[39] Green, *The Politics of Exclusion: Institutions and immigration policy in contemporary Germany*, 117.
[40] Ibid., 116.

attend cannot be imposed against all immigrants."[41] These proposals were intended to be non-partisan in the hope of promoting cross-party consensus. As such, the commission had a cross-party membership, formed by Interior Minister Otto Schily of the SPD but chaired by former speaker of the *Bundestag*, CDU member Rita Süssmuth.

This occurred against the backdrop of a new discourse taking shape in Germany, advocated by Friedrich Merz, then leader of the CDU in the Bundestag, on promoting *Leitkultur*, or "guiding/lead culture." Merz spoke of immigrants being required to accept German culture, which has its "foundation in the Constitution as the most important expression of German moral order guaranteeing the coherence of German society."[42] Where this definition resembles a type of constitutional patriotism, the interpretation by the CSU – the CDU's Bavarian sister-party – was a little more assimilationist, where "adoption of 'Leitkultur must [involve] more than just acquisition of the language and the recognition of laws', it required 'tolerance and consideration for the norms and customs' of the native population."[43] As a strategy to gain political ground for the right and simultaneously weaken the SPD, the CDU set up an alternative immigration commission. This alternative, CDU-led immigration commission began to set a new tone for new criteria for permanent residence, not trusting that the SPD-led government could effectively handle the issue. The term "*Leitkultur*" was eventually dropped from the commission's final reports, but according to Hartwig Pautz, it had already fulfilled its role by "triggering a debate about identity that totally eclipsed the aims of the Süssmuth Commission."[44] He continues: "Whereas the Süssmuth Commission's intention was to provide practical guidelines for immigration and integration, such as a detailed programme concentrating on language acquisition, the CDU and CSU managed to shift the focus of the debate on to questions of national identity and to query the loyalty of non-European immigrants in particular."[45] By setting the tone of the discourse, the CDU/CSU opposition was also successful in setting the agenda itself. In terms of tone, while the left was "uneasy about the concept of a German 'lead culture'," there was a "broad consensus that immigrants and aspiring citizens need to adapt to the legal, cultural and linguistic norms of the host nation, even if there is acute disagreement about what precisely these consist of."[46] In the end, while both commissions diverged in terms of asylum and other areas, they were in agreement that the key to integration was in learning the host society language. They

[41] Independent Commission on Migration to Germany (Süssmuth Commission), *Structuring Immigration, Fostering Integration*, 254.

[42] Hartwig Pautz, "The politics of identity in Germany: The Leitkultur debate," *Race & Class* 46, no. 4 (2005), 45.

[43] Ibid.: 46. [44] Ibid.: 47. [45] Ibid.

[46] Jan Palmowski, "In search of the German nation: Citizenship and the challenge of integration," *Citizenship Studies* 12, no. 6 (2008), 559.

both produced similar proposals on this front, supporting the introduction of 600 hours of compulsory integration courses.[47]

The 2004 Immigration Act (in force January 1, 2005) introduced a number of major integration policies for immigrants in obtaining permanent residence.[48] Immigrants were required to demonstrate both oral (a requirement since 1990) and written language skills, obtained through attendance at an integration course (*Integrationskurs*), as well as knowledge of society, conveyed through a civic education course (*Orientierungskurs*). The content of the orientation course touches on several themes including politics (e.g., voting system, welfare state), history (including Nazism), and individuals and society (e.g., education, child-raising, religious diversity).[49] Integration requirements have evolved to include participation in an integration course of (at most) nine hundred units of language courses and forty-five units of civic orientation, culminating in both language and civic tests.[50]

While representing an unquestionable new restriction for immigrants to obtain permanent residence, there are some elements of design that suggest requirements also aim to foster a modicum of integration. First, a migrant can obtain a one-year residency reduction toward citizenship if he or she successfully completes the integration course. Second, completion in a timely manner (within two years of eligibility) enables the immigrant to claim back half the costs of the course (see below). Finally, in contrast to Denmark, for example, permanent residence is slightly more connected to citizenship in that a migrant is exempt from the language requirement for citizenship if they complete it for permanent residence. Plans to exempt immigrants from the citizenship test with successful completion of the civic orientation course and test were introduced in 2012. This makes the German model closer in kind to the Dutch and British models than their more restrictive citizenship counterparts, in which citizenship is a reward for – and not a process of – integration. Defining belonging in citizenship through the conditionality of permanent residence effectively joins these membership categories together and diminishes distinctions between them. This makes permanent residence more difficult (an unsurprising outcome in that it is regulated by immigration policy), while simultaneously making citizenship

47 Green, *The Politics of Exclusion: Institutions and immigration policy in contemporary Germany*, 128.

48 The Immigration Act, of course, was about more than integration requirements as it was the first comprehensive legal framework for immigration policy in Germany. The primary objective – in which it had little success – was to increase the immigration of highly skilled workers. Additionally, through parallel changes to the Residence Act there was consolidation of a number of resident statuses into two categories: temporary status and permanent status.

49 These examples are pulled from the official curriculum, "45 hours Germany."

50 A migrant with sufficient German (defined at or above the B1 level) also does not need to complete the language course and may produce certification of proficiency instead of sitting for the standardized exam. The migrant is still required to attend the civic orientation component of the integration course and, since 2009, to take the culminating exam, unless they have certification of completing German secondary school. See Seveker and Walter, "Country Report Germany."

easier and, importantly, more inclusive in the long run, a more surprising and not an insignificant achievement.

However, alongside these reprieves – which we might call "positive sanctions" – there are a number of negative sanctions, including fines and the denial of a residence permit.[51] Perhaps the most pervasive sanction is that third-country nationals who fail to attend these courses or pass the end-of-course exam could see a suspension of payment of social welfare benefits during their period of non-attendance. Even long-term residents could be obligated to attend courses if they received the long-term unemployment benefit (known as *Hartz IV*). This touches on a greater problem of structural dependency: while immigrants without permanent residence enjoy significant social and welfare rights, benefit utilization and a lack of economic self-sufficiency can affect an immigrant's chances of obtaining both long-term statuses of residence and citizenship. So while immigrants benefit from policy arrangements earlier on, improving their footing and security in society, it can create a vicious dependency that makes status even more unobtainable. In sum, welfare benefits became conditional on integration, while status became conditional on welfare independence. We also witness in this "rights and responsibilities" contract a compromise between approaches, where the government engages more actively in immigrant integration (as per left preferences) while also demanding more active participation from the immigrants (as per right preferences).

This mixed result but overall restrictive tone was produced not by accident or mutual preference, but out of necessity. By 2004, the CDU/CSU captured an overwhelming majority in the *Bundesrat*. Therefore, support for the law was needed from both houses, severely weakening the extent to which the SPD–Green coalition could liberalize. Once the CDU had succeeded in mainstreaming elements of restriction into the SPD-led program, the only remaining discussion on integration was whether it was to be funded by the federal government or by the states.[52] As a result of this gained political leverage by the right, as well as general antipathy in public opinion toward immigration – especially but not exclusively from 9/11 and the connection of the assailants to Germany, this phrase of policy adaptation is comparatively restrictive. Here we also see another limitation to the ideological orientation of government approach. Governments operate in environments of concession and bargaining, particularly in federal systems with bicameral legislatures. While immigrants were certainly enabled to be self-sustaining in society through language and country knowledge, and integration opportunities were balanced with positive

[51] Course fees themselves can be seen as a type of sanction. According to the Federal Office for Migration and Refugees (BAMF), fees start at €792 (approximately $1070) but can cost more if immigrants require additional language training or take special courses. There are possible fee exemptions for the unemployed, those receiving social assistance, or those who demonstrate hardship. http://www.bamf.de (accessed September 25, 2013).

[52] Michalowski, "Integration tests in Germany: A communitarian approach?," 190.

sanctions, a migrant's ability to reap the benefits of integration was limited to their ability to succeed in the course. Integration requirements for permanent residence were able simultaneously to satisfy both liberal and restrictive demands.

The final stage to the unfurling of integration requirements in Germany occurs by returning to citizenship, standardizing language assessment, and introducing a naturalization test. The primary focus of civic integration in this case study, as well as other cases of restrictive citizenship orientation, observes the concentration of integration requirements for residence first and foremost. This is deliberate. Integration is very much tied to the issue of immigration, and in front-loading the expectations of integration to the acquisition of residence permits, German policymakers are able to create both the right and the duty to integrate. On the one hand, this can have the effect of improving an immigrant's life chances, while on the other hand failure to achieve integration can produce decisive and enduring exclusion. All this vetting takes place outside of the realm of citizenship, which remains insulated from politics following the 1999 Act. This changed in 2006. But, again, it was not because the now-center government, comprising a CDU/CSU–SPD grand coalition, deliberately pursued language standardization and tests. Rather, these policies were reactively adopted to counterbalance more restrictive alternatives. Unlike residence, integration was not a central concern for citizenship and, as we shall see, its still-comparatively restrictive orientation remains unaffected by new requirements. This does not equate to liberalization of citizenship, but rather neutrality, even indifference.

If the 1999 Act could be classified by its liberalizing reform (symbolic if not in practice), the 2007 citizenship amendments might be described as standardizing and procedural. There were a number of factors that impelled the federal government into a decision on language assessment and citizenship tests. We see, again, integration requirements were not a proactive decision but rather a response to external and incremental pressures. First, there existed the need to standardize the level of language assessed for citizenship across the states. Originally, there was no specification of language level for citizenship, only that an applicant demonstrate "adequate" German. In a 2005 court decision, the Federal Administrative Court ruled that an applicant did not need to be able to write German provided that he or she was able to understand a simple text and dictate letters in German.[53] This was not a standard across the *Länder*. where each state maintained discretion in practice. Second, there was a lingering problem of compatibility with other requirements. The Immigration Act introduced standardized language assessment for permanent residence at the B1 level. This was a higher target than was demanded in most *Länder* for citizenship, thus creating direct, upward pressure for reform.

[53] Hailbronner, "Germany," 10.

In terms of knowledge assessment for citizenship, a groundswell of state-level practices foisted the issue onto the national stage. In addition to the absence of guidelines on assessing "adequate" German, states also had discretion in evaluating "commitment to basic liberal democratic order and constitution."[54] To this end, the *Länder* of Baden-Württemberg and Hesse both found the declaration of loyalty as required by the 1999 Act to be inadequate. The conservatively governed *Land* of Baden-Württemberg was the first to unveil a formal citizenship test on January 1, 2006. This interview test began to be referred to as a "Muslim test" because it asked leading questions for a specific profile. For example: "Shall a woman be permitted to be alone in public or to go on holiday on her own – what is your opinion about that?"[55] Other questions inquired as to the applicant's views on forced marriage, terrorism, women's rights, and homosexuality. Moreover, the test was explicitly and exclusively for applicants from Organization of Islamic Cooperation (OIC) countries as, according to a statement by the Interior Ministry in Stuttgart, "All Muslims are suspect."[56] This discriminatory focus was quickly taken back after protest. Later that year in Hesse, also a CDU-led *Land*, a similar citizenship test was proposed. In contrast to the interview, this exam would not only assess liberal values, but use a written exam to assess general knowledge of German history and culture. While never implemented, it set the tone for a discussion on national standardization.

In both of these cases, the CDU succeeded in setting a new agenda for testing. In raising the issue of assessment through state-level decisions, where the implementation of the Citizenship Law is relegated owing to Germany's federal structure and can create a divergence of practices that could be constitutionally problematic, the question could no longer be ignored at the federal level. These independent state practices led to a meeting of CDU/CSU interior ministers that called for a national values test. This then led to a recommendation for a federal-level test by the Interior Ministers Conference (IMK) that produced a compromise to prevent further individual practices and naturalization "tourism." Recommendations included the standardization of written and oral German assessment at the B1 level that would equalize language expectations of citizenship with that of permanent residence. No recommendations were made for the nature of citizenship testing, thus preserving state-level discretion on assessment.

54 "*Freiheitlich demokratische Grundordung*" appears in s.10 ss.1 No.1 StAG Naturalisation Law.

55 Gerard-Rene de Groot, Jan-Jaap Kuipers, and Franziska Weber, "Passing citizenship tests as a requirement for naturalisation: A comparative perspective," in *Illiberal Liberal States: Immigration, citizenship and integration in the EU*, ed. Elspeth Guild, Kees Groenendijk, and Sergio Carrera (Farnham, Surrey; Burlington, VT: Ashgate, 2009), 60.

56 Heribert Prantl, "Alle Muslime sind Verdaechtig," *Süddeutsche.de*, May 17, 2010. Available at http://www.sueddeutsche.de/politik/baden-wuerttemberg-alle-muslime-sind-verdaechtig-1.785482 (accessed February 2, 2014).

Formal amendments to the Citizenship Law were made as part of a package of changes to implement a series of EU Directives in 2007. The government went further than the IMK recommendations by proposing a formal and standard citizenship test for all the *Länder* to assess "knowledge of the legal and social system and the way of life in the Federal territory." It also required the new test for spouses of German citizens. Implemented in September 2008, the civic test requires an applicant to correctly answer 17 out of 33 multiple-choice questions. Thirty questions are derived from a general catalogue of naturalization test questions and assess three areas of knowledge: "living in a democracy," "history and responsibility," and "people and society."[57] The remaining three questions assess the *Land* of main residence. Test-takers can prepare for the exam through free on-line practice tests, tutorials, and obtaining copies of the catalogue of questions for both the general section and specific *Land* section. Finally, the law provides for citizenship courses as a way to prepare for the test, but these have not been implemented across all states because of lack of demand.[58]

The introduction of the citizenship test certainly makes naturalization more procedural if perfunctory by adding another requirement to the process. But does it make it more difficult? In cases of restrictive retrenchment, we see both citizenship and permanent residence become more difficult – thus preserving a restrictive orientation toward outsiders – through civic integration and other requirements. In the case of Germany, however, we do not see civic integration exclusively as a way to maintain exclusion but also as a means to update membership to the realities of intake in the context of liberalizing-oriented governments. Where there was significant pressure to liberalize citizenship across the ideological spectrum, integration requirements have offset this opening by transforming the effective barrier of admission from citizenship to permanent residence through robust integration programs and testing. The effect of cross-party and cross-institution politics has been to mitigate the degree of both proposed restriction and liberalization that can be achieved, resulting in contained liberalization for citizenship and moderate restriction for permanent residence.

Implementation and variegated effects on settlement and citizenship

This final section examines the extent to which these divergent policy outputs match up with policy outcomes. In this view, permanent residence is unambiguously the new, decisive barrier of membership. Despite disagreements about the actual degree of liberalization produced by the 1999 Act, one can see evidence that implementation of a mild citizenship test has neither eroded liberalizing

[57] See website for Federal Office for Migration and Refugees (BAMF) at bamf.de (accessed September 30, 2013).

[58] Seveker and Walter, "Country Report Germany."

gains nor made citizenship more difficult. On average, 98.9 percent of applicants pass the German citizenship test.[59] This is one of the highest rates in Europe and globally (the United States, for example, boasted a pass rate of 95.8 percent in 2010; Australia, 98.9 percent).

Alongside this minimal effect on citizenship acquisition – owing in large part to its negotiated origins and insulated position due to investments in permanent residence – we see language and country knowledge requirements successfully work to preserve an unequivocal shade of restriction through permanent residence. Pre-empting the filtering power once preserved to citizenship, permanent residence has been structured to be a consequential, prohibitive barrier to "promote and also demand" integration. Table 5.1 shows low pass rates of the language test among candidates for permanent residence. In the first few years we see significantly low pass rate rates among course graduates reaching B1 (between 38 and 44 percent), and among those who passed were mainly highly qualified migrants.[60] It also shows that before the 2007 reforms to the integration program, course graduates were performing far worse on the language exam than those who did not complete the course. These figures have since improved, and as early as 2009 two-thirds of course graduates were passing the language exam at the B1 level.

These figures are far below the citizenship pass rate, leaving a large segment of immigrants in need of more language training and reaffirming the shift in authoritative barriers from citizenship to permanent residence. Still, in 2012, BAMF declared a great success for the integration course, which had been taken

TABLE 5.1. *Pass rates for integration course and language requirement for permanent residence in Germany, 2005–2011*[61]

	2005	2006	2007	2008	2009	2010	2011
Number who finished integration course	31478	76401	67052	73557	70968	83818	73647
Number who took language exam	17482	50952	43853	78163	104387	103875	92547
Pass rate among test participants (%)*	69.5	71.8	67.4	47.9	45.2	49.9	53.8
Pass rate among course graduates (%)*	38.6	47.9	44.1	50.9	66.4	61.8	67.6

* Percentages apply only to people who passed at the B1 level, as this is the required level for completing integration requirements for a permanent residence permit.

59 "Who wants a passport? Minuscule fail rate for German citizenship test," *Spiegel Online*, February 1, 2009 (accessed September 30, 2013).

60 van Oers, "Citizenship tests in the Netherlands, Germany and the UK," 75.

61 BAMF, "9. Lagebericht Der Beauftragten Der Bundesregierung Für Migration, Flüchtlinge Und Integration über Die Lage Der Ausländerinnen Und Ausländer in Deutschland," (July 2012), 677.

by over one million new participants since inception.[62] And pass rates have generally not only increased over time, but remain significantly higher than for non-graduates. This reflects not only the high number of applicants who sit through the language test with insufficient knowledge but also the positive effects of sustained language education.

A formal consequence of not meeting the integration requirement is the refusal of a permanent residence permit. In practice, however, failure to complete the integration course only re-feeds applicants back into the integration cycle: sitting for more exams and obtaining more language training until the B1 level is met, not to mention waiting longer to obtain permanent residence. The alternative side to this argument is that immigrants who do not succeed invariably enjoy a longer exposure to these subsidized programs of integration that, ultimately, improve their economic and social prospects in Germany. However, access to permanent residence, and hence political inclusion and security of status, is significantly delayed.

This view of practice shows how permanent residence has become the new, decisive barrier for admission to the national political community. With future changes that will exempt immigrants from sitting through the citizenship test if they successfully complete integration for permanent residence, the former is clearly diluted by the latter. The citizenship test can ultimately be described as a symbolic and neutral addition, a result of upward pressure both to standardize state-level practice and to equate expectations of belonging with that of permanent residence. It does not make naturalization more difficult, but neither does it ameliorate existing difficulty or add opportunities for acquisition. It certainly does not produce the kind of immediate, negative effect on naturalizations that other additions have had, like unemployment and welfare dependency conditions. Of course, it is worth considering that even though high pass rates suggest that the citizenship test is not difficult, it may still yield some exclusionary effects as applicants might be discouraged from applying for citizenship because they do not feel adequately prepared. Despite the liberalizing reforms of the 1999 Act, naturalizations have steadily decreased. Hailbronner suggests this precipitious drop – of more than 40 percent between 2000 and 2010, "needs to be taken as a serious sign that the nationality legislation has not reached its goal in the long run."[63] The citizenship test has only a minor, perhaps even insignificant, effect in this decline. Meanwhile, the uptick in naturalizations before the implementation of language and knowledge requirements in 2006 and 2007 (evident in Figure 5.1) may be evidence of its disincentivizing character.

[62] BAMF, "Erfolg bei Integrationskursen: Millionen-Marke erreicht," (January 19, 2012). Available at http://www.bamf.de/SharedDocs/Pressemitteilungen/DE/2012/20120118-0001-pressemitteilung-integrationskurs-millionste-teilnehmer.html (accessed September 27, 2013).

[63] Hailbronner, "Germany," 21.

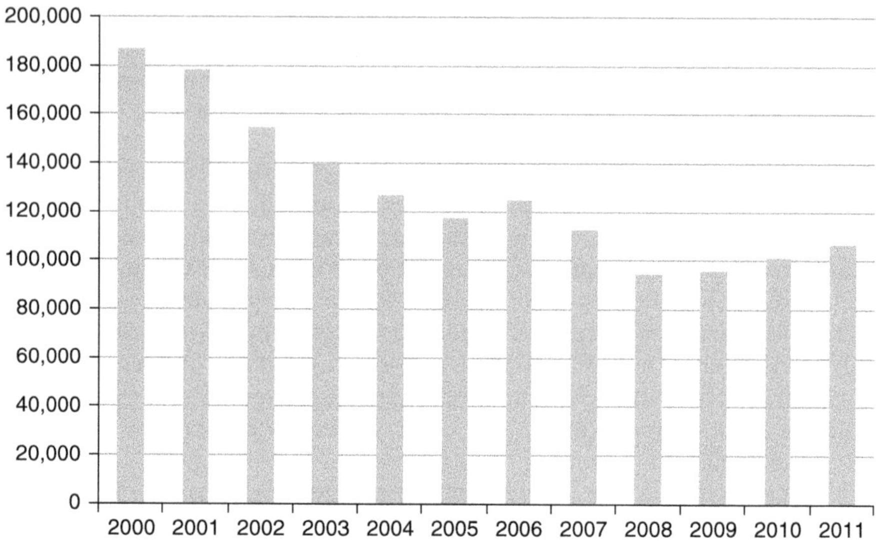

5.1 Acquisition of citizenship in Germany, 2000–2011

CONCLUSION

The German case lays out a number of points of comparison. First, in contrast to cases where integration requirements were decisive instruments for restrictive retrenchment in uncontested political settings (e.g., in Austria and Denmark), new integration requirements in Germany were achieved through political maneuverings and were part of a deliberate strategy to offset change. Center-right political actors, first in opposition and later in *Land* government, offered counterbalancing measures to maintain a comparatively restrictive orientation toward outsiders, through a strengthened permanent residence. Mandatory integration was a mechanism by which opposition or regional interests were pushed to the fore of political debates, setting a decisive agenda for new policy. Resulting from these political processes – between insiders and outsiders and across different levels of government – the design and the implementation of civic requirements are more moderate, though they still maintain the unmistakable hue of exclusion.

Second, and perhaps more consequential, we see a central preoccupation with requirements at permanent residence, through robust requirements and ties to non-utilization requirements. By comparison, citizenship remains relatively untouched, and new integration requirements reveal themselves to be nothing more than a neutral addition that neither liberalizes nor adds restriction, whereas permanent residence becomes a more decisive barrier of control. A strict path dependence approach might note this outcome as a result of stasis, missing the intervening story and unique processes of political maneuvering and bargaining.

In the end, Germany still maintains an exclusive understanding of belonging, in both law and practice, made ever more restrictive not by changes to citizenship *per se* but by conditionality established at earlier barriers of admission. Moreover, despite the significant liberalization to citizenship that occurred in 1999, we see that this change makes little difference if all the barriers preceding eligibility are so formidable. While, in principle, the act of articulating explicit contours of membership suggests accessibility, the wall is high and the road to it is long.

THE UNITED KINGDOM

The attachment of integration requirements to naturalization and the promotion of newly defined "British values" have been described as part of a "quiet citizenship revolution."[64] Like Germany, the UK has adopted membership requirements, namely the language and knowledge of life (KOL) test for settlement and citizenship. In addition, it adopted and adapted civic integration under a left government. Labour's long run in government lasted from 1997 until the 2010 General Election. While this period was marked by escalating concerns about immigration, the issue was never central in an election. Nor did the Conservatives gain support in opposition on the issue in particular. More significant than opposition actors in the British system is the nature of institutional design itself. As such, in a single-actor institutional system, policies are made with a view to continually win over public opinion.

Despite similarities between Germany and the UK, we see significant divergence in the purpose, design, and outcome of new membership policies. Unlike its counterpart on the continent, the UK adopted and maintained a civic integration strategy for the purpose of promoting, not detering, access to full membership through citizenship. In fact, even when restrictive political pressure was first present, following the 2005 General Election and until the 2009 introduction of the Borders, Citizenship and Immigration Act (BCIA), the ultimate abandonment of new restrictions is testament to the high price of change. And while neighboring effects, learning, and a change in government have recently made civic integration – a once stalwart model of positive citizenship promotion – more restrictive, differences persist which can largely be understood as a product of different conceptions of and objectives for belonging, as measured in citizenship policy orientation.

Despite recent restrictions, the UK still stands in contrast to previously examined cases on a number of related fronts. First, unlike Austria, Denmark, and Germany, which all adopted civic integration policy in the context of restrictive citizenship starting points, reflecting insular, ethnocultural concepts of membership, the UK started with a liberal citizenship policy, reflecting an inchoate concept of the "British citizen" that remains vague and is regularly

[64] Ruth Kelly and Liam Byrne, "A common place" (London: Fabian Society, 2007).

redefined.[65] Second, unlike these restrictive regimes that have used membership requirements since inception to maintain restriction by decreasing acquisition of status, mainly through permanent residence, the UK initially used civic requirements to maintain its liberal orientation, incentivizing acquisition of citizenship and simultaneously diminishing the appeal of permanent residence. This strategy was directed at both improving the integration "journey"[66] as well as articulating a clear conception of membership for British citizenship for the first time, evident not only in the insulated and relatively uncontested origins of civic integration policy adoption, but also in its design, where the UK relies on the individual to self-assess and obtain integration. By maintaining a minimal role for the state in directing or facilitating integration, in contrast to the contracts and courses used by other European countries, British integration remains largely self-directed and liberal in both senses of the word.

This case study traces the UK's distinct phases of membership policy: (1) a long period of enriching change that includes successful rebuffing of institutionally costly, restrictive change; and (2) recent steps of restriction. It begins by examining the content of citizenship, followed by an examination, similar to previous case studies, of extant demographic and political conditions that influence civic integration policy adoption. The case highlights Labour leaders pursuing citizenship enrichment in an insulated policy environment, employing idea entrepreneurs to shape policy without contestation or politicization. Following this first policy change (integration for citizenship), I then trace the evolution of civic integration policies through its contemporary practice. This includes the extension of integration to settlement, attempted but ultimately unsuccessful restrictions through "probationary citizenship," as well as recent, successful changes ending the course-based route of completing language and KOL under a Conservative-led government. Whereas policies were initially designed to address problems of cohesion and incentivize naturalization, we see more emphasis on control and conditionality in later practices. These later restrictions have less to do with government preferences, however, and are more accurately described as the result of neighboring effects and learning.

In the end, however, the UK illustrates that, under different conditions (namely inclusion-oriented actors in a liberal citizenship context), civic integration can represent something other than restriction or assimilation. Of course, the notion that any requirement is equal to a new restriction is not only problematic to the concept of citizenship as a contract relationship but also asserts a liberal bias into the contract by denying that the state can ask *any* conditions of

[65] See David Cesarani and Mary Fulbrook, *Citizenship, Nationality, and Migration in Europe* (London; New York: Routledge, 1996), 57–73; James Hampshire, *Citizenship and Belonging: Immigration and the politics of demographic governance in post-war Britain* (Houndmills, Balsingstoke, Hampshire; New York: Palgrave, 2005).

[66] Dina Kiwan, "A journey to citizenship in the United Kingdom," *International Journal on Multicultural Societies* 10, no. 1 (2008), 60–75.

an immigrant without seeming exclusionary or tight-fisted. Tracing the causal path of membership policy in the UK reveals that civic integration can be more than one thing, given policy context and government preferences. It also shows that it can be more than one thing over time, where conditions and governments change.

Easy to join, but join what?

While civic integration is not the first attempt to positively define a sense of Britishness, John Greenwood and Lynton Robins point out that "Its importance on today's political agenda, however, suggests that previous initiatives have borne little fruit."[67] The UK has maintained a historically liberal set of citizenship policies, typified by low-residence duration for naturalization (5 years; 3 years for spouses), allowance for dual citizenship, and the conferring of citizenship through *jus soli* at birth as a right. English has been a formal requirement for naturalization of non-British subjects since 1914, reaffirmed with the British Nationality Act (BNA) of 1981 (effective in 1983) that applicants demonstrate "sufficient knowledge of the English, Welsh or Scottish Gaelic language."[68] The practice of assessing language, as in other states, was always *ad hoc*, and the successful completion of naturalization paperwork was often evidence of sufficiency.[69]

This inclusivity is notably juxtaposed to what many scholars and politicians have identified as an incomplete and ill-defined concept of belonging in British citizenship. The United Kingdom is, first and by definition, the unification of multiple national communities. It sews together the different nations of England, Scotland, Wales, and Northern Ireland. Multiculturalism (and multiracialism) may have "officially" begun with the arrival of Jamaican immigrants on the *Empire Windrush* ship in 1948,[70] but Britain has been multinational for much longer, precluding a shared national identity. Moreover, as Joppke notes, by virtue of Britain being a post-colonial state – where nation-centered concepts of

[67] John Greenwood and Lynton Robins, "Citizenship tests and education: Embedding a concept," *Parliamentary Affairs* 55, no. 3 (2002), 507.

[68] This 1981 language requirement did not apply to naturalizing spouses of British citizens, as reported in the House of Commons Written Answers, *Hansard*, 2 June 1997, column 3.

[69] Also, similar to early Danish and German practices, language requirements were not instruments of immigrant integration. Citizenship, according to Randall Hansen, was fashioned to preserve different categories of membership based on subjecthood. Randall Hansen, *Citizenship and Immigration in Post-War Britain: The institutional origins of a multicultural nation* (Oxford; New York: Oxford University Press, 2000), 37–45.

[70] Of course, the UK received non-European migrants before this much-publicized event. In fact, many of the migrants on the *Empire Windrush* were "returnees," having fought with the Royal Air Force during World War II. See Leo Lucassen, *The Immigrant Threat: The integration of old and new migrants in Western Europe since 1850* (Urbana: University of Illinois Press, 2005), 113.

immigration are eclipsed by liberal-state ones – citizenship "no longer can explicitly and directly reproduce and reinvigorate particular nationhood."[71]

Resulting from this inherent diversity as a starting point, even the 1948 BNA did not positively define a category of British citizenship as membership, but instead, as Randall Hansen describes, preserved connections of subjecthood with other Commonwealth states as they were breaking off to define their own categories of citizenship.[72] Persons with British nationality were divided into three categories: "Citizen of the United Kingdom and Colonies" (CUKCs), "Citizen of Independent Commonwealth Countries" (CICCs), and Irish Citizens with British subjecthood. In sum, political and residence rights differed based on status and "almost the only common bond which the vast array of British 'citizens' throughout the world enjoy is allegiance to the Crown."[73] The law established very little in terms of reflecting a common membership into citizenship for Britons; overseas subjects and Commonwealth citizens were even more removed from belonging than even European migrants to Britain, as the former groups were exempt from the oath of allegiance to the monarch.[74] In fact, the 1981 Act was the first time a definition of a British citizen formally appeared, and it was for the purpose of creating a distinction with Commonwealth citizens.

Subjecthood obviated the establishment of membership through citizenship, or a sense of common belonging. As such, Caroline Sawyer refers to the British citizenship relationship as one of "individual rather than national membership."[75] Brubaker also employs this type of distinction to contrast Britain to other European countries: "The concept of citizenship as membership of a legal and political community was foreign to British thinking. Legal and political status were conceived instead in terms of allegiance – in terms of the vertical ties between individual subjects and the king. The ties of allegiance knit together the British empire, not the British nation."[76] As then-Prime Minister David Cameron said in 2011, in regard to the problem of Muslim extremism in Britain, "We have failed to provide a vision of society to which they feel they

71 Christian Joppke, *Selecting by Origin: Ethnic migration in the liberal state* (Cambridge, MA: Harvard University Press, 2005), 2.

72 Hansen draws this argument out by looking at Canadian citizenship. The Canadian government introduced a citizenship act that "would define Canadian citizens and declare that they possessed British subjecthood *in consequence* of their status as Canadian citizens" (emphasis added). It reversed the logic of allegiance. See Hansen, *Citizenship and Immigration in Post-War Britain: The institutional origins of a multicultural nation*, 37–45.

73 Greenwood and Robins, "Citizenship tests and education: Embedding a concept," 512.

74 From the Nationality and Status of Aliens Act, 1914, reprinted in Richard W. Flournoy and Manley O. Hudson, *A Collection of Nationality Laws of Various Countries, as Contained in Constitutions, Statutes and Treaties* (New York: Oxford University Press, 1929), 61–72.

75 Caroline Sawyer, "The United Kingdom," in *EUDO Citizenship Country Reports* (Florence: EUDO Citizenship, Robert Schuman Centre for Advanced Studies, EUI, 2010), 5.

76 William Rogers Brubaker, ed. *Immigration and the Politics of Citizenship in Europe and North America* (Lanham, MD: University Press of America; German Marshall Fund of the United States, 1989), 10.

want to belong." Moreover, the inclination of many Scots to vote in favor of independence only underlines the thinness of shared identity.

MULTIPLE TRIBUTARIES TO CIVIC INTEGRATION POLICY ADOPTION

A relatively accessible citizenship paired with a minimal definition of belonging enabled Britain to flourish in its postwar and post-Empire years into a multicultural society in both composition and policy. Britain today is significantly more diverse than it was 50 years ago. In 1961, non-whites comprised only about 1.5 percent of the population in England and Wales.[77] By 2001, they comprised over 8 percent.[78] The increase in ethnic heterogeneity, coupled with official policies of multiculturalism, maintained diversity as a British reality, but as political events in the first years of the new millennium would highlight, the omission of promoting cohesion alongside this diversity – or balancing inclusion with a common civic identity – created a number of problems for Labour party policymakers. As a result, as Sawyer notes, "The atmosphere and rhetoric of recent general elections have [...] focused not so much on citizenship in the sense of nationality as either on citizenship in the sense of a conception of reciprocal rights and obligations (especially obligations) or else on the concept of Britishness."[79]

The first impetus for re-examining citizenship as a membership category was the period of significant demographic change in the 1980s and 1990s. On top of general changes in migration patterns during a period of economic booms and the continuation of family-based migration, asylum proved to be a significant demographic and political factor in defining the immigration agenda. By 2004, and after some high-profile incidents involving asylum,[80] humanitarian-based migration accounted for 19 percent of total intake. This influx highlighted asylum as a divisive political issue not simply as an immigration matter but also because it impacted on settlement and welfare benefits. Consequently, "the category of 'bogus asylum seeker' has acquired particular resonance in British public debate."[81]

[77] "The West Indian-born population of England and Wales was 171,796; Indian nationals numbered 46,575, and Pakistanis 19,250," in Ceri Peach and Relations Institute of Race, *West Indian Migration to Britain: A social geography* (London; New York: Published for the Institute of Race Relations by Oxford University Press, 1968), xv.

[78] Commission for Racial Equality, *Ethnic Minorities in Great Britain, Factfile* 2 (London: CRE, 2007).

[79] Sawyer, "The United Kingdom," 26.

[80] Politics were exacerbated in the summer of 2001 as pictures and stories of asylum seekers trying to reach Britain though the Channel Tunnel were splashed across the news. Newspapers ran headlines like "Stop the Invasion," "We can't take any more asylum seekers," "Asylum invasion reaches 12,000 a month," and "Asylum: we're being invaded." L. Schuster, "Asylum seekers: Sangatte and the Tunnel." *Parliamentary Affairs* 56, no. 3 (2003), 511.

[81] Andrew Geddes, *The Politics of Migration and Immigration in Europe* (London; Thousand Oaks, CA: Sage Publications, 2003), 40.

In May 2001, The Research, Development and Statistics directorate of the Home Office published a report titled "Migration: an economic and social analysis," which looked at long-term consequences of large-scale migration to the UK. It noted the deep connection between a lack of English proficiency and social exclusion.[82] The report also stressed the importance of citizenship in "strengthen[ing] good race and community relations."[83] Incoming Labour Home Secretary David Blunkett's self-declared "first task" was to "get to grips with problems that affect social cohesion."[84] Thus, he and his policy advisor, Nick Pearce, began to devise plans to promote English language skills and common citizenship.[85]

If overall immigration and the perceived lack of skills presented a prominent but diffuse cause for the civic identity agenda, the Northern Riots of 2001 provided a second, more acute impetus. In July 2001, violent clashes erupted between the police, and white and Asian youth in the towns of Oldham, Burnley, and Bradford. In response, the Community Cohesion Review Team was convened to investigate the causes of the violence. The team's report (known as the Cantle Report) concluded that despite – or perhaps because of – the difference-friendly reception of newcomers and diversity under multiculturalism, "many communities operate on the basis of a series of parallel lives."[86] It further noted that there had been "little attempt to develop clear values which focus on what it means to be a citizen of a modern multi-racial Britain."[87]

Many scholars point to the Northern Riots as the sole impetus for the UK's citizenship agenda,[88] but it is imperative to contextualize this event among other pressures, recognizing that there was a confluence of factors. There was an overlap in theme and population, but Blunkett and Cantle were talking about distinct phenomena. Cantle's report addressed policies on community cohesion, defined as connecting existing ethnic minority communities to other groups in society. Blunkett, drawing from the economic analysis report, focused on skills for immigrant integration, in other words, incorporating newcomers into society.[89] However, timing, not design, would unite these agendas. Blunkett came to speak on his "English for passports plan" only a few weeks after the Northern Riots,[90] obfuscating henceforth the different integration challenges of *new*

[82] Stephen Glover et al., "Migration: An economic and social analysis," in *RDS Occassional Paper No 67* (London: Home Office, 2001), 26.

[83] Ibid., 31. [84] Stephen Pollard, *David Blunkett* (London: Hodder & Stoughton, 2005), 251.

[85] Sarah Spencer. Interview with the author. August 7, 2007. London, UK.

[86] Ted Cantle, "Community cohesion: A report of the Independent Review Team," ed. Home Office (London: HMSO, 2001), 9.

[87] Ibid., 19.

[88] See, for example, Dora Kostakopoulou, "Why naturalisation?," *Perspectives on European Politics and Society* 4, no. 1 (2003), 85–115.

[89] See Will Somerville and Sara Wallace Goodman, "The role of networks in the development of UK migration policy," *Political Studies* 58, no. 5 (2010), 951–970.

[90] "Blunkett 'English for Passports Plan'," in *Independent on Sunday*, 19 August 2001.

immigrants and *settled immigrants*. While the differences between these agendas would eventually become evident in the institutional bifurcation of community cohesion (under the Department for Communities and Local Government) and citizenship and integration (under the Home Office), there was this period of what former Commissioner of the Council for Racial Equality Sarah Spencer describes as "regrettable overlap."[91] Blunkett, for his part, was adamant to maintain a distinction: "We really needed to win people over that naturalization and integration was the obvious thing to do ... We want integration and cohesion in its own right, because it is right for our society."[92] In other words, where a response to an event like the Northern Riots or 9/11 was widely expected and accepted, Blunkett saw he had some serious convincing to do, especially of the Liberal Left in his own party, that citizenship values and integration were important. And as integration became more and more linked to Muslim extremism in the post-9/11 climate, Blunkett asserted: "I used to say, 'Rooting out terrorism is not the same thing as prioritizing integration and cohesion'."[93] In the end, September 11th proved a decisive catalyst to unite early initiatives. In a speech a couple weeks afterwards, Blunkett himself made the connection, identifying citizenship and immigration as a viable and popular strategy to combat cultural integration problems: "We must ... do more to articulate and secure the common values that underpin our democracy. We have allowed parts of our society to become effectively segregated. Mutual understanding and respect have weakened, particularly among the young. We have done too little in the past to articulate our common values and democratic commitments, or to promote positive induction into citizenship for those settling here."[94]

Last, but certainly not least, perhaps the most pronounced influence on the introduction of civic integration requirements for immigrants seeking citizenship was the introduction of a statutory citizenship curriculum for schools in England. Here we see the UK as an interesting contrast to other states, as the ideational origin for new requirements was born from a problem of citizenship among British-born children, and not out of examining the immigrant integration problem. This only further reflects the vague understanding of citizenship that existed at the time, insufficient not only to newcomers but also to the native-born. Following New Labour's 1997 landslide electoral victory at the helm of Tony Blair, one of its first initiatives was introducing citizenship studies into the National Curriculum. This curriculum design was guided by Sir Bernard Crick, an academician who later returned in a similar advisory capacity at the request of Home Secretary David Blunkett to transform the idea of "citizenship for schools" into "citizenship for immigrants" by way of promoting requirements for naturalization. By using similar experts for immigration, drawn largely from

[91] Spencer, Interview with the author.

[92] David Blunkett, Interview with the author. August 3, 2007. London, UK. [93] Ibid.

[94] David Blunkett, "Are civil liberties at risk? No, promises the Home Secretary David Blunkett," in *The Observer (Guardian)*, September 30, 2001.

education circles, Dina Kiwan concludes that "not only are the policy rationale and means of assessment for the UK naturalization requirements presented in distinctly educative terms, but so too is the actual content of both the course and test significantly influenced by citizenship education policy developments that preceded the introduction of the naturalization requirements in 2002."[95]

Stepping back to examine these initial conditions, there are a number of factors behind the adoption of civic integration, but none were to make membership restrictive. Moreover, citizenship debates remained at the elite level among a set of dedicated policy entrepreneurs and insulated from the public. When Blunkett was promoted from Education to Home Secretary in May 2001, he brought with him an ideological inclination toward communitarianism and a staff consisting of Crick and other educators to shape the new citizenship agenda, signaling a deliberate shift from the consumerist, "passport citizenship" that prevailed under Margaret Thatcher's premiership.[96] Blunkett would later reflect on his citizenship achievements, speaking specifically about citizenship ceremonies, that "Rare as these occasions may be, I think I can say, hand on heart, that this was one of those policies that certainly would not have happened when it happened if I had not been Home Secretary."[97]

The 2002 Nationality, Immigration and Asylum Act (NIA) not only strengthened the language requirement but also introduced "sufficient knowledge about life in the United Kingdom" and citizenship ceremonies. The assessment of language became standardized through the "Life in the UK" citizenship test, implemented in 2005. If applicants already had a sufficient level of English, they were subject to this 24-question computerized test. If their English needed improvement, they could instead pursue a course-based route through the English Speakers of Other Languages (ESOL) "Skills for Life" curriculum and certification program for adult learners, where potential citizens learn English in the context of citizenship content. Finally, a citizenship ceremony was implemented in February 2004, where new citizens pledge to uphold British *qua* "democratic values" and swear an oath of allegiance to the monarchy.

When the White Paper for this bill – "Secure Borders, Safe Haven: Integration with Diversity in Modern Britain" – entered parliamentary debate in late spring of 2002, the discussion was relatively benign. Simon Hughes, a Liberal Democrat MP from North Southwark and Bermondsey, described it as characterized by "moderate language," further noting that this tone was imperative if Britain did not want "to risk in the near future provoking extreme political reactions like those they have provoked across the channel. We all have an interest in making sure that that does not happen here."[98] Here, Hughes is

[95] Dina Kiwan, "'National' citizenship in the UK? Education and naturalization policies in the context of internal division," *Ethnicities* 11, no. 3 (2011), 271.

[96] Greenwood and Robins, "Citizenship tests and education: Embedding a concept," 507–10.

[97] David Blunkett, *The Blunkett Tapes: My life in the bear pit* (London: Bloomsbury, 2006), 601.

[98] *Hansard*, House of Commons debates for 24 April 2002, column 375.

referencing the success of Jean Marie Le Pen in the first round of the French Presidential election that occurred only three days prior, on April 21, 2002. Despite the relative insulation of policymaking, fear of politicization was ever-present. In the 2002 local elections, the British National Party (BNP – the UK's most prominent far-right party) gained three council seats in Burnley by capitalizing on racism only a year after that city's three-day riot. The following year, the BNP became the second-largest party in the city, and the official opposition, by winning eight council seats.[99] Thus, the ability of the far-right to gain electoral popularity by exploiting problems with integration cast a significant shadow over the tone of citizenship reform. For example, Keith Vaz, a Labour MP from East Leicester, stated "We should note what has happened in France and deal with it in the right way. We need to do several things, including confronting the far-right openly and positively . . . We have a particular responsibility as we have the largest settled black and Asian population in Europe, and need to continue our leadership role.[100]

Opposition mainly came from pro-immigrant organizations. Compulsory English lessons were decried as "linguistic colonialism" by the Joint Council for the Welfare of Immigrants (JCWI), and Blunkett even risked a potential "backlash from MPs in his own party."[101] Yet, the debates in the parliamentary houses largely focused on the content, such as what "Life in the UK," "British," and "sufficient" really meant, rather than the requirements of the instruments of civic integration. For example, Lord Navnit Dholakia recommended getting rid of the "Knowledge of Life in the UK" requirement because "[t]here are legitimate concerns that such knowledge cannot be tested. Moreover, the Government have nowhere provided their definition of the term, 'life in the United Kingdom.'"[102]

Here we see a second important distinction between the UK and other European states with regard to civic integration requirements. In addition to the educational roots of civic integration in the UK, membership requirements were introduced under a well-entrenched, left government, where policymakers were insulated not only from public mobilization but also from significant opposition or veto players. Consequently, references to keeping the public at the "heart of the changes"[103] and "maintain[ing] public confidence" appear all over this policy.[104] Therefore, on the relatively non-politicized issue of

[99] BBC News, "Local elections, council, Burnley," available at http://news.bbc.co.uk/2/shared/bsp/hi/vote2003/locals/html/42.stm (accessed January 12, 2009).

[100] *Hansard*, House of Commons debates for 24 April 2002, column 376–77.

[101] Severin Carrell, "Blunkett 'English for passports' plan," in *The Independent*, 19 August 2001.

[102] *Hansard*, House of Lords debate for 8 July 2002, column 440.

[103] Home Office, "The path to citizenship. Next steps in reforming the immigration system," (London: Border and Immigration Agency Communications Directorate, 2008), 11.

[104] Home Office, "Controlling our borders: Making migration work for Britain," (London: TSO, 2005), 6.

citizenship, we see little difference between Labour and Conservative parliamentarians and no role played by party spoilers. Debates in Parliament largely focused on content rather than the instruments themselves.

The job of defining this content as well as designing the unique dual paths to citizenship – course advancement or the test – was tasked to the Life in the United Kingdom Advisory Group, created in September 2002, to "advise the Home Secretary on the method, conduct and implementation of a 'Life in the United Kingdom' naturalisation test." This insulated policy group, consisting of Crick, ESOL teachers, and other idea entrepreneurs on facets of immigrant integration, had a straightforward task: transitioning British citizenship from a bureaucratic process to a "significant life event" that is "meaningful and celebratory."[105] Where other countries, such as Germany and Denmark, could boast tacit "guiding cultures" to underscore their citizenship projects, the UK had to deliberately create one through membership requirements and education.[106] As such, the Group's definition of Britishness as an inclusive set of common values and stripped of cultural or historical cues is both notably wide and purposefully shallow:

> To be British ... mean[s] that we respect the laws, the elected parliamentary and democratic political structures, traditional values of mutual tolerance, respect for equal rights and mutual concern; and that we give our allegiance to the state (as commonly symbolized in the Crown) in return for its protection. To be British is to respect those over-arching specific institutions, values, beliefs and traditions that bind us all, the different nations and cultures together in peace and in a legal order.[107]

By design, common British values were to indicate "how we behave towards each other collectively and that is what binds us together, rather than assertions of national, ethnic or religious priorities or particular interpretations of history."[108] And, importantly, the clear starting point for crafting definitions of Britishness, and subsequent membership requirements to promote it, was accommodating existing diversity, not resurrecting some concept of national-cultural assimilation.

Central to their remit, members of the Life in the UK Advisory Group used this positive definition of citizenship in order to "encourage people to apply for British citizenship at an earlier stage" because naturalization evidence showed

[105] Home Office, "The new and the old: The Report of the 'Life in the United Kingdom' Advisory Group," (London: Home Office Communication Directorate, 2003), 8.

[106] For more, see Eva-Maria Asari, Daphne Halikiopoulou, and Steven Mock, "British national identity and the dilemmas of multiculturalism," *Nationalism and Ethnic Politics* 14, no. 1 (2008), 1–28; Nasar Meer and Tariq Modood, "The multicultural state we're in: Muslims, 'multiculture' and the 'civic re-balancing' of British multiculturalism," *Political Studies* 57, no. 3 (2008), 473–497.

[107] Home Office, "The new and the old: The report of the 'Life in the United Kingdom' Advisory Group," 11.

[108] Ibid., 12.

flagging rates,[109] particularly among long-term residents. Specifically, the group identified that applicants from New Commonwealth countries, the Middle East, and the rest of Asia are one-third more likely to naturalize than Old Commonwealth applicants.[110] Also, evidence showed applicants from New Commonwealth countries are twice as likely to naturalize as Europeans after 6 years of residence.[111] Hence, for the Advisory Group, the two paths to citizenship promoting language and "knowledge of life" in the UK, as well as the citizenship ceremonies, are specifically and explicitly designed to "incentivize" citizenship and encourage more people to acquire citizenship.[112] In terms of how this directly translated to Home Office goals, policymakers did not seek wholesale increases in naturalization rates per se. Rather, to quote Blunkett, it was to include values and skills of citizenship that would "promote the acceptable absorption of the uptake."[113]

Restrictive adaptation: Failed attempts and ultimate success

The early days of membership policy in the UK are dramatically in contrast to those of states with restrictive citizenship policy starting points, in terms of both purpose and political process. Instead of beginning civic integration with permanent residence, using integration requirements to create an alternative and durable status to citizenship, in the UK we see citizenship prioritized first and foremost as the location of new requirements. And from the initial work of the Advisory Group through to the expansion of requirements to permanent residence, we see a divergence in strategy: not to make permanent residence more prominent but to diminish it.

Following the introduction of membership requirements to citizenship (implemented by November 2005) to promote a more meaningful naturalization process, the "knowledge of life and language" requirements were secondarily extended to the settlement stage in 2007. The catalyst in extending the language requirement to permanent residence is typically attributed to Tony Blair's statement in reaction to the London Bombings of July 7, 2005, in which he states:

> We should share a common language. Equal opportunity for all groups requires that they be conversant in that common language. It is a matter both of cohesion and of justice that we should set the use of English as a condition of citizenship. In addition, for those who wish to take up residence permanently in the UK, we will include a requirement to pass an English test before such permanent residency is granted.[114]

[109] Ibid., 7. [110] Ibid., Appendix A, 39. [111] Ibid.
[112] See Kiwan, "A journey to citizenship in the United Kingdom."
[113] Blunkett, Interview with the author.
[114] Tony Blair, "The duty to integrate: Shared British values," December 8, 2006, available at http://www.prime-minister.gov.uk/output/Page10563.asp (accessed December 9, 2006)

However, the groundwork for a settlement test appeared as early as the 2002 White Paper, in which the government recognized that it was "necessary for all those who are seeking long term resident status to be provided with the opportunity (where they do not already have the capacity) to receive language training and to receive an easy to understand and practical guide in the form of both print and video, about Britain and its institutions relevant to an understanding of the society they are entering."[115] This reflects the reality that – even after the "citizenship revolution" – immigrants may still not see incentives to naturalize but still require integration as permanent participants in the national polity. For example, in 2005, approximately 160,000 persons obtained citizenship, while 180,000 obtained permanent residence.[116]

There also were political circumstances that began to shift the balance of rhetoric in a more restrictive direction. While immigration played no significant role in the 2001 General Election, it increasingly moved to become a central political issue. After Michael Howard became leader of the Conservatives in 2003, immigration became one of the keys areas where he and the Conservative Party managed to score some points against Tony Blair, forcing, for instance, the Labour government to concede that the UK's asylum system was broken. Immigration then became a key plank of the Conservative Manifesto in 2005, with Blair and others in Labour accusing the Tories of exploiting the immigration issue, in part because they were afraid it was winning them votes. The success of the far-right British National Party (BNP) in the 2002 local council elections also played a key role in raising the profile of migration. Finally, the change in Labour leadership from Tony Blair to Gordon Brown is also significant for tracing a change in tone. Derek McGhee identifies new civic requirements for permanent residence as marking a decisive shift to a different phase in civic attitude, from David Blunkett's "model of civic assimilation" to Gordon Brown's broader "model of civic nationalism with its post-7/7 emphasis on loyalty, duty and responsibility."[117] It is suggested that this nationalist turn by Brown was strategic, to downplay "his own Scottishness, to allay English fears about his suitability to be Prime Minister."[118]

Indeed, the London terrorist attack is the apex of a second phase of British immigration politics, where issues of diversity and citizenship play a far more visible role in political rhetoric and underscored a succession of policy changes to "manage migration" that began with the 2005 Five-Year government strategy, "Controlling Our Borders: Making Migration Work for Britain," which

[115] Home Office, *Secure Borders, Safe Haven: Integration with diversity in modern Britain* (London: HMSO, 2002), 31.
[116] Philip Johnston, "Migrants face new 'Britishness' test," *The Telegraph*, December 5, 2006.
[117] Derek McGhee, "The paths to citizenship: A critical examination of immigration policy in Britain since 2001," *Patterns of Prejudice* 43, no. 1 (2009), 43.
[118] Frank Bechhofer and David McCrone, "Being British: A crisis of identity?," *The Political Quarterly* 78, no. 2 (2007), 251.

extended language and "knowledge of life" requirements for spouses and applicants seeking Indefinite Leave to Remain (i.e., permanent residence).

In 2008, the Green Paper "Path to Citizenship" laid out a radical reimagining of citizenship and its connection to permanent residence. Noting the disparity between acquisition of residence versus citizenship, this proposal set the groundwork for the 2009 Borders, Citizenship and Immigration Act (BCIA) that raised the residency duration from five to eight years and reconceptualized the progression from temporary residence to citizenship, where permanent residence was eliminated as a middle status and reserved only for those whose sending country does not grant dual citizenship. This necessitated an interim stage called "probationary citizenship." One could exit this purgatory stage and get a reduction in residency through "active citizenship," which included participation in "community service," "improving command of English," "working hard and paying taxes," and "obeying the law."[119] The central purpose of this new restriction was a "vehicle for 'increasing public confidence' in immigration policy,"[120] namely the introduction of a managed migration scheme. In this restrictive-hued policy, we see a much stronger and explicit connection between issues of citizenship and immigration than in the initial civic integration legislation of 2002.

This new policy highlights conditions of a contained restriction strategy where a traditionally liberal citizenship orientation can become more restrictive, or in the words of Home Secretary Jacqui Smith, reformed "in order to reinforce our shared values."[121] Bowing to political pressures in a post-7/7 climate and the politicization of integration as a result, Labour leaders reformed the process of citizenship to uphold that "alongside strengthening the rights of citizenship, citizenship must be earned."[122] There is also a keen sense in the Green Paper that a potent mechanism behind the overhaul was awareness of other European practices; chapter 2 of the document is dedicated not only to "the view of the British public" but also to "what other countries are doing."[123]

These new proposals represent the first attempt at restriction, to transform instruments of inclusion into devices of control. In the end, however, the Conservative-led coalition government decided against implementation of these requirements, rejecting them not because public opinion on immigration had changed but because these Labour-led reforms were "too complicated,

[119] Home Office, "The path to citizenship. Next steps in reforming the immigration system," 25.

[120] McGhee, "The paths to citizenship: a critical examination of immigration policy in Britain since 2001," 55.

[121] Home Office, "The path to citizenship. Next steps in reforming the immigration system," 5.

[122] Ibid., 11.

[123] Also see Dora Kostakopoulou, "Matters of control: Integration tests, naturalisation reform and probationary citizenship in the United Kingdom," *Journal of Ethnic and Migration Studies* 36, no. 5 (2010), 834.

bureaucratic and, in the end, ineffective."[124] This highlights two dimensions of abandoned restriction: (1) The Conservatives were only symbolically pressing the immigration issue for electoral gain, abandoning avenues of real restriction once in power; and (2) immigration is a salient political issue and vote-getter, but citizenship is not seen as a meaningful part of this electoral platform. The abandonment of these proposed restrictions is also evidence of a public-oriented majoritarian government being sensitive to opposition before policies even enter politics, i.e., at the stage of planning. For example, in response to the government's 2008 "Path to Citizenship" Green Paper, a majority of respondents opposed the condition of active citizenship as a requirement for the acquisition of permanent residence or British citizenship.[125] The government took this opposition seriously in underscoring the abandonment of probationary and earned citizenship.

Finally, it is worth considering that in the comparative scope of civic requirements, and despite the clearly restrictive tone of these new requirements for permanent residence, there is some evidence to suggest that these additions were not designed to be entirely exclusionary in the first place. As Bernard Ryan points out, this policy was not to restrict access to citizenship *per se*, but to "favour direct progression to British citizenship" as opposed to stopping incorporation at permanent residence.[126] In other words, the requirements to "earn" citizenship may have constituted new restriction, but it did so to promote a decidedly inclusive objective. "Active citizenship" requirements would have added an extra burden to the process of naturalization, but in doing so it would have also lessened the new, considerably restrictive residency period (from 8 to 6 years). In sum, and unlike cases of restrictive retrenchment, requirements did not create an alternative status and impediment to citizenship but rather, in Gordon Brown's words, "enough of a distinction between those who want to reside here temporarily and those who want to become full British citizens."[127] This provides further evidence for the point that not all requirements in the "civic turn" are created equal: additions in restrictive settings can be quite different to additions in liberal ones.

Whereas this first wave of attempted restriction by Labour was ultimately abandoned, a second series of efforts, this time by a new Conservative–Liberal Democrat coalition, would prove to be more successful. Public dissatisfaction with the way Labour handled immigration was "significantly worse than for

[124] Theresa May, "The Home Secretary's immigration speech," November 5, 2010. http://www.homeoffice.gov.uk (accessed February 2, 2014).

[125] Home Office, "The path to citizenship: Next steps in reforming the immigration system: Analysis of consultation responses," (London: Border and Immigration Agency Communications Directorate, 2008), 25–27.

[126] Bernard Ryan, "Integration requirements: A new model in migration law," *Journal of Immigration Asylum and Nationality Law* 22, no. 4 (2008), 289.

[127] Gordon Brown, "Speech on managed migration and marned citizenship," February 20, 2008, http://www.pm.gov.uk (accessed February 21, 2008).

their handling of the economy even in the midst of the financial crisis," so much so that it supported defection from supporting incumbents in the 2010 General Election.[128] Therefore, in this context, the Conservatives needed to assert their credentials and competence in immigration control. And while Liberal Democrats served as junior partners in the coalition, and held drastically different views of immigration, James Hampshire and Tim Bale point out that the Conservatives set the agenda.[129] As such, Bale interprets Conservative strategy as one that "dialed down the rhetoric but pumped up the policy."[130]

As part of an overall goal to reduce immigration to the "tens of thousands" by 2015, the coalition government introduced a series of changes that emphasize language and integration. Perhaps the most consequential of these Conservative-led changes was the introduction of an English language qualification *alongside* the "Life in the UK" knowledge test as a condition for settlement and naturalization. Introduced in the 2011 Consultation, "Family Migration," this new requirement (effective from October 28, 2013) mandates that all applicants hold a speaking and listening qualification in English at the B1 level or higher, thus eliminating the ESOL qualification as an alternative route to fulfilling the "knowledge of life and language" requirement, as well as the one-step improvement below the B1 level.[131] This was a reflection of a type of public skepticism of multiculturalism that gave increasing support for policies that would promote, even compel, integration. This change had a moderate impact on settlement and naturalization – as approximately 20 percent of immigrants used the ESOL qualification to meet the knowledge and language requirement – and even less impact as an immigration policy. On the other hand, it does send a strong signal to a skeptical public that the government is active on the issue of integration. Even the new English language requirement for entry – a policy that can actually limit immigration – was couched in integrationist terms: "everyone coming to this country must be ready to embrace our core value and become a part of their local community."[132] Aside from public opinion, these changes were also made in the context of financial and administrative pressures. For example, in the

[128] Geoffrey Evans and Kat Chzhen, "Explaining voters' defection from Labour over the 2005–10 electoral cycle: Leadership, economics and the rising importance of immigration," *Political Studies* 61 (2013), 142.

[129] James Hampshire and Tim Bale, "New administration, new immigration regime: Do parties matter after all? A UK case study" (paper presented at the Conference of the Council for European Studies, Amsterdam, 2013), 6.

[130] Tim Bale, "More and more restrictive – but not always populist: Explaining variation in the British Conservative Party's stance on immigration and asylum," *Journal of Contemporary European Studies* 21, no. 1 (2013): 32.

[131] Since April 2011, the ESOL route ceased to be available to people who entered the UK on a work visa (e.g., highly skilled, ministers, innovators, artistes, etc.). Home Office, "Knowledge of language and life in the UK for settlement and naturalisation: Statement of Intent, changes to the requirement from October 2013," (London: Crown Copyright, 2013), 3.

[132] Conservative Party, *The Conservative Party Manifesto* (Uckfield, East Sussex: Pureprint Group, 2010), 21.

shadow of the 2015–2016 spending review, Chancellor George Osborne indicated that welfare claimants who do not speak English could have benefits cut if they fail to attend a language course. This change is estimated to affect approximately one million people.[133]

Finally, the Conservative-led government made some important changes to the content of the "Knowledge of Life in the UK" test. When the test was originally adopted in 2005, New Labour intentionally designed the test to avoid history and culture. In fact, policymakers and test writers were deliberate in distinguishing the citizenship test from the so-called "cricket test," in which Conservative politician Norman Tebbit suggested that immigrants who cheer for their native country rather than England in cricket are not sufficiently integrated. After a number of updates, history content was eventually included, but the test became primarily oriented around practical information and facts to enable "active citizenship," as it came to be called. It was this test that the Conservatives replaced in March 2013, excising the existing test of "Labour spin"[134] and installing a new exam that places more emphasis on British history, achievements, and culture, with questions ranging from the number of seats in the Welsh Assembly to famous British films. Education Secretary Michael Gove framed the content change as follows: "if we can develop a better understanding of our past – how *institutions* have evolved and changed – then we'll have a better understanding . . . of how *institutions* can give expression to our shared sense of identity."[135] Mark Harper, Minister for Immigration, provided a decidedly more colorful rationale, noting the new test "strip[s] out mundane information about water meters, how to find train timetables, and using the internet. The new test rightly focuses on values and principles at the heart of being British. Instead of telling people how to claim benefits it encourages participation in British life."[136] Here we see a logic to content that really differs from other states, the Netherlands in particular. Whereas a significant portion of the integration test in the Netherlands is preoccupied with everyday knowledge, the new British test deliberately opted against this kind of content in favor of more history and culture.

In contrast to civic integration policy adoption, these adaptations represent a clear departure from earlier purpose. The initial adoption of the test and ESOL course routes to citizenship, and later to settlement, were clearly designed to promote naturalization, incentivizing citizenship by adding meaning. Later changes, including elimination of the course-route, the addition of an English

[133] "Spending Review: George Osborne targets benefits and slashes public sector jobs." *The* Guardian, June 26, 2013, http://www.theguardian.com/politics/2013/jun/26/george-osborne-spending-review-benefits (accessed October 2, 2013)

[134] Jack Grimston and David Leppard, "God Save the Queen test for migrants," *The Times (UK)*, July 1, 2012 (accessed October 2, 2013).

[135] Varun Uberoi and Tariq Modood, "Inclusive Britishness: A multiculturalist advance," *Political Studies* 61, no. 1 (2012), 34.

[136] Home Office. "New Life in the UK test goes live." https://www.gov.uk/government/news/new-life-in-the-uk-test-goes-live–2. March 25, 2013 (accessed October 2, 2013).

language qualification at a higher level, and revisions to the citizenship test, indicate more conditionality and, as a result, more exclusion. This change in purpose is mirrored in change of rhetoric. For example, Uberoi and Modood look at discourse employed by Conservative Prime Minister David Cameron, who "said in *opposition* that to 'strengthen Britishness' immigrants must learn English' and those now applying to join their partner in the UK 'must demonstrate basic command of English', but in *government* this is not justified by referring to Britishness."[137] One reading of this shift is that while membership promotion and inclusion may be a motivation behind policy adaptation, immigration control and restriction prove to be more rhetorically popular. The growing popularity of the United Kingdom Independence Party (UKIP), which is now as much xenophobic as it is Euroskeptic, has only further impelled major parties to reassert their credentials on immigration.

Interpreting performance data

Turning from policy design to policy outcome, the practice of British civic integration policy maintains an overall liberal citizenship orientation. However, the UK is also liberal in a second sense, as laissez-faire with maximal autonomy for the individual. The pass rate for the "Life in the UK" test for citizenship is low in comparison to other states at 68.6 percent. One interpretation of this pass rate is that it is a significant barrier. However, it also directly raises questions about what a "fair" citizenship test looks like. States have the prerogative to ask immigrants to complete requirements for citizenship, but there is no sense about what a fair or unfair test resembles. The opposite of an easy test with a 99 percent pass rate (e.g., Germany) is not necessarily a hard test where the pass rate is anywhere lower than total inclusion and perfunctory assessment.

In the British design, we see pass rates for citizenship as lower than in other countries, but there is insufficient evidence to support a claim that this is the result of test design and not individual self-assesment. For instance, until October 2013, immigrants seeking permanent residence or citizenship could either complete the "Knowledge of Life in the UK" test (offered at the B1-equivalent level) or attend courses including language and civic content to proceed at their own pace, required only to improve one level, e.g., A1 to A2. In making this choice, immigrants in the UK *self-assessed* their language ability. The Home Office formally collects information on how many applicants for Indefinite Leave to Remain (ILR) met the requirement via the course route versus the KOL test. Table 5.2 presents these numbers. We see a majority of applicants take the test route to settlement: 93 percent (2008), 83.5 percent (2009), and 82.3 percent (2010). And while the Home Office does not formally collect this information for citizenship, "on the one or two occasions [the Home Office] has asked caseworkers to keep a 'five bar gate' type tally of cases passing over their

[137] Uberoi and Modood, "Inclusive Britishness," 34.

TABLE 5.2. *Number of grants of settlement by integration requirement*[138]

	2008	2009	2010
Grant ILR – ESOL course	5,879	16,175	17,607
Grant ILR – KOL test	78,138	81,870	81,688

desks [they] have established that the division is roughly 80% take the test and 20% take a course."[139]

The overwhelming use of the test route as opposed to the course route was presumably because it was less time consuming and cheaper, even if a migrant is not sufficiently prepared (i.e., at the B1 proficiency level). However, the laissez-faire approach toward assessment, where the immigrant self-evaluated their ability to take the test, artificially inflates the fail rate. For example, the inability to read the exam study guide, which is written at the B1 level, will render the immigrant unable to adequately prepare for the KOL test. In fact, the most typical reason for test failure is not confusing content, but lack of language proficiency.[140] Moreover, these figures do not convey how many times a test was taken by a single applicant. The increase in the ESOL course usage over time suggests slight learning effects, that it is both a possible option for fulfilling the language and knowledge requirement as well as a more feasible route for obtaining settlement for those with limited English. Yet, the pass rate of the KOL test for settlement is at 77 percent in 2011, which is higher than citizenship. It is also higher than pass rates of the integration test in Germany among both test participants that take the course (67.6 percent in 2011) and participants who do not (53.8 percent).

The 2013 changes eliminated the course option for both settlement and citizenship. Under new rules, every migrant must obtain B1-level proficiency in English-speaking and listening and pass the KOL test. Migrants are encouraged to take an optional class to improve their English and prepare for the exam, but it no longer counts as a substitute for the exam. This brings the British policy directly in line with the Dutch design, but with a more simplified test. It also seems that while this only affects a small number of applicants, it is not insignificant in terms of principle.

In terms of citizenship, the effects of the KOL test on citizenship acquisition are ultimately low, despite the low pass rate. As Table 5.3 shows, on average only a small percentage (2.7 in 2009) of applicants for citizenship are rejected annually for reasons of insufficient language or knowledge of life in the UK. Acquisition of citizenship actually doubled in the period between 2000 and 2007.[141] This suggests

[138] FOI #20784. December 8, 2011. On file with the author. [139] Ibid.

[140] BBC News, "British Citizenship test: One in three immigrants fails," http://news.bbc.co.uk/2/hi/8707152.stm (accessed January 2, 2012).

[141] Home Office, "*Home Office Statistical Bulletin: British Citizenship Statistics, United Kingdom 2009*," (London: Home Office Statistics, 2010).

TABLE 5.3. *Integration reasons for refusal of British citizenship, 2002–2011*[142]

	2002	2003	2004	2005	2006	2007	2008	2009	2010	2011
Oath not taken in time	70 (1%)	115 (1.3%)	186 (1.5%)	339 (2.3%)	105 (0.7%)	38 (0.3%)	37 (0.4%)	26 (0.3%)	9 (0.1%)	10 (0.15%)
Insufficient knowledge of English and KOL	n/a	n/a	n/a	234 (1.6%)	502 (3.7%)	2,365 (16%)[143]	608 (7%)	267 (2.7%)	382 (5%)	143 (2.2%)
Total refusals	6927	8976	12118	14531	13610	14723	8734	9902	7593	6576

142 Home Office, "Citizenship data tables: Immigration Statistics July to September 2012." Available at https://www.gov.uk (accessed October 2, 2013).

143 There are two, interrelated explanations for this outlier. First, English and KOL requirements were extended to acquiring Indefinite Leave to Remain (permanent residence) on April 2, 2007. Second, fees were raised this year at both stages: citizenship (from £200 to £575) and permanent residence (from £335 to £750). As permanent residence cost more, and the language and KOL requirements were now equal, significant demand for citizenship was generated among otherwise unprepared applicants. Additionally, a third reason that may have caused this aberrant percentage was the introduction of a revised test and handbook. After April 2, 2007, the KOL test was based on different material from the new handbook. Immigrants may not have obtained the new material, and were therefore inadequately prepared for the exam.

that applicants for citizenship are taking the test more than once to meet the requirement, at a price of £50 ($80) each attempt.

Finally, it is interesting to reflect on the number of persons taking the test for citizenship versus settlement in light of the initial goal of civic integration adoption: to promote naturalization. Since the "Life in the UK" test was introduced in November 2005 for citizenship, 741,938 have taken the test. This is in contrast to the 506,706 who have taken it for settlement purposes since the requirement was expanded in April 2007.[144] This is still a significant number of immigrants taking the test to seek permanent residence instead of citizenship. As the requirements are equivalent, this does not suggest that holders of permanent residence will not become citizens, as indefinite leave to remain is not a requirement for citizenship. However, it remains an open question what might impel someone to take further steps for naturalization in light of additional fees and full entitlement at permanent residence to welfare benefits.

CONCLUSION

Over the timeline of civic integration policy in the UK, we witness two distinct but parallel logics. First, there is the prominent and continued emphasis on inclusion and citizenship promotion. This manifests not only in the conditions of policy adoption but also in laissez-faire preparation. Moreover, the UK maintains a fluid, coordinated system where the status of permanent residence is not seen as a solution but instead the source of the problem. Through elite-level idea entrepreneurship in a context where citizenship is de-politicized, integration tests are promoted to establish common values and knowledge that can support cultural diversity, not to subsume multiculturalism. To that end, the UK is a critical case for challenging the "cultural assimilation" hypothesis, where scholars interpret requirements as a type of cultural instrumentalism in which the "ideas of ... citizenship ... are increasingly dependent on a reassertion of the need for cultural homogeneity and the demand for assimilation."[145] As such, Meer and Modood describe these policies not as assimilationist but as representative of a "civic-rebalancing."[146] Moreover, the fact that Labour-designed restrictive policies to create a decisive path from temporary residence to citizenship were ultimately rejected – by a Conservative-led coalition no less – is

144 FOI #20784. December 13, 2011. On file with the author. An additional 10,946 indicated they were taking the KOL for "other" reasons.

145 Claire Alexander, Rosalind Edwards, and Bogusia Temple, "Contesting cultural communities: Language, ethnicity and citizenship in Britain," *Journal of Ethnic and Migration Studies* 33, no. 5 (2007), 785; Patricia White, "Immigrants into citizens," *The Political Quarterly* 79, no. 2 (2008), 221–231; Dora Kostakopoulou, "Thick, thin and thinner patriotisms: Is this all there is?," *Oxford Journal of Legal Studies* 26, no. 1 (2006), 73–106.

146 Meer and Modood, "The multicultural state we're in: Muslims, 'multiculture' and the 'civic re-balancing' of British multiculturalism."

illustrative that costs of policy change are high, endowing citizenship with continued relevance.

On top of this promotion, we witness a second, recent turn toward restriction. This does not diminish the inclusive thrust of promoting common identity and citizenship, but addresses pressures for migration control in a different political context. Where policy was adopted in an insulated, de-politicized environment of general cross-party consensus, policy adaptation has come about in a far more politicized and polarized environment in which integration is no longer tied to debates on citizenship but rather migration control. Moreover, UKIP's rising prominence only exacerbates political polarity. From a comparative perspective, this change could be viewed as a type of regularization, bringing the UK in line with other state practices and possibly even a result of learning effects. However, it also represents unambiguous restriction for immigrants who do not possess English proficiency or who will be challenged in doing so. In the end, it is hard to imagine British identity becoming thinner or "lighter" than what it started with, which was essentially a legal concept of belonging void of membership altogether. Therefore, the questions remain at what point are British policymakers "normalizing" membership by overcoming a content deficit and at what point do these additions amount to exclusion.

Examining Germany and the UK side by side has revealed a number of important observations. Both have undergone a 'civic turn' in translating implicit or inchoate definitions of membership into formally articulated and standardized measured benchmarks. And, by the very nature of requirements being conditional aspects of status acquisition, these membership additions include some and exclude others. On the whole, however, these states have each articulated definitions of state identity for different reasons, under different conditions, and – through differences in design and sequencing – to different effect.

In Germany, we see integration additions achieved through conservative political leveraging, as well as oppositional and state-level politicization. Light and externally provoked changes to preserve restrictive citizenship bookend concentrated changes at permanent residence, in which comprehensive courses and testing became formidable barriers. Moreover, through linkages with benefit utilization and additional conditions between settlement and citizenship (the "chain of conditionality"), integration criteria only elongate time spent obtaining permanent residence and, potentially, preserving dependency. In sum, Germany has interpreted a new and closer role for the state in relation to the immigrant by managing coordination, in which exclusive membership is promoted and preserved through instrument design and settings.

By contrast, the UK introduced a citizenship test for the purposes of increasing naturalization, with the hopes that potential citizens would see the benefits of full membership and not remain permanent residents. In contrast to Germany and other European countries, politicization over immigration inevitably followed political choices not made in defence against Conservative pressure but, rather, by the Labour government itself. Extension of the test to settlement and attempted restrictions through "probationary citizenship" were attempts by Labour to appear "in control" over the issue of immigration, a perennially disappointing source of public frustration. And Conservative-led changes that make the test more difficult (removing the course-based route and changing test content) ultimately pale in comparison to the effects of self-assessment, where misperceptions of ability or preferences for expediency produced low test results. However, because the British approach to civic integration asserts a minimal role for the state in coordinating or facilitating integration directly – prizing and preserving, instead, a laissez-faire approach – it produces outcomes that may resemble those of Germany on the surface.

What is the analytical purchase gained by comparing these two systems? If they both produce varieties of restriction in the end, is it not sufficient to conclude that these are two states that have adopted requirements simply to promote exclusion and limit immigration? No, because as this paired comparison shows, we see different outcomes stemming from different designs, produced out of different causal paths. Germany's approach yields restriction from dense, state-coordinated requirements in which requirements are tied to benefit utilization, while the UK's restriction is produced primarily from errors of self-assessment. This outcome was arguably unintentional, where public and private statements by policymakers explicitly support the interpretation that knowledge and language aimed to promote, not hinder citizenship. But, also, where a liberal integration scheme is consistent with – and not a departure from – other institutional configurations, the "market," and not coordinative efforts and government facilitation, determine outcomes. As such, these cases are marked by significant causal equifinality.

Chapters 4 and 5 illustrated the effects of citizenship orientation on government behavior, contextualizing ideologically informed preferences with parameters of membership to produce both similarities (Chapter 4) and differences (Chapter 5) of policy design. Chapter 6 pushes beyond initial conditions to emphasize it is not merely the presence of certain settings but also how they operate, i.e., causal mechanisms, that determine policy outcome. It makes this case by examining the final paired comparison of the book: the Netherlands and France.

6

Examining interactions and processes: the Netherlands and France

This chapter presents the book's third and final paired comparison. Whereas Chapter 4 illustrated the effects of the legacy of citizenship by observing shared and constrained decisions in the adoption of integration policy by differently oriented governments, and Chapter 5 illustrated the differentiated effects of the context of citizenship on policy evolution under similar, left-oriented but right-influenced governments, this chapter illustrates how even when both conditions – the context of citizenship and the ideology of governments – are similar we can still observe different civic integration outcomes as a result of causal mechanisms. Causal mechanisms characterize the process by which conditions produce outcome. As such, qualitative methodologists maintain that it is not sufficient to identify relevant conditions to account for certain outcomes; strong explanation requires identifying *how* these conditions interact to produce certain outcomes of interest.

The Netherlands and France serve as rich case studies for examining the way in which different causal mechanisms can produce divergent policy, despite similar causal conditions. Beginning with these similarities, both the Netherlands and France have added not only civic integration requirements to permanent residence and citizenship in the context of a liberal *qua* inclusive citizenship, but also vibrant immigration politics where the role of far-right parties is pronounced. They also maintain similar political stories. Left governments introduce mild, non-coercive, and uncontested versions of civic integration policy. Right parties then come to power, in a context conducive to a strong rightist influence, whereby instruments get "repurposed" into mechanisms of exclusion as civic requirements constitute real, decisive barriers to status (particularly permanent residence).

Nevertheless, differences in both design and practice can be observed as a result of *how* these political actors operate in context. In the Netherlands, a policy instrument of integration – crafted by a left-led coalition – quickly becomes an entrenched instrument of immigration control in the context of a broad consensus for restriction and under successive right coalitions that included the far-right. It is arguably the only case study that successfully shifts the initial starting point through incremental reform, establishing new parameters of debate more accepting of policies once considered radical. In France, politicization did not produce consensus, but rather polarization. In the absence of a restrictive consensus, many of the exclusive overtones of membership would be stripped away with the rise of other issues and a change in government. These divergent pathways stem from differences in political institutional design; the Netherlands maintains the archetypal "consociational" democracy, where cooperation is facilitated across cleavages,[1] while France's political structure maintains majority rule by strengthening ideological families. In sum, where institutional layering in the context of consensus yielded a series of entrenched restrictions in the Netherlands, polarized French politics produced policies that are far milder and, as a consequence, more easily changed.

It is interesting to note that it is these two cases that have probably had the most influence in defining the field of civic integration studies, despite the complexity of within-case factors and change in civic integration strategy. Much of this influence has to do with timing, and the fact that these two states were the first adopters. In 1998, the Netherlands was the first country to introduce a law pertaining to obligatory civic integration – the Civic Integration for Newcomers Act (*Wet Inburgering Nieuwkomers;* WIN). This piece of legislation soon became a model for other states. By 1998, France had already implemented voluntary integration platforms for new immigrants to learn the French language and about French society, with language education funded by the state for over a decade previously. Both of these cases also maintained coherent but distinct models of integration – multiculturalism and assimilationism, respectively, which underscores the argument that new requirements represent something as an alternative to existing integration practices.

But while these two cases are central to the study of civic integration, they have also served to shape some of its central problems. These include the assumption that all civic integration policies represent a departure from – instead of a compatibility to or means of repair for – national models. In other words, because we see adoption across cases of otherwise most-different integration models, we are seeing a pattern of policy convergence, where requirements are synonymous with restrictive goals through sanctions. I submit that these assumptions are born from a segmented view of policy change, looking at one snapshot or iteration of policy and not the entire policy strategy over time. This reductive treatment obviates the possibility that different rationales change over time, much less account for degrees of difficulty or differences in design. This chapter aims to illustrate this story. Methodologically, I present a paired-comparison in order to test and ultimately highlight divergent effects of the

[1] Arend Lijphart, *The Politics of Accommodation; Pluralism and democracy in the Netherlands* (Berkeley: University of California Press, 1968).

far-right in liberal citizenship contexts[2], namely that of producing real versus symbolic exclusion in political contexts of consensus versus polarization.

THE NETHERLANDS

Describing the adoption and evolution of civic integration policy in the Netherlands is no small feat. Methodologically, as the primogenitors of civic integration – a phrase derived from the Dutch word *inburgering*, which means to "citizenize" without connoting naturalization – it arguably constitutes a crucial case for hypothesis-testing.[3] Having said that, nuance in both citizenship policy and ideological orientation of government prevents a neat fitting within a 2x2 typology.[4] On ideological orientation, several governments (particularly the second purple coalition under the Wim Kok II cabinet, which was responsible for membership policy adoption) consisted of both left *and* right parties. While these instances can be classified by leadership (in this case, a left-led government), and left–right orientation measures affirm a "left" classification (recall Figure 3.3), the nature of compromise might *a priori* moderate or contain the degree of liberalization or restriction a party can pursue.[5] On citizenship orientation, the extent to which this starting point was entirely liberal to begin with is a matter of debate. As this case has many moving parts, this chapter follows the same format as previous chapters, but it is a little longer to accommodate and sufficiently discuss these many, complex dynamics.

Additionally, perhaps because it is one of the earliest practitioners of immigrant integration in Europe, there is a seemingly insurmountable quantity of research on the matter. To quote Dutch scholar Maarten Vink, "Dutch integration policy has been well documented and one can safely say that, for a medium-sized country, the Netherlands is one of the most over-studied cases in the international

[2] As Sidney Tarrow argues, one of the unique achievements of the paired comparisons is "its ability to compare the impact of a single variable or mechanism on outcomes of interest." Sidney Tarrow, "The strategy of paired comparison: Toward a theory of practice," *Comparative Political Studies* 43, no. 2 (2010), 244.

[3] Cf. John Gerring, "Is there a (viable) crucial-case method?," *Comparative Political Studies* 40, no. 3 (2007), 231–253.

[4] N.B. Chapter 3 highlights this complexity in its discussion of concept identification and measurement and, ultimately, in its presentation of a dynamic alternative to a 2x2 typology. Acknowledging these types of cases is also valuable for the purposes of calibration.

[5] Consistent with Dutch political institutions, coalitions not only reflect but foster additional consensus. Lijphart, *The Politics of Accommodation; Pluralism and democracy in the Netherlands*.

migration literature."[6] These studies range from examining the "retreat" or "backlash" from multiculturalism to assimilation[7] and discourse shifts[8] to details of policy design itself[9] and political party preferences.[10] This industry of analysis is so robust that analytical consensus is hard to come by. Also, there remains an omission in the critical examination and explanation of civic integration policy from adoption to adaptation. In this chapter, I causally examine the evolution of membership policy through three distinct phases: group-oriented multiculturalism (context before adoption), skill-oriented civic integration (adoption), and restrictive-oriented integration today (adaptation).[11] The mid-range perspective taken here, between on-the-ground detail and macro-theorizing, acknowledges and argues that there can be more than one logic behind policy design given extant political circumstances. With this perspective, we observe policy originally adopted under an integration-oriented consensus to promote self-sufficiency and meaningful participation successfully re-purposed under a new, immigration-oriented consensus as an instrument of restriction and control. We also observe how the far-right did not create this second consensus, but successfully accelerated and capitalized on it in a policy environment where center-right (and, to an extent, leftist) parties saw competition over the "foreigner issue" as electorally advantageous.[12]

In primarily conditioning access to entry and permanent residence, civic integration establishes direct linkages between integration and immigration

[6] Maarten P. Vink, "Dutch 'multiculturalism' beyond the pillarisation myth," *Political Studies Review* 5, no. 3 (2007), 337.

[7] See, for example, Stephen Castles and Mark Miller, *The Age of Migration: International population movements in the modern world* (New York, NY: Guilford Press, 2009 [2003]), 275; Han Entzinger, "The rise and fall of multiculturalism: The case of the Netherlands," in *Toward Assimilation and Citizenship: Immigrants in liberal nation-states*, ed. Christian Joppke and Ewa T. Morawska (Houndmills, Basingstoke, Hampshire; New York: Palgrave Macmillan, 2003), 59–86; Christian Joppke, "The retreat of multiculturalism in the liberal state: Theory and policy," *British Journal of Sociology* 55, no. 2 (2004), 237–257; Ellie Vasta, "From ethnic minorities to ethnic majority policy: Multiculturalism and the shift to assimilationism in the Netherlands," *Ethnic and Racial Studies* 30, no. 5 (2007), 713–740; Han Entzinger, "The growing gap between facts and discourse on immigrant integration in the Netherlands," *Identities* (2013), 1–15. For a criticism of these perspectives, see Vink, "Dutch 'multiculturalism' beyond the pillarisation myth."

[8] Peter Scholten and Ronald Holzhacker, "Bonding, bridging and ethnic minorities in the Netherlands: Changing discourses in a changing nation," *Nations and Nationalism* 15, no. 1 (2009), 81–100.

[9] Tineke Strik, Maaike Luiten, and Ricky van Oers, "Country Report the Netherlands," in *The INTEC Project: Integration and naturalisation tests: The new way to European citizenship* (Nijmegen, the Netherlands: Centre for Migration Law, Radboud University, 2010).

[10] Saskia Bonjour, "Governing diversity. Dutch political parties' preferences on the role of the state in civic integration policies," *Citizenship Studies* 17, no. 6/7 (2013), 837–851.

[11] This is consistent with other periodizations and framing of Dutch integration policy over time. See Entzinger, "The growing gap between facts and discourse on immigrant integration in the Netherlands."

[12] Kees van Kersbergen and André Krouwel, "A double-edged sword! The Dutch centre-right and the 'foreigners issue'," *Journal of European Public Policy* 15, no. 3 (2008), 399.

control. Meanwhile, changes produce variegated effects on citizenship. Therefore, while the literature rightly debates the degree with which we can classify the Dutch starting point as liberal or not, we see similar ambiguity in outcome. Citizenship and permanent residence are equalized through the integration test, leaving citizenship as "liberal" as before. At the same time, little incentive is identified for foreigners to pursue citizenship. Is preserving inclusion through lack of use really inclusion? This case offers no clear answers, but even asking the question raises significant democratic concerns. Yet, against the long timeline and many iterations of civic integration content, we see the contemporary integration obligation (in 2013) as still close to its original, neo-liberal objective in emphasizing language and skills of participation, not culture. Restriction and inclusion prove to be two sides of the same coin.

The Netherland's liberal citizenship starting point: A debate

Dutch citizenship policy is a moving picture. Starting in the 1980s, liberalization was part of a larger policy initiative to improve the legal status of ethnic minorities, known as the Minorities' Policy (*minderhedenbeleid)*. The Netherlands established naturalization as a procedure of entitlement, not discretion like most other states, in which naturalization transformed from a grant of the government to a right claimed by an immigrant. A second major change introduced the allowance of dual citizenship in 1992, which produced a direct and dramatic increase in the acquisition of citizenship. However, offsetting these ebbs of liberalization were some major backflows of restriction. Dual citizenship turned out to be an experiment that did not last long as the renunciation requirement was reintroduced in 1997. The original allowance resulted from a compromise between the right–left coalition government of Labour (*Partij van de Arbeid*; PvdA) and Christian Democrats (*Christen-Democratisch Appel*; CDA), the former agreeing that there would be no extension of voting rights for non-nationals beyond the local level (previously established in 1985 for immigrants with five years of residence) in exchange for facilitating more naturalizations by dropping the renunciation requirement.[13] Dual citizenship was also a strategic counterbalance to restrictive immigration policies, especially family and labor migration.

These dynamics and policy trade-offs present a challenge for depicting policy as liberal or restrictive. In most categorizations, the Netherlands is classified as liberal, but only marginally. For example, Howard classifies policy in the 1980s as "medium," as it prohibited dual citizenship but allowed double *jus soli* (where citizenship is automatically obtained by a third-generation immigrant child where one parent is born in the Netherlands), and had a five-year residence

[13] In a classic move, once the CDA moved to a right-wing majority with the VVD in the Senate – they prevented the PvdA-led Kok I Cabinet from codifying dual citizenship. Thus, in 1997 the practice of dual citizenship formally ended.

requirement, which it maintains today. Excluded from Howard's study, but significant to a liberal classification, second-generation immigrants also had access to citizenship through a process of declaration, without further conditions of naturalization or renunciation of other citizenships. By contrast, Howard classifies contemporary citizenship policy on the low end but decidedly over the threshold of "liberal" citizenship countries, as liberalizing change includes *jus soli* after birth for third-generation immigrants born on Dutch soil by option (since 1985) and manifold exemptions to the renunciation requirement.[14] In fact, in 63 percent of all naturalizations applicants are able to retain their citizenship of origin.[15] MIPEX coding for policy in 2010 reveals a similar sort of ambiguity, coding the Netherlands' "access to nationality" score as 66 out of 100. Dual citizenship and eligibility conditions tracks receive scores around 80, but they are "dragged down" by conditions of acquisition (being one of the only countries that does not fully accept *jus soli* for first-generation immigrants) and security of status.[16] These dynamics show where aggregate scores – and even bimodal classification – can be misleading. As a coherent whole, these studies coalesce around an interpretation of Dutch citizenship as exhibiting a starting point (t_o) that is internally moderate but comparatively liberal.

Given this debate over interpretation, it is perhaps not surprising that the very notion of belonging to Dutch national identity is also in dispute and "up for grabs." Dutch identity is defined by a series of contrasts. Rogier van Reekum cites a number of different views on Dutch nationalism, noting a continuum in interpretations between a nationalism that is "weak, thin, procedural and pluralist" to a nationalism that is "strong, thick, cultural and monist."[17] It is – at the same time – ethnically homogeneous and based on deep historical tradition, while it also purposefully cultivates "recognition of public difference."[18] This accommodation stems from both ideological and religious differences over time as well as the heterogeneity that has come to define the modern Netherlands through large-scale migration. Moreover, because of immigration as well as other cultural changes, the Netherlands is described by Frank Lechner as "a nation that has begun to worry again about what it means to be Dutch," in

[14] Exemptions include if a person is born in the Netherlands, for spouses of Dutch citizens, if children are born to parents of different citizenships, and if a naturalizing person's native country does not permit them to renounce their citizenship. See Sara Wallace Goodman, "Naturalisation policies in Europe: Exploring patterns of inclusion and exclusion," in *EUDO Citizenship Comparative Reports* (Florence: EUDO Citizenship, Robert Schuman Centre for Advanced Studies, EUI, 2010), 44.

[15] Ricky van Oers, Betty de Hart, and Kees Groenendijk, "The Netherlands," in *EUDO Citizenship Observatory Country Reports* (Florence: EUDO Citizenship, Robert Schuman Centre for Advanced Studies, EUI, 2013), 19.

[16] Migration Policy Group, "The Migrant Integration Policy Index (Mipex)," (Migration Policy Group & British Council, 2011). http://www.mipex.eu/netherlands (accessed June 18, 2012).

[17] Rogier van Reekum, "As nation, people and public collide: Enacting Dutchness in public discourse," *Nations and Nationalism* 18, no. 4 (2012), 584.

[18] Ibid., 597.

which the "arrival of culturally distinct newcomers" has "complicated the effort to redefine that identity."[19]

Historically, to reconcile diversity within the context of one national identity, the Dutch invoked "pillarization" (*verzuiling*) to structure participation and belonging in the context of deep pluralism. Pillarization enabled religious and ideological differences to thrive by allowing each group to have its own trade unions, schools, newspapers, sports clubs, etc. The basic idea is that political and religious denominations were vertically divided into institutions of self-regulating sovereignty. Designed in the nineteenth century to enable integration of the Netherlands' Catholic minority, pillarization allowed for both the preservation of one's original culture and coexistence in the same society. Unifying this institutional diversity was a top-level of horizontally-connected elites, which would regularly gather in the realm of politics to reach consensus, ameliorate conflict, and make decisions.[20] This elite-level integration was often the only contact between the pillars, as it tended to entrench differences between groups.

Pillarization might have been an ideal institutional pretext for immigrant integration as, like multiculturalism, it allowed individuals to retain elements of their cultural identity while feeling part of a national project. Like other European countries, the Netherlands received a significant number of guest workers into its flourishing labor market in the 1960s and early 1970s, mainly from Turkey and Morocco. And, consistent with the tradition of the "guest worker myth," neither Dutch politicians nor the immigrants of the first generation assumed that they would ever consider permanent residency in the Netherlands and thus never promoted assimilation. Instead, efforts were made to promote the retention of their own cultural traditions and identity. This approach also applied to a majority of post-colonial immigrants, especially Surinamese and Moluccans, who were expected to return home in time.[21] But in tandem with this increase in immigration and diversity, pillarization was suffering its own decline because of increased social mobility and secularization. It was not, therefore, a tool to stimulate the integration of immigrants.

This institutional backdrop locates definitions of Dutch belonging not only in citizenship but also in the unique practice of accommodation. Multiculturalism emerged in the context of the decline of pillarization and the rise of permanent immigrant populations as a new, practical model for incorporating diversity into a shared identity. In this model, van Reekum notes "the recognition of group claims was certainly not meant to preserve or nurture immigrant cultures.

[19] Frank J. Lechner, *The Netherlands: Globalization and National Identity* (New York: Routledge, 2008), 26.

[20] Lijphart, *The Politics of Accommodation: Pluralism and democracy in the Netherlands.*

[21] This is in contrast to postcolonial migrants from Indonesia, who were encouraged to rapidly assimilate as "repatriates," even if they had never lived in the Netherlands.

Group recognition was established as a means of collective integration ... [and] was never a goal itself."[22]

Multiculturalism and beyond: The political context of civic integration policy adoption

In 1979, the Scientific Council for Government Policy (WRR), a government think tank, wrote that "just as minorities and the majority need to respect one another's attitudes, both have to recognize that an optimal participation in society by minorities will necessitate cultural change from both sides."[23] Addressing permanent migrant populations as "ethnic minorities" for the first time, the Minorities Policy was adopted in 1983. This was not a wholesale acknowledgment that they had become a country of immigration (which the government only officially acknowledged in the early 1990s), but rather a recognition that permanent residents faced meaningful, structural problems and these problems could be addressed by targeting specific needs as a minority group.

Characterizing Dutch society as multicultural, the Minorities Policy allowed for immigrants to retain their own culture while improving their social and economic integration into Dutch society.[24] Combating permanent marginalization consisted of welfare-oriented policies and improving an immigrant's legal position, which occurred through a series of anti-discrimination measures and the adoption of a new Dutch Nationality Act in 1985 that established that a strong legal position – i.e., naturalization – enabled integration. Initially though, immigrants were not encouraged to take up Dutch citizenship as it might be perceived as an assault on their individual identity; thus the extension of local voting rights for non-nationals instead of a campaign to change their legal status and, much later, removing the renunciation requirement. For those who decided to obtain citizenship, the Act was also amended to include integration as the first condition for naturalization, which measured a "reasonable knowledge" of Dutch on the basis of an informal interview with a civil servant. Importantly, the implementation of these liberalizing reforms spanned a decade of Christian Democrat-led government, with Ruud Lubbers forming his third cabinet in 1989 with the Labour party.

Just as the Minorities Policy gained momentum it also showed signs of stress as the migrant population continued to grow and diversify, almost doubling in size. By the early 1990s it became a central topic of criticism and public debate. The Scientific Council published another report that unequivocally saw the

[22] Van Reekum, "As nation, people and public collide: Enacting Dutchness in public discourse," 593.

[23] Cited in Peter Scholten and Ronald Holzhacker, "Bonding, bridging and ethnic minorities in the Netherlands: Changing discourses in a changing nation," ibid.15, no. 1 (2009), 89.

[24] Explicitly rejected, however, was the idea that immigrants would "integrate with the retention of identity" ("integratie met behoud van eigen identiteit"), as this was associated with the assumption of return. See Vink, "Dutch 'multiculturalism' Beyond the pillarisation myth," 344.

Minorities Policy as having failed in areas of education and the labor market, particularly given evidence of exacerbated unemployment gaps between native and immigrant populations.[25] It criticized the government's implementation of its previous report, charging they put too much weight on multiculturalism and not enough on participation.[26] Among many recommendations, the Scientific Council proposed to repair this problem through Dutch language training instead of mother-tongue teaching and replacing multiculturalism with integration.[27]

Politically, there was significant polarization over the issue of multiculturalism by this point. In 1991, Frits Bolkestein of the conservative Liberals (*Volkspartij voor Vrijheid en Democratie*; VVD)[28] – the largest opposition party at the time – capitalized on the recent energy produced by the British Rushdie Affair and the Headscarf Affairs in France, challenging multiculturalism by speaking out against the presumed incompatibility between Islam and Western values. By positioning Islam as a threat to liberal democracy, he triggered a public debate that underscored a new public discourse on the problem of immigrant integration. The VVD's success in the 1994 election validated this skepticism of multiculturalism by pointing to a "silent majority" in agreement.[29] As a consequence, the "minorities' policy was rebaptised integration policy."[30] But when the VVD joined in Labour leader Wim Kok's "purple coalition" along with the Social Democrats (*Democraten 66;* D66), a consensus between the left and the right can be observed, in which integration policy shifted from group-oriented accommodation to individual-oriented responsibility.[31] This was the context for the

[25] In 1987, native Dutch workers experienced unemployment of 7.5 percent of the total workforce, while immigrant workers were at 19.5 percent. By 1992, the gap had not diminished (at 5.6 and 16.5 respectively). And, among immigrant workers, we saw further variation. According to 1992 figures, Surinamese workers had lower unemployment (at 18 percent), compared to Turkish (26 percent) and Moroccan (32 percent) workers. Still, all of these categories paled in comparison to native Dutch workers. Ruben Gowricharn, "Integration and social cohesion: The case of the Netherlands," *Journal of Ethnic and Migration Studies* 28, no. 2 (2002), 266.

[26] Entzinger, "The rise and fall of multiculturalism: The case of the Netherlands," 70. The report stated that "the prevailing multicultural policies had treated immigrants too much as 'care categories' and had failed to offer immigrant opportunities to become self supportive." Jeanine Klaver and A. W. M. Odé, *Civic Integration and Modern Citizenship: The Netherlands in perspective* (Groningen: Europa Law Publishing, 2009), 43.

[27] Entzinger, "The rise and fall of multiculturalism: The case of the Netherlands," 70–71.

[28] To clarify, the official name is the People's Party for Freedom and Democracy. They are an economically liberal but socially conservative party on the right.

[29] Entzinger, "The rise and fall of multiculturalism: The case of the Netherlands," 71.

[30] Ibid., 72.

[31] A1994 policy document (*Contourennota)* proposed a move from targeting ethnic minority groups and toward focusing on individuals, specifically on education and skills for the labor market. Academics and government consultants Arie van der Zwan and Han Entzinger developed a set of proposals designed to improve the skills of immigrants entering the labor market, including "to organize mandatory language and social skills training for new arrivals." Ibid., 76. For more, see Arie van der Zwan and Han B. Entzinger, *Beleidsopvolging Minderhedendebat* (Den Haag: Ministerie van Binnenlandse Zaken, 1994).

Newcomers Integration Act (WIN). This consensus also moved the Christian Democrats into opposition for the first time in fifteen years, and created fertile ground for politicization that populists would soon exploit.

The explicit purpose of the Newcomers Integration Act was to "increase the self-sufficiency of newcomers."[32] To do so, it obligated newcomers to participate in a civic integration program so that migrants would "achieve a certain level of capability to live independently, in a social, educational and/or professional sense."[33] Migrants would attend approximately 600 hours of language training, as well as integration courses (*inburgeringsprogramma*) to enable participation in everyday life, mainly orientated toward the labor market. Courses were organized and financially supported by the government and run by local municipalities.[34] Course attendance was compulsory for newcomers and voluntary for "*oudkomers*" (oldcomers – immigrants with long-term residence). As Klaver and Odé describe, the obligation was that a newcomer "has to make an effort to actively participate in the courses," not attain a level of proficiency or pass a test.[35] Finally, knowledge of Dutch was assessed at the beginning and end of the course with the objective that migrants improve proficiency, but there was no set standard. In other words, Dutch language improvement was a goal, not a requirement. This policy was not only the first step toward a formalized integration test for settlement, it was also the model that other European countries looked to as inspiration for their own civic integration programs.

In this design, the emphasis of Dutch integration undergoes a neoliberal shift from the group to the individual, stressing the importance of acquiring socio-economic skills, like language and employment training, rather than catering to cultural or religious concerns of accommodation. Crafted in the context of a left–right consensus, the integration obligation was based on an individual's capacity, where the goal was self-improvement and participation, not acculturation or exclusion (e.g., limiting access to residence). And because the only requirement was participation, there were few sanctions in place for non-compliance.[36] Of course, one of the problems that stemmed from this was the "relatively high drop-out rates and slow progress in language skills,"[37] which merited a policy overhaul that would take on a compulsory character.

At the same time as the WIN was debated and designed, a revision to the Dutch Nationality Act was taking place to supplant the informal interview with

[32] Ministry of Justice (the Netherlands), "Wet Inburgering Nieuwkomers (Newcomers Integration Act)," (The Hague 1998).

[33] Strik, Luiten, and van Oers, "Country Report the Netherlands," 13.

[34] This built off an established institutional structure in which cities were on the forefront of providing integration courses before there was a legal basis for compulsory education by extending reception courses for immigrants receiving a social assistance allowance. Klaver and Odé, *Civic Integration and Modern Citizenship: The Netherlands in perspective*, 44.

[35] Ibid., 62.

[36] The only sanctions were financial, and included potential social cuts or fines.

[37] Klaver and Odé, *Civic Integration and Modern Citizenship: The Netherlands in perspective*, 69.

a naturalization test to assess language and country knowledge. Adding a more rigid language requirement to citizenship was discussed throughout the 1990s, framed not as a mechanism to make citizenship more difficult, but to improve the fairness of the process and make language assessment more "objective."[38] In other words, when the renunciation requirement was removed, the concern for parliamentarians was that the language and integration requirement were not applied uniformly, with some interviews also requiring reading or written comprehension.[39] However, once the door of dual citizenship had been re-closed – the initial opening of which the governing-VVD in particular was always against – language as well as the need for immigrants to integrate into Dutch society became central subjects of discussion. In this debate, the Christian Democrats played a more prominent role as vocal advocates for new requirements, proposing an amendment with support from the VVD to test an applicant's proficiency in the Dutch language, including written ability, and knowledge of Dutch society. The CDA view was that naturalization should represent the "legal and emotional completion of the integration" process.[40] The majority in parliament tipped toward a naturalization test when MPs of D66 – also members of the coalition – came out to support sufficient reading skills as a requirement for citizenship.

Yet while citizenship reform was debated and designed alongside WIN, proposals for change gained traction only after the 1998 election. There are three reasons for this delay. First, soon after the passage of WIN, political pressure was exercised by the CDA and VVD, supported by small Christian parties, to strengthen requirements for naturalization by stressing a "desire to demand written language skills for immigrants who wanted to become Dutch nationals."[41] In essence, WIN exerted a type of upward pressure to promote integration elsewhere, not just for newcomers but also for potential citizens. It especially generated a concern for appropriate expectations, where more is not asked of a newcomer than of a potential citizen in terms of language level and integration. Second, the dual citizenship experience – lasting between 1992 and 1997 – left a sour taste in both the opposition CDA's and the coalition-partner VVD's mouths. As Strik et al. observe, they "did not draw the conclusion that the experiment of not applying the renunciation requirement had been successful, but rather that acquiring Dutch nationality had become 'too easy.'"[42] Finally, while a naturalization test was part of a long-term agenda in which the test design was prepared by the late 1990s, the delay in implementation could also be chalked up to a personal objection by the then Minister of

[38] Kees Groenendijk and Eric Heijs, "Immigration, immigrants and nationality law in the Netherlands, 1945–98," in *Towards a European Nationality: Citizenship, immigration and nationality law in the EU*, ed. Randall Hansen and Patrick Weil (Houndsmills, Basingstoke, Hampshire: Palgrave, 2001), 150.

[39] Strik, Luiten, and van Oers, "Country Report the Netherlands," 69. [40] Ibid., 70.

[41] Ibid., 10. [42] Ibid., 70.

Migration Job Cohen (PvdA). It was suspected that Cohen – who later became mayor of Amsterdam and was referred to as "the integrationist" when he ran as head of Labour in the 2010 general election – was reluctant to push forward restrictive policies that he did not stand behind, like the naturalization test.[43] Each of these factors underlined the late transition to formal language and integration requirements through the naturalization test, which required sufficient knowledge of Dutch society and being able to speak, understand, read and write Dutch at the A2 level. (In 2007, the naturalization test was replaced with the more rigorous, modular integration test for settlement.) Alongside the naturalization test, citizenship ceremonies were introduced to make the moment of acquisition more meaningful.

Both of these reforms – the 1998 WIN and the Revised Dutch Nationality Act of 2003 – were designed by a left–right coalition to promote individual self-sufficiency first and foremost. This enrichment strategy predated the rise and influence of far-right parties in Dutch politics, which were able both to capitalize and to accelerate a shift in consensus from individual-oriented integration to supporting restriction.

Policy adaptation: Repurposing integration requirements for restriction

In contrast to the first phase of membership enrichment, Dutch civic integration policy ever since can be understood by its second, more dominant phase of contained restriction. This primarily includes a transformation of the Newcomers's Integration Act into an Integration Act, introducing comprehensive integration testing for new and old immigrants alongside meaningful sanctions for enforcement. The electoral success of center- and far-right parties, concomitant with a series of high-profile political events, underscored change in consensus that Entzinger labels as moving from an "integrationist" framework to an "assimilationist" framework, or what Ellie Vasta describes more poignantly as a switch from a "minorities policy" to a "majority policy."[44]

A series of events leading up to the 2002 local and general elections proved decisive in fomenting a new consensus behind contained restriction. For a start, it had become apparent that the coalition was facing problems on a variety of issues. Discontent on social and particularly security issues was largely fuelled by the events of 9/11. Second, the coalition parties had underestimated the general

[43] This is not to say that Job Cohen did not support restriction in other migrant-related issues. For example, he developed the Aliens Act of 2000 (Vreemdelingenwet) as a junior minister, which restricted asylum and family migration policies. This is perhaps an indicator that restrictive immigration policies were supported by consensus, unlike restrictions for citizenship. It also suggests there is no philosophical contradiction in promoting integration but supporting the regulation and restriction of immigration.

[44] Entzinger, "The growing gap between facts and discourse on immigrant integration in the Netherlands"; Vasta, "From ethnic minorities to ethnic majority policy: Multiculturalism and the shift to assimilationism in the Netherlands."

dissatisfaction with immigration and multiculturalism. Dutch sociologist Paul Scheffer wrote a controversial article in the *NRC Handelsblad* called "the multicultural drama" (*Het multiculturele drama)*, in which he observed that policies of multiculturalism and a culture prizing diversity did not transform a growing gap between natives and foreign-born into a cohesive society but, instead, produced an ethnic underclass that was both unwilling and unable to integrate. He opined for Dutch elites to give up their "cosmopolitan disillusion" and promote language, culture, and history among ethnic minorities.[45] As a prominent member of the Labour party, Scheffer's scathing critique of Dutch integration was not decried as racist or conservative, but this was also indicative that Dutch politics had entered a new era of discourse, where even liberals became openly critical of degrees of tolerance, successes of multiculturalism, and, above all, the influx of immigrants. In essence, Scheffer legitimized a new, cross-party discourse criticizing integration. Add to this that there were some persistent problems with the Newcomers Integration Act. Only two years after the adoption of WIN, van Boxtel led an integration task force that looked at the issue of reducing wait time on Dutch language classes for immigrants. The task force proposed a number of policies that included introducing an integration test as well as financial and legal consequences for not passing.

It was in this context that the populist politician Pim Fortuyn managed to turn dissatisfaction to his political advantage. Campaigning as a conservative under an eponymously named party, Fortuyn warned that as a result of "our disinterest in our own identity and in the essence of our society, our original culture is in danger of perishing."[46] To that end, he described the Netherlands as a "full country" and called for closed borders, not to mention famously calling Islam a "backward" religion. The populist ideas of Fortuyn matched perfectly with the public debate about the multicultural society that had intensified since Scheffer's essay. On May 6, 2002, Fortuyn was assassinated by an animal rights activist. He quickly became a martyr for the cause of Dutch identity and immigration control. In the parliamentary election 9 days later, his party won 17 percent of the votes (26 seats out of 150), while the Christian Democrats became the largest party with 27.9 percent (43 seats). With this, the second purple coalition lost their majority and a new rightist coalition consisting of the CDA, VVD, and Lijst Pim Fortuyn (LPF) members came to power under Jan Peter Balkenende. The LPF secured a cabinet post in their most meaningful issue portfolio – Integration and Immigration – as well as place security issues, immigration control (particularly in reference to asylum seekers and family formation), and stricter, compulsory integration at the center of political debates.

Yet while the far-right became an electoral force to be reckoned with after 2002, a more accurate assessment of their impact could be to say they accelerated and capitalized on existing events and predispositions toward restriction.

[45] Paul Scheffer, *Immigrant Nations* (Cambridge, UK; Malden, MA: Polity, 2011), 325.

[46] Lechner, *The Netherlands: Globalization and national identity*, 67.

One would be hard-pressed to find a policy reform of the Balkenende government – or even later of Mark Rutte's government (2010 onward) – that was not already on the "wish list" of the CDA and VVD, respectively (and often of the PvdA and D66, as the left were part of the consensus). On the left, van Boxtel had already proposed the aforementioned changes in January 2002. On the right, the CDA, having been stuck in opposition for eight years, immediately seized upon the anti-immigrant momentum to push forward an agenda of "re-establishing the norms and values of society."[47] In fact, in Sjordje van Heerden et al.'s examination of party manifestos, the CDA coverage doubles in "the percentage of sentences dedicated to [immigration] issues between 1994 and 1998," while "the increase in salience of the immigration issue in the programmes of most other parties was less spectacular, but still observable."[48] As for the VVD, their position in manifestos in 2002 is "noteworthy since it is almost identical to that of the LPF."[49] When the CDA and VVD government reformed with D66 after the Balkenende I cabinet collapsed (lasting only 87 days, owing to internal arguments and power-struggles in the LPF), for example, it maintained in the new, Balkenende II coalition agreement that "anyone who wants to permanently settle in our country must be active participants in society, consider Dutch language your own, and be aware of and comply with Dutch values and norms."[50] Thus, we see how these preferences not only outlasted but existed before the far-right capitalized on them. This does not diminish the degree to which far-right politicization impacted this discourse. In 2004, eager to mark a radical turning point in its integration policies, the government presented its plans for a new law on civic integration.

The new Civic Integration Act was the embodiment of "new style integration policy" (*integratiebeleid nieuwe stijl*). Conceptually, it formally shifted integration as primarily concerned with autonomy and self-responsibility to a concept connected to regulation and immigration policy.[51] This is visible not only in the policy adopted, where sanctions for failure to integrate include

[47] Van Kersbergen and Krouwel, "A double-edged sword! The Dutch centre-right and the 'foreigners issue'," 405.

[48] Sjoerdje van Heerden et al., "The immigration and integration debate in the Netherlands: Discursive and programmatic reactions to the rise of anti-immigration parties," *Journal of Ethnic and Migration Studies* 40, no. 1 (2014): 127.

[49] Ibid.: 14.

[50] This language is similar to that of the Balkenende I Cabinet Outline Agreement, in which "any person who wishes to settle permanently in the Netherlands must actively take part in society, learn Dutch, be aware of Dutch values and abide by the rules." Ministry of Justice (the Netherlands), "*The Civic Integration Abroad Act: Information package*," (Den Haag, 2006).

[51] This was made explicit in the corresponding government position paper: "According to the government, immigration and integration are inextricably bound up with each other. It is unthinkable that sustainable results in the field of integration can be achieved if immigration is not regulated. And vice versa, immigration is not well regulated if the necessary conditions for integration of newcomers are not taken into consideration. Therefore the government will link

rejection of temporary (entry) or permanent (settlement) residence, but also in the institutional shift of the integration portfolio itself, from the Ministry of the Interior to the Ministry of Justice.[52] The central change of the Act was in replacing a course participation requirement with an integration exam.[53] This test was comprised of two parts. The first is a practical exam in which immigrants produce a portfolio of evidence of integration skills (e.g., locating a doctor, looking for work, contacting the municipality, etc.) or participate in a simulation (i.e., role-playing) of practical situations demonstrating language skills in an integrated context. The second part is a centralized exam that consists of three components: (1) a speaking exam (*Toets gesproken Nederlands*, TGN), which assesses oral Dutch skills; (2) an electronic practical exam (*Elektronisch praktijkexamen*, EPE), where a test-taker demonstrates language comprehension in different everyday situations, such as how to read a gas or electric bill, or fill out an application for a mobile phone; and, (3) a "Knowledge of Dutch Society" test (*Kennis van de Nederlandse Samenleving*, KNS), which poses questions to the candidate to assess their knowledge of Dutch society, values, and norms of behavior. The KNS covers such specific areas as employment and income, norms and values, living, healthcare, history and geography, institutions, the legal system, and raising children. Newcomers must demonstrate Dutch proficiency at the A2 level, while oldcomers (newly required to "integrate" under the 2007 Act) are required to meet the A1 level. In this scheme, courses were still available and even modified to accommodate an immigrant's specific integration needs, focusing on: education, health, and child-raising; labor; social participation for people who neither work nor raise children; and entrepreneurship for the self-employed.[54] However, they were voluntary; an immigrant could elect to do the integration course as a means of preparation for integration, but participation was not mandatory. In this design, we see the dual objectives of promoting restriction but also retaining an emphasis on skills and participation. The two goals were layered and overlapping, not mutually exclusive. And through applying legal sanctions for noncompliance, namely denial of a permanent residence permit, financial penalties, and potential

immigration to integration demands by means of civic integration." Klaver and Odé, *Civic Integration and Modern Citizenship: The Netherlands in perspective*, 59.

52 In 2002, the management of integration moved from the Big Cities division of the Ministry of Interior Affairs, a department largely focused on municipality function to the Ministry of Justice, which oversees immigration and citizenship, and placed under a newly created Minster for Immigration & Integration.

53 Applicants were able to earn exemption from the integration exam by obtaining a diploma, such as passing the "Dutch as a second language" exam (NT2). This exemption also applies to the new 2013 integration test.

54 The social participation and entrepreneurship tracks were not offered until July 1, 2009. Significant, "Evaluation report integration in the Netherlands (*Evaluatierapport Inburgering in Nederland*)," (Barneveld, the Netherlands: Significant, 2010), 126.

withholding of social benefits, the obligation to participate was replaced by an obligation to pass the exam.[55]

A final change was in shifting economic responsibility for integration exclusively into the migrant's hands. All of this was part of a renewed emphasis on individual autonomy and personal responsibility. Migrants now self-prepare for the exam, identifying whether courses are relevant and necessary as well as funding this preparation.[56] But while the municipality was formerly responsible for both providing and funding integration courses, under the new scheme it only directly oversaw and subsidized integration for certain categories of migrants (e.g., unemployed, refugees).

In an unambiguous sign of the new consensus, the 2007 Civic Integration Act (WI) passed with 149 "yes" votes in a parliament of 150 seats.[57] With an upcoming election, no party wanted to be seen as "multiculturalist" and vote against it.[58] Left-wing parties were concerned about the financial burden on the immigrant, and that civic integration courses are offered to everyone and not only targeted groups, but in principle there were no objections to the introduction of language and society knowledge measures. As Saskia Bonjour points out, "the most contentious issue in Dutch political debates about civic integration is not the role of the state in cultural matters, but the role of the state in economic distribution."[59] In other words, politicians did not debate the content or merit of civic integration, but whether the state or the market vis-à-vis commercial providers would be responsible for organizing civic integration.

With that, the integration exam became a condition for obtaining permanent residence, and since the test was at the same language level as the naturalization test, the latter has replaced the former. And while permanent residence is a condition for citizenship, as one of the conditions for naturalization is that there are no objections against indefinite residence in the country, they were equalized as membership statuses. Completing the test for residence exempts an immigrant from completing the test for citizenship, thereby linking the two statuses in terms of integration. In sum, it requires newcomers to meet the

55 Kees Groenendijk would disagree with the nuanced interpretation of integration as a series of overlapping goals. In a harsh indictment of sanctions, he concludes that "language and knowledge tests are no longer an instrument of training (establishing the level the immigrant has acquired). They became an instrument of immigration control and a condition for more secure residence status." Kees Groenendijk, "From assisting to requiring integration: Selective citizenship policies in the Netherlands," in *Naturalisation: A Passport for the Better Integration of Immigrants?*, ed. OECD (Paris: OECD Publishing, 2011), 338.

56 Loans from the government were made available so immigrants could afford more comprehensive preparatory courses, and there is remuneration for a portion of the costs of integration if an immigrant completes the obligation within a certain time frame.

57 The one "no" vote came from Koser Kaya, a Turkish-born member of the Liberal party D66. In the Senate, D66, Greens, and the Socialist party all voted no.

58 Interview with author. April 1, 2009. Den Haag, NL: Ministry of Justice.

59 Bonjour, "Governing diversity. Dutch political parties' preferences on the role of the state in civic integration policies," 12.

same expectations and standards of ability as naturalizing citizens. There are, of course, other requirements that keep these statuses distinct (such as fees and a citizenship ceremony), but in terms of integration they are equal. If anything, it makes the acquisition of an already liberal citizenship that much more within reach, compared to Austria or Denmark, as requirements do not alter a migrant's timeline.

Throughout this period of incremental restriction, in which residence became significantly more conditional, the left did not express significant opposition to change, as indicated by their total support in the Integration Act vote. A second sign of consensus is that when the 2006 elections forced a change in the government, the Labour and Christian Union parties joined the Christian Democrats in the Balkenende IV cabinet. The flexibility in coalition-forming, where a left and a right party frequently join together, prizes ideological accommodation and mitigates against polarization. With this reformation, some of the potent populist fervor of the early decade began to die down. First, the integration portfolio was moved again, from the Ministry of Justice to the formerly titled Ministry of Housing, Spatial Planning and the Environment. Summarily, the minister in charge also changed hands, from the hardline Rita Verdonk (VVD) to Ella Vogelaar of the Labour party. This new institutional housing and leadership of civic integration suggests it is – once again – part of an integral approach to improving immigrant neighborhoods.

Indeed, perhaps the biggest predictor for the direction and tone of membership policy in the Netherlands is found by looking not at who governs but at who is invited to join the coalition. Other "softening" reforms came when the left joined the right again in government, namely in the form of the 2007 Deltaplan. While the Civic Integration Act passed with an overwhelming majority in parliament, it was a complicated law with a lot of problems. The Deltaplan aimed at improving the quality of language courses, simplifying the legislation, and improving on what was observed to be flagging integration rates. The new plan brought participation back as a central theme: "Integration and participation are inextricably linked: integration promotes involvement and the integration program has a greater chance of success if the participant participates. This is a refinement of the vision of integration ... achieving the desired goal [of integration] does not stop at achieving the (compulsory) integration exam." The Deltaplan also shifted the financial burden back to the municipality, which can ask for different contribution levels from an individual migrant, including free provision. Strik et al. point out that the fee from the migrant usually pertains to instances of re-examination.[60] By paying for integration courses for all those with an integration obligation (and not merely those who do so voluntarily), municipalities significantly lifted the individual financial pressure of course fees, which are estimated to cost around €5,300.[61]

[60] Strik, Luiten, and van Oers, "Country Report the Netherlands," 49.

[61] van Oers, de Hart, and Groenendijk, "The Netherlands," 27.

And, true to form, just as softening measures were achieved during a period of a "populist low tide," a resurgence by a new face would impel another reverse wave of reform. Geert Wilders, of the Freedom Party (*Partij voor de Vrijheid*, PVV) gained popularity through an unambiguously anti-Islamic agenda, advocating a substantial reduction in family migration and a burqa ban, raising the level of the integration abroad exam, etc. Both the PVV and the VVD began to suggest that the immigrant bear all the costs of integration and language courses, as well a new sanction – the withdrawal of a temporary residence permit – for not passing the integration exam within a specific period of time.[62] By 2010, Wilders' party had achieved 15.5 percent of the total vote, resulting in a 15 seat gain in parliament (increasing their seat holding to 24). While they did not formally join the government by receiving cabinet seats under Rutte (VVD), they provided voting support for the VVD–CDA minority government. The early dissolution of this cabinet in 2012 by the Freedom Party's exit over budget issues limited the extent of Wilders' restrictive reach, but many amendments to the Civic Integration Act – submitted in November 2011 and in force from January 2013 – maintain and reinforce the overall restrictive tone of Dutch civic integration. This moved the financial obligation back to the migrant, with limited state assistance ("soft loans"), the need to pass a new test within three years upon penalty of residence permit revocation, and a restructured integration exam. Gone is the emphasis on practical skills through both the electronic practical exam and the decentralized exam of the portfolio and/or simulation exercise (as of January 2015), and in its place there is a greater comprehensive emphasis on Dutch language, wherein the central exam now assesses reading, listening, and writing skills along with continued assessment of speaking skills (TGN) and knowledge of Dutch society (KNS). While these exams assess language skill through materials on work, education, and daily life, they are unequivocally more rigorous for the migrant with limited education and experience in taking exams. On the other hand, the migrant will be able to complete the entire integration exam in one day and the cost has been significantly reduced. The new standardized exam (as of August 2013) costs €250, while the practical components of the former decentralized test alone ranged in price from €104 to as high as €1200.[63]

In sum, we see predictable vacillation between restriction and softening measures, and there is nothing to suggest that these policies are immune to future politicization and potential change. Membership policies in the Netherlands prove to be effective political instruments. On the one hand, they are consistently used to leverage restriction where coalition-preservation and popular opinion

[62] Groenendijk, "From Assisting to Requiring Integration: Selective Citizenship Policies in the Netherlands," 338.

[63] J. Stouten and M. Bring, "Doorstroom Praktijkexamen Inburgering," (Amsterdam: Regioplan, 2010), 16.

demand it. On the other hand, they are also among the first policies softened when a left-oriented government resumes power or enters government. In aggregate, it is hard to make an overall assessment of the impact of policies that are so often changed. However, it would seem that over time, contained restriction has incrementally produced what now stands as a dense web of conditionality through a process of layering. These policies are likely to be eased with a change in government, but not eradicated. This cumulative effect has moved the parameters of membership discourse and inched the moderately liberal orientation of the Netherlands (already a contested concept) closer than ever to restriction.

Implementation: Variegated outcomes of practice

To what extent is this shift in tone – from enrichment to conditionality – reflected in practice? It is too early to examine the effect of the 2013 changes, but beginning with the naturalization test – before it was replaced with the integration exam in 2007 – we see that testing itself naturally creates a barrier. As van Oers et al. note, "Prior to the formalisation of the [language and integration requirement], only 1–2 percent of all applicants were turned down because of insufficient integration."[64] After the test was introduced, approximately 60 percent of those who registered eventually completed it.[65] And in examining a breakdown of the pass rates based on nationality, we see that some groups were more disadvantaged than others (see Table 6.1). Turkish and Moroccan immigrants, especially, have the highest rates of registration for citizenship but among the lowest pass rates. For these groups, the test can be viewed as a significant deterrent to applying for citizenship. However, a number of citizenship applicants were actually exempt from the naturalization to begin with. Around 85 percent of all applicants for naturalization were exempt on the

TABLE 6.1. *Pass rates percentages for Dutch naturalization exam by nationality, 2003–2007 average*[66]

Nationality	Pass Rate (in percent)
Chinese	71
Afghan	63
Iraqi	59
Moroccan	56
Turkish	52
Somali	51
Unknown	40

[64] van Oers, de Hart, and Groenendijk, "The Netherlands," 33.
[65] Strik, Luiten, and van Oers, "Country Report the Netherlands," 78. [66] Ibid., 80.

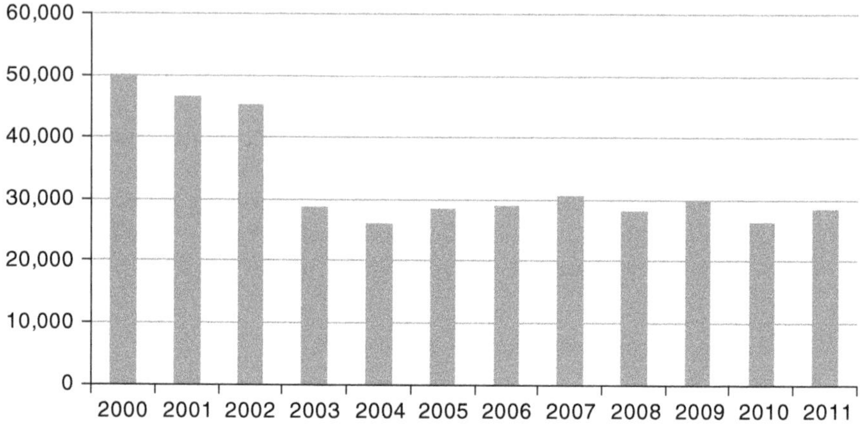

6.1 Acquisition of citizenship in the Netherlands, 2000–2011[67]

basis of a diploma, indicating that their education was primarily received in the Netherlands.[68] While this left only a small proportion of the potential citizenship population who were required to take the test, for this group the test had more drastic consequences. In sum, the test produced variegated results.

In looking at the pattern of citizenship acquisition in the past decade (Figure 6.1), we see a steady decline occurring after the introduction of the naturalization test in 2003. From that point, naturalization rates level off on average. This translates to a significant change in which the percentage of eligible foreigners obtaining citizenship was cut in half (7.7 percent of the foreign population was obtaining citizenship in 2000, compared to 3.8 percent in 2011). This change cannot be entirely explained by civic integration; new income requirements, conditions of continuous residence, and fees also significantly affect naturalization. However, it does show the immediate impact of the threat of civic integration assessment on citizenship acquisition, with a precipitous drop from 2003 onward.

The replacement of the naturalization test with the integration exam has introduced more rigor, but not more restriction for citizenship. A similar drop-off to 2003 is not evident; instead we see consistent rates of acquisition. This is primarily because the integration test is now for both permanent residence and citizenship. And since permanent residence is a condition for citizenship,[69] the test gets completed at this earlier stage. Moreover, additional non-integration barriers between residence and citizenship (for example, the cost of obtaining

[67] OECD, *International Migration Outlook: SOPEMI 2013*. [68] Ibid., 75.
[69] Not formally, but an applicant for citizenship must be compliant with all the requirements for permanent residence.

TABLE 6.2. *Full integration exam results, Jan–July 2012*

	Total participants	Successful	Success Rate (%)
Municipality-facilitated	14,595	9,341	64
Without facilitation	876	699	80
Others	667	538	81
Total	16,139	10,578	66

permanent residence is €150 to naturalization's €810) and negligible differences in terms of benefits and identity may lead even fewer to citizenship in the end.

Therefore, looking at the effects of the integration test for permanent residence offers a more precise vision of its total effect. We see the integration test as a barrier for a significant number of immigrants, namely those who choose to do the municipality-facilitated course in order to complete the integration obligation and test. Table 6.2 shows test results for the first half of 2012.[70] While the overall *average* pass rate for the integration exam is 66 percent (a slight decrease from the first half of 2011, at 70 percent), this figure obfuscates the asymmetry between test-takers who complete facilitated integration (at 64 percent) and applicants that do not (at 80 percent). Moreover, we see that an overwhelming number of applicants take the test through the municipality provision, where the proportion of participants in this exam group constitutes 90 percent of total test-takers.[71]

While one interpretation of this result suggests wholesale restriction, we also need to look at these figures within context. First, pass rates are suspected to naturally decrease over time not because the test becomes more difficult but, as Strik, Luiten, and van Oers observe, more motivated candidates take the exam earlier on, whereas less-motivated candidates will have lower levels of education and require more training.[72] For example, when the test was first implemented, the pass rate for first-time test-takers was 85 percent.[73] Second, while restrictive, the standards set by the integration exam represent a clear improvement upon the previous requirement of course participation. Under the old scheme, as Klaver and Odé point out, "the majority of newcomers and [voluntary] oldcomers who finished their integration course in 2006 did not achieve a language level sufficient to become socially self-reliant" – the overall objective of civic integration.[74] Finally, in looking more closely at the different modules of the integration exam in Table 6.3, the most difficult portions are

[70] Dutch Government (August 2012)."Integration newsletter" (Nieuwsbrief Inburgering), vol. 45, no. 28, p. 3 Available at https://abonneren.rijksoverheid.nl (accessed September 20, 2013).

[71] Ibid.: 4. [72] In Strik, Luiten, and van Oers, "Country Report the Netherlands," 56.

[73] Significant, "Evaluation report integration in the Netherlands (*Evaluatierapport Inburgering in Nederland*)," 129.

[74] Klaver and Odé, *Civic Integration and Modern Citizenship: The Netherlands in perspective*, 70.

TABLE 6.3. *Pass rates for integration exam components, 2007–2009*[75]

Part of test	Pass rate at first exam	Pass rate at last exam (cumulative)	Average exams taken before pass
Practical exam	72	83	1.15
Electronic practical exam (EPE)	69	77	1.14
Knowledge of society (KNS)	88	91	1.04
Test on spoken Dutch (TGN)	81	85	1.06

the practical tests – both the decentralized portfolio assignment and the electronic practical exam. The removal of these two sections in the 2013 changes to the Civic Integration Law portend an increase in pass rate over time, where the pass rates for remaining knowledge and language portions remain high. It remains an open question as to what sort of effect raising the language level for naturalization (from A2 to B1), as the 2013 government has favored, will have on pass rates.

In the end, the integration exam is certainly a new formidable barrier to the population of family-based and unskilled migrants that the government seeks to limit. It may even be successful in doing so by reverting personal responsibility of paying for integration courses back to the individual, a necessary means of preparation for the integration exam for the majority of test-takers. However, for a large percentage of test-takers, it seems to be rigorous but not restrictive. Thus, wholesale condemnation of the exam as difficult and unfair is misplaced.[76] Indeed, we see stratification in outcome that prioritizes certain migrant groups over others. The outcomes of policy are therefore an apt reflection of design, pairing integration with migration control.

[75] Significant, "Evaluation report integration in the Netherlands (Evaluatierapport Inburgering in Nederland)," 131.

[76] See, for example, Ricky van Oers, *Deserving Citizenship: Citizenship tests in Germany, the Netherlands and the United Kingdom* (Martinus Nijhoff Publishers, 2013). Van Oers focuses, in particular, on the discriminatory nature of the exam on "weaker" groups, including the illiterate, applicants over the age of 65, and "dark numbers" of persons who do not even take the exam for fear of failure or prohibitive costs. While the exclusion of the former two is certainly concerning, it does not render the test unfair as a whole. I maintain that van Oers' critique misses the point. It is not merely about integration – where status begets inclusion – but about *civic* integration, in which work begets status, which begets inclusion. The key is earned status and, as such, there has to be an arbitrary but fair bar of difficulty where some migrants are included and others are excluded.

Conclusion

This detailed, longitudinal examination of the changing paradigms of integration policy in the Netherlands reveals the direct and moderating effect of civic integration requirements on a liberal citizenship context as a result of a restrictive-oriented consensus and incremental policy layering over time. Before the early 2000s, integration requirements for citizenship and permanent residence were minimally restrictive and primarily oriented to improving autonomy and the socioeconomic and legal statuses of ethnic minorities. In the context of a liberal citizenship orientation, these integration requirements serviced inclusive ends by enabling a migrant's political and social incorporation. However, in a new political context where political parties are reshaped around an anti-immigrant discourse, we see conclusive alteration to membership requirements where old instruments were repurposed to new, restrictive ends. Difficult barriers and decisive sanctions transformed the integration obligation into an instrument of immigration control and restriction and, therefore, a formidable barrier to legal incorporation. This adds some true restrictive coloring to the Netherlands' already-contested liberal starting point.

However, one should not go so far as to interpret incremental, contained restriction as a wholesale overhauling of citizenship. Crucially, the process of change occurred through layering, where integration goals were placed on top of individual participation goals. Each restriction moved the parameters of acceptable change to a new median, and consistent with Dutch political institutional design, this incremental reorientation was produced in the context of numerous cross-party consensuses. In sum, the parameters for change today are slightly more toward exclusion than fifteen years ago. But also crucial is that policy was made through layering, not replacement. Therefore, we still see the elements of individual participation and enablement from initial policy adoption. Policy adaptation, however, has made it significantly more conditional.

FRANCE

Where the Netherlands presented a challenge to analyze because of ambiguity in independent variables, France is a challenge because of ambiguity in outcome. France receives a CIVIX score of five, placing it on the low-end of civic integration practicing countries and directly in the middle in the sample of Western Europe. In this view, it remains only a step or two away from Austria and the UK. That said, no comparative qualitative analysis of the French civic integration program would conclude it is close in either intensity or design. France "ticks all the boxes" in terms of requiring civic education, language assessment, and value commitments, but CIVIX scoring rules do not account for subvariation in requirements, such as the length of coursework, and thus overestimates difficulty in this instance.[77] There is also significant difference in France between policy design and practice. The restrictive tone of policy is quite loud, but its application is much softer.

This ambiguity in membership policy is not surprising. France is the only country to start the civic integration process with a consolidated definition of state identity already in place, inclusive in principle if not in practice. In other words, French citizenship – by definition – is based on values ("*Liberté, égalité, fraternité*") that already reflect a logic of togetherness. The principle of assimilation has long been a cornerstone to promote this identity. Since 1927, skills (i.e., language) and values of Republicanism have been formal requirements for citizenship. As France is widely touted as Europe's first country of immigration, the recognition that assimilation in naturalization can produce equality of membership positions France as distinct from other liberal citizenship case studies examined here, in which membership is characterized by either dense religious diversity (the Netherlands) or nothing at all (the UK). Any revisions to this sacrosanct concept might appear an admission of failure.

Moreover, where there have been changes to citizenship, they have largely been symbolic, coming much later in the order of reform, almost as an afterthought. In the French case, we see civic integration serve as an extension – and not a replacement – of assimilation, updating Republicanism for a new generation. As a result, and because of the embedded nature of membership-making in France, civic integration policies are nearly exclusively targeted at non-citizens as an immigration policy. Language and value commitments have been primarily unfurled at the stages of temporary and permanent residence through the introduction of a "welcome and integration contract" (*contrat d'accueil et d'intégration*; CAI), henceforth the integration contract. These contracts are service-oriented, in which evaluation and sanctions are considerably milder than the practices of other European counterparts.

In accounting for this policy configuration, we see a number of similarities to the Netherlands. First, policies initially adopted to promote enrichment and participation get adapted into instruments of restriction. Second, far-right parties play a significant role in reshaping major party positions through politicization and agenda-setting. Third, there is a broad consensus among centrist parties, built in the shadow of a dominant and growing far-right presence over immigrant-related issues. This legitimizes a narrower rhetoric for discussing diversity and immigration. Finally, there are also numerous flashpoints, from the Headscarf Affairs of 1989 and 1993 to the riots in suburbs of Paris among

[77] For example, a one-day civic education course in France is scored equal to Germany's 30 units. CIVIX uses dichotomous rules for courses in tests, where the presence of a requirement is scored as "1" and its absence as "0." France is the exception rather than the rule in terms of policy design. Adding weights for course length would drive other country scores up and create a greater distance between scores with France, but this information is not available in all cases (e.g., language) to be a practical scoring rule.

French youth of African and Maghrebi origin, which all bring the question of identity and membership to the fore of public debate, and have supported successive government reforms to make immigration and settlement more restrictive.

While both countries experience far-right politicization in the context of a broad, restriction-oriented consensus and political events that raise the saliency of the immigration issue, we also see some crucial differences emerge from this paired comparison. First, while the far-right National Front was an effective agenda-setter, politicization occurred exclusively through electoral competition, not active lobbying, vote blocking, petition campaigns, or participation in legislative planning. This necessarily makes the impact more ephemeral. Second, the effect of politicization of the far-right in France was polarization, in which a governing consensus endured not merely because of this agenda but because of the weakness of the left. This is unlike in the Netherlands and its accommodationist institutions. Thus, when a new left government came back to power, it was simpler to unravel restrictive and undesirable elements of policy. Therefore, we can observe distinct changes in membership strategy that correspond to changes in government: mild enrichment during cohabitation, followed by contained restriction under successive rightist governments, and culminating with recent liberalization (i.e., reversal of restriction) with the return of a leftist government.

As a result, France is an example of a milder restrictive membership strategy. As it stands, new requirements primarily target the status of long-term residence, adding restrictions to make family reunification and settlement more difficult. Settlement becomes a process of integration, while full membership remains reserved and, in principle, accessible only through citizenship. As such, the practice of new requirements reveals a more complex reality where rhetoric and output is harsh but practice and outcome are subdued. In this final difference with the Netherlands, we therefore see increased conditionality but not the same intensity of restriction.

A community of citizens

Alongside Germany, no other European case has been as scrutinized as France when it comes to examining the origins, meaning, and significance of citizenship.[78] Uniting all of these studies, however, are two observations: (1) in spite of more restrictive periods in history, France has one of the most liberal citizenship

[78] For only a sample, see Rogers Brubaker, *Citizenship and Nationhood in France and Germany* (Cambridge, MA: Harvard University Press, 1992); Adrian Favell, *Philosophies of Integration: Immigration and the idea of citizenship in France and Britain* (New York: St. Martin's Press in association with the Centre for Research in Ethnic Relations, University of Warwick, 1998); Miriam Feldblum, *Reconstructing Citizenship: The politics of nationality reform and immigration in contemporary France* (Albany: State University of New York Press, 1999); Riva Kastoryano, *Negotiating Identities: States and immigrants in France and Germany*

policies today, with a comparatively low residency duration, acquisition via double *jus soli*, toleration of dual citizenship, generous socialization-based policies for resident minors, and expansive rights of justification and appeal; and (2) the formal designation of citizenship is constitutive to defining the concept of membership in the French Republic.

France differs from other liberal citizenship orientation states namely because an inclusive citizenship is defined and supported by a well-articulated concept of state belonging, a type of coherence and continuity across generations more common to ethnocultural societies. Here France represents an outlier to the dichotomy of national and state identity, as in France they are one and the same. Forged from its revolutionary experience and the philosophy of the Enlightenment, republicanism maintains the idea that a national political community is supported by a citizen-based identity, instead of ethnic, sectarian or other variations. Each citizen is directly engaged in a relationship with the state, and citizens are equal to one another in the public sphere as a "community of citizens."[79] This public equality obviates the need for group identity politics, much less religious or racial cleavages. Belonging to the nation means belonging as a *citizen*, defined by rights and obligations, and not as an *individual*, which carries personalistic connotations and interests. This civic identity is universalistic, where – in principle – anyone willing to commit to the values of the community can join. It is also assimilationist, where one must forgo other notions of political fidelity or identity (including the role of particularism or privatized identity in the public sphere) if they are in conflict with the political unity and values of France's national political community.

Finally, belonging is elective and volitional. Like Ernst Renan's concept of the (French) nation as a "daily plebiscite," one must choose to take on the values and become a member of the political community. In fact, according to Adrian Favell, "the 'autonomy' to choose and become one's French nationality," thus recognizing republican values as superseding pre-existing ones, is "the first precondition to the possibility of integration, since it is only through this act of individual *volonté* that the moral requirements of political and social integration can become possible."[80] Through this choice and the adherence to republican values, in Sergio Carrera's words, "the non-national becomes the juridical being incarnated in the status of French citizen."[81]

(Princeton: Princeton University Press, 2002); Dominique Schnapper, *Community of Citizens: On the modern idea of nationality* (New Brunswick, NJ: Transaction Publishers, 1998); Charles Tilly, "The emergence of citizenship in France and elsewhere," in *Citizenship, Identity and Social History*, ed. Charles Tilly (Cambridge: Cambridge University Press, 1996), 223–236; Patrick Weil and Catherine Porter, *How to be French: Nationality in the making since 1789* (Durham: Duke University Press, 2008).

79 Schnapper, *Community of Citizens: On the modern idea of nationality*.

80 Favell, *Philosophies of Integration: Immigration and the idea of citizenship in France and Britain*, 69.

81 Sergio Carrera, *In Search of the Perfect Citizen? The intersection between integration, immigration and nationality in the EU* (Leiden; Boston: Martinus Nijhoff, 2009), 300.

The goal of immigrant integration fits quite cleanly into this framework of inclusive, formal membership. In fact, immigration was not seen as a sensitive matter until the 1980s – conceived primarily beforehand as an economic/labor issue – because integration was a natural part of the process of *becoming* French.[82] Yet, when politicized (as we see in the 1980s by a growing far-right National Front), immigration starts to challenge the simultaneity of republican values, namely assimilation, nationalism, and the public/private divide.[83] Specifically, as Christophe Bertossi and Abellali Hajjat point out, French citizenship for outsiders highlights the "tension between colour-blind principles of inclusiveness – an inclusiveness which ought not to take account of different origins, in particular ethnic origins – and a culturalised conception of French integration."[84] In other words, despite a civic ideology that forces the elimination of difference from the public sphere through socialization and assimilation, there also appears to be a strong, underlying sense of national identity that draws on a more cultural or even ethnic identity.[85]

The republican tradition is institutionally maintained through a formal assimilation requirement for citizenship, in addition to the institutional separation of the public and the private (*laïcité*). For decades, the original formulation of this condition required "assimilation into the French community, in particular a sufficient knowledge, upon his condition, of the French language, history, culture and society." Today, after a series of changes concurrent to the "civic turn," the requirement has expanded beyond linguistic assimilation to include not only knowledge of "rights and duties conferred by French nationality" (since 2003) but also "adherence to the principles and essential values of the Republic" (since 2011). This clause of the Civil Code articulates broad goals for the applicant, though they are not measured with any systematization. Unlike language, which since 2012 requires an applicant to acquire a language diploma at the B1 level,

[82] For more on this process, see Gérard Noiriel, *The French Melting Pot: Immigration, citizenship, and national identity* (Minneapolis: University of Minnesota Press, 1996); Eugen Weber, *Peasants into Frenchmen: The modernization of rural France, 1870–1914* (Stanford, CA: Stanford University Press, 1976).

[83] Daniel Brunstetter, "Rousseau and the tensions of France's Contrat d'Accueil et d'Integration," *Journal of Political Ideologies* 17, no. 1 (2012), 109.

[84] Christophe Bertossi and Abdellali Hajjat, "France," in *EUDO Citizenship Observatory Country Reports* (Florence: EUDO Citizenship, Robert Schuman Centre for Advanced Studies, EUI, 2013), 6.

[85] Carrera provides a Foucauldian reading here: "Any identity(ies) diverging from 'the canon' or the 'perfect citizenry' are considered to be a deviation in need of correction, discipline and naturalization. They are treated as a threat to the nation, which is 'one', of the foundations of universalism, unitarism, secularism and homogeneity, and which is legitimised to practice a series of corrective actions against any fragmentation from its sacral wholeness." His is a type of essentialist view of French membership, divergent from an ethnic concept of nationhood only in its lack of being organic. Sergio Carrera, "Nationality, immigration and 'the Republican Integration' in France: Normativisation, expansionism and externalisation," in *Illiberal Liberal States: Immigration, citizenship and integration in the EU* ed. Elspeth Guild, Kees Groenendijk, and Sergio Carrera (Farnham, Surrey; Burlington, VT: Ashgate, 2009), 316–17.

thus replacing the informal assessment by a civil servant,[86] cultural assimilation and value adherence continue to be measured through an interview by a civil servant at a local prefecture. An immigrant must also sign a Charter of Rights after the interview, committing to an adherence of "the principles, values and essential symbols of the French Republic."[87] Though subjective and highly discretionary, these imprecise objectives do not constitute a significant barrier to acquisition for the average applicant.

Politicization and resolution of citizenship before the adoption of civic integration

While a liberal citizenship context defines the parameters for debating membership, the issue of citizenship itself was not particularly controversial at the time of civic integration policy adoption. Citizenship emerged as a major political issue in the 1980s and Miriam Feldblum describes it as a "reconstruction" of a "new nationalist citizenship" through: (1) changes in immigration; (2) an increasingly central role of the National Front in raising issue saliency and thus creating competition for the center-right; and (3) restrictive citizenship change that shifted a general discourse about membership from one focusing on a "right of difference" to the reintroduction of republican *qua* assimilationist themes and values.[88] I will briefly examine these three factors as they are integral to establishing the context for the adoption of civic integration policy.

Particularly notable about the impact of immigration in the early 1980s is not the influx of new migrants *per se*, but the policies that enabled a growing number of immigrants to become citizens. The effect of "increasingly strict laws on temporary stays and return visits to home countries gave long-term residents the incentive to become French, secure the right to travel as much as possible, and improve their position in an economic marketplace increasingly marked by recession."[89] A second inclusive policy was that of double *jus soli*, which allowed children born in France to French-born non-nationals to gain French citizenship. These young people – mainly Muslims from Algeria and the Maghreb – were portrayed as inassimilable, especially by the National Front,[90] who referred to them as "French without being aware of it or wanting it"

86 Completion of a language course as part of the integration contract at the B1 level is sufficient to meet this requirement. Abdellali Hajjat, "Naturalisation procedures for immigrants: France," in *EUDO Citizenship Observatory Naturalisation Procedures Reports* (Florence: EUDO Citizenship, Robert Schuman Centre for Advanced Studies, EUI, 2013), 3.

87 This is part of the interview and does not constitute a separate obligation equivalent to an oath or ceremony. Since 2006, a citizenship ceremony has also been offered. However, this occurs after the acquisition of citizenship and is not obligatory. Bertossi and Hajjat, "France," 32.

88 Feldblum, *Reconstructing Citizenship: The politics of nationality reform and immigration in contemporary France.*

89 Bertossi and Hajjat, "France," 13.

90 Noiriel, *The French Melting Pot : Immigration, Citizenship, and National Identity.*

("*Français sans le savoir et sans le vouloir*") and as "*Français de papier.*" Through this rhetoric and in criticizing easy access to citizenship through *jus soli*, they successfully maneuvered to the center-stage of politics. Naturalization rates support this perception of accessibility and incentivization for citizenship, as a significant amount of immigrants became citizens – from 2.7 percent of the total foreign population in 1991 to 4.5 percent in 1999.[91]

Second, the popularization of criticism against automatic citizenship – typified by the slogan "*Etre Français, ça se mérite*" – not only strengthened the National Front, it also created heated competition with the largest center-right party, Rally for the Republic (*Rassemblement pour la République*, RRF). As the numbers of French citizens with non-European origins increased under the left-wing presidency of François Mitterrand, both the center and the far-right had ammunition to attack citizenship. And while the far-right were certainly the most vocal entrepreneurs of new restriction, Howard notes that "Not to be outdone, and in an attempt to prevent the division of the political right into two camps that would help to ensure a long-term Socialist majority, the center-right quickly moved to capitalize on this hot-button topic.[92] One such early move included the Pasqua Law of 1986, stewarded by the then-Prime Minister Jacques Chirac, which aimed to eliminate the automaticity of French acquisition by adding an act of willingness and formal request at the age of 16. The National Front pushed for further restrictions, including knowledge of French and a loyalty oath, but this was rejected for being too exclusionary, as "highlighted by public protests and government impediments in the bill passage."[93] In contrast to the Netherlands in 2002, where far-right rhetoric echoed consensus sentiments, here the far-right speaks from the margins. The fact that these proposals would later be seen not as exclusionary but as broadly desirable by a spectrum of political parties is indicative of both a discourse shift in integration and a new norm of citizenship.[94] Despite differences among major parties, none supported the degree of restriction that the far-right supported at the time, a reflection of the parameters defined by national citizenship understandings.

With the failure of a number of restrictive proposals, Chirac (now President), not wanting to be seen as giving in to the left and in order to maintain competition with the far-right, set up both a Nationality Commission, chaired by Marceau Long (vice-president of the *Conseil d'État*) and a High Council on

[91] OECD, *International Migration Outlook: SOPEMI 2003* (Paris: OECD Publishing).

[92] Marc Morjé Howard, *The Politics of Citizenship in Europe* (Cambridge: Cambridge University Press, 2009), 151–52.

[93] Carrera, *In Search of the Perfect Citizen? The intersection between integration, immigration and nationality in the EU*, 310.

[94] As Feldblum notes, "Despite the lack of an actual restrictive reform, the discourse and public practices of the new nationalist citizenship were already shaping French politics." Feldblum, *Reconstructing Citizenship: The politics of nationality reform and immigration in contemporary France*, 144.

Integration (*Haut Conseil à l'intégration*; HCI), which clarifies integration needs for a legal framework. Both of these institutions offered proposals that would become the basis for citizenship restrictions in 1993, abolishing the category of automatic acquisition at the age of majority and creating a more discretionary naturalization to include an expression of will ("*manifester leur volunte de devenir francais*").

Third, and finally, by invoking republican philosophy alongside new restriction, the National Front would over the next decade set not only a tone for new restriction but also a new discourse on integration, transitioning from a "right of difference" ("*droit à la différence*") to what Rogers Brubaker describes as a "return of assimilation."[95] Favell regards Le Pen's "turning of the issues to his advantage" as skillful and monumental in terms of altering the debate on citizenship. He notes how in Jean Marie Le Pen's hands, the "*droit à la difference*" was interpreted not as an innocuous nod of diversity but "as the bottom line of Muslim claims in France, and taken to mean: '*différence*' = 'not one of us', and therefore not truly French." Furthermore, "by emphasizing their diverse cultural or religious background, and blurring the lines between new immigrants with full citizenship and those still foreign or illegal residents, the crudely identified *immigrés* were all thereby said to enjoy overly easy and unproblematic access to social rights and welfare. This was then argued to have debased the institution of French citizenship."[96] This sort of shift was legitimized and echoed in work by the HCI as well, which in a 1991 report specified that the "French conception of integration must obey a *logic of equality and not a logic of minorities*."[97] Moreover, it galvanized the base of what Brunstetter describes as "*la République du centre*" (the Republican center), a consensus between the left and the right that "established republican integration as the immigration model in France" in direct response to the nationalist and culturally exclusive tone of the far-right.[98]

Many of the 1993 restrictions would eventually be stripped away by the 1998 liberalizing reforms under cohabitation, where a newly elected Socialist government led by Lionel Jospin offset a conservative presidency held by Chirac. While both of the citizenship policy changes "attracted strong parliamentary and intragovernmental critique from the opposition, they did not suscitate much visible outcry" in that they were "coupled with the partisan politics of re-election and with more divisible immigration bills, which sustained much of the attention."[99] Therefore, perhaps the most enduring accomplishment of two decades

[95] Rogers Brubaker, "Return of assimilation? Changing perspectives on immigration and its sequels in France, Germany, and the United States," *Ethnic and Racial Studies* 24, no. 4 (2001), 531–548.

[96] Favell, *Philosophies of Integration: Immigration and the idea of citizenship in France and Britain*, 53–54.

[97] Feldblum, *Reconstructing Citizenship: The politics of nationality reform and immigration in contemporary France*, 144.

[98] In Brunstetter, "Rousseau and the tensions of France's Contrat d'Accueil et d'Integration," 110.

[99] Feldblum, *Reconstructing Citizenship: The politics of nationality reform and immigration in contemporary France*, 147.

of citizenship reform was in fusing the immigration–integration policy nexus, around which future elections would pivot. As Bertossi and Hajjat describe, the "re-politicisation of citizenship ... was no longer about the entry of diversity through French nationality, but about perceived cultural and religious deviance among groups who were already formal members of the 'national community of citizens.'"[100] For citizenship to remain inclusive and accessible, as it underwent no significant reforms after 1998, there needed to be a concurrent process of committing to French values. In this context, we see the adoption of civic integration.

As in the Dutch case, civic integration in France started as a voluntary scheme. According to Patrick Weil, the motivation behind suggesting the integration contract was the cessation of funding for the Association for the Rights of Foreigners (*L'association pour le droit des étrangers; ADDE)*, which provided language courses to immigrants. As a member of the HCI, Weil explains that as it "was the last year of my term [on the HCI], I decided to focus on that issue. If [immigrants] did not speak the language, they did not play a role. Their children who learned the language would play the role of administration for parents, and cannot focus on work or child things. They shouldn't do what adults should do."[101] Language acquisition was a voluntary scheme and, according to Weil, there was no debate about making it compulsory at this time.

By 1998, introductory platforms *(plate-forme d'accueil)* had been set up, which included voluntary half-day instructions on life in France for family and other migrants. This civic instruction would take place right after immigration, and therefore was offered in several languages to suit the needs of new immigrants. In other words, it was not civic education in the context of French learning, but a functional opportunity to learn rules and culture for everyday living. As such, classes were organized around country-of-origin. It would be only a short period of time before these instruments were "re-purposed" into devices of migration control.

Policy adaption: From voluntary to mandatory contracts

Obligatory measures, an emphasis on values, and the extension of civic integration requirements to spouses shortly followed a change in government. After contentious campaigning in the 2002 presidential election, Jean-Marie Le Pen unexpectedly received the second-most votes in the first round, placing him above the Socialist candidate Lionel Jospin and moving him to the second ballot run-off election against Chirac. The embarrassing knock-out of Jospin indicated not only the importance of immigration to the public but the weaknesses of

[100] Bertossi and Hajjat, "France," 28.
[101] Patrick Weil. Interview with the author. July 16, 2007. Paris, France.

the existing government on this issue[102], exacerbated by Jospin's strategic error of moving the party to the already-crowded political center on issues like social policy and immigration and away from the social democratic core voter.[103] This move reflected a tacit consensus that, in Virginie Guiraudon's description, "privileges the restriction function of immigration policy" and in which "France's political left and right appear to have agreed not to disagree."[104] In the second round, Chirac received a landslide 82 per cent of the vote, but Le Pen's second-place finish was the spark that lit the tinder of a new decade of immigration politics, preoccupied not only with control but also, and especially, with integration.

Chirac's party – reformed in late 2002 as the Union for a Popular Movement (*Union pour un Mouvement Populaire*, UMP) – moved substantially to the right on issues of immigration, attempting to restrict both intake and access to citizenship. As such, the far-right's greatest achievement from this election was in reshaping the center, pushing the UMP to the right in a preservationist strategy to prevent vote-drift and gain legitimacy as the party of migrant control. In contrast to the Netherlands, this politicization of immigration produced polarization, not consensus. This new center proved conducive to passing a series of reforms that can be described as contained restriction. In sum, the election not only signaled the reinvigoration and normalization of value debates but also the expansion of membership values from its traditional status (citizenship) into the policy field of immigration.

This broader scope for integration was concretized in the Sarkozy Law of 2003 (nicknamed after then-Minister of the Interior, Nicolas Sarkozy), which introduced the integration contract. Immigrants were invited to sign the contract, which made the granting of a legal permanent residence and the 10-year residence card conditional on "knowledge of the French language and of the principles that constitute the French Republic" *("l'intégration républicaine")*. At the time, it was still a voluntary contract, creating an obligation only if a migrant chooses to sign it. To fulfill the language component of the contract, immigrants are required to take a basic exam comprised of writing and oral assessment. If an immigrant does not demonstrate adequate French, the state provides free language courses in which attendance is required (thus the incentive for signing the contract). The course culminates with a second evaluation exam. Immigrants are

102 Jospin and Chirac, having governed in a period of cohabitation, were seen as indistinguishable and shared the blame for government frustrations. Dissatisfaction inevitably turned into electoral support for anti-state parties on both the left and the right. See Alistair Cole, "A strange affair: The 2002 presidential and parliamentary elections in France," *Government and Opposition* 37, no. 3 (2002), 317–342.

103 Michael Laver, Kenneth Benoit, and Nicolas Sauger, "Policy competition in the 2002 French legislative and presidential elections," *European Journal of Political Research* 45, no. 4 (2006), 685.

104 Virginie Guiraudon, *Immigration Policy in France* (Brookings Institution Center on the United States and France, 2001), 3.

not required to reach a specified level above introductory (CEFR A1.1), which is the lowest threshold of any European country.

To fulfill the values component of the contract, an immigrant must attend a day course on civic education, covering subjects that range from national history to the role of France in Europe. As Brunstetter describes, "The purpose of the civic education class is not just to teach immigrants, but to signal to those who seek to reside in France what French identity is (and what it is not)."[105] Immigrants partake in a half-day orientation, part of which is dedicated to watching a PowerPoint presentation titled "Civic Education" (*formation civique*). The content of this initial presentation is dedicated to the values, rights, and duties of French citizenship, with lengthy sections on symbols, principles, and institutions of the Republic. There are also sections on the Rights of Man, rules for accessing citizenship, the role of France in Europe, and the integration contract. Obtaining information on everyday needs and the functioning of public services is available in an optional, secondary training class lasting between one and six hours. Both of these courses are organized and paid for by the state. This is directly in contrast to the nature of civic education in the Netherlands, which is both preoccupied with practical information and individual functionality and requires individual financial contributions. Aside from attendance, further integration measures are not specified. The contract is considered fulfilled when an immigrant can present a certificate of attendance and a *Diplôme Initial de Langue Française* test. In order to reach the A1.1 level, an immigrant may have to attend language training. There is no formal assessment of country knowledge, an otherwise major feature of most civic integration policies. Non-compliance with the terms of the contract could lead to negative sanctions that include withholding of a permanent residence permit or the inability to renew a short-term residence permit.

In the strictest sense, the contract not only binds an immigrant to attend civic training, follow language classes as prescribed, and go to any interviews that may be set for monitoring the contract, it also binds the state to an obligation of providing services to ensure the contract be fulfilled. These, according to the language of the contract, include an "individual meeting with a social assessor for social and language diagnosis," "language assessment (if required)," "civic training," "language training," "specific information on access to the public employment service and to professional training," as well as "monitoring and assessment of experiences and problems encountered (training, housing, schools, health)."[106]

While the contract and its components appear mild, even innocuous, the reason it is classified as a type of contained restriction and control mechanism becomes evident by looking at the user. The clear target population of this program is family migration, as Sarkozy states: "What we want is to oblige

[105] Brunstetter, "Rousseau and the tensions of France's Contrat d'Accueil et d'Integration," 119.
[106] Contrat d'Accueil et d'Intégration. Available at www.ofii.fr (accessed September 24, 2013).

someone who wants to be joined by a close family member (from abroad), which is generally his wife, to permit her to learn French and insert herself into our society."[107] But while the integration contract in the 2003 law was voluntary and therefore insignificant as a deterrent, there were other aspects of the law that were more impactful for limiting settlement, including extending the minimum waiting period for receiving permanent residence from three to five years. It also re-establishes a two-year wait period for spousal acquisition of citizenship, previously eliminated in the 1998 reforms, as well as encourages the prefecture to assess language as well as investigate if the couple have lived together as a married couple.[108]

To summarize, the new integration contract was transposed from a voluntary scheme to a formal but voluntary obligation with the 2003 Sarkozy law, extending republican values to non-citizens by targeting permanent residence. The 2003 law did not stir much public debate. Restrictive elements of the law were directed not toward citizenship but migration – a relatively uncontested area for control. It instrumentalized the sacrosanct symbol of the social contract to promote integration and values to outsiders. And while new language was included to citizenship policy that required "sufficient knowledge of right and duties," this signified little real change to the practice of assessing assimilation for citizenship.

The 2003 law formalized the integration contract while maintaining the voluntary color of the 1998 introductory platforms, but additional policy and secondary legislation in the context of an unambiguously xenoskeptic political environment transformed this instrument into its current, obligatory incarnation. A 2005 circular extended the contract from 12 practicing départements to the whole of France. And with the second Sarkzoy Law of 2006 (in force in 2007), the contract became mandatory for non-EU immigrants wishing to settle or renew residence permits, including spouses of French citizens and specifically targeting so-called "marriages of convenience." The contract operates in much the same way as the voluntary one. Language is evaluated through a multiple-choice exam, as well as through oral and written proficiency. If the immigrant does not meet a certain level of adequacy, they are required to attend free French language classes (at a maximum of 400 units) and undergo assessment upon completion. Migrants are also required to take civic training and attend an information session, both free of charge, in which attendance – not participation – is required. To meet the "professional integration" requirement, immigrants can have a skills assessment. Immigrants have one year to complete the contract conditions, and failure to comply can lead to a denial of a permit.[109]

107 Christian Joppke, "Transformation of immigrant integration: Civic integration and antidiscrimination in the Netherlands, France, and Germany," *World Politics* 59, no. 2 (2007), 253.

108 Bertossi and Hajjat, "France," 17.

109 The INTEC synthesis report indicates instead that there are "indeterminate consequences for entitlement to long-term residence or renewal of temporary residence," presumably because the consequences are formal but have rarely been applied. As the authors note, "It is not clear how

The explanatory memorandum details that the contract was to ensure, as is clearly stated in the Entry and Residence Code, foreign nationals arriving in France "assimilate into French society." Assimilation is defined as "good mastery of the French language," "good knowledge of the institutions and values of the French republic," "good knowledge about daily life in France," and "good professional integration." This emphasis on assimilation was framed not as a departure from existing tropes of belonging, but as a way to reaffirm them, particularly in light of France's neighbors. In the Stasi Commission report, a committee charged with examining the practice of laïcité, the French integration project is drawn in direct contrast to the Dutch, which followed "the path of communitarianism pushed to the extreme [...]; the strength of our French cultural identity can favor the melting pot of integration."[110] Patrick Simon defines "communitarianism" as closely akin to the idea of British or American multiculturalism in that it sees cultural separatism as "the inevitable outcome of group recognition and the promotion of cultural differences." This, Simon argues, is "perceived as the opposite of the French model of integration. It is seen to conflict with Republican values and national cohesion."[111]

Despite the rhetorical strength of the contract and its emphasis on obligation, there are a number of dimensions that mitigate against its restrictive bent. No fines or consequences for social benefits are levied for non-compliance. There are also several exempt categories in addition to EU and EEA migrants, including applicants for temporary or seasonal work, and foreign nationals who have had three years of secondary education in a French *lycée*. In sum and by way of contrast to the arduous integration schemes of some other states, the French contract is comparatively service-oriented with soft sanctions.

Despite the context of the center-right political consensus, political actors on the left as well as human rights groups and NGOs opposed the move from voluntary to compulsory contracts, particularly the introduction of integration conditions. The Socialist-led opposition objected to the "'non-equilibrated' character of this 'forced contract.'"[112] However, there was little public outcry. Contentious elements of the contract targeting immigrant settlement were no doubt obfuscated by the strategic linking of integration to larger, more

much weight they attach to the fulfillment of the welcoming contract in deciding on applications for permanent permits ... [but] There appear to have been no cases where immigrants were refused a renewal of their temporary permit on this ground." Tineke Strik et al., "Synthesis report," in *The INTEC Project: Integration and naturalisation tests: The new way to European citizenship* (Nijmegen, the Netherlands: Centre for Migration Law, Radboud University, 2010), 55–56.

110 Bernard Stasi, "Rapport au President de la Republique. Rapport de la Commission de Reflexion sur l'Application du Principe de Laïcité dans la Republique," (Paris: La Documentation française, 2003), 35.

111 Patrick Simon, "French national identity and integration: Who belongs to the national community?," (Washington, DC: Migration Policy Institute, 2012), 14.

112 Christian Joppke, "Beyond national models: Civic integration policies for immigrants in Western Europe," *West European Politics* 30, no. 1 (2007), 12.

controversial immigration issues, such as the question of DNA testing for family reunification or the collection of statistics on ethnicity.

The cachet gained by Sarkozy in pushing forward a succession of unambiguously restrictive immigration policies underscored his successful presidential bid in the 2007 election. It also created a political mandate for restriction, including: the launching of a national debate on "What it means to be French?"; a new, controversially-titled ministry to institutionalize the linkages between immigration and integration called the Ministry of Immigration, National Identity, Integration and Co-Development;[113] and a rhetorically striking distinction between "*immigration subie*" (suffered; i.e., family migrants) and "*immigration choisie*" (chosen; i.e., highly skilled migrants). Immigration and concomitant integration policies flowed directly from this distinction. In addition to promoting civic integration abroad (see Chapter 7), the government strived to limit family migration by creating a "reception and integration contract for the family" (*Contrat d'accueil et d'intégration pour la famille*; CAIF). This adaptation signified that there is not only an individual obligation to integrate but also "rights and duties of parents in France" (e.g., schooling, conveying values of equality, etc.). It carries similar penalties to the individual contract. And to encourage skilled migration, the second Sarkozy Law created a new "Skills and Talents Card" (*Carte Compétences & Talents*) for highly skilled migrants who would make a "significant or lasting contribution, through your skills or talents, to France's economic development."[114] These persons are exempt from signing the integration contract. In the short term, one of the clearest objectives of the "immigration choisie" policy was establishing integration as a pre-condition for residence permits to limit certain intake categories (generally, family-based migrant, which in 2008 constituted approximately 44 percent of the intake[115]). Only in the long run does this have an effect on citizenship, as residents eventually qualify for naturalization. By promoting integration in the context of a debate over immigration, Sarkozy was able to skim off supporters from and stave off desertion to the National Front. Notably, citizenship remained untouched in this series of changes.

The integration contract in France was a deliberate push to promote assimilation at an earlier, non-citizen stage. Facilitating attachment to values and knowledge of language before citizenship, even if required at the lowest proficiency level, distinguishes residence (both temporary and permanent) not as a transitional status but as a potentially stable alternative. Furthermore, adding assimilation to residence – particularly in the French case – conceptually expands

113 Around the same time, the process of citizenship decisions also moved from the Ministry of Social Affairs to this new institutional home. In 2010, it would move again to the Ministry of Interior.

114 http://www.consulfrance-washington.org/spip.php?article519 (accessed May 30, 2012)

115 OECD, *International Migration Outlook: SOPEMI 2011*, 281. (2011), Work migration accounted for 12 percent; humanitarian 6 percent; free movement 30.4 percent, and others 7.2 percent.

the political community outside of citizenship status. This potential dilution of citizenship's special status underscores some of the recent – and comparatively belated – changes to citizenship. Evaluation has become more objective but not necessarily more restrictive. Primarily, linguistic assessment now takes place by the applicant obtaining a language diploma. Specifically, an applicant must demonstrate oral and written comprehension of French at the B1 level. But attempts to replace the assimilation assessment interview with a citizenship test were unsuccessful.[116] Moreover, these changes have not been controversial. In contrast to the public debates around the 1993 restriction and 1998 liberalization, modifications to citizenship have not been contested because "the law of 2003 [for immigrants] has aspects that are much more restrictive."[117] Restriction at earlier barriers has both deflected attention from citizenship – where "NGOs, left wing activists or political parties" have directed their attention[118] – and also created a type of internal pressure to equalize expectations of integration for citizens to that of immigrants. Finally, the Socialist government under Françoise Hollande has committed to a number of citizenship changes, rolling back some restrictions made under Sarkozy in order to make naturalization easier, such as standardizing the review processing across regions.[119] This, of course, reflects the same positions as before the politicization of citizenship that began almost three decades ago. Restrictive changes to immigration policy and not citizenship between 2002 and 2012 show the impact of starting points *a fortiori*. In the end, the expectations of citizenship have not changed, in contrast to those of immigration, which have been significantly colored by the contract as part of a mild, but unambiguous strategy of contained restriction.

A mismatch between policy and practice

Turning to implementation, policymakers employ forceful language to articulate their goal of counterbalancing immigration with assimilation conditions, but neither the design nor the practice appear to be onerous, either on their own merits or in comparison to other states. In terms of design, recall that all information sessions and French language classes are free and paid for by the state. The level of assessed language is the lowest in Europe, and the civic education and information session lasts only one day, in contrast, for example, to the 30 hours of civic orientation we see in Germany. Moreover,

[116] While the Civil Code dictates that an applicant recall "principles, values and essential symbols of the French Republic," attempts to adopt a multiple-choice questionnaire were stymied when a new Interior Minister, Manual Valls, came to power, maintaining assessment should be assessed through "natural conversation and not through an 'artificial' questionnaire." Hajjat, "naturalisation procedures for immigrants: France," 3–4.

[117] Bertossi and Hajjat, "France," 18. [118] Ibid.

[119] "French citizenship to become more accessible." *France* 24. August 28, 2013. Available at: http://www.france24.com/en/20130828-france-immigration-valls-naturalisation-citizenship-integration-government (accessed September 22, 2013).

TABLE 6.4. *Participation and success rate of French language evaluation sessions, 2008*[120]

Number of candidates registered (i.e., required to take language training)	14,265 (21.5% of total contract signatories)
Number of candidates who attended	12,457 (87.3%)
Number of candidates who did not attend	1,808 (12.7%)
Number of successful candidates	11,123 (89.3%)
Number of unsuccessful candidates	1,334 (10.7%)

while the contract is obligatory, a sizable number of third-country nationals originate from francophone countries like Algeria, Morocco, Tunisia, Mali, etc. that, according to the conditions of the contract, are exempt from following the language training portion if they demonstrate adequate knowledge. This amounts to only "about one in four or five newcomers" requiring language training.[121]

In looking at the minority of migrants who are required to take language courses, we see high rates of attendance and successful completion. Table 6.4 presents figures for 2008 for migrants attending language courses: 89.3 percent of persons completing the language training end up completing the language component of the contract, which includes course attendance and a cumulative exam. Finally, by examining raw figures of first issuance of residence permits, new requirements have not proved to be a significant barrier here in either practice or as a pre-emptive disincentive. Family-based migration has remained relatively stable (in 2007: 91,106; in 2010: 89,065; in 2012: 91,441), with declines primarily among labor migrants and students.[122]

In turning to the assimilation requirement for citizenship, while it has been conceptually expanded over the past decade to include not only language but cultural assimilation and value adherence, the likelihood of rejection as a result of *défaut d'assimilation*, or failure to assimilate, is quite narrow. A failure to assimilate is generally identified where lifestyle choices are deemed incompatible to republican values, namely by engaging in a polygamous relationship, wearing a burqa to the interview, or demonstrating a degree of obedience by a female applicant to her husband that suggests a lack of personal independence. And while these instances of citizenship rejection are visible and highly politicized, they amount to only a handful of applicants. As Weil notes, of the 16,355 foreigners that acquired French citizenship by marriage in 2009, "There were

120 Yves Pascouau, "Country Report France," in *The INTEC Project: Integration and naturalisation tests: The new way to European citizenship* (Nijmegen, the Netherlands: Centre for Migration Law, Radboud University, 2010), 17.

121 Strik et al., "Synthesis Report," 48.

122 Institut national de la statistique et des etudes économiques (INSEE) website. http://www.insee.fr/fr/themes/tableau.asp?reg_id=0&ref_id=TITSEJ (accessed July 23, 2013).

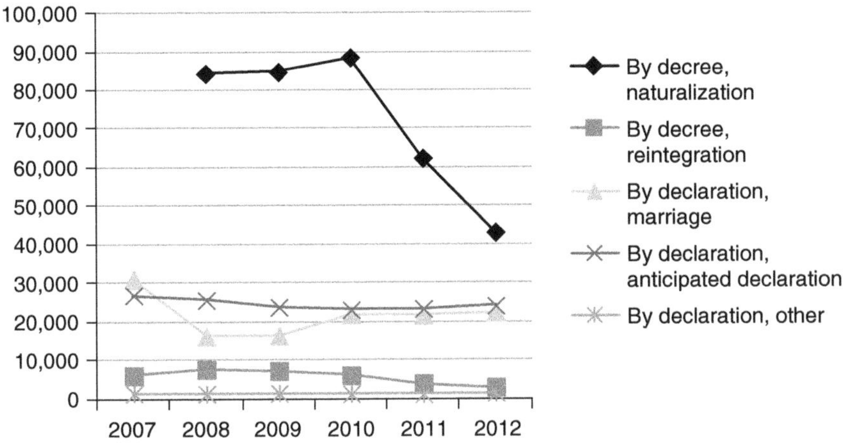

6.2 Acquisition of French citizenship by category[123]

about twenty refusals, 90% for failure to assimilate."[124] In other words, only 18 out of 16,355, or 0.11%, of spouses seeking citizenship were denied on the grounds of assimilation. And, in looking at acquisition rates in Figure 6.2, acquisition on the basis of marriage has only increased since 2008. General naturalization has decreased significantly, not as a result of the assimilation or language requirements but by a harsher interpretation of the job contract requirement by the then conservative government. Bertossi and Hajjat explain that "78 percent of the rise in negative decisions recorded in 2011 is due to the lack of 'professional integration': applicants who did not have a [sic] permanent job contract were systematically rejected."[125] Removing this requirement is another of the "softening" measures proposed by a leftist government. While restrictive outcomes are achieved through other policy manipulations, integration measures, as Yves Pascouau concludes, "do not constitute a huge obstacle."[126]

CONCLUSION

France has unequivocally ratcheted up integration requirements in the past decade, in line with the trends of neighboring European countries. By promoting

[123] Secrétariat général à l'immigration et à l'intégration – Ministère de la justice. Available at http://www.immigration.interieur.gouv.fr (accessed July 23, 2013).

[124] "Le refus de nationalité pour "défaut d'assimilation, *Le Nouvel Observateur*, June 10, 2011.

[125] Bertossi and Hajjat, "France," 23.

[126] Yves Pascouau, "Integration measures in France: An evolving process between integration and migration issues," in *A Re-Definition of Belonging? Language and integration tests in Europe*, ed. Ricky van Oers, Eva Ersbøll, and Theodora Kostakopoulou (Leiden; Boston: Martinus Nijhoff, 2010), 166.

assimilation through the contract and expanded expectations of belonging, integration has emerged as a strategic device of a center-right government intent on appearing tough on immigration by making acquisition of status – first residence, then citizenship – conditional on knowledge and adherence to republican values. Unlike the UK or the Netherlands, integration measures do not newly define the content of French membership, but serve as the extended arm of an already entrenched, coherent concept of membership in which integration has been "transferred from nationality law to the rules regulating the conditions for admission and residence of [third-country nationals]."[127] Adding the expectation of assimilation to residence establishes equivalence in the expectations of integration between residence and citizenship as membership categories, despite the central role of the latter in defining national belonging and Republicanism. By creating this equality, if only through symbolic instruments, we see France as a case of contained restriction. It uses integration requirements to temper the inclusivity of French belonging by conditioning the acquisition of status with barriers earlier on, all the while leaving citizenship relatively untouched.

Yet, evidence suggests that these requirements are formidable in rhetoric only, marking France as only a mild example of contained restriction. The courses are free, language level is low, compliance is high, and the population that undergoes the full rigor of the contract is quite limited. On the one hand, the divergence of rhetoric and design is a testament to the lasting impact of citizenship understandings, where a liberal starting point constricts the range of potential change. Of course, one can speculate that *any* changes to this inclusive notion of civic membership might suggest weakness in managing and incorporating immigrant-related diversity. On the other hand, the gap between outcome and output is also a product of its political system, in which the far-right exacerbated party polarization instead of creating cross-party consensus to sustain incremental and layered restriction (as in the Netherlands). Pursuing civic integration goals through uniquely French instruments, membership requirements are clearly directed to influence immigration directly (and citizenship only indirectly and abstractly, as immigrants become eligible down the line). The fact that these prove to be strong in rhetoric but mild in design and practice says a lot about how the French state views its role in impacting social change. And that citizenship has changed so little speaks volumes to how the existing Republican approach remains durable against the winds of change.

This comparison of the Netherlands and France illustrates that it is not simply the presence of similar conditions and the setting of those conditions – in these cases, liberal citizenship orientation and the path of left-then-right governments with far-right influence – that produce policy output. The strongest and most accurate explanation of unique policy design requires paying attention to causal mechanisms, or how political processes unfold in a liberal citizenship context.

[127] Carrera, "Nationality, immigration and 'the republican integration' in France: Normativisation, expansionism and externalisation," 332.

This is especially necessary when initial conditions are similar but outcomes are not. In the Netherlands, a process of incremental, restrictive layering in the context of right-wing consensus produced real but variegated change on the practice of status acquisition. In France, politicization in a polarized political environment still defined by a liberal citizenship orientation made restrictions less entrenched and easier to unravel with a change in government.

The different processes by which civic integration policy was established in both states not only accounts for policy design, it is consistent with differences in implementation, where the Netherlands maintains a far more robust and restrictive membership policy than France. French design remains consistent with state understandings of membership based on the social contract, while the Dutch interpret quite a managerial role for the state in controlling – but not facilitating – opportunities for integration. As a result, while both cases boast similar citizenship policy contexts and similar political trends, they proceed down quite distinct causal paths. One might counter this interpretation by suggesting that it is the nature of the far-right party itself, where the National Front and the Pim Fortuyn List draw on different constituencies, or where the former enjoys different kinds of establishment effects having been an actor on the French political scene for decades, while LPF was an ephemeral, zeitgeist party. This may very well be the case, but as these case studies show, far-right parties are responsible for exacerbating and accelerating, but – crucially – not originating new membership requirements. Differences in party reputation, platform, or constituency characteristics only underscore the importance of mechanisms, whereby similar conditions are filtered through different political processes to, ultimately, produce different policy outcomes.

Previous chapters provided nuanced comparisons to illustrate the effects of citizenship context similarities (Chapter 4) and differences (Chapter 5) in defining parameters for government actors to pursue membership policy. This chapter adds to these insights by arguing that even in the presence of similar conditions, different policy outcomes can be observed as a result of different interaction effects and unique causal processes. All of these observations underscore the book's central argument: states undergo unique causal paths to produce ultimately unique membership policy outcomes. These different paths primarily reflect different constraints on policymakers and discourse, namely citizenship understandings. The next chapter (Chapter 7) transitions from internal membership regulation to external immigration regulation by examining factors shaping pre-departure civic integration policies. Where internal civic integration is characterized by difference, external civic integration is established through commonality, of purpose (requirements as a selection mechanism) and process (the EU as the policy venue of establishment and transfer/learning effects from initial Dutch implementation).

7

External dimensions of civic integration: requirements for entry

This chapter marks a conceptual shift in the book by turning away from the examination of internal dimensions of civic integration – how obligatory integration requirements condition permanent residence and citizenship – toward the external dimension of civic integration, or how language and country knowledge requirements become conditions of entry.[1] This conceptual distinction is meaningful. The previous case study chapters have illustrated how states adopt and adapt membership policies for various yet oftentimes overlapping purposes, namely promoting participation or achieving exclusion of (primarily family-based) migrants. Both of these represent distinct forms of regulation, facilitating the terms of inclusion and the conditions of exclusion in the modern polity, respectively. As such, the phenomenon of regulating membership itself to both potential citizens *and especially* potential long-term residents represents an unambiguous reconceptualization and expansion of the "national political community." In this broader category, it remains within the policymakers' purview – consistent with the contractual framework of citizenship – to define what they see as "best practices" for succeeding in that community. These expectations may be more difficult for some than others, but setting the bar in and of itself to this expanded population suggests the state takes the prospects of permanent membership seriously.

It is, of course, one thing to enact membership practices *within* a territory (internal), tying compliance to sanctions, targeting the settlement of family members in particular, but the robust practice of civic integration policy is also defined by the attempt to regulate access from *outside* the territory (external). Immigration control is a perennial concern for European states, and the past quarter century has been littered with headlines lamenting government

[1] The identification of the internal (territorialized) versus external (deterritorialized) dimensions of civic integration's anatomy comes from Dora Kostakopoulou, "The anatomy of civic integration," *Modern Law Review* 73, no. 6 (2010), 933–958.

ineffectuality on this front. That civic integration is one of the many schemes employed by governments to limit immigration – even if only symbolically – as well as defensively combat perceptions of ineptitude, is not particularly surprising. Costs associated with policy failure are low. And even if policies for promoting integration fail in this objective, they may still produce ancillary gains in limiting immigration or, at the very least, project even a vague sense of government regulatory competence.

The external application of civic integration is part and parcel to the "civic turn." As such, measures of these policies are presented alongside internal policies in the CIVIX policy tables in Chapter 2 (Tables 2.1 and 2.2), under the column of immigration. However, I position these policies as distinct in the analysis by separating their discussion from the case studies. This division is driven by three reasons. The first is a concern for maintaining conceptual precision, in which states internally impose integration requirements as part of the metaphorical (or, oftentimes, literal) contract. As such, both the individual and the state have guarantees of the other in the form of obligations and rights. These guarantees do not exist for the entry-seeking migrant. The relationship is entirely asymmetrical, in which the state exercises full sovereignty over admittance (though, as we will see, this authority is sometimes checked through judiciary rulings). Secondly, civic integration-from-abroad is empirically distinct from civic-integration-from-within, as we might distinguish it, in that the European Union serves as a meaningful venue for the policymaking process, specifically through the Directives on the Right to Family Reunification (2003/86/EC) and on the Status of the Third-Country Nationals Who are Long-Term Residents (2003/109/EC). This underscores a further distinction between internal and external civic integration: when it comes to migrant-related policies, border issues continue to involve interstate cooperation or, at least, consensus. Finally, where the previous case studies illustrated different objectives for membership policy adoption, informed by existing citizenship policy orientation and distinct political configurations of government, we can observe a shared, uniform objective: qualified and controlled family-based migrant intake of third-country nationals. Internal integration requirements certainly impact family-based migration, particularly where the acquisition of permanent residence relates to the ability to sponsor family members, but the external dimension of civic integration prizes the regulation and conditioning of family-based migration as its primary and central objective. Where integration as a selection mechanism is only a subset of the many goals of internal civic integration, external civic integration requirements decisively fuse together immigrant integration to migration control.

This chapter critically examines the distinct purpose, as well as the design and implication of integration requirements for immigration in Western Europe. It illustrates how states adopt external integration requirements – also referred to as "integration-from-abroad" or deterritorialized integration – as a new mechanism for selection, specifically regulating family-forming migration (bringing a spouse from another country) and family unification (reuniting a family from abroad). It is structured around examining two experiences that account for the robust adoption of integration-from-abroad: (1) the use of supranational institutions as a venue, creating the legal opportunity for national implementation, and (2) the design and practice of pre-arrival integration, as for example in the Netherlands through the Dutch Basic Integration Exam (*basisexam inburgering*). This pre-arrival requirement created a legitimate model for policy transfer,[2] as well as a learning opportunity for subsequent state practices, particularly in regard to degree of restriction. While subsequent permutations of integration-from-abroad reveal variation, resulting from a process of policy learning and domestic institutions, including courts and politics, all maintain the central, shared objective of migration control. Finally, in the conclusion, I consider the political leverage gained by politicians and policymakers in using the language of integration to achieve a decidedly non-inclusive outcome of immigration restriction.

EXAMINING EXTERNAL DIMENSIONS OF CIVIC INTEGRATION

External civic integration deterritorializes assessment of integration, using tests, interviews, and other evaluation mechanisms to assess language, country knowledge, and society values in an immigrant's point of origin. The requirements are administered by consulates and embassies abroad as well as private institutions that certify language acquisition, and access to the territory through a granting of entry or a temporary residence visa is contingent on successful completion.

Mandatory integration-from-abroad is not just a new policy, it is a relatively new idea. Only Germany maintained a type of language requirement for entry before the recent "civic turn" (see Chapter 6). The paradoxical extension of obligatory civic integration beyond the archetypical civic status – the citizen – is justified by policymakers as a way of promoting integration from the first step, not that an immigrant needs to be integrated already but that they have a baseline for obtaining skills for succeeding in the labor market (e.g., linguistic proficiency). However, despite this discourse, new obligatory requirements at the stage of pre-entry most clearly serve to limit immigration, specifically family-forming migrants. The most salient effect of pre-entry integration and high pre-entry barriers is exclusion by way of self-selection, cost, and unsuccessful completion of requirements. For whereas an applicant for citizenship may be sufficiently prepared to demonstrate his or her extent of integration at the time of naturalization, having resided in the host country for an extended period of time, integration requirements for entry assesses a potential newcomer without any cultural or linguistic exposure. The onus for self-preparation and integration is

[2] The Dutch were the first to practice *civic* integration as a pre-departure requirement, but Germany was an earlier practitioner of language for select categories (e.g., a requirement for *Ausseidler* in 1997).

entirely on the migrant, particularly in the absence of meaningful preparatory schemes. Pre-entry integration requirements mandate a degree of integration into the state while the applicant is physically and conceptually – vis-à-vis legal status – *outside* the state.

The states that have introduced the most robust, internal membership policies are also the states that have extended integration requirements to the border: Austria (2011),[3] Denmark (2010), France (2007), Germany (2007), the Netherlands (2006), and the UK (2010). There are a number of broadly similar features to these integration requirements. First and foremost, each state assesses language, primarily to target family migration sponsored by third-country nationals, including family-members of citizens. Second, a number of states (Denmark, the Netherlands, the UK) also explicitly require religious leaders to complete the requirement. The UK, in particular, has maintained a language requirement for immigrant religious leaders since 2004, and for highly skilled migrants since 2006,[4] still a full four years before it extended it to family members. Third, the language level in each state is set at the A1 "breakthrough" level, in which immigrants are expected to have a command of "very basic phrases" and "can interact in a simple way." This shared attribute in particular echoes the oft-cited rationale for integration-from-abroad, in which requirements are packaged as devices to assist newly arrived spouses find "productive employment"[5] and as the "first step toward successful participation...in society."[6] In this view, immigrating with basic knowledge of the host society language enables an immigrant to be more autonomous and functional, and serves as a base from which to build more skills. Fourth, and finally, with the exception of France,[7] the consequence of failing in each is denial of a residence permit (in the case of Denmark, as I discuss below, the penalty is removal as the exam is taken within the state).

Alongside these similarities are a number of design differences. The Netherlands stands out in this regard by running a formal test that assesses both language (speaking and reading) and country knowledge at embassies and consulates abroad. It does not provide language training or other facilitated preparation. Potential migrants can purchase a study guide and must take the

[3] Belated adoption has been attributed to court blockage. See Kees Groenendijk, "Legal concepts of integration in EU migration law," *European Journal of Migration and Law* 6, no. 2 (2004), 120–21.

[4] I exclude, however, in this analysis these types of programs that incentivize language proficiency as part of a points-based system. These requirements do not exclusively determine eligibility, but exist as part of a configuration of policies in which a migrant can accrue sufficient points by other means. Language assessment for student visa applications also is omitted as their immigration is viewed as temporary and does not foray to integration concerns.

[5] UK Border Agency, "Impact assessment of pre-application English language requirements," ed. UKBA (London: Home Office, 2009), 1.

[6] Ineke Hoekstra and Koen Bron, "Andersson Elffers Felix jaarboek," (Utrecht, the Netherlands), 161.

[7] Failure of a language exam abroad obliges the immigrant to participate in mandatory French language classes upon immigration.

computerized exam at the nearest embassy or consulate in their home country.[8] By contrast, immigrants seeking a temporary visa to Germany or Austria need to either complete an exam at the Goethe Institute or obtain other language certification. Similarly, the UK also "outsources" language training to the private market. It does not mandate or offer any specific language training abroad, but a migrant spouse must take a spoken English language tests to fulfill the "pre-application English language requirement." In each of these three countries, a privately enrolled language course is not mandatory to gain entry, but it might be necessary in order to pass the exam.

In a third design, France provides language training from abroad, with only an evaluation as evidence of proficiency. Applicants must demonstrate written and oral knowledge of French at the lowest level, and undergo a short oral interview about values of the Republic in their native language. If a sufficient level of knowledge and French proficiency is shown, a visa is issued. If a migrant's knowledge proves to be insufficient, he or she is obliged to take a course that is offered in the country of origin, financed and organized by the *Office Français de l'Immigration et de l'Intégration* (OFII). If, after this course, they are still insufficient in knowledge, they are not denied an entry visa to France, but are required to attend courses as part of their integration contract in France. In sum, admission to France – like integration *in* France – is based not on achieving a pass mark but on participation.

Finally, Denmark only recently abandoned a Dutch-styled integration exam that assessed both basic Danish and country knowledge, as it was deemed too costly, and moved to an exclusive assessment of language. The Danish also differ from other practicing states in that they do not formally assess integration before entry, but rather immigrants are granted a short-term stay and are required to pass a language test within three months of entry *in Denmark* (this was also true for the former integration exam). If an immigrant does not pass the test at this time, the residence permit is refused and the applicant must leave Denmark. In contrast to the Dutch practice, offering a test once the immigrant has already entered the host country offers the opportunity to practice the Danish language with family and in society, as opposed to the more isolated setting abroad.

This speaks to another issue: the relationship between integration and socialization. In France and Germany, arbitrary language proficiency levels subject potential immigrants to attend classes that serve to socialize new immigrants in networks of other immigrants in their situation. These networks may be transferrable and of use after relocation. However, the Dutch approach is highly atomized, placing the responsibility of preparation solely on the shoulders of the migrant and the family they are joining. Moreover, in terms of socialization, mass exemptions for other categories of migrants, including highly skilled

[8] The preparatory material was originally only available for purchase at stores in the Netherlands and not available online. The idea behind this limited distribution was that the sponsoring spouse would purchase the materials and assist the migration-seeking spouse in preparation.

workers, paternalistically suggest that language acquisition (or, worse, language acquisition *and* country knowledge) is a skill that is valuable only to some and not to others.

To reiterate, the instrumental use of integration requirements as this earliest barrier of admission is not altogether surprising. Civic requirements such as language acquisition and country knowledge are extensions of citizen objectives, and citizenship is an "object and instrument of closure" where people are defined as included by simultaneously identifying people who are excluded. On the other hand, it is revealing that states strategically refer to this migration control policy as a type of integration policy. The next section examines the origins of this policy.

CREATING AN OPPORTUNITY FOR PRE-ENTRY INTEGRATION: EXAMINING SUPRANATIONAL PRECEDENT

One of the most significant differences between the internal and external dimensions of civic integration is the origin of policy. The roots of integration-from-abroad requirements are located in supranational rules. The process of adding integration requirements to EU Directives was intergovernmental where entrepreneurial member states were the main actors. However, the codification of their preferences in the form of EU Directives – as opposed to individual state adoption of practices first – is notable. First, it invested states in the shared problem of regulation of family-based migration and connected to it the idea that integration measures were part of a shared response. Second, this supranational platform for ideational entrepreneurship in EU Directives created the legal precedent for states to adopt and potentially go further in policy practice than domestic politics might have allowed. This is especially the case where the Dutch became the first implementers of integration-from-abroad, defining what turned out to be the most aggressive practice in comparison with that of other states.

EU-level decision-making and the EU arena generally have been identified as playing an increasingly prominent role in the process of immigration policy-making. Virginie Guiraudon describes migration policy shifting from the national to the supranational level as a form of "venue-shopping," in that it allows national governments to "circumvent national constrains on migration control," including courts, other political parties, or even pro-migrant organizations.[9] Martin Schain also points to the EU as a "relatively protected space" that "rather than constraining states in Europe, has enhanced their abilities both to control immigrant entry and to develop more forceful policies on integration, essentially defined at the Member State level."[10] Moreover, the powers of the

[9] Virginie Guiraudon, "European integration and migration policy: Vertical policy-making as venue shopping," *Journal of Common Market Studies* 38, no. 2 (2000), 251–52.

[10] Martin A. Schain, "The state strikes back: Immigration policy in the European Union," *European Journal of International Law* 20, no. 1 (2009), 106.

EU as a supranational entrepreneur in informal agenda-setting are significantly circumscribed to the availability of informational asymmetry and windows of opportunity to exercise privileged access.[11]

In this vein, a number of scholars have focused on the November 2004 European Council agreement on "common basic principles" as the central influence explaining widespread convergence on immigrant integration.[12] The Common Basic Principles (CBPs) of immigrant integration for third-country nationals recognizes a European-wide objective of "mutual understanding and accommodation," with strategies including the promotion of basic values of the European Union (i.e., rule of law), access to employment, and a "basic knowledge of the host society's language, history, and institutions."[13] It was introduced by Dutch ministers, most notably the hardline and controversial Minister for Integration and Immigration Rita Verdonk, responsible for the legislation for the Civic Integration from Abroad Act (*Wet Inburgering in Het Buitenland*, WIB) in September 2005. However, this attribution is not correct. The CBPs, as part of the EU Framework on Integration (a non-legally binding set of guidelines for national practices), can be described as a reflection, but not a motive, for mandatory integration. Moreover, they are typified by their inclusive bent, suggesting strategies that would enable integration. They do not mention integration-from-abroad or conditional criteria for family reunification, which are restrictive in character.

Instead, the origins of integration requirements for family migrants can be found in negotiations for the EU Family Directive, starting in December 1999 and adopted by the Council in September 2003, all predating the CBPs. The Family Directive was the first piece of community law to pertain to family migration. In general, it advises a "set of rules governing the procedure for examination of applications for family reunification and for entry and residence of family members" to be laid down, whereby "family reunification may be refused on duly justified grounds."[14] The Directive introduced a number of restrictions, including proof of sufficient evidence of adequate accommodation, health insurance, an income requirement, as well as minimum-age requirement in order to – according to Article 4(5) – "ensure better integration and to prevent forced marriages." In addition, and central to our concern, Article 7(2) also states that "Members States may require third country nationals to comply with

[11] Andrew Moravscik, "A new statecraft? Supranational entrepreneurs and international cooperation," *International Organization* 53, no. 2 (1999), 267–306.

[12] Christian Joppke, "Beyond national models: Civic integration policies for immigrants in Western Europe," *West European Politics* 30, no. 1 (2007), 3–5. Also see Elspeth Guild, Kees Groenendijk, and Sergio Carrera, eds., *Illiberal Liberal States: Immigration, citizenship, and integration in the EU* (Farnham, Surrey; Burlington, VT: Ashgate, 2009).

[13] Council of the European Union, "*Immigrant Integration Policy in the European Union*," (Brussels, 2004), 15–16.

[14] 2003/86/EC, p. 13, par. 13–14.

integration measures, in accordance with national law."[15] At the same time, perhaps with the other side of its hand, the Directive also recognizes family migration as a way of creating "sociocultural stability" to facilitate integration for third-country nationals.[16] In other words, family reunification of a spouse and minor children *promotes* integration, and yet impediments to reunification, like tests and language requirements – which work against the goal of integration – are set into motion. The Directive does not state explicitly *how* states should interpret integration measures, nor does it bind them to implement integration measures as it contains the "may" clause. The Directive also does not make a distinction between family reunification and family-forming migration,[17] but the perceived logic of bringing spouses from abroad is that it is more likely to reinforce counterproductive cycles to integration, marginalizing third-country nationals into insular and potentially divisive community affiliations and networks. With independent status via a temporary residence permit, the immigrating spouse is responsible for his or her own integration.

The insertion of integration measures was a product of intergovernmental cooperation. Laura Block and Saskia Bonjour describe how national governments were driven by the "same overarching goal in the negotiations: to ensure that the new Directive would require as little change to national family migration policies as possible."[18] As such, regarding integration, Kees Groenendijk observes that Austria initiated the insertion of integration measures in "November 2002 ... later supported by Germany and the Netherlands."[19] Member states including Sweden and Belgium were against this initiative, out of concern about the impact it might have on refugees and their families. In terms of the European Commission, reticence was expressed, noting that the admissibility of national integration "can be questioned on the basis of the accessibility of such courses or tests, how they are designed and/or organized (test materials, fees, venues, etc.), whether such measures or their impact serve purposes other than integration (e.g., high fees excluding low-income families)."[20] Also in opposition stood the French delegation, which instead supported the Commission's proposal to strengthen family reunification rights. Block and Bonjour suggest that they were ultimately "unable to impose their views in the

15 Art. 7 further stipulates that integration requirements can only be applied to refugees "once the persons concerned have been granted family reunification."

16 2003/86/EC, 12.

17 Family reunification is defined in Art. 2(d) as "the entry into and residence in a Member State by family members of a third country national residing lawfully in that Member State in order to preserve the family unit, whether the family relationship arose before or after the resident's entry."

18 Laura Block and Saskia Bonjour, "Fortress Europe or Europe of rights? The Europeanisation of family migration policies in France, Germany and the Netherlands," *European Journal of Migration and Law* 15 (2013), 212.

19 Groenendijk, "Legal concepts of integration in EU migration law," 119.

20 European Commission, "Report from the Commission to the European Parliament and the Council on the Application of Directive 2003/86/EC on the Right to Family Reunification," ed. Commission of the European Communities, COM (2008) 610 (Brussels, 2008), 7–8.

negotiations, however, mostly because they failed to win support among the Member States, but perhaps also because their defense of migrants' rights became somewhat less fervent after the UMP Raffarin government replaced the PS Jospin government in 2002."[21] The Commission was aware in its 2008 impact report on the implementation of the Family Reunification Directive that there were alternative objectives to integration-from-abroad, reminding Member States that the purpose of integration requirements should be "to facilitate the integration of family members" and questioning the "principle of proportionality" in existing practices, including high fees and test accessibility.[22] This awareness demonstrates an *ex ante* understanding that policies labeled to achieve one goal (integration) are designed to achieve something ulterior (immigration control).

Pre-arrival integration was extended to third-country nationals seeking long-term resident status (defined by legally and continually residing in the EU for a minimum of five years prior to the submission of the relevant application) in the eponymously titled Directive. Article 5(2) states: "Members States may require third-country nationals to comply with integration conditions in accordance with national law." This, too, can be a significant impediment to the goal of integration. Long-term residence status is permanent under Article 8(1) and guarantees the holder to "equal treatment with nationals" in areas including access to employment, education, social security, tax benefits, and other democratic freedoms. Without this, a migrant may face continual discrimination or disadvantage under the law and in society. Third-country nationals who hold an EC long-term residence permit and move from one EU member state to another do not need to complete additional civic integration measures, but may still be subject to language classes according to Article 15(3).

These Directives establish a legal background for integration requirements for both new immigrants seeking temporary residence and old immigrants seeking long-term residence. They create an allowance, but not an obligation, for new integration provisions. As such, a number of states directly invoked the Family Directive in particular in the national adoption of pre-integration requirements. Germany introduced new family restrictions, including pre-integration, in the unambiguously titled "Directive Implementation Act." The French government, now firmly under the rightist government of Sarkozy, defended pre-departure as "fully in line with the Family Reunification Directive."[23] Finally, and perhaps most significantly for understanding policy-in-practice, the Dutch government referenced its own negotiation success in codifying integration for family

[21] Block and Bonjour, "Fortress Europe or Europe of rights? The Europeanisation of family migration policies in France, Germany and the Netherlands," 213.

[22] European Commission (2013). DG Home Affairs, Immigration and Integration Infringements (http://ec.europa.eu/dgs/home-affairs/what-is-new/eu-law-and-monitoring/infringements_by_policy_immigration_and_integration_en.htm): 7 (accessed July 1, 2010).

[23] Block and Bonjour, "Fortress Europe or Europe of rights? The Europeanisation of family migration policies in France, Germany and the Netherlands," 214.

reunification. In presenting its proposal for civic integration-from-abroad, the Dutch government "emphasized that 'the new integration requirements fit with recent developments in European migration law.'"[24]

A majority of member states have chosen not to exercise these optional clauses. At the same time, Denmark and the UK are not even bound by EU directives, and yet both adopted pre-entry integration. However, the Directives have made it possible for Member States to make strategic use of EU law by linking integration requirements to restrictive reform, particularly for its first adopter, the Netherlands. Highlighting this supranational opportunity – forged out of intergovernmental decision-making – not only sheds light on the process of legitimacy leveraging through EU Directives, it also underlines significant differences in the origins of external and internal dimensions of civic integration. Where internal civic integration is born from existing political configurations, mindful of the existing citizenship context that promotes or hinders inclusion, the regulation of family migration through pre-departure conditions and measures[25] appears more of a shared problem, thus necessitating a shared solution, at least in principle.

ESTABLISHING LEGITIMACY FOR A NEW POLICY: DUTCH CIVIC INTEGRATION FROM ABROAD

Even more so than the legal opportunity created by the EU Directives, the Dutch implementation of pre-entry integration established both legitimacy and a model for the adoption of integration-from-abroad in other EU states. Each state that adopts external dimensions invokes references to the Dutch model. In fact, "Dutch politicians actively engaged in turning integration aboard into a common practice among Member States."[26] This marks another distinction between the origins of external integration requirements and the origins of internal requirements. Since the Dutch model is central as a source of legitimation, diffusion, and learning, this section examines the motives, process, successes, and failures of this program. After describing the political landscape that made restrictive integration requirements for family-based entry possible, I look at the immigration test more closely. The direct connection between testing and targeting family-forming migration is visible in three dimensions: (1) design; (2) excluded categories; and (3) explicit language of policy papers that identify family-forming migration as problematic.

Since the early 2000s, migration control in the Netherlands has largely focused on limiting family-based migration (both family reunification following asylum or

24 Ibid.

25 See Groenendijk, "Legal concepts of integration in EU migration law" for the subtle but important differences between integration "measures" for family reunification and integration "conditions" for third-country nationals.

26 Block and Bonjour, "Fortress Europe or Europe of rights? The Europeanisation of family migration policies in France, Germany and the Netherlands," 218.

labor-based migration and family formation, i.e., spouse-based migration). This is not solely because family-based migration is believed to yield deleterious effects on integration. Discernible problems related to family migration began to become more apparent following initial government successes in reducing asylum-based migration. Asylum and migration control were part of an early ambition to comprehensively streamline immigration under the second purple coalition government (Kok II cabinet), consisting of the Labour Party, Conservative Liberals (VVD), and Social Democrats (D66). Streamlining began with asylum, in which the new Aliens Act of 2000 effectively decreased asylum admissions from 18,388 in 2002 to 8,262 in 2003, and has leveled off since at around 3,000 per year.[27] Having accomplished this first goal, the next focus for streamlining was the so-called "normal immigration routes," which involved effective controls against family-based migration and against "import brides" in particular.[28]

A second context for interpreting the adoption of external integration requirements was the proliferating notion of internal assessment. The idea for introducing language and country knowledge assessment at other admission barriers had been floating around since the mid-1990s. The VVD reached agreement with the CDA on the issue of a naturalization test under the purple coalition, and testing was already part of a long-term agenda by the time Job Cohen (PvdA) became Minister of Migration in 1998 (a Royal Decree in 2003 finally implemented the long-delayed roll-out of this test). And in 2002, the Balkenende I coalition agreement floated the idea of an integration test for permanent residence. To this, the amplifying role played by Pim Fortuyn's party on restriction could not be denied. Even though the party's tenure in office was short, a civil servant has stated that "everything became possible after Pim Fortuyn."[29] For example, the head of the Ministry for Integration and Immigration, previously occupied by an LPF minister, was replaced by Verdonk (of the VVD) when the government collapsed. This secured a continuity of restrictive, hardline policy in an atmosphere becoming highly conducive to restrictive migration controls.

Under Verdonk's leadership, concomitant to other proposals to strengthen restrictions in the Family Directive,[30] and overlapping with a second assassination, this time of filmmaker Theo Van Gogh by Moroccan-born, Dutch national

[27] Central Bureau for Statistics (the Netherlands), "Statline Cbs Databank," (2009). Some changes in the Aliens Act that produced this decline include raising the burden of evidence for applicants, establishing more leeway to the government in determining safe conditions for repatriation to the sending country, and abolishing the administrative review process for rejected asylum applications. Instead, applications are sent directly for court review while the asylum seeker must leave the Netherlands to await a decision.

[28] Marc de Leeuw and Sonja van Wichelen, "Civilizing migrants: Integration, culture and citizenship," *European Journal of Cultural Studies* 15, no. 2 (2012), 200.

[29] Interview with the author. April 1, 2009. Den Haag, NL: Ministry of Justice.

[30] In particular, this included raising the income requirement from 100 percent to 120 percent of minimum wage. After the EU Court's *Chakroun* ruling (2010), the government was forced to lower it to its pre-2004 level.

Mohammad Boyeri, government actors identified sufficient political capital to create further restrictions against immigration, specifically of marital partners.[31] The Civic Integration Abroad Act was passed by the Dutch parliament on March 22, 2005 (entering into force in March 2006). Passing the Civic Integration Abroad exam became required for obtaining a temporary residence permit (*Machtiging tot Voorlopig Verblijf*; MVV). The pre-arrival test was initially comprised of two parts: a 15-minute, 50-question Dutch language exam (an oral exam assessing listening and speaking skills, *Toets Gesproken Nederlands*) and a separate Knowledge of Dutch Society exam (*Kennis van de Nederlandse Samenleving*), in which the applicant answers 30 questions on Dutch life and society. It is taken over the phone and administered at the Dutch embassy in the applicant's country of origin. The applicant listens to a computer and responds through voice recognition software. The government designed the test so that it would "not select based on level of education but rather on motivation and perseverance of the migrant."[32]

As of April 2011, a 55-question Reading and Comprehension Skills test (*Toets Geletterdheid en Begrijpend Lezen;* GBL) was added. It consists of sentence completion and answering questions on a short text. A change was also made in 2011 that raises the spoken Dutch exam level from A1-minus to A1. Preparation was also changed, whereby one can obtain the video titled "Coming to the Netherlands" (*Naar Nederland*) and the accompanying pack of photographs and battery of questions online.[33] Formerly, this preparatory pack could only be purchased in-person in the Netherlands, as part of a deliberate strategy to encourage the migrant to practice speaking and understanding Dutch with the sponsoring spouse over the phone.

The clear purpose of the requirement was to control immigration through integration. Recognizing that "immigration and integration are inherently connected," the government noted that "no sustainable effects can be achieved [in the sphere of integration] as long as immigration is not regulated and immigration is not well regulated if it takes no consideration of the conditions for integration of newcomers."[34] It continued in specificity: "ongoing immigration in combination with a lack of integration can lead to processes of marginalization of specific groups in the sense of declining capacities to social participation, weak chances on the labor market and structural dependence on income support."[35] As such, the government explicitly referred to the test as a "selection criterion."[36]

The main target of the pre-entry test was family-based migrants, a growing group of applicants receiving temporary resident permits. In 2006, it

[31] Interview with the author. April 2, 2009. Utrecht, NL. [32] TK 2003–2004, 29700, nr.3: 11.

[33] The video is a one-hour and forty-five minute presentation on life in the Netherlands. It touches on a wide range of issues, including cold Dutch weather, the history of William of Orange, and the Dutch monarchy. It also includes more controversial topics including honor killings, topless beach bathing, and homosexuality.

[34] TK 2003–2004, 29700, nr. 3: 2. [35] TK 2003–2004, 2900, nr. 3: 4.

[36] TK 2003–2004, 2900, nr. 3: 6.

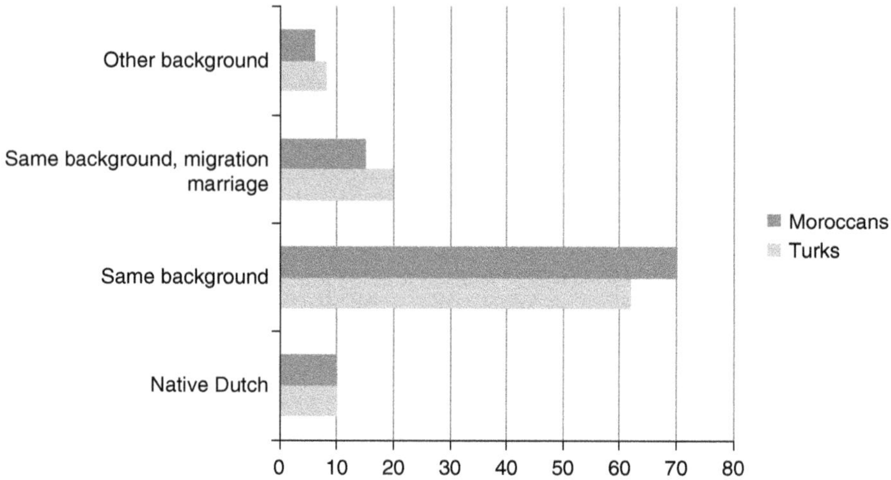

7.1 Partner choice of Turks and Moroccans, 2007

constituted about 50 percent of total migration to the Netherlands (60 percent when excluding intra-European movement). And of this figure, a significant percentage was family-forming. If the family was the general target group, family-migrants from Turkey and Morocco were a particular focus. As Figure 7.1 shows, about 20 percent of Turks and 15 percent of Moroccans who married in 2007 brought in marriage partners from Turkey and Morocco.[37] Also note that a disproportionate number of new migrants (about 67 percent) who took the civic integration abroad exam in 2007 were women, indicating a significant level of marriage-based migration.[38]

The second area in which we see the integration test specifically targeting family-forming migration is in terms of exempt categories. The question of who is subject to and who is exempt from taking the immigration test is a contentious issue, and one criticized by Human Rights Watch as discriminatory.[39] Exemptions are based on nationality, specifically persons from the European Union, European Economic Community, Australia, Canada, Japan, New Zealand, South Korea, Switzerland, and the United States, as well as migrants and spouses from the Netherlands Antilles and former Dutch colony of Surinam. The difference in treatment based on nationality is

[37] Central Bureau for Statistics (the Netherlands), "Decline in number of Turkish and Moroccan immigration brides continues," *Web Magazine* (2008), http://www.cbs.nl/en-GB/menu/themas/dossiers/allochtonen/publicaties/artikelen/archief/2008/2008-9015 6-wk.htm (accessed July 1, 2010).

[38] Informatie-en Analyses Centrum (INDIAC), "Monitor Inburgeringsexamen Buitenland" (Den Haag: Immigratie- en Naturalisatiedienst, 2008), 16.

[39] Human Rights Watch, "The Netherlands: Discrimination in the name of integration" (Human Rights Watch, 2008).

one that the government failed to justify.[40] Marc de Leew and Sonja van Wichelen describe these exemptions as a form of discrimination that is "internally contradictory and therefore normatively objective."[41] Finally, there are exemptions for persons coming to the Netherlands with a work (labor) permit, knowledge (highly-skilled) migrants, self-employed persons, as well as asylum seekers. In addition to family-based migration, the only other target of civic integration includes religious leaders, regardless of nationality or skill. This is deliberate, as radicalization by imams in Dutch mosques, and anxiety about religious clergy generally, was a key impetus to initial policy adoption where the imams were characterized by their "unwillingness to integrate to Dutch norms and values (such as shaking hands with women)."[42] In addition to the pre-entry test, religious leaders from all denominations and faiths also take a special *inburgeringscursus* (integration course) together for long-term residence.

Given these exemptions and where family-based migration at its peak makes up only approximately half of the total intake to the Netherlands, a full half of the new immigrant population, including free movement, humanitarian, and work-based migrants, enter without a foothold for integration. Integration is not sold as an opportunity to these migrants, who start out with more skills and ostensibly better start positions; in their exemption, policymakers clearly recognize that obligatory requirements would be a potentially disincentivizing factor to *desired* migrants. And while exam candidates from Turkey and Morocco made up 15 percent and 22 percent of total test takers in 2007,[43] and have consistently been the largest groups of nationalities receiving temporary resident permits, they only represent a fraction of total immigration in any given year. For example, of the 67,000 immigrants the Netherlands received in 2006, only 2,748 (4 percent) were Turkish and 1,713 (2.5 percent) were Moroccan.[44]

Finally, the language of policymaking itself indicates a clear emphasis on targeting immigrants with established "entry problems."[45] Family-forming migrants from non-excluded countries – like Turkey and Morocco – are said to bear "characteristics that are unfavorable for a good integration in Dutch society."[46] These reasons span socioeconomic and cultural attributes:

Almost half of the family migrants come from Morocco and Turkey. These migrants have a poor starting position in Dutch society ... Approximately 40% of the Turkish and

[40] Tineke Strik et al., "Synthesis Report," in *The INTEC Project: Integration and naturalisation tests: The new way to European citizenship* (Nijmegen, the Netherlands: Centre for Migration Law, Radboud University, 2010), 23.

[41] de Leeuw and van Wichelen, "Civilizing migrants: Integration, culture and citizenship," 203.

[42] Ibid.: 200.

[43] Informatie-en Analyses Centrum (INDIAC), "Monitor Inburgeringsexamen Buitenland," 19.

[44] OECD, *International Migration Outlook: SOPEMI 2008* (Paris: OECD Publishing, 2008).

[45] Ministry of Justice (the Netherlands), "*The Civic Integration Abroad Act: Information Package,*" ed. MOJ (Den Haag, 2006), 8.

[46] Ibid., 7. Also see TK 2003–2004, 2900, nr. 3: 4

almost 60% of the Moroccan family migrants have basic education as their maximum education level. The unemployment rate of Turkish and Moroccan marriage migrants in this period is about 12% for both nationalities, as against 3% for the native Dutch working population ... Marriage migrants lag behind in the language area compared to the second generation, whereby speaking and reading is a problem for many marriage migrants. The level of sociocultural integration of Turkish and Moroccan marriage migrants is closer to that of the first generation of migrants than of the second generation. They have little contact with Dutch people, identify mainly with their own group and orient themselves mainly to their own language and culture.[47]

It is worth noting that this exclusive focus on non-Western, Muslim-sending countries raises the specter of assimilation and even racism as a motivation behind new requirements. This allegation is particularly salient where far-right parties bear influence on legislation and coalition-formation. In the case of the Netherlands, Turkish and Moroccan migration is hardly new. In fact, the problem as previously described is that second- and third-generation migrants from these countries are still exhibiting socioeconomic and behavioral patterns inimical to first-generation migrants, despite having grown up in the Netherlands and, in many cases, with Dutch citizenship. Pre-entry requirements may proactively try to course-correct a spiraling trend of integration problems across the generations, but the requirements are too limited and insufficient to be its primary function. In fact, another explicit objective of abroad requirements was as a strategy to pragmatically address low completion rates of integration programs mandatory for permanent residence.[48] Promoting integration from abroad does not achieve integration directly; rather it indirectly links a newcomer into their integration course for settlement. Integration-from-abroad promotes the civic integration program, not integration itself.

In the end, we see the Dutch civic integration from abroad policy as designed and oriented toward the explicit objective of "postponement or even cancellation of the intended settlement in the Netherlands," where the test yields an "immigration-limiting effect as a selection mechanism."[49] The political successes of integration-from-abroad, which passed in Parliament with a total of 118 "yes" votes out of a total of 150, affirms the collective goal of control. Despite some of the lip service in opposition to Verdonk's restrictive agenda, it saw widespread support not only among the right but on the left as well. The only parties to vote "no" were the Socialists (with 25 votes) and the Greens (with 7 votes). Even members of the Labour party, who are typically

[47] Ibid.

[48] Completion of this course is marked with a comprehensive language test and assessment of active engagement with the wider Dutch society, e.g., through volunteer work. The program lasts three-and-a-half years, but for asylum seekers and previously settled migrants it is five years. Spiritual leaders such as imams, whose visas are limited to three years, also have to take the integration course.

[49] Ministry of Justice (the Netherlands), "*The Civic Integration Abroad Act: Information Package*," 16–17.

more pro-immigrant than restrictive-leaning, came out in support of Civic Integration from Abroad. Green opposition against the immigration test was not even about the content of the exam, but the instrument of assessment (i.e., issues over voice recognition software). And even where the government invoked rhetoric indicating that reduction in immigration was not a primary goal, it "nevertheless welcomed the 'side effect' that [civic integration abroad] was expected to result in a decrease in family migration flows by an estimated 25 percent."[50]

COMPARING DESIGN AND EFFECTS OF DUTCH INTEGRATION-FROM-ABROAD

Given its clear objective and broad-based support, and taking into account the test design and category exemptions, what has been the effect of integration-from-abroad? Pass rates (in Table 7.1) indicate that an overwhelming number of applicants pass on their first attempt. The introduction of the reading and comprehension (GBL) test at the A1 level drove down percentages in 2011, where speaking (TGN) and knowledge (KNS) scores remained high. However, the 2012 rebound suggests its effect is short lived. These figures might suggest that the integration test is more symbolically restrictive than it is restrictive in practice. But a closer look at application figures, before and after the new requirement, support the interpretation that the test – alongside other restrictions – serves as a decisive instrument to limit family-based immigration. This suggests pass rates are so high because the *threat* of the test yields a selection effect that disincentivizes the process of immigration for candidates less likely to score well.

TABLE 7.1. *Results of civic integration from abroad for first-time takers, Jan. – Jun. 2008*[51]

	2008			2011			2012		
	Pass	Fail	Other	Pass	Fail	Other	Pass	Fail	Other
Total %	89	8	2	75	25	0	79	21	0
TGN %	91	7	2	85	15	0	88	12	0
KNS %	95	3	2	96	4	0	97	3	0
GBL %	–	–	–	84	15	0	87	13	0

50 Saskia Bonjour, "Between integration provision and selection mechanism. Party politics, judicial constraints, and the making of French and Dutch policies of civic integration abroad," *European Journal of Migration and Law* 12, no. 3 (2010), 306.

51 Informatie-en Analyses Centrum (INDIAC and the Netherlands), "Monitor Inburgeringsexamen Buitenland" (Den Haag: Immigratie- en Naturalisatiedienst, 2008), 22; Significant, "Monitoring the Integration from Abroad Exam ('Monitor Inburgeringsexamen Buitenland')," (Barneveld, the Netherlands: Ministerie van Sociale Zaken en Werkgelegenheid, 2012), 23.

TABLE 7.2. *Pass rate of civic integration from abroad tests for first-time takers by nationality*[52]

	2011					2012				
	Number of test takers	Total %	*TGN* %	*KNS* %	*GBL* %	Number of test takers	Total %	*TGN* %	*KNS* %	*GBL* %
Moroccan	427	70	90	98	75	929	84	92	98	84
Turkish	356	66	74	95	88	n/a	–	–	–	–
Indonesian	186	87	91	96	99	229	99	93	99	99

First, to stay on the analysis of test results, we can more accurately assess impact on defined target populations by looking at pass rates by nationality. Table 7.2 presents 2011 and 2012 pass rates for Turkish and Moroccan applicants. I also include Indonesian applicants to serve as a point of comparison. There are no scores recorded in 2012 for Turkish immigrants, after a 2011 Central Court of Appeals decision ruled the integration-abroad test for immigrants and their spouses from Turkey seeking either permanent or temporary residence was a violation of the EU–Turkey Association Agreement.[53] In looking at these percentages, we see a moderately lower pass rate among Moroccan first-time test-takers in 2011 (70 percent) compared to the national average (75 percent), but a significantly lower success rate among Turkish applicants (at 66 percent). By 2012, perhaps after a period of learning (which may inform a different preparation for second-time test takers), the Moroccan average climbs above the national average. The knowledge component (KNS) proves to be an ineffective barrier to all categories, while language creates the most difficulty. In particular, Moroccans struggle the most with Dutch reading comprehension, while Turks score significantly lower on the spoken Dutch component. In contrast to the Indonesian applicants, both groups fared worse, suggesting the test has variegated effects based on pre-existing traits.

As such, there are identifiable changes in family migration as a result of new requirements, not only the test in 2006 but also the income requirement between 2004 and 2011. Table 7.3 presents family-based migration as a share of total intake. We observe a decrease between 2005 and 2011 of 53 percent (thus meeting and exceeding the government's goals). The disincentivizing effect of the test itself also is evident, as the numbers of applications between 2006 and 2007 drop dramatically. In raw figures, more than 11,000 fewer family-based migrants applied for entry in 2007, representing a change of 42 percent. And

52 Significant, "Monitoring the integration from abroad exam ("Monitor Inburgeringsexamen Buitenland")," 37–38.

53 Turkish immigrants are also exempt in Austria.

TABLE. 7.3. *Change in family-based migration by year*[54]

	Number (in thousands)	Category % of Total
2005	28.1	45.0
2006	27.7	46.6
2007	16.1	23
2008	30.4	58.8
2009	29.3	61
2010	20.8	21.7
2011	22.4	21.2

where application figures rebounded in 2008, a continued decline in applications can be witnessed: family migration declines from comprising almost 60 percent of immigration in 2008 to 21 percent in 2011. This represents a change of almost 64 percent, and a real alteration to the composite profile of Dutch immigration today. In offering an alternative to the "passive" reception of immigrants, the Dutch model is without precedent.

POLICY TRANSFER AND LEARNING EFFECTS: VARIATION ACROSS PRACTICING STATES

The final section of this chapter examines how the other European practitioners of external civic integration requirements learned from the Dutch experience. Subsequent permutations by neighboring states have altered the structure or content of the Dutch model, but the intent of limiting migration has remained constant. As evidenced in Table 7.4 (taking a snapshot year in 2006), family-based migration reveals to be among the largest category in every state, second only to intra-EU free movement. Yet, most significantly, the state with the most pressing family-to-skilled labor ratio – France – maintains the least invasive and coercive policy.

The diffusion of ultimately different civic integration practices as a mechanism to control family-based migration results from a process of domestic-level policy learning, defined as lesson-drawing as a type of voluntary policy transfer that allows policymakers to use a variety of instruments, content, and goals.[55] The Human Rights Watch report is illustrative in this case. After its chastisement of civic integration from abroad, one Dutch policymaker observed that other countries felt that if the "liberal Dutch" could get admonished for perceivably

[54] OECD, *International Migration Outlook: SOPEMI 2008; 2010; 2011*, p. 205; *2013*, p. 279.

[55] David P. Dolowitz and David Marsh, "Earning from abroad: The role of policy transfer in contemporary policy-making," *Governance* 13, no. 1 (2000): 9.

TABLE 7.4. *Migration inflow by type, percentage distribution for 2006*[56]

	Work	Family *(including accompanying family)*	Humanitarian	Free movement	Other
Austria	1.5	41.0	11.1	46.2	.3
Denmark	15.2	23.8	5.0	50.5	5.5
France	6.1	59.0	4 .4	20.0	10.5
Germany	6.1	23.3	2.8	64.2	3.6
Netherlands	5.4	46.6	24.3	23.6	–
UK	28.9	31.8	8.9	24.3	6.0

discriminatory policies, they would fare far worse.[57] A British policymaker reaffirmed this suspicion, noting that "We got a sense of what excessive was perceived as."[58] On the other side of this argument, Block and Bonjour note the Netherlands' strategic interest in model diffusion: "Having other Member states follow its lead gave Dutch civic integration policy the legitimacy of serving as a role model, rather than remaining an extreme and exceptional case."[59] It follows, therefore, across the remaining five states, that we see a variety of institutions – from domestic courts to legal precedent to party politics – play a role in altering the original Dutch template to national specification.

The most direct adaptation of the Dutch model occurred in Denmark. Strik et al. note that "during the debate in parliament, it was stressed that the immigration test had not been invented by the government; it had been, allegedly, successfully implemented in the Netherlands."[60] Using the Dutch example as a legitimizing baseline, the Danish introduced a similar integration test in 2010. While the test rhetorically aimed to promote rapid integration, it was also the hope that "based on the test some migrants might change their opinion about staying in Denmark – having discovered 'what it is all about' (learning about Danish sexual morality, etc.)."[61] And while the Danish People's Party was not interested in creating any exemptions based on nationality, immigrants from OECD countries are exempt because they have a "considerable similarity to Denmark and therefore have better prerequisites to become integrated in Danish society."[62] As such, citizens of the EU, Australia, Canada, Israel, Japan, New Zealand, Switzerland, South Korea, and the United States were exempt.

56 OECD, 2008. 57 Interview with the author. March 21, 2009. Den Haag, NL: VROM.
58 Interview with the author. August 3, 2009. London, UK: Home Office.
59 Block and Bonjour, "Fortress Europe or Europe of rights? The Europeanisation of family migration policies in France, Germany and the Netherlands," 219.
60 Strik et al., "Synthesis Report," 28. 61 Ibid.
62 Silvia Adamo, "What Is the point? Policies on immigration and the language issue in Denmark," in *RECODE Working Paper Series* (2012), 7.

However, the Danish part company from the Dutch model in several respects. First, immigrants complete the immigration test *after* immigration. As previously mentioned, in order to receive a residence permit, immigrants and their spouses/partners must pass the immigration test as well as provide a financial guarantee ("collateral requirement"). This shift enables an immigrant to practice Danish in a wider circle than just their spouse (as structured in the Dutch model). Second, in 2012, the new center-left government replaced the immigration test with a language test, effectively removing the country knowledge component. Finally, alongside this change was the removal of exemptions, where the aforementioned nationalities are now required to demonstrate proficiency of Danish at the A1 level.

Germany had a number of influences for shaping its pre-entry language requirement, drawing on past experiences, EU precedent (the language requirement was adopted as part of legislation titled the "Directives Implementation Act"), as well as other state models.[63] The Christian Democrats advocated a German language test as a way to prohibit forced and arranged marriage, as well as prevent misuses of family reunification generally. Policymakers also saw the Dutch incur significant costs of state-run assessment.[64] As a result, they adopted a more cost-effective program of integration-from-abroad by delegating-out training and assessment. Instead of taking on the costs of running an exam themselves, assessment of German proficiency takes place through the Goethe Institute, a private (but state-funded) organization that is globally situated in order to proliferate German language and culture. There is also no German test requirement per se, rather a requirement of language proficiency. This creates an easy avenue for admission for proficient German speakers, who can obtain certification through a degree or diploma granted by a secondary institution (for immigrants who have independently studied German) or through the passing of an A1-compatible German test, called *Start Deutsch 1*, at the Goethe Institute.[65] Austria also makes use of the Goethe Institute to prepare migrants in German proficiency and provide the A1-level test. Those who are not proficient and need to take this test may opt to take a language course as well, though a majority of migrants who take the test at the Goethe Institute (approximately 80 percent) do not take part in a course.[66] The German government does not

[63] Block and Bonjour, "Fortress Europe or Europe of rights? The Europeanisation of family migration policies in France, Germany and the Netherlands," 217.

[64] The Dutch themselves also recognized the inherently high costs of providing language and integration courses in countries of origin, opting instead to write the "Welcome to the Netherlands" preparation material and shift the onus of integration on the individual. Embassies were ill-equipped to run such intensive programs, and nothing exists for Dutch-language training like the Goethe Institute.

[65] There is minimal variation in the price of certification; the San Francisco office charges $60 and the Istanbul office charges $66 (100 TL). However, one can obtain certification only at an Institute with language departments.

[66] P. W. A. Scholten et al., "Integration from abroad? Perception and impacts of pre-entry tests for third country nationals," in *Promoting Sustainable Policies for Integration (PROSINT)*, ed. ICMPD (2012), 63.

subsidize any of this training or assessment. The certification process also does not require country knowledge. And despite a traditionally active role by domestic courts in impacting immigration law, decisions in 2007 (Administrative Court in Berlin) and 2010 (Federal Administrative Court in Leipzig) confirmed that the requirement to demonstrate a basic knowledge of German did not violate German Basic Law's protection of marriage and family or equality. Other challenges to the policy through individual suits have been countermanded thus far through the strategic issuing of visas, rendering decisions on legality of requirements moot.

Adoption in the UK was inspired by similar impetuses as the former cases, referencing other country measures and presenting the pre-entry language requirement in a 2007 UK Border Agency document titled "Marriage Visas: the way forward." It ended up adopting a requirement similar to Germany, requiring that applicants for leave to remain demonstrate a basic level of spoken English prior to arrival. Inspired by the Dutch, but structurally modeled off their own Points Based System (PBS) where skill-based applicants demonstrate English competence in listening, speaking, writing and reading, the British system requires marriage-based migrants to demonstrate only listening and speaking proficiency. There are myriad qualifications and test providers through which an individual can fulfill the language requirement at the A1 level, including the TOEFL ("Test of English as a Foreign Language") and Pearson Test of English Academic (PTE Academic). Given the minimal level of assessment and maximal level of outward delegation to private institutions, the UK Border Agency estimates that the total cost of introducing a language requirement will yield a negative net loss between 3.2 and 28.8 million pounds.[67] This estimate factors in transitional costs for the UK Border Agency, as well as costs for the applicant in tuition and testing, and third/private sector actors that provide training and familiarization. And while a case was brought to the High Court in 2011 challenging the English test as having a discriminatory effect on a couples' right to a family life, the policy was maintained.

Austria's pre-entry language requirement explicitly followed the "successful models" of its European neighbors.[68] Like the Netherlands, we also see domestic courts play a role in influencing policy output. In this case, courts delayed implementation. Political discussion for pre-entry German proficiency occurred alongside discussion of a new, comprehensive points-based migration system (the Red-White-Red Card scheme), which differentiated between wanted migration (skilled) and unwanted migration (unskilled, adult TCNs). This latter category was seen as disruptive to social integration because of high unemployment rates and lack of basic competence in German. And as an interesting product of business and employer representative lobbying, exemptions were

[67] UK Border Agency, "Impact assessment: English language requirement for spouses," ed. UKBA (London: Home Office, 2010), 2.

[68] Scholten et al., "Integration from abroad? Perception and impacts of pre-entry tests for third country nationals," 57.

secured for family members of very highly skilled migrants, but not for skilled migrants.[69] Moreover, in an interesting difference to Germany, Austria maintains a strict quota system for family reunification. In this system, where German certification is only valid for one year after issuance, migrants must renew their certification if the quota for that year has already been met.

Finally, the French were keen to learn from both the Dutch and subsequent German model when designing their integration-from-abroad policy.[70] As a result, the Immigration Law of 2008 (also referred to as the Hortefeux Law) requires a family-forming migrant to demonstrate a sufficient level of French proficiency not exclusively through assessment (i.e., testing), but primarily through evaluation (i.e., conversation and interview).[71] Additionally, foreigners applying for family reunification must also have knowledge of republican values.

Like Austria, France also faced a number of legal issues in implementing integration-from-abroad, particularly because the "right to a normal family life" is a constitutional right ("*principe général du droit*'), and therefore protected by the Constitutional Council. The left-wing parties – especially the Socialists – used this principle to oppose external requirements. There were also ambitions to make the integration requirement more rigorous; Sarkozy, while campaigning for President in 2007, proposed the idea of an integration test to demonstrate knowledge of the French language. However, amendments for greater restrictions were withdrawn upon the advice of the government, who suggested that "the Constitutional Council would most certainly censor a provision that would thus infringe upon the right to family reunification."[72] As a result, French integration-from-abroad measures are much milder than intended and designed. Cost and domestic legal constraints have retarded implementation, but they have not tabled robust integration ambitions. For example, a separate integration contract for the family (*Contrat d'Acceuil et d'Integration pour la famille*) was implemented in 2009 for immigrating spouses and families, and legislation for some form of integration test was passed but not implemented.[73]

Observing the diffusion of the Dutch model and subsequent adaptations not only legitimates the initial practice, it also reveals how European states amend

[69] Ibid., 56.

[70] See Thierry Mariani, "Rapport sur les politiques d'intégration des migrants dans l'union Européenne," in *Report 3502 of the National Assembly* (2006).

[71] Foreigners who have studied at a French secondary school or have one year of higher education of French are exempt (Article R 311-30-2).

[72] Bonjour, "Between integration provision and selection mechanism," 313.

[73] Arrêté du 1er décembre 2008 relatif à l'évaluation dans leur pays de résidence du niveau de connaissance, par les étrangers, de la langue française et des valeurs de la République et aux formations prescrites dans ces domaines conformément aux articles R. 311-30-1 à R. 311-30-11 du code de l'entrée et du séjour des étrangers et du droit d'asile, IMIC0827547A, *Journal Officiel de la République française*, December 5, 2008.

integration-from-abroad in terms of difficulty, practice, and coordination as a result of domestic institutions, from politics to courts. This variation does not reaffirm the outdated analytical tool of national models of immigrant integration (i.e., multiculturalism, assimilation), but shows the strength of the policy-learning process. It also underscores the shared goal of family-migration control, and that there are any number of avenues states can take to get there.

CONCLUSION

In light of this important fusion between immigration control and integration policy in a handful of important countries of immigration in Western Europe, a question looms for consideration. If the connections between migration control objectives and integration-from-abroad are so concrete, why do politicians and policymakers refer to it as an integration tool in the first place? In other words, why do elites use the language of integration and inclusion for what appears to be a decidedly non-inclusive outcome?

One possible answer sees the two not as a trade-off but as complementary goals, whereby selective immigration policies at the border enable successful integration policies in the country. This suggests a dual functionality to external integration; requirements are not only mechanisms of control, but there is the sense that controlling intake can lead to better integration internally. This may be because immigrants are better prepared to integrate having already taken initial steps. It may also be because resources are more concentrated with lower intake figures, producing a better quality of integration courses and other services and increasing the possibility for migrants to engage in the labor market or with new social networks. Language and knowledge requirements for residence and citizenship can start the work of integration, especially where migrants must begin right away with integration courses and contracts, while an initial, selective vetting at the pre-entry stage makes sure that the immigrants are prepared to begin such a rigorous process of integration.

A second, less-tangible answer to the question of why policymakers frame a potentially objectionable and contentious policy with the language of mutual beneficence, where integration is a public good in which the newcomer and receiving society prosper, is that governments are devising new and effective strategies to reduce unwanted immigration (i.e., low-skilled) without incurring accusations of illiberal or discriminatory behavior. Supranational opportunity and precedent set by one of the most famously tolerant societies in Europe contributes a degree of endorsement for other states to pursue variations on the theme. In this answer we see the greatest difference between external and internal civic integration. While external civic integration allows for more blunt policies and effective regulation of persons coming in, internal civic integration requires more nuanced approaches where the goal is control and limitation.

Each of these answers is simultaneously possible. Civic integration proves not only to be multi-faceted but also influenced by a multitude of domestic, supranational, and international factors. Without minimizing some significant, well-intentioned aims of policymakers to ensure new spouses can operate independently in their new home, integration-from-abroad conditions appear to be distinct from the processes establishing thorough and lasting integration as a permanent resident or a citizen, prioritizing regulation of intake for its own sake. They are principally connected by subject and objective (integration requirements connect the external to the internal as a means to best prepare an immigrant for integration upon arrival), but we see distinctly different political processes and conditions impact each policy. Additional speculation can be made as to the relationship between internal and external dimensions of civic integration, but suffice it to say it is evident they are oftentimes motivated by different objectives and, therefore, serve potentially overlapping but conceptually distinct ends.

This chapter has shown how deterritorialized requirements are shaped out of supranational opportunity and lesson-learning following Dutch legitimization for the purposes of regulating, qualifying, and, indeed, limiting family-based migration. By contrast, states have demonstrated myriad reasons, conditions, and mechanisms for introducing civic requirements internally. States have patently fewer obligations toward potential immigrants than they do toward settlement-seeking immigrants, where inclusion (or, at the very least, acknowledgment) is unavoidable in advanced democracies. That states juggle both internal and external dimensions only underscores the complexity and importance of civic integration policy today.

Conclusion: the anchoring of citizenship

The widespread adoption of mandatory integration requirements has unequivocally raised the profile of membership in European societies. New state articulations of belonging through language, country knowledge, and value requirements have not only defined a script of membership for newcomers to follow, they also signify a "waking up" of the European nation-state to twenty-first century realities of immigrant-related ethnic and cultural heterogeneity. This important updating of national membership reveals the nation-building project to be an ongoing one and one that, perhaps, is even more vibrant than ever. Membership as a category of belonging contains an intrinsic and unique set of values to the state that are distinct from values of national citizenship as a legal status (see Chapter 1), and the current, almost obsessive focus on membership suggests that citizenship alone is insufficient for keeping European societies together.

This book has taken a critical look at this new process of membership definition by examining both the root causes for civic integration policy adoption as well as processes of policy adaptation. Existing explanations for civic integration policy across European nation-states have drawn on similar macro-explanations, propping up a consensus view of convergent policy change, where states with most-different concepts of national belonging become more similar by adopting a common integration approach. This is one version of the civic integration story in which, as Christian Joppke describes it, "everything and everyone flees the center," demoting the value of citizenship and national belonging by liberalizing access and expanding rights to residence.[1] Convergence and national diminution accounts serve as a useful jumping-off point for the analysis presented in this book in that they offer a series of testable

[1] Christian Joppke, *Citizenship and Immigration* (Immigration & Society series) (Cambridge; Malden, MA: Polity, 2010), 148.

propositions. In examining these accounts, however, a second, more nuanced version of the civic integration story comes to light, in which policymakers identify common pressures but are influenced and constrained by the institutional setting in which they play out, including both existing citizenship orientations and domestic politics. Examining this version of the civic integration story not only required robust case study analysis and a series of paired comparisons to examine the effects of conjunctural causation, but also developing a systematic measure of civic integration policy to accurately characterize the phenomenon of civic integration, identifying degrees of similarity and difference, and moving beyond anecdotal or qualitative descriptions.

Therefore, the contributions of this book signify a break with previous work in a number of respects. First, by developing a Civic Integration Policy Index (CIVIX) to measure configurations of membership requirements in a period before change and after, I have provided evidence that pushed beyond dichotomous change and convergence accounts to reveal that we actually see *degrees* of adoption (developed in Chapter 2). Some states offer robust practices of civic integration, whereas others are more modest. Still others, such as Sweden and Ireland, have not adopted any civic integration policies. We also see variation in change, where some states went from zero policies to extensive buffets of membership requirements (Denmark) and others had some legal precedent or experience in membership from which to build upon (Germany). While not a fully comprehensive measure of policy, CIVIX provides an efficient means of scoring and comparing policies, which enables analysis and comparison across both space and time.

CIVIX conveys the size of civic integration policy change, but not the nature of it. As the case studies in this book have shown, states with high CIVIX scores have all made a "civic turn," but policies bear significant divergence in design, scope, and sequencing. As such, identification of policy diversity is the second major contribution of this book. I moved "closer to the ground" to triangulate quantitative observations gleaned from CIVIX and other indices with qualitative descriptions of membership policy to reveal this diversity, in both policy outcome and practice. This evidence of policy variety then pointed to the possibility that there are a variety of reasons behind policy adoption, a hypothesis I went on to develop theoretically and test empirically through within-case analysis. In sum, identifying significant difference in membership policies led to the central research question of the book: Why do states adopt civic integration requirements?

The third major contribution of this book – and the centerpiece of analysis – is in answering this question. I have established that states may have all made a turn toward obligatory integration, but they have done so under different conditions and for distinctly different reasons. Specifically, I argue (in Chapter 3) that state strategies for implementing civic integration requirements are determined by citizenship orientation, or existing policies that define degrees of access to citizenship, and government preferences of membership, i.e., whether left/inclusionary or right/exclusionary governments are in power. The effects of citizenship orientation cannot only be seen in defining the parameters of debate and change (where both left and right are theoretically constrained) and thus shaping party preferences, but also in strategic changes to permanent residence, where exclusionary ends can be accomplished by creating a more formidable chain of conditionality. As a result, while we see a similar set of instruments in the form of tests, courses, oaths, etc., across European states, we see them used for different reasons. Citizenship context can lead differently oriented governments to define and pursue similar policy paths (Chapter 4). Citizenship context can also lead similarly oriented governments to define and pursue distinct policy paths (Chapter 5).

But context does not tell the whole story, and this is not merely a retelling of the path dependence narrative. Political parties are agents of change and can maneuver any number of ways within a given institutional framework. Therefore, similar conditions may not always yield similar policy outcomes or practices where political actors operate differently. Chapter 6 illustrates this scenario, where far-right politicization in the context of consensus in the Netherlands contributed to a layering – and eventual embedding – of restriction, while politicization by similar forces in France only exacerbated polarization between major parties, rendering policy more superficial – and thus reversible – when a new party comes to power. Moreover, governments are not always the source of change. Opposition parties may use civic integration requirement to offset proposed changes or currents of thinking they view as undesirable, making strategic use of integration to improve their own political fortunes. In-depth case studies illustrated these different strategies of civic integration policy and fleshed out the various mechanisms for policy change, including agenda-setting, leverage gained from coalition membership, and insulation of policy entrepreneurs from the political process.

Finally, we have seen that where there are variable guiding strategies for attaching new membership requirements to processes of settlement and naturalization, there is an altogether separate – and shared – rationale: membership regulation at the border. In distinguishing between internal and external dimensions of civic integration (Chapter 7), I showed that internal civic integration can achieve a number of different objectives – depending on the aforementioned domestic conditions – but external civic integration is largely governed by the goal of immigration control, especially that of family-based migration. In the spirit of providing a comprehensive account of the civic integration phenomenon, I presented a separate argument to account for this shared logic, identifying opportunities created by supranational EU Directives and legitimacy provided by early Dutch practices as central explanatory factors to account for external convergence. By distinguishing between internal and external policy and the different reasons behind their adoption, this study draws attention to the complex and dynamic nature of this new policy, one that is too multifaceted to be reduced to dichotomous treatments or explained away by potentially reductive accounts.

Overall, this book has been structured with two goals in mind. The first is methodological: to systematically examine new membership requirements with the tools of comparative political science and an eye toward causality. In providing the first analytically driven comparison of civic integration policies, combining medium-N analysis and within-case analysis of six case studies, presented through three paired comparisons, it is my hope that the study lays a rigorous foundation for further research among citizenship and immigration scholars. By deriving analysis from empirical observation and comparison, not thick descriptions or normative positions, further studies can contribute to the joint enterprise of theory testing and development, mapping in particular potential extensions of civic integration in and beyond Western Europe. The possible extension of scope in both space and time enables greater consideration of whether common instruments (tests, courses, etc.) are indicative of common problems or goals, whether obligatory integration changes the meaning of citizenship and belonging for citizens, as well as whether immigrants – in the long run – perceive of themselves as more included vis-à-vis their own functionality built out of language skills and country knowledge.

Moreover, the groundwork laid here makes possible the consideration of what effect civic integration policies actually have on immigrants. Do civic integration courses make a difference in the lives of immigrants? Do course and test graduates feel a greater sense of understanding – and therefore attachment and loyalty – to their adoptive home as a result of obligatory integration? It is still too early to examine overall and long-term effects of civic integration, but asking questions in this direction is possible with the foundation laid here. There is no reason to believe that the value of membership and autonomy-promoting skills will go unnoticed in other advanced democracies, particularly as they continue to face the challenge of preparing immigrants for the labor market in times of recession. Nor is there any reason to believe membership is going away any time soon.

The second goal was conceptual: to turn the spotlight on membership as a critical and complementary component of citizenship. We witness the state (re) turning to membership through new articulations of state identity as a way of addressing problems associated with immigration, which some ascribe as a type of state response to the "clash of civilizations" in reference to the rise of Islam in Europe. This articulation resurrects the very idea of membership from the annals of history, even though it is different in form and content from traditional national identity. Nation-states are not merely reasserting what they already have, but defining new parameters of belonging under the banner of liberalism. This act of definition is not particularly surprising. Benedict Anderson famously describes the nation as an "imagined political community," where the nation is not merely imagined but "once imagined, modeled, adapted and transformed."[2]

[2] Benedict Anderson, *Imagined Communities: Reflections on the origin and spread of nationalism* (London; New York: Verso, 1991), 145.

Rogers Smith forwards a similar thought in suggesting "the politics of people-building is always an ongoing as well as a competitive politics, even within apparently well-established and unified political communities."[3] In other words, nation-building is not merely about foundational moments; it is an ongoing process that requires maintenance.

While change to definitions of belonging is not novel, the content of its most current iteration is. Connecting skill and value acquisition to the process of obtaining permanent legal status within the state represents a type of reinvestment in the idea that establishing a formal relationship between an individual and a state is meaningful. As such, these new membership commitments signify that states are still heavily vested in belonging, through the logic of togetherness and the concept of state identity, not sameness as embodied in national identity. This is an important insight that I hope this book contributes to migration studies specifically and the comparative study of advanced democracies generally. Especially where we see growing integration gaps between immigrants and natives, including but not limited to a democratic deficit where lack of skills hinders participation and therefore representation, state efforts to forge superordinate identification and unity become significant not only for membership but also for questions of designing and maintaining viable democratic regimes in ethnically divided societies.

Moreover, the promotion of state identity through civic integration and reinvestment in national citizenship through membership does not mean states are reverting to the kind of flat, assimilationist trope of belonging often characterized of nation-states.[4] Instead, re-asserting the importance of membership suggests states find a value to it as a category that binds people together in a community of like values, skills, and goals (or, on the other side of the coin, membership makes citizenship a more coherent identity that can justify exclusion in the context of liberalizing norms). It is not sameness but togetherness, or, more specifically, the balance of autonomy with connectedness that matters in twenty-first century democratic nation-states defined by ethnic diversity. Belonging is not valuable in the abstract; membership matters in concrete and unique ways to both the individual and the state.

The rest of this concluding chapter discusses broader implications of civic integration policy in Europe today and the book's central finding: states adopt membership requirements under different conditions, for different purposes, and, inevitably, for different effect. Specifically, I focus on two themes. First, I discuss what I interpret as the "anchoring" of national citizenship through membership. Contrary to descriptions of the "lightening" of citizenship or post-national predictions of a bifurcation of citizenship and belonging, I identify

[3] Rogers M. Smith, "Citizenship and the politics of people-building," *Citizenship Studies* 5, no. 1 (2001), 76.

[4] See, for example, Ashutosh Varshney, "Discovering the 'state-nation'," *Journal of Democracy* 23, no. 2 (2012), 163.

a strengthening and renewing of citizenship through membership content and norms. This occurs through one of two processes: either citizenship is directly strengthened through new content, or it is indirectly buttressed by changes to adjacent or peripheral policies. This buttressing includes the expansion of citizen-like expectation to non-citizen stages. Finally, and particularly because states adopt different membership requirements to address different membership problems, we see that acts of citizenship anchoring remain nationally distinct. This conceptual overhaul reflects a new generation of thinking about citizenship and membership, not as an inherent relationship but as a dynamic, ongoing, and purposeful one.

In this section, I also consider the extent to which the "civic turn" represents an alternative to or departure from liberal ideals. Many scholars, namely political theorists, have challenged the extent to which the liberal defense of obligatory integration is valid or consistent with the tenets of liberalism. Others ascribe the widespread adoption of active service-based citizenship as not merely a departure from liberalism to illiberalism, but also concomitant to a "republican turn." I suggest that the latter premise is a false choice. Meanwhile, as liberal-democratic value ascription becomes involuntary and states identify a new, closer role in facilitating integration, I maintain that civic integration remains liberal in practice, but barely.

Third, and finally, I consider the extent to which membership requirements impact the immigrant–state relationship. While civic integration has its own objectives, it remains insufficient for addressing larger issues of immigrant integration, xenophobia, and inequality. These concerns have democratic consequences for the liberal democratic nation-state, which become increasingly difficult to avoid over time.

THE NATION-STATE'S NEW LEASE ON LIFE

Conflict over identity and immigration are two of the most prominent issues defining European politics today. As conflicts of perceived national interest – from diffuse threats of immigration to immediate conflicts over the Eurozone debt crisis – pull states further and further apart, complicating and potentially undermining achievements in European integration over time, states are turning inward. There is not a small amount of irony in this turn. Alan Milward describes how, in the immediate postwar period, when economic crises were rife, the nation-state was "rescued" by coming together in the European Community.[5] Today, policymakers seem firmly of the belief that salvation and national survival lies not in Europe, but in a return to the nation-state. To that, the most important and significant consequence of membership-promoting policies in Europe is the unique and innovative way in which it is rescuing national citizenship and, by extension, the nation-state. This book has so far

[5] Alan S. Milward, *The European rescue of the nation-state* (London; New York: Routledge, 2000).

provided ample evidence to show how citizenship policies and politics impact policymakers' decisions to introduce membership requirements. In turn, we saw in the evolution and application of membership requirements the fortification of existing approaches to citizenship, recognizing that even ambitious change is only moderate in effect given the larger parameters of existing understanding of belonging. This conclusion provides an opportunity to expand on this insight, to explore how membership ultimately preserves citizenship as the keystone category of belonging in the nation-state. I address three important questions. How does membership strengthen, or anchor, national citizenship? What sort of identity is civic integration actually promoting? And, how does this novel membership identity qualify as nation-building and, therefore, nation-state saving?

How does membership anchor citizenship? The strengthening of citizenship through membership occurs through one of two ways: citizenship is directly changed through the layering of new membership content, or citizenship is indirectly affected by changes to related policies. Both processes – often at the same time – are visible in the case studies examined in this book. The case studies illustrate states following distinct national paths to civic integration policy. In so doing, the anchoring of citizenship is also non-uniform. Civic integration policy in Austria, Denmark, and Germany ultimately has a more exclusionary effect than policy in the Netherlands, France, and the UK. All make status acquisition more conditional, but they illustrate that there is a difference between *qualified* and *restrictive* acquisition procedures.

Beginning with direct changes, membership requirements primarily serve to strengthen and preserve citizenship as the central category of national belonging without necessitating changes to some of the foundations of citizenship policy itself. This process is referred to as "institutional layering," in which there is "partial renegotiation of some elements of a given set of institutions while leaving others in place."[6] In fact, it is interesting to note that in many of these cases (e.g., France, Germany) citizenship debates were largely settled before civic integration moved to the forefront of the domestic agenda. Layering occurs when new elements are attached to existing institutions and these can gradually change the structure over time. It does not replace existing institutions, but adds to them, "thereby changing the ways in which the original rules structure behavior."[7] The addition of formal integration requirements significantly "thickens" the identity of citizenship without altering existing tenets of citizenship, like residency duration, procedure of acquisition, dual citizenship, etc. In fact, only in Germany do we see civic integration requirements

[6] Kathleen Thelen, "How institutions evolve: Insights from comparative historical analysis," in *Comparative Historical Analysis in the Social Sciences*, ed. James Mahoney and Dietrich Rueschemeyer (Cambridge: Cambridge University Press, 2003), 225–26.

[7] James Mahoney and Kathleen Ann Thelen, *Explaining Institutional Change: Ambiguity, agency, and power* (Cambridge, UK; New York: Cambridge University Press, 2010), 16.

negotiated as a means to offset change to citizenship (specifically, liberalization). In most cases, integration requirements get added to – not traded for – existing policies. Citizenship policy is the institutional context in which policymakers understand the parameters of belonging, and, by and large, the past decade has been defined not as one of citizenship policy change, but one of membership policy change in the form of civic integration requirements. While the trend in scholarship has been to interpret membership policy changes as a type of restrictive backlash to citizenship liberalization (employing the trade-off mentality of obligations for rights), the case studies provided in this book illustrate that restriction is not always the primary or exclusive aim of integration requirements. They can preserve existing restriction (Austria, Denmark), create new politically motivated restriction (the Netherlands), and recalibrate liberalization (Germany) to produce a zero-sum outcome, but they can also promote integration (France and the Netherlands before 2002) or promote citizenship uptake (the UK).

The anchoring of citizenship also occurs indirectly through changes to related policies. These membership changes secure the importance of citizenship as a cantilever. In this capacity, we observe layering, but also a process of institutional conversion, where "existing institutions are redirected to new purposes."[8] Through this mechanism, citizenship is indirectly strengthened by building up permanent residence as a durable and meaningful membership status. Repurposing permanent residence to become a formidable barrier of integration directly impacts citizenship without necessitating changes to citizenship itself. In some cases, permanent residence is transformed into a portico to facilitate and promote progression to citizenship, especially where we see integration requirements "double count" for permanent residence and citizenship (the Netherlands, the UK) or where permanent residence is not a requirement for citizenship. Notably, in the Dutch case, standards of integration for citizenship were eventually even replaced with the assessment of integration for permanent residence, rendering permanent residence the centrifugal point for defining inclusion and membership, not citizenship. In other cases, we see permanent residence transformed to serve as an impediment to or substitute for citizenship, promoting integration as a stable, alternative legal status. This is especially the case where permanent residence becomes yet another prerequisite for obtaining national citizenship (Austria), or where the integration barriers to permanent residence do not obviate additional integration requirements for citizenship (Denmark). In repurposing permanent residence, drawing it into a deliberately strategic relationship to citizenship, policymakers can avoid direct changes to citizenship but still achieve citizenship-related goals of maintaining inclusive–exclusive distinctions in the population. This is particularly advantageous where political debates over citizenship *qua* membership can be more controversial than debates addressing permanent residence, which are typically related to immigration control and colored by a more restrictive-oriented consensus.

[8] Thelen, "How institutions evolve: Insights from comparative historical analysis," 225–26.

Both of these mechanisms – layering and conversion – represent dynamic and nuanced readings of policy change. It is my desire that this book, therefore, pushes the practice of analysis beyond a linear reading of access requirements, where liberal gains in the latter are negated by restrictive changes in the former, and toward a more complex, configurative view of policy.[9] Through layering, citizenship is infused with new dimensions of identity without fundamental changes to or trade-offs with existing rules. Through conversion, primarily focusing on permanent residence, citizenship can indirectly increase in value as an incentive but also as a prize. Membership requirements may certainly make citizenship more difficult or desirable to obtain, but it is through the layering of new policies on top of old ones and not by altering existing policy parameters. In this, membership requirements have rejuvenated citizenship by infusing a sense of meaning in defining not only new elements of the acquisition process but what the end point of that process looks like. In sum, both processes strengthen citizenship with new meaning. But what kind of meaning? Can only certain kinds of identity anchor national citizenship against tides of change and irrelevance? What kind of identity does civic integration actually promote?

A number of civic integration studies examine the type of membership or belonging that civic integration requirements ostensibly promote.[10] Some interpret a cultural, thick identity, while others see a liberal, thin identity. Does only a certain type of identity qualify as nation-building and, therefore, nation-state saving? A narrow definition of national identity, one grounded in cultural essentialism, would answer "yes." Rising from the ashes of nineteenth-century European empires, nation-states are politically demarcated territories that reflect a coherent or singular culture, defined by language, shared history, etc. The citizen, or *national*, is the political identity that connects the individual member of that community to the political entity of the state that claims to represent this group's interests. Therefore, the death knell of national identity and, by extension, the nation-state is the disappearance of *national* difference. Promoting liberal democratic values and skills that could enable an immigrant to function in interchangeable, advanced democracies, according to this perspective, is decidedly non-national. Joppke expounds on this view by interpreting current attempts to "renationalize citizenship" as just "smoke and mirrors – a 'symbolic politics' if ever there was one," concluding that "the future of citizenship is

[9] For a prior articulation of this argument, see Sara Wallace Goodman, "Integration requirements for integration's sake? Identifying, categorising and comparing civic integration policies," *Journal of Ethnic and Migration Studies* 36, no. 5 (2010): 753–772. For a more disaggregated perspective of policy "constellations" see Gary P. Freeman, "Immigrant incorporation in Western democracies," *International Migration Review* 38, no. 3 (2004): 945–969.

[10] For some examples, see Christian Joppke, "Immigration and the identity of citizenship: The paradox of universalism," *Citizenship Studies* 12, no. 6 (2008): 533–546; Dora Kostakopoulou, "Thick, thin and thinner patriotisms: Is this all there is?," *Oxford Journal of Legal Studies* 26, no. 1 (2006): 73–106; Ines Michalowski, "Required to assimilate? The content of citizenship tests in five countries," *Citizenship Studies* 15, no. 6/7 (2011): 749–768.

bound to be light, and lighter still with the help of 'Europe.'"[11] This view holds that a state cannot maintain a specific national identity while invoking or building membership around universal principles and values espoused by liberalism. The lightening of citizenship here is a thin denationalizing identity, juxtaposed to what Joppke sees as a thick, culturally laden national identity, where, aside from the specificities of national language, there is nothing particularly British, Dutch, or German to the content of membership requirements.

I offer two critiques of this position. First, these views take an excessively purist, even nostalgic, view of identity. Nation-states are not what they once were – and this is a good thing – but that does not mean that a modern nation-state cannot persevere, where membership in one state is distinguished from membership in another. Distinction is not achieved by rehashing an arcane identity, but in manufacturing a new one. As Will Kymlicka argues (see Chapter 1 for a lengthier discussion), immigrants necessarily integrate into greater society while preserving what he describes as a "societal culture." At a minimum, this identity is thin and may include only linguistic integration or knowledge of history and other social institutions.[12] State articulations of common culture, according to Kymlicka, are not violations of liberalism or a desecration of state neutrality, but a necessary minimum for contemporary states. Others, including Jürgen Habermas and Jan-Werner Müller, even propose a type of third way to the thick versus thin identity debate, noting that a type of national or constitutional patriotism can exist that promotes liberal values in a national context.[13] In sum, it is unnecessarily reductionist to draw a line in the sand where only thick national identity can infuse national citizenship with significance or a distinctive meaning of belonging. There is room for a skill- and value-laden civic identity to replace the role formerly played by traditional national identity, now defunct as a source for membership, having been so thoroughly delegitimized after the atrocities of World War II. A state or civic identity also supports national citizenship where historical alternatives, like subnational or city identities, do not appear to be competition for a newcomers' affection and affinity.

Second, critiques of civic integration as expressions of "repressive liberalism" or "illiberal liberalism" are also unnecessarily simplistic, casting too broad a negative shadow over the entire civic integration project. The chief accusations against the liberality of integration tests is not that they are hard (though there

[11] Joppke, *Citizenship and Immigration*, 172.

[12] Will Kymlicka, *Politics in the Vernacular: Nationalism, multiculturalism, and citizenship* (Oxford; New York: Oxford University Press, 2001), 155–74.

[13] See Jürgen Habermas, "Citizenship and national identity: Some reflections on the future of Europe," in *Theorizing Citizenship*, ed. Ronald Beiner (Albany, NY: State University of New York Press, 1995): 255–282; Jan-Werner Müller and Kim Lane Scheppele, "Constitutional patriotism: An introduction," *International Journal of Constitutional Law* 6, no. 1 (2008): 67–71. Also see Liav Orgad, "Illiberal liberalism: Cultural restrictions on migration and access to citizenship in Europe," *American Journal of Comparative Law* 58, no. 1 (2010): 53–106.

are proponents like Joseph Carens who suggest "the most liberal test is none at all"[14]); states are within their right to expect a certain degree (even a high degree) of knowledge. Rather, the critique is that there is a fine line between assessing knowledge of values and assessing beliefs (as well as virtue through active behavior). There is also a critique laid where there is perceived lack of neutrality in application. In other words, the argument is not that tests are hard, but that they are unfair. Both of these critiques suggest that the appropriate distance between the state and the individual has been breached. To this, I suggest that the case studies have provided ample evidence where lines *could* be crossed, but very little evidence to show they actually have been. The quick abandonment of the so-called "Muslim tests" in southern German states, as well as the ultimate rejection of the requirement of "active citizenship" for naturalization in the UK, in fact, show that states effectively police the line between liberal and illiberal. Even citizenship oaths and ceremonies that require naturalized citizens to swear fidelity or loyalty to a set of liberal-democratic values are not really an assessment of belief, much less a measure of behavior. An immigrant may profess one view, believe another, and act another way still. Where the state is drawing closer to the individual is also an area that – given the slippery slope of the contemporary surveillance state – has the propensity to violate liberality, but it has not done so thus far. Even in regard to defining culturally inappropriate aspects of religion, states can take a minimal (the United States) or maximal (France) role in regulating personal religious choice, but rarely do they take no role. Tests may be difficult, and they may have uneven effects, but raising barriers of membership is not the same thing as violating core liberal values of the state.

This also raises an interesting issue about alternative political ideals, specifically whether these debates about liberalism and interpretations of restrictive change are instead an unpackaged assertion of a "republican turn." Liberalism refers to the individual as a passive bearer of status (i.e., a bundle of rights), while republican citizenship emphasizes experience as practice, and values and rights in society are maintained through active participation. To wit, the addition of requirements may, on the one hand, be construed as restriction, while, on the other hand, it may signify the assertion of duty as a guarantor of rights. Drawing on work by Adrian Oldfield further qualifies republicanism, in which both the *desire* and the *capacity* to participate constitute one's civic virtue and are not only an expression of but also a condition for citizenship.[15] In this sense, civic integration may merely be a way in which to build up an individual's capacity to participate, which, in turn, may foster the desire. That said, the rise

[14] See also the contribution by Dora Kostakopoulou in Rainer Bauböck and Christian Joppke, eds., *How Liberal are Citizenship Tests?*, vol. 2010/41, EUI Working Papers (Florence, Italy: Robert Schuman Centre for Advanced Studies, EUI, 2010).

[15] Adrian Oldfield, *Citizenship and Community: Civic republicanism and the modern world* (London: Routledge, 1990).

of republicanism does not mean a departure of liberalism.[16] Yoav Peled has illustrated that the two coexist, particularly in the context of ethnic division. In looking at Israel, he identifies a republican political culture of citizenship for Jews and a liberal one for Israeli-Arabs.[17] Rogers Smith makes a similar argument about concurrent identities – including illiberal ethnoculturalism – in the United States.[18] In looking at European practices today, one sees belonging for immigrant outsiders expressed and obtained through active participation in integration schemes, while belonging for insiders maintains no expectation of participation, obligation, or service. This is particularly notable where civic integration is a requirement at permanent residence, in which integration courses and contracts teach an immigrant how to be a good citizen without actually being a citizen. In the end, we see that membership makes citizenship matter, but matter differently for different groups of people.

Third, and finally, while Joppke devalues these recent attempts to invest meaning to national citizenship as merely "symbolic politics," we see that they have a consequential impact on elections and political party popularity, direct impact on acquisition and application rates, and play a significant role in coloring the tenor of national politics. In other words, membership investments in citizenship can be just as "game changing" as whatever the opposite of symbolic politics is. They may not make a Moroccan turn Dutch or an Algerian turn French, but they unequivocally signal to those newcomers, and to the general Dutch and French populations, that membership is an important organizing principle in society. Therefore, to the immigrant, the parameters of new identity are not symbolic but functionally consequential. Even if the barrier is easy, it may involve time and procedural commitments. It can also vastly alter their opportunities in accessing and advancing in the labor market. For the general population, it shows the government playing a role in "managing" the continued challenges of migration and immigrant integration, which is seldom measured by achievable goals. In sum, decrying the updating of citizenship as nothing more than a symbolic gesture that dilutes identity, simultaneously underestimates the importance of symbolism to national belonging and overestimates the benchmark for possibilities of national belonging in a postwar era.

Deciding who can become a member of the national political community has long been and continues to be a core feature of the modern nation-state. Through a new, civic identity, citizenship is reinvigorated with new articulations of state membership and, as a result, national citizenship is more meaningful now than ever before. This reinvigoration of citizenship reveals the truly

[16] Empirical studies that treat them as opposites are therefore incorrectly specified.

[17] Yoav Peled, "Ethnic democracy and the legal construction of citizenship: Arab citizens of the Jewish state," *American Political Science Review* 86, no. 2 (1992): 432–443.

[18] Rogers M. Smith, "The 'American Creed' and American identity: The limits of liberal citizenship in the United States," *Western Political Quarterly* (1988): 225–251.

"resilient" nature of the nation-state.[19] Not resurrecting old tropes of nationalism but instead identifying new parameters of membership, nation-states are providing a script for belonging that safely falls between the bookends of necessity for the liberal democratic state: maintaining neutrality and promoting cohesion. Even the application of constitutional patriotism, which in principle is a postnational value, illustrates the creative problem-solving characteristic of civic integration, where these values do not replace but get coupled alongside existing national understandings.[20] Moreover, new citizenship paints a picture of what the minimum of internal inclusion looks like, even if it is not achieved in practice. States can set up the gauntlet for inclusion, but it is very much up to the immigrant to decide whether he/she wants to commit to this new membership category or not. This reflects not a blunt suggestion of an uncaring state, but the limits of liberalism that prize autonomy and tolerance.

Counter to those who argue that the European state has become less "Westphalian," owing to the extension of rights to non-citizen statuses, trends of globalization, European integration, the increased movement of people – and therefore cultures – across borders, to mention only a few changes, this book has illustrated that through membership development in the past decade, states in Europe have held firm to the authority of determining who can attain full membership and how they must achieve it. The hard fact is that citizenship is here to stay. We see variation in different European countries in terms of the specifics of membership-crafting reflecting these different political conditions and institutional starting points, but all this membership change reflects a basic intent to reassert the community-defining competence of the modern nation-state.

Moreover, instead of witnessing the "end of national models," the view across Europe shows states using new tools in variable ways to address national membership problems. These new civic requirements represent real innovation – articulating clear definitions for belonging and laying out arbitrary steps for outsiders to become insiders in principle, if not always in practice – without fundamental alterations to the parameters of what the state already has. In other words, these articulations of belonging, expressed through requirements and achieved through mechanisms of layering and conversion, do not replace or dilute but revive national citizenship as a politically salient and relevant category of belonging. In anchoring citizenship, the nation-state has found a new – though perhaps its last – lease on life. The European nation-state is in endgame, and its ability to (re)define national belonging through a contorted

[19] This was Joppke's conclusion in 1999. Christian Joppke, *Immigration and the Nation-State: The United States, Germany, and Great Britain* (Oxford; New York: Oxford University Press, 1999). After a decade of policy change, his assessment of the "lightening of citizenship" seems less optimistic about this conclusion.

[20] Moreover, states adopt constitutional patriotism in light of nationally specific values, not at the provocation of EU or international norms.

liberalism shows that while it is not "relegated to the dustbin of history," it is today something different from its ancestors. It is different in kind, not type. In the end, through state identity and membership requirements promoting knowledge and skill, a new understanding of belonging – but one still plainly national – invigorates citizenship.

RAMIFICATIONS FOR THE IMMIGRANT–STATE RELATIONSHIP

Given the resurgence of national citizenship and the resulting endurance of the nation-state, how does the assertion of civic identity through membership requirements impact the immigrant experience itself? On a practical level, this is the most important question of all. The previous section discussed shifts in the concept of national identity and membership by examining change at the state level. While this aforementioned discussion is also an important concern, it is largely an academic one. Do new requirements make any real difference in the lives of immigrants? Membership requirements are categorized under the umbrella of "civic integration policies," but do they actually achieve immigrant integration? Scholars are divided on this question.

On the one hand, there is deep skepticism that the benefits of integration requirements outweigh the costs incurred by the individual. As Dora Kostakopoulou writes, "The language of participation and the institutional format of the 'integration contract' cannot conceal the unidirectional, disciplinary and exclusionary character of the contemporary civic integration paradigm. Pressuring people to follow designated curricula, sit integration tests, learn about national values and ways of life and, in some cases, to change their minds is likely to produce precisely the opposite of the desired effect: it will make them more estranged, apprehensive, fixated and resistant."[21] In her estimation, civic integration does not draw immigrants closer to the state but creates greater alienation. I would also characterize some of the aforementioned indicator scoring projects that categorize "more requirements" as equal to "more restriction," as part of this perspective. As the outcome evidence from the case studies shows, these practices are not particularly exclusive if one only focuses on the end point, where a majority of applicants eventually achieve status through integration over time. However, a more qualitative focus on the means of integration, looking at how immigrants participate in courses and prepare for exams, may provide more insight into whether mechanisms foster feelings of resentment or aspiration. This is a particularly fertile field of research for ethnographic and comparativist scholars to explore. In particular, it could identify the specific mechanisms by which an outsider actually *becomes* an insider, and what role institutions play in fostering or impeding that process. I also anticipate this to be a ripe research question to take on from a quantitative

[21] Dora Kostakopoulou, "The anatomy of civic integration," *Modern Law Review* 73, no. 6 (2010), 957.

perspective, examining the impact of integration policies on different indicators ranging from economic performance to political participation, social capital, and identity.

A second, broader interpretation of civic integration sees requirements not as a "devious plot against immigrants but embedded within a general restructuring of the welfare state, from public to private responsibility, which is causally disconnected from the fact of immigration."[22] From this perspective, civic integration for immigrants is similar to other "new paternalist" welfare policies, in which welfare programs are premised on the idea that service users lack certain capacities and require "supervisory" programs to guide them toward self-sufficiency. When required for permanent residence, membership requirements can produce positive results for integration by affecting access to the labor market, unlike when required only for naturalization, which is too late in a migrant's residency to substantially or meaningfully impact access. State "intrusion," as Elizabeth Ben-Ishai describes, is "potentially an enabling mechanism for the development and exercise of autonomy."[23] However, even this functional interpretation can be linked to Kostakopoulou's interpretation of requirements in observing that state paternalism and autonomy-promoting policies are ultimately incompatible. As Ben-Ishai continues, "The assumptions that underlie the theory of new paternalism and the techniques of conditionality, including those regarding the concept of autonomy, serve to replicate relations of power that are themselves implicated in the structural causes of poverty and inequality, the very problems new paternalist policies claim to address."[24]

The issue at hand is what role the state can and should play in promoting autonomy-enabling skills in an immigrant. Where is the line between support and force? And does the state have the right to cross that line in the name of integration as a matter of national interest? There are no clear answers here. These kinds of questions present a number of interesting theoretical considerations for political theorists to take up, examining not just the limits of liberalism (and when it crosses into "illiberal liberalism" and whether this is normatively acceptable) but also state prerogatives of control, and to what extent this can evolve under changing circumstances. These lines of questioning, much like examining processes of immigrant integration, draw this policy story outside of the European context and toward a whole host of other cases, including advanced democracies that are forever consolidating to achieve more inclusivity and participation to democracies in transition, which are only beginning to ask questions about how appropriately to manage issues of diversity.

What is plainly apparent, and perhaps one of the reasons civic integration gets accused of being nothing more than a set of symbolic policies that pacify

[22] Joppke, *Citizenship and Immigration*, 150.
[23] Elizabeth Ben-Ishai, "The new paternalism," *Political Research Quarterly* 65, no. 1 (2012), 151.
[24] Ibid., 152.

xenoskeptic populations and express the influence of far-right political parties, is that new membership requirements are insufficient by themselves for addressing larger issues of immigrant integration and inequality. While the state plays an authoritative role in ensuring immigrants obtain skills for autonomy and participation, these policies do not address the other, manifold contextual factors that impact an immigrant's integration outcome, such as the neighborhood in which they live, the kind of education they receive, and other socio-economic variables, not to mention their existing social or familial networks that may have a negative influence on bridge-building across communities. Indeed, the ultimate limitation of the liberal state in promoting integration is that it can provide the skills – even make them obligatory – but it cannot mandate the practice. In other words, an individual can self-elect into segregation. On the flip side, we see this as the ultimate freedom of the individual migrant; an individual can make an oral commitment that they understand and swear to uphold liberal democratic values, but they are not obliged to believe it.

The short-term story of civic integration is one of building skills and strengthening citizenship and identity, preserving national differences in state approaches to belonging by articulating concrete definitions of membership. However, a long-term view of policy change makes other alternatives possible. With more iterations of policy change over time, this could be the first juncture of a slow-moving process that changes the ultimate arrangement of state membership. As Theda Skocpol notes: "Policies transform or expand the capacities of the state. They therefore change the administrative possibilities for official initiatives in the future."[25] For example, one of the real changes that comes with new requirements is bringing the state closer to the individual. Requirements secure a tighter relationship between the individual and the state in a paternalistic relationship; the state takes a responsibility for ensuring integration, while the individual is directly accountable to the state at increased stages of interaction. Giving the state a more prominent role in the lives of newcomers and pulling the immigrant ever closer to the state sets a precedent for a bevy of potential illiberal possibilities – ranging from surveillance to the conditionality of rights. These serious extremes may be unintended outcomes of a causal chain that begins here. Indeed, a feature of historical institutionalism is the possibility that long-term outcomes are often "by-products of social processes rather than embodying the goals of social actors."[26] While, for the time being, membership requirements promote integration and reaffirm national approaches to citizenship, it is possible that this may be the first step of the adaptive nation-state to altering not only the orientation of citizenship but the citizen–state relationship altogether.

[25] Cited in Paul Pierson, "When effect becomes cause: Policy feedback and political change," *World Politics* 45, no. 4 (1993): 603.

[26] Paul Pierson, *Politics in Time: History, institutions, and social analysis* (Princeton: Princeton University Press, 2004), 15.

This book has strived to systematically establish and analytically illustrate that membership, once again, matters to nation-states. The major immigrant-receiving states of Europe have all turned to membership-promoting integration tests, courses, and assessment in order to address unique challenges of belonging, defined by existing parameters of belonging and driven by domestic politics. Whether aiming to achieve real gains by improving the lives of immigrants or obtain symbolic "wins" with a population already nervous and skeptical toward outsiders, civic integration is the mark of a responsive and resilient nation-state coming to terms with the changing realities of twenty-first-century Europe. And against the backdrop of a continued demographic and cultural impact of immigration, from which ensue emotionally charged debates over national identity, the compatibilities of Islam in Europe, terrorism on European soil, and the perceived threat of outsiders to a continued "European" way of life, as well as the economic debt crisis that pervades every area of policymaking and discourse, there is no indication that states will abate in these membership-promoting practices or cease in the continued project of nation-building. Membership will continue to be an enduring feature of citizenship and, therefore, the contemporary nation-state, so long as states continue to believe that the answer to problems of diversity and community cohesion are to be found at home.

APPENDIX I

Common European Framework of Reference (CEFR) on languages

The Common European Framework of Reference (CEFR) provides a mutual recognition for language qualifications, including language syllabuses, curriculum guidelines, and exams, across Europe. It employs a "hypertext" branching principle, expanding on the classic typology of beginner, intermediate, and advanced. A more advanced version of this schema includes additional levels, including A2+, B1+, and B2+.

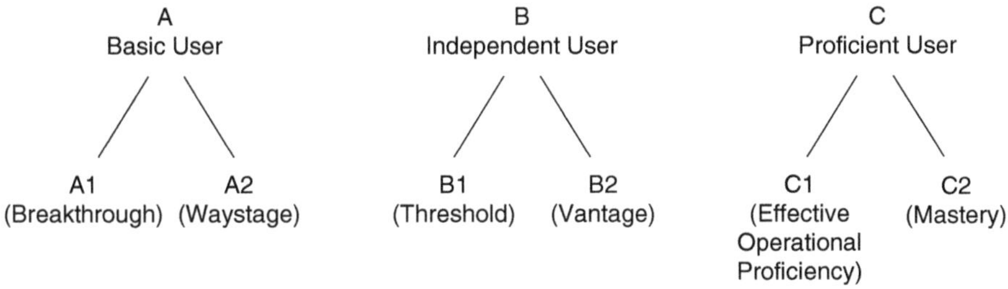

A.1 CEFR Language Levels

These CEFR levels standardize language comprehension for listening, writing, reading, speaking, and conversation/interaction, with slight modifications for each. For more, see *The Common European Framework of Reference for Language: Learning, teaching, assessment* (Cambridge: Cambridge University Press, 2001).

APPENDIX II

Other indices for civic integration policy and calculated correlations

Koopmans et al.'s Indicators for Citizenship Rights of Immigrants (ICRI): Measurement of cultural requirements

TABLE IIA. *Policy scores of cultural requirements across three legal stages*

	Marriage migration				Residence				Nationality acquisition			
	1980	1990	2002	2008	1980	1990	2002	2008	1980	1990	2002	2008
AUT	1	1	1	1	1	1	1	−1	0.5	0.5	0	−1
DEN	1	1	−1	−1	1	1	−1	−1	0.5	0.5	0	−0.5
FRA	1	1	1	0	1	1	1	−1	−1	−1	−1	−1
GER	1	1	1	0	−1	−1	0	−1	−1	−1	0	−0.5
NET	1	1	1	0	1	1	1	−1	−1	0.5	0.5	−0.5
SWE	1	1	1	1	1	1	1	1	1	1	1	1
UK	1	1	1	1	1	1	1	−1	0.5	0	−0.5	−0.5

TABLE IIB. *Calculated sum for comparability to CIVIX*

	1980	1990	2002	2008
AUT	2.5	2.5	2	−1
DEN	2.5	2.5	−2	−2.5
FRA	1	1	1	−2
GER	−1	−1	1	−1.5
NET	1	2.5	2.5	−1.5
SWE	3	3	3	3
UK	2.5	2	1.5	−0.5
Correlation with CIVIX 1997		−0.66		
Correlation with CIVIX today				−0.93

Migrant Integration Policy Index (MIPEX): Integration Requirements

TABLE 11C. *Policy scores across three legal stages (averages)*

	Family reunion		Residence	Nationality			
Dimension no.	22	23	79	99	100		
	Pre-departure *(average)*	Upon arrival *(average)*	*(average)*	Language and exemptions *(average)*	Citizenship and integration *(average)*	Average	Sum
AUT	100.00	50.00	50.00	65.00	75.00	68.00	340.00
BEL	100.00	100.00	100.00	100.00	100.00	100.00	500.00
DEN	35.71	32.14	32.14	30.00	41.67	34.33	171.67
FIN	100.00	100.00	100.00	35.00	100.00	87.00	435.00
FRA	71.43	82.14	82.14	10.00	16.67	52.48	262.38
GER	57.14	32.14	32.14	45.00	83.33	49.95	249.76
GRE	100.00	100.00	3 9.29	40.00	25.00	60.86	304.29
IRE	100.00	100.00	100.00	100.00	100.00	100.00	500.00
ITA	100.00	100.00	42.86	100.00	100.00	88.57	442.86
LUX	100.00	100.00	100.00	45.00	83.33	85.67	428.33
NET	14.29	39.29	39.29	45.00	41.67	35.91	179.52
POR	100.00	100.00	60.71	65.00	100.00	85.14	425.71
SPA	100.00	100.00	100.00	10.00	16.67	65.33	326.67
SWE	100.00	100.00	100.00	100.00	100.00	100.00	500.00
UK	100.00	100.00	67.86	65.00	41.67	74.91	374.52
Correlation with CIVIX today						−0.87	−0.87

For individual measures on various policy facets behind these composite averages (including level of language requirement, conductor of requirement, cost, and support, etc.), see www.mipex.eu

APPENDIX III

Citizenship indicator scores

TABLE IIIA. *Janoski's Barriers to Nationality Index (BNI)*

	BNI – original				Compatible scores *(inverted for consistency in direction)*			
	1970	1980	1990	2002	1970	1980	1990	2002
AUT	0.88	0.88	0.82	0.87	0.12	0.12	0.18	0.13
DEN	0.79	0.74	0.74	0.75	0.21	0.26	0.26	0.25
FRA	0.54	0.54	0.58	0.5	0.46	0.46	0.42	0.5
GER	0.94	0.89	0.55	0.47	0.06	0.11	0.45	0.53
NET	0.56	0.51	0.49	0.49	0.44	0.49	0.51	0.51
UK	0.19	0.21	0.16	0.16	0.81	0.79	0.84	0.84

TABLE IIIB. *Koopmans et al.'s Indicators for Citizenship Rights of Immigrants (ICRI): Nationality acquisition indicators*

	Nationality acquisition scores for ICRI			
	1980	1990	2002	2008
AUT	−0.4	−0.3	−0.4	−0.8
DEN	0.1	0.1	0	−0.5
FRA	0.4	0.4	0.2	0.2
GER	−0.7	−0.7	0.1	0
NET	−0.2	0.2	0.4	0.2
UK	0.8	0.6	0.5	0.5

For full indicators data set, see http://www.wzb.eu/en/persons/ruud-koopmans?s=12394 (accessed September 4, 2013).

TABLE IIIC. *Howard's Citizenship Policy Index (CPI):*

	CPI – original		
	1980	1998	2008
AUT	0.5	1.25	0
DEN	1.43	0.93	0
FRA	4.22	4.72	4.97
GER	0	1	2.04
NET	2.72	3.72	4.22
UK	5.47	4.97	4.97

Note: 1998 calculations are made by Goodman and are available upon request.

References

Adamo, Silvia. "The legal position of migrants in Denmark: Assessing the context around the 'Cartoon Crisis'." *European Journal of Migration and Law* 9 (2007): 1–24.

"Northern exposure: The new Danish model of citizenship tests." *International Journal on Multicultural Societies* 10, no. 1 (2008): 10–28.

"What is the point? Policies on immigration and the language issue in Denmark." In *RECODE Working Paper Series*, no.4 (2012): 1–18.

Akkerman, Tjitske. "Comparing radical right parties in government: Immigration and integration policies in nine countries (1996–2010)." *West European Politics* 35, no. 3 (2012): 511–29.

"Immigration policy and electoral competition in Western Europe. A fine-grained analysis of party positions over the past two decades." *Party Politics* (2012): DOI: 10.1177/1354068812462928.

Aleinikoff, Thomas Alexander, and Douglas B. Klusmeyer. *Citizenship Policies for an Age of Migration.* Washington, DC: Carnegie Endowment for International Peace: Migration Policy Institute; Brookings Institution Press, distributor, 2002.

Alexander, Claire, Rosalind Edwards, and Bogusia Temple. "Contesting cultural communities: Language, ethnicity and citizenship in Britain." *Journal of Ethnic and Migration Studies* 33, no. 5 (2007): 783–800.

Anderson, Benedict. *Imagined Communities: Reflections on the origin and spread of nationalism.* London; New York: Verso, 1991.

Aristotle, and Carnes Lord. *The Politics.* Chicago: University of Chicago Press, 1984.

Asari, Eva-Maria, Daphne Halikiopoulou, and Steven Mock. "British national identity and the dilemmas of multiculturalism." *Nationalism and Ethnic Politics* 14, no. 1 (2008): 1–28.

Bale, Tim. "Turning round the telescope. Centre-right parties and immigration and integration policy in Europe 1." *Journal of European Public Policy* 15, no. 3 (2008): 315–30.

"More and more restrictive – but not always populist: Explaining variation in the British Conservative Party's stance on immigration and asylum." *Journal of Contemporary European Studies* 21, no. 1 (2013): 25–37.

BAMF. "9. Lagebericht der Beauftragten der Bundesregierung für Migration, Flüchtlinge und Integration über die Lage der Ausländerinnen und Ausländer in Deutschland." July 2012.

Banting, Keith, and Will Kymlicka. "Is there really a retreat from multiculturalism policies? New evidence from the Multiculturalism Policy Index." *Comparative European Politics* 11, no. 5 (2013): 577–98.

Bauböck, Rainer, and Dilek Çinar. "Nationality law and naturalisation in Austria." In *Towards a European Nationality: Citizenship, immigration and nationality law in the EU*, edited by Randall Hansen and Patrick Weil, 255–72. Basingstoke, Hampshire: Palgrave, 2001.

Bauböck, Rainer, and Christian Joppke, eds. *How Liberal Are Citizenship Tests?* Vol. 2010/41, EUI Working Papers. Florence, Italy: Robert Schuman Centre for Advanced Studies, EUI, 2010.

Bauböck, Rainer, Eva Ersbøll, Kees Groenendijk, and Harald Waldrauch, eds. *Acquisition and Loss of Nationality in Fifteen EU States. Volume 2: Country Analyses. Policies and trends in 15 European countries.* Amsterdam: Amsterdam University Press, 2006.

Bechhofer, Frank, and David McCrone. "Being British: A crisis of identity?" *The Political Quarterly* 78, no. 2 (2007): 251–60.

Beiner, Ronald. *Theorizing Citizenship*. Albany: State University of New York Press, 1995.

Ben-Ishai, Elizabeth. "The new paternalism." *Political Research Quarterly* 65, no. 1 (2012): 151–65.

Bertossi, Christophe, and Abdellali Hajjat. "France." In *EUDO Citizenship Observatory Country Reports*. Florence: EUDO Citizenship, Robert Schuman Centre for Advanced Studies, EUI, 2013.

Betz, Hans-Georg. *Radical-Wing Populism in Western Europe*. Basingstoke, Hampshire: Macmillan, 1994.

Bleich, Erik. "The legacies of history? Colonization and immigrant integration in Britain and France." *Theory and Society* 34, no. 2 (2005): 171–95.

Block, Laura, and Saskia Bonjour. "Fortress Europe or Europe of rights? The Europeanisation of family migration policies in France, Germany and the Netherlands." *European Journal of Migration and Law* 15, no. 2 (2013): 203–24.

Bloemraad, Irene. "Who claims dual citizenship? The limits of postnationalism, the possibilities of transnationalism, and the persistence of traditional citizenship." *The International Migration Review* 38, no. 2 (2004): 389–426.

Blunkett, David. *The Blunkett Tapes: My Life in the Bear Pit*. London: Bloomsbury, 2006.

Böcker, Anita, and Tineke Strik. "Language and knowledge tests for permanent residence rights: Help or hindrance for integration?" *European Journal of Migration and Law* 13, no. 2 (2011): 157–84.

Bonjour, Saskia. "Between integration provision and selection mechanism. Party politics, judicial constraints, and the making of French and Dutch policies of civic integration abroad." *European Journal of Migration and Law* 12, no. 3 (2010): 299–318.

"Governing diversity. Dutch political parties' preferences on the role of the state in civic integration policies." *Citizenship Studies* 17, no. 6/7 (2013): 837–51.

Bosniak, Linda. *The Citizen and the Alien: Dilemmas of contemporary membership*. Princeton, NJ: Princeton University Press, 2006.

"British Citizenship Test: One in three immigrants fails." *BBC News Online*, May 27, 2010.

Brown, Gordon. "Speech on Managed migration and earned citizenship." pm.gov.uk. February 20, 2008, http://www.pm.gov.uk (accessed February 21, 2008)

Brubaker, Rogers. *Citizenship and Nationhood in France and Germany*. Cambridge, MA: Harvard University Press, 1992.

"Return of assimilation? Changing perspectives on immigration and its sequels in France, Germany, and the United States." *Ethnic and Racial Studies* 24, no. 4 (2001): 531–48.

Brubaker, William Rogers, ed. *Immigration and the Politics of Citizenship in Europe and North America*. Lanham, MD: University Press of America; German Marshall Fund of the United States, 1989.

Brunstetter, Daniel. "Rousseau and the tensions of France's Contrat d'Accueil et d'Integration." *Journal of Political Ideologies* 17, no. 1 (2012): 107–26.

Buley, Jennifer. "Government proposes end to 'points system'." *The Copenhagen Post*, 2012.

Cağlar, Ayse S. "German Turks in Berlin: Social exclusion and strategies for social mobility." *Journal of Ethnic and Migration Studies* 21, no. 3 (1995): 309–23.

Calvo, Vera Guitiérrez. "Los extranjeros que pidan la nacionalidad Pasarán un test de españole "integración"." *El Pais*, March 28, 2013.

Cantle, Ted. "Community cohesion: A report of the independent review team," edited by Home Office. London: HMSO, 2001.

Carens, Joseph H. "Aliens and citizens: The case for open borders." *Review of Politics* 49, no. 2 (1987): 251–73.

Carrera, Sergio. "A typology of different integration programmes in the EU." in T. Balzacq and S. Carrera (eds.), *Security versus Freedom? Security* (Ashgate: Aldershot, 2006).

In Search of the Perfect Citizen? The intersection between integration, immigration and nationality in the EU. Leiden; Boston: Martinus Nijhoff, 2009.

"Nationality, immigration and 'the Republican Integration' in France: Normativisation, expansionism and externalisation." In *Illiberal Liberal States: Immigration, citizenship and integration in the EU*, edited by Elspeth Guild, Kees Groenendijk, and Sergio Carrera, 315–36. Farnham, Surrey; Burlington, VT: Ashgate, 2009.

Castles, Stephen, and Mark Miller. *The Age of Migration: International population movements in the modern world*. New York: Guilford Press, 2009 [2003].

Central Bureau for Statistics (the Netherlands). "Decline in number of Turkish and Moroccan immigration brides continues." *Web Magazine* (2008), http://www.cbs.nl/en-GB/menu/themas/dossiers/allochtonen/publicaties/artikelen/archief/2008/2008-90156-wk.htm (accessed July 1, 2010).

"Statline Cbs Databank." 2009.

Cesarani, David, and Mary Fulbrook. *Citizenship, Nationality, and Migration in Europe*. London; New York: Routledge, 1996.

Çinar, Dilek. "Austria." *EUDO Citizenship Observatory Country Reports*. Florence: EUDO Citizenship, Robert Schuman Centre for Advanced Studies, EUI, 2010.

"Citizenship Classes: The Austrian Way." *BBC News Online*, October 26, 2001.

Cole, Alistair. "A strange affair: The 2002 presidential and parliamentary elections in France." *Government and Opposition* 37, no. 3 (2002): 317–42.

Common European Framework of Reference for Languages. *The Common European Framework of Reference for Language: Learning, teaching, assessment*. Cambridge: Cambridge University Press, 2001.

Conservative Party. *The Conservative Party Manifesto*. Uckfield, East Sussex: Pureprint Group, 2010.

Council of the European Union. "*Immigrant Integration Policy in the European Union.*" Brussels, 2004.

Dahl, Robert A. "What political institutions does large-scale democracy require?" *Political Science Quarterly* 120, no. 2 (2005): 187–97.

Dalton, Russell J. *The Good Citizen: How a younger generation is reshaping American politics*. Washington, DC: CQ Press, 2008.

Davy, Ulrike. "Integration of immigrants in Germany: A slowly evolving concept." *European Journal of Migration and Law* 7, no.2 (2005): 123–44.

de Groot, Gerard-Rene, Jan-Jaap Kuipers, and Franziska Weber. "Passing citizenship tests as a requirement for naturalisation: A comparative perspective." In *Illiberal Liberal States: Immigration, citizenship and integration in the EU*, edited by Elspeth Guild, Kees Groenendijk, and Sergio Carrera, 51–78. Farnham, Surrey; Burlington, VT: Ashgate, 2009.

de Leeuw, Marc, and Sonja van Wichelen. "Civilizing migrants: Integration, culture and citizenship." *European Journal of Cultural Studies* 15, no. 2 (2012): 195–210.

Diez, Thomas, and Vicki Squire. "Traditions of citizenship and the securitisation of migration in Germany and Britain." *Citizenship Studies* 12, no. 6 (2008): 565–81.

Dolowitz, David P., and David Marsh. "Earning from abroad: The role of policy transfer in contemporary policy-making." *Governance* 13, no. 1 (2000): 5–24.

Entzinger, Han. "The rise and fall of multiculturalism: The case of the Netherlands." In *Toward Assimilation and Citizenship: Immigrants in liberal nation-states*, edited by Christian Joppke and Ewa T. Morawska, 59–86. Houndmills, Basingstoke, Hampshire; New York: Palgrave Macmillan, 2003.

"The growing gap between facts and discourse on immigrant integration in the Netherlands." *Identities* (2013): 1–15.

Ersanilli, Evelyn, and Ruud Koopmans. "Rewarding integration? Citizenship regulations and the socio-cultural integration of immigrants in the Netherlands, France and Germany." *Journal of Ethnic and Migration Studies* 36, no. 5 (2010): 773–91.

Ersbøll, Eva. "Nationality law in Denmark, Finland and Sweden." In *Towards a European Nationality: Citizenship, immigration and nationality law in the EU*, edited by Randall Hansen and Patrick Weil, 230–54. Houndmills, Basingstoke, Hampshire: Palgrave, 2001.

"On trial in Denmark." In *A Re-Definition of Belonging? Language and integration tests in Europe*, edited by Ricky van Oers, Eva Ersbøll and Dora Kostakopoulou, 107–52. Leiden; Boston: Martinus Nijhoff, 2010.

"Denmark." *EUDO Citizenship Observatory Country Reports*. Florence: EUDO Citizenship, Robert Schuman Centre for Advanced Studies, EUI, 2013.

Ersbøll, Eva, and Laura Katrine Gravesen. "Country Report Denmark." In *The INTEC Project: Integration and naturalisation tests: The new way to European citizenship*. Nijmegen, the Netherlands: Centre for Migration Law, Radboud University, 2010.

Etzioni, Amitai. "Citizenship tests: A comparative, communitarian perspective." *Political Quarterly* 78, no. 3 (2007): 353–63.

"Citizenship in a communitarian perspective." *Ethnicities* 11, no. 3 (2011): 336–49.

European Commission. "Report from the Commission to the European Parliament and the Council on the Application of Directive 2003/86/Ec on the Right to Family Reunification." Brussels, 2008.

Evans, Geoffrey, and Kat Chzhen. "Explaining voters' defection from Labour over the 2005–10 electoral cycle: Leadership, economics and the rising importance of immigration." *Political Studies* 61, no. S1 (2013): 138–57.

Fahrmeir, Andreas. "Coming to terms with a misinterpreted past? Rethinking the historical antecedents of Germany's 1999 citizenship reform." *German Politics & Society* 30, no. 1 (2012): 17–38.

Faist, Thomas, Jürgen Gerdes, and Beate Rieple. "Dual citizenship as a path-dependent process." *International Migration Review* 38, no. 3 (2004): 913–44.

Falleti, Tulia G., and Julia F. Lynch. "Context and causal mechanisms in political analysis." *Comparative Political Studies* 42, no. 9 (2009): 1143–66.

Favell, Adrian. *Philosophies of Integratio: Immigration and the idea of citizenship in France and Britain*. New York: St. Martin's Press, 1998.

Feldblum, Miriam. *Reconstructing Citizenship: The politics of nationality reform and immigration in contemporary France*. Albany: State University of New York Press, 1999.

Flournoy, Richard W., and Manley O. Hudson. *A Collection of Nationality Laws of Various Countries, as Contained in Constitutions, Statutes and Treaties*. New York: Oxford University Press, 1929.

Foblets, Marie-Claire. "Legal aspects of the multicultural society. Tensions and challenges for policy making." In *New Citizens, New Policies? Developments in diversity policy in Canada and Flanders*, edited by Leen d'Haenens, Marc Hooghe, Dirk Vanheule, and Hasibe Gezduci, 89–104. Gent, Belgium: Academia Press, 2006.

Freeman, Gary P. "Modes of immigration politics in liberal democratic states." *International Migration Review* 29, no. 4 (1995): 881–902.

"Immigrant incorporation in Western democracies." *International Migration Review* 38, no. 3 (2004): 945–69.

Friedkin, Noah E. "Social cohesion." *Annual Review of Sociology* 30 (2004): 409–25.

Gaertner, Samuel L., and John F. Dovidio. *Reducing Intergroup Bias: The common ingroup identity model*. Hove, East Sussex, UK; New York: Psychology Press, 2000.

Geddes, Andrew. "Migration and the welfare state in Europe." In *The Politics of Migration: Managing opportunities, conflict and change*, edited by Sarah Spencer, 150–62. Oxford: Blackwell, 2003.

The Politics of Migration and Immigration in Europe. London; Thousand Oaks, CA: Sage Publications, 2003.

George, Alexander L., and Andrew Bennett. *Case Studies and Theory Development in the Social Sciences*. Cambridge, MA: MIT Press, 2005.

Gerring, John. "Is there a (viable) crucial-case method?" *Comparative Political Studies* 40, no. 3 (2007): 231–53.

Social Science Methodology. 2nd edn. Cambridge: Cambridge University Press, 2012.

Givens, Terri E. *Voting Radical Right in Western Europe*. Cambridge: Cambridge University Press, 2005.

Givens, Terri, and Adam Luedtke. "European immigration policies in comparative perspective: Issue salience, partisanship and immigrant rights." *Comparative European Politics* 3, no. 1 (2005): 1–22.
Glover, Stephen, Ceri Gott, Anais Loizillon, Jonathan Portes, Richard Price, Sarah Spencer, Vasanthi Srinivasan, and Carole Willis. "Migration: An economic and social analysis." In *RDS Occassional Paper No. 67*. London: Home Office, 2001.
Göktürk, Deniz, David Gramling, and Anton Kaes. *Germany in Transit: Nation and migration, 1955–2005*. Berkeley: University of California Press, 2007.
Goodman, Sara Wallace. "Integration requirements for integration's sake? Identifying, categorising and comparing civic integration policies." *Journal of Ethnic and Migration Studies* 36, no. 5 (2010): 753–72.
"Naturalisation policies in Europe: Exploring patterns of inclusion and exclusion." In *EUDO Citizenship Comparative Reports*. Florence: EUDO Citizenship, Robert Schuman Centre for Advanced Studies, EUI, 2010.
"Fortifying citizenship: Policy strategies for civic integration in Western Europe." *World Politics* 64, no. 4 (2012): 659–98.
"Measurement and interpretation issues in civic integration studies: A rejoinder." *Journal of Ethnic and Migration Studies* 38, no. 1 (2012): 173–86.
"Concluding remarks: What can we learn from citizenship policy indices?" *Migration and Citizenship. Newsletter of the American Political Science Association. Organized Section on Migration and Citizenship* 1, no. 2 (2013): 48–54.
Goodman, Sara Wallace, and Marc Morjé Howard. "Evaluating and explaining the restrictive backlash in citizenship policy in Europe." *Studies in Law, Politics, and Society* 60 (2013): 111–39.
Gordon, Susan M. "Integrating immigrants: Morality and loyalty in US naturalization practice." *Citizenship Studies* 11, no. 4 (2007): 367–82.
Gowricharn, Ruben. "Integration and social cohesion: The case of the Netherlands." *Journal of Ethnic and Migration Studies* 28, no. 2 (2002): 259–73.
Green, Simon. *The Politics of Exclusion: Institutions and immigration policy in contemporary Germany*. Manchester; New York: Manchester University Press, 2004.
"Much ado about not-very-much? Assessing ten years of German citizenship reform." *Citizenship Studies* 16, no. 2 (2012): 173–88.
Green-Pedersen, Christoffer, and Jesper Krogstrup. "Immigration as a political issue in Denmark and Sweden." *European Journal of Political Research* 47, no. 5 (2008): 610–34.
Greenwood, John, and Lynton Robins. "Citizenship tests and education: Embedding a concept." *Parliamentary Affairs* 55, no. 3 (2002): 505–22.
Grimston, Jack, and David Leppard. "God Save the Queen test for migrants." *The Times (UK)*, 2012.
Groenendijk, Kees. "Legal concepts of integration in EU migration law." *European Journal of Migration and Law* 6, no. 2 (2004): 111–26.
"From assisting to requiring integration: Selective citizenship policies in the Netherlands." In *Naturalisation: A passport for the better integration of immigrants?*, edited by OECD, 335–52. Paris: OECD Publishing, 2011.
"Pre-departure integration strategies in the European Union: Integration or immigration policy?" *European Journal of Migration and Law* 13, no. 1 (2011): 1–30.
Groenendijk, Kees, and Eric Heijs. "Immigration, immigrants and nationality law in the Netherlands, 1945–98." In *Towards a European Nationality: Citizenship,*

immigration and nationality law in the EU, edited by Randall Hansen and Patrick Weil, 143–72. Houndsmills, Basingstoke, Hampshire: Palgrave, 2001.

Guibernau, Montserrat. "Anthony D. Smith on nations and national identity: A critical assessment." *Nations and Nationalism* 10, no. 1/2 (2004): 125–41.

Guild, Elspeth, Kees Groenendijk, and Sergio Carrera, eds. *Illiberal Liberal States: Immigration, citizenship, and integration in the EU*. Farnham, Surrey; Burlington, VT: Ashgate, 2009.

Guiraudon, Virginie. "Policy change behind gilded doors: Explaining the evolution of aliens' rights in contemporary Western Europe." Ph.D. Dissertation, Harvard University, 1997.

"European integration and migration policy: Vertical policy-making as venue shopping." *Journal of Common Market Studies* 38, no. 2 (2000): 251–71.

Immigration Policy in France. Washington, DC: Brookings Institution Center on the United States and France, 2001.

Habermas, Jürgen. "Citizenship and national identity: Some reflections on the future of Europe." In *Theorizing Citizenship*, edited by Ronald Beiner, 255–82. Albany, NY: State University of New York Press, 1995.

Hagedorn, Heike. "Republicanism and the politics of citizenship in Germany and France: Convergence or divergence?" *German Policy Studies* 1, no. 3 (2001): 243–72.

Hailbronner, Kay. "Germany." In *EUDO Citizenship Observatory Country Reports*. Florence: EUDO Citizenship, Robert Schuman Centre for Advanced Studies, EUI, 2012.

Hainmueller, Jens, and Dominik Hangartner. "Who gets a Swiss passport? A natural experiment in immigrant discrimination." *American Political Science Review* 107, no. 1 (2013): 159–87.

Hajjat, Abdellali. "Naturalisation procedures for immigrants: France." In *EUDO Citizenship Observatory Naturalisation Procedures Reports*. Florence: EUDO Citizenship, Robert Schuman Centre for Advanced Studies, EUI, 2013.

Hall, Peter A. *Governing the Economy: The politics of state intervention in Britain and France*. Cambridge, UK; Oxford, UK: Polity Press, in association with B. Blackwell, 1986.

"Policy paradigms, social learning, and the state: The case of economic policymaking in Britain." *Comparative Politics* 25, no. 3 (1993): 275–96.

Hampshire, James. *Citizenship and Belonging: Immigration and the politics of demographic governance in post-war Britain*. Houndmills, Basingstoke, Hampshire; New York: Palgrave, 2005.

Hampshire, James, and Tim Bale. "New administration, new immigration regime: Do parties matter after all? A UK case study." Paper presented at the Conference of the Council for European Studies, Amsterdam, 2013.

Hansen, Randall. *Citizenship and Immigration in Post-War Britain: The institutional origins of a multicultural nation*. Oxford: Oxford University Press, 2000.

"Diversity, integration and the turn from multiculturalism in the United Kingdom." In *Belonging? Diversity, recognition and shared citizenship in Canada*, edited by Keith G. Banting, Thomas J. Courchene, and F. Leslie Seidle. Montreal: Institute for Research on Public Policy, 2007.

"A new citizenship bargain for the age of mobility? Citizenship requirements in Europe and North America." Washington, DC: Migration Policy Institute, 2008.

"The poverty of postnationalism: Citizenship, immigration, and the new Europe." *Theory and Society* 38, no. 1 (2009): 1–24.

Hansen, Randall, and Patrick Weil, eds. *Towards a European Nationality: Citizenship, immigration and nationality law in the EU*. London: Palgrave-Macmillan, 2001.

Hartnell, Helen Elizabeth. "Belonging: Citizenship and migration in the European Union and in Germany." *Berkeley Journal of International Law* 24, no. 1 (2006): 330–400.

Heater, Derek Benjamin. *Citizenship: The civic ideal in world history, politics, and education*. Manchester; New York: Manchester University Press, 2004.

Helbling, Marc. "Validating integration and citizenship policy indices." *Comparative European Politics* 11, no. 5 (2013): 555–76.

Hoekstra, Ineke, and Koen Bron. "Andersson Elffers Felix Jaarboek." Utrecht, the Netherlands.

Hollomey, Christina, Alfred Wöger, and Albert Kraler. "The national policy frame for the integration of newcomers in Austria." In *Promoting Sustainable Policies for Integration (PROSINT)*. Vienna: ICMPD, 2011.

Home Office. "The new and the old: The report of the 'Life in the United Kingdom' Advisory Group." London, 2003.

"Controlling our borders: Making migration work for Britain." London: TSO, 2005.

"The path to citizenship: Next steps in reforming the immigration system: Analysis of consultation responses." London: Border and Immigration Agency Communications Directorate, 2008.

"*Home Office Statistical Bulletin: British citizenship statistics, United Kingdom 2009*." London, 2010.

"Knowledge of language and life in the UK for settlement and naturalisation: Statement of intent, changes to the requirement from October 2013." London: Crown Copyright, 2013.

"Life in the United Kingdom: A guide for new residents." London: Home Office, 2013.

Howard, Marc Morjé. *The Politics of Citizenship in Europe*. Cambridge: Cambridge University Press, 2009.

Human Rights Watch, "The Netherlands: Discrimination in the name of integration." Human Rights Watch, 2008.

Huo, Yuen J., Heather J. Smith, Tom R. Tyler, and E. Allan Lind. "Superordinate identification, subgroup identification, and justice concerns: Is separatism the problem; is assimilation the answer?" *Psychological Science* (1996): 40–45.

Independent Commission on Migration to Germany (Süssmuth Commission). "Structuring immigration, fostering integration." Berlin: Druckerei Conrad GmbH, 2001.

Informatie-en Analyses Centrum (INDIAC). "Monitor Inburgeringsexamen Buitenland." Den Haag: Immigratie- en Naturalisatiedienst, 2008.

Jacobs, Dirk, and Andrea Rea. "The end of national models? Integration courses and citizenship trajectories in Europe." In *European Union Studies Association Annual Conference*. Montréal, Quebec, 2007.

Janoski, Thomas. *The Ironies of Citizenship. Naturalization and Integration in Industrialized Countries*. Cambridge, UK: Cambridge University Press, 2010.

Jeffers, Kristen, Iseult Honohan, and Rainer Bauböck. "CITLAW indicators: How to measure the purposes of citizenship laws." In *Comparing Citizenship Across Europe: Laws, implementation and impact*. EUI and University College Dublin, 2012.

Johnston, Philip. "Migrants face new 'Britishness' test." *The Telegraph*, 2006.

Joppke, Christian. *Immigration and the Nation-State: The United States, Germany, and Great Britain*. Oxford; New York: Oxford University Press, 1999.

"Citizenship between de- and re-ethnicization." *European Journal of Sociology* 44, no. 3 (2003): 429–58.

"The retreat of multiculturalism in the liberal state: Theory and policy." *British Journal of Sociology* 55, no. 2 (2004): 237–57.

Selecting by Origin: Ethnic migration in the liberal state. Cambridge, MA: Harvard University Press, 2005.

"Beyond national models: Civic integration policies for immigrants in Western Europe." *West European Politics* 30, no. 1 (2007): 1–22.

"Transformation of immigrant integration in Western Europe: Civic integration and antidiscrimination policies in the Netherlands, France, and Germany." *World Politics* 59, no. 2 (2007): 243–73.

"Immigration and the identity of citizenship: The paradox of universalism." *Citizenship Studies* 12, no. 6 (2008): 533–46.

"Limits of integration policy: Britain and her Muslims." *Journal of Ethnic and Migration Studies* 35, no. 3 (2009): 453–72.

Citizenship and immigration (Immigration & Society series). Cambridge, UK; Malden, MA: Polity, 2010.

"'Rejoinder', review symposium of Christian Joppke's Citizenship and Immigration." *Ethnicities* 12, no. 6 (2012): 859–63.

Joppke, Christian, and Ewa T. Morawska. *Toward Assimilation and Citizenship: Immigrants in Liberal Nation-States* (Migration, Minorities, and Citizenship series). Houndmills, Basingstoke, Hampshire; New York: Palgrave Macmillan, 2003.

Kastoryano, Riva. *Negotiating Identities: States and immigrants in France and Germany*. Princeton: Princeton University Press, 2002.

Kelly, Ruth, and Liam Byrne. "A common place." London: Fabian Society, 2007.

Kesler, Christel, and Irene Bloemraad. "Does immigration erode social capital? The conditional effects of immigration-generated diversity on trust, membership, and participation across 19 countries, 1981–2000." *Canadian Journal of Political Science* 43, no. 2 (2010): 319–47.

Kitschelt, Herbert. *The Radical Right in Western Europe: A comparative analysis*. Ann Arbor: University of Michigan Press, 1997.

Kiwan, Dina. "A journey to citizenship in the United Kingdom." *International Journal on Multicultural Societies* 10, no. 1 (2008): 60–75.

"'National' citizenship in the UK? Education and naturalization policies in the context of internal division." *Ethnicities* 11, no. 3 (2011): 269–80.

Klaver, Jeanine, and A. W. M. Odé. *Civic Integration and Modern Citizenship: The Netherlands in perspective*. Groningen: Europa Law Publishing, 2009.

Klusmeyer, Douglas B. *Immigration Policy in the Federal Republic of Germany: Negotiating membership and remaking the nation*: Oxford; New York: Berghahn Books, 2009.

König, Karin, and Bernhard Perchinig, "Austria." In *EU and US Approaches to the Management of Immigration*, edited by Jan Niessen, Yongmi Schibel, and Raphaele Magoni, Brussels: Migration Policy Group, 2003.

Koning, Edward A. "Ethnic and civic dealings with newcomers: Naturalization policies and practices in twenty-six immigration countries." *Ethnic and Racial Studies* 34, no. 11 (2011): 1974–94.

Koopmans, Ruud, Ines Michalowski, and Stine Waibel. "Citizenship rights for immigrants: National political processes and cross-national convergence in Western Europe, 1980–2008." *American Journal of Sociology* 117, no. 4 (2012): 1202–45.

Koopmans, Ruud, Paul Statham, Marco Giugni, and Florence Passy. *Contested Citizenship. Immigration and cultural diversity in Europe*. Minneapolis, MN: University of Minnesota Press, 2005.

Kostakopoulou, Dora. "Why naturalisation?" *Perspectives on European Politics and Society* 4, no. 1 (2003): 85–115.

"Thick, thin and thinner patriotisms: Is this all there is?" *Oxford Journal of Legal Studies* 26, no. 1 (2006): 73–106.

"Introduction." In *A Re-Definition of Belonging? Language and integration tests in Europe*, edited by Ricky van Oers, Eva Ersbøll and Dora Kostakopoulou, 1–23. Leiden; Boston: Martinus Nijhoff, 2010.

"Matters of control: Integration tests, naturalisation reform and probationary citizenship in the United Kingdom." *Journal of Ethnic and Migration Studies* 36, no. 5 (2010): 829–46.

"The anatomy of civic integration." *Modern Law Review* 73, no. 6 (2010): 933–58.

Krzyzanowski, Michal, and Ruth Wodak. *The Politics of Exclusion: Debating migration in Austria*. New Brunswick, NJ: Transaction Publishers, 2009.

Kymlicka, Will. *Politics in the Vernacular: Nationalism, multiculturalism, and citizenship*. Oxford, UK; New York: Oxford University Press, 2001.

"The rise and fall of multiculturalism? New debates on inclusion and accommodation in diverse societies." *International Social Science Journal* 61, no. 199 (2010): 97–112.

"Multiculturalism: Success, failure, and the future." Washington, DC: Migration Policy Institute, 2012.

Laver, Michael, and Ian Budge. *Party Policy and Government Coalitions*. New York: St. Martin's Press, 1992.

Laver, Michael, Kenneth Benoit, and Nicolas Sauger. "Policy competition in the 2002 French legislative and presidential elections." *European Journal of Political Research* 45, no. 4 (2006): 667–97.

"Le refus de Nationalité pour "défaut d'assimilation"." *Le Nouvel Observateur*, June 10, 2011.

Lechner, Frank J. *The Netherlands: Globalization and national identity*. New York: Routledge, 2008.

Lijphart, Arend. *The Politics of Accommodation: Pluralism and democracy in the Netherlands*. Berkeley: University of California Press, 1968.

Lipset, Seymour Martin, and Stein Rokkan. *Party Systems and Voter Alignments: Cross-national perspectives*. New York: Free Press, 1967.

Lucassen, Leo. *The Immigrant Threat: The integration of old and new migrants in Western Europe since 1850*. Urbana: University of Illinois Press, 2005.

Löwenheim, Oded, and Orit Gazit. "Power and examination: A critique of citizenship yests." *Security Dialogue* 40, no. 2 (2009): 145–67.

Mahoney, James. "After KKV: The new methodology of qualitative research." *World Politics* 62, no. 1 (2009): 120–47.

Mahoney, James, and Kathleen Ann Thelen. *Explaining Institutional Change: Ambiguity, agency, and power*. Cambridge: Cambridge University Press, 2010.

Mann, Michael. "The social cohesion of liberal democracy." *American Sociological Review* 35, no. 3 (1970): 423–39.

The Rise and Decline of the Nation State. Cambridge, MA: Blackwell, 1990.

Mariani, Thierry. "Rapport sur les politiques d'intégration des migrants dans l'Union Européenne." In *Report 3502 of the National Assembly*, 2006.

Marks, Gary, and Marco Steenbergen. "Understanding political contestation in the European Union." *Comparative Political Studies* 35, no. 8 (2002): 879–92.

Marshall, Thomas. *Citizenship and Social Class and Other Essays*. Cambridge, UK: Cambridge University Press, 1950.

May, Theresa. "The Home Secretary's immigration speech." November 5, 2010. http://www.homeoffice.gov.uk (accessed February 2, 2014).

McGhee, Derek. *The End of Multiculturalism? Terrorism, integration and human rights*. Milton Keynes: Open University Press, 2008.

"The paths to citizenship: A critical examination of immigration policy in Britain since 2001." *Patterns of Prejudice* 43, no. 1 (2009): 41–64.

Meer, Nasar, and Tariq Modood. "The multicultural state we're in: Muslims, 'multi-culture' and the 'civic re-balancing' of British multiculturalism." *Political Studies* 57, no. 3 (2008): 473–97.

Messina, Anthony M. *The Logics and Politics of Post-WWII Migration to Western Europe*. Cambridge: Cambridge University Press, 2007.

Michalowski, Ines. "Integration tests in Germany: A communitarian approach?" In *A Re-Definition of Belonging? Language and integration tests in Europe*, edited by Ricky van Oers, Eva Ersbøll, and Dora Kostakopoulou, 185–210. Leiden; Boston: Martinus Nijhoff, 2010.

"Required to assimilate? The content of citizenship tests in five countries." *Citizenship Studies* 15, no. 6/7 (2011): 749–68.

Migration Policy Group. "*The Migrant Integration Policy Index (MIPEX)*." Migration Policy Group & British Council, 2011.

Miller, David. *On Nationality*. Oxford: Oxford University Press, 1997.

Milward, Alan S. *The European Rescue of the Nation-State*. London; New York: Routledge, 2000.

Ministry of Justice (the Netherlands). *Wet Inburgering Nieuwkomers* (Newcomers Integration Act). The Hague, 1998.

The Civic Integration Abroad Act: Information package. Den Haag, 2006.

Ministry of Refugee Immigration and Integration Affairs (Denmark). *Denmark Past and Present*, edited by Ministry of Refugee Immigration and Integration Affairs (Denmark), 2007.

"New to Denmark." Available at http://www.nyidanmark.dk/en-us/frontpage.htm (accessed June 18, 2013).

Ministry of Social Affairs Children and Integration (Denmark). *Fakta Om Integration: Status Og Udvikling*. Copenhagen: Schultzboghandel, 2011.

Money, Jeannette. *Fences and Neighbors: The political geography of immigration control*. Ithaca, NY: Cornell University Press, 1999.

Mouritsen, Per. "The particular universalism of a Nordic civic nation: Common values, state religion and Islam in Danish political culture." In *Multiculturalism, Muslims and Citizenship: A European approach*, edited by Tariq Modood, Anna Triandafyllidou, and Ricard Zapata-Barrero, 70–93. London: Routledge, 2006.

"Political responses to cultural conflict: Reflections on the ambiguities of the civic turn." In *Constituting Communities. Political solutions to cultural conflict*, edited by Per Mouritsen and Knud Erik Jørgensen, 1–30. London: Palgrave, 2008.
"Beyond post-national citizenship: Access, consequence, conditionality." In *European Multiculturalisms*, edited by Anna Triandafyllidou, Tariq Modood, and Nasar Meer, 88–115. Edinburgh: Edinburgh University Press, 2011.
Mouritsen, Per, and Tore Vincents Olsen. "Denmark between liberalism and nationalism." *Ethnic and Racial Studies* 36, no. 4 (2013): 691–710.
Müller, Jan-Werner. "Is Europe converging on constitutional patriotism? (and if so: is it justified?)." *Critical Review of International Social and Political Philosophy* 10, no. 3 (2007): 377–87.
Müller, Jan-Werner, and Kim Lane Scheppele. "Constitutional patriotism: An introduction." *International Journal of Constitutional Law* 6, no. 1 (2008): 67–71.
Nascimbene, Bruno. *Nationality Laws in the European Union = Le droit de la nationalité dans l'Union Européenne.* Milano; [London]: A. Giuffrè; Butterworths, 1996.
Noiriel, Gérard. *The French Melting Pot: Immigration, citizenship, and national identity.* Minneapolis: University of Minnesota Press, 1996.
OECD. *International Migration Outlook: SOPEMI 2003*. Paris: OECD Publishing, 2003.
International Migration Outlook: SOPEMI 2008. Paris: OECD Publishing, 2008.
International Migration Outlook: SOPEMI 2011. Paris: OECD Publishing, 2011.
International Migration Outlook:SOPEMI 2013. Paris: OECD Publishing, 2013.
Oldfield, Adrian. *Citizenship and Community: Civic republicanism and the modern world*: London: Routledge, 1990.
Orgad, Liav. "Illiberal liberalism: Cultural restrictions on migration and access to citizenship in Europe." *American Journal of Comparative Law* 58, no. 1 (2010): 53–106.
Palmowski, Jan. "In search of the German nation: Citizenship and the challenge of integration." *Citizenship Studies* 12, no. 6 (2008): 547–63.
Pascouau, Yves. "Country Report France." In *The INTEC Project: Integration and naturalisation tests: The new way to European citizenship*. Nijmegen, the Netherlands: Centre for Migration Law, Radboud University, 2010.
"Integration measures in France: An evolving process between integration and migration issues." In *A Re-Definition of Belonging? Language and integration tests in Europe*, edited by Ricky van Oers, Eva Ersbøll, and Theodora Kostakopoulou, 153–84. Leiden; Boston: Martinus Nijhoff, 2010.
Pautz, Hartwig. "The politics of identity in Germany: The Leitkultur debate." *Race & Class* 46, no. 4 (2005): 39–52.
Peach, Ceri, and Relations Institute of Race. *West Indian Migration to Britain: A social geography*. London; New York: Oxford University Press, 1968.
Peled, Yoav. "Ethnic democracy and the legal construction of citizenship: Arab citizens of the Jewish state." *The American Political Science Review* 86, no. 2 (1992): 432–43.
Perchinig, Bernhard. "All you need to know to become an Austrian: Naturalisation policy and citizenship testing in Austria." In *A Re-Definition of Belonging? Language and integration tests in Europe*, edited by Ricky van Oers, Eva Ersbøll, and Dora Kostakopoulou, 25–50. Leiden; Boston: Martinus Nijhoff, 2010.
"Country Report Austria." In *The INTEC Project: Integration and naturalisation tests: The new way to European citizenship*. Nijmegen, the Netherlands: Centre for Migration Law, Radboud University, 2010.

Permoser, Julia Mourão. "Civic integration as symbolic politics: Insights from Austria." *European Journal of Migration and Law* 14, no. 2 (2012): 173–98.

"Redefining membership: European Union policy on the rights of third-country nationals." Ph.D. Dissertation, University of Vienna, 2010.

Pettigrew, Thomas F. "Intergroup contact theory." *Annual Review of Psychology* 49, no. 1 (1998): 65–85.

Pierson, Paul. "When effect becomes cause: Policy feedback and political change." *World Politics* 45, no. 4 (1993): 595–628.

Politics in Time: History, institutions, and social analysis. Princeton: Princeton University Press, 2004.

Pollard, Stephen. *David Blunkett*. London: Hodder & Stoughton, 2005.

Prantl, Heribert. "Alle Muslime Sind Verdaechtig." *Süddeutsche.de*, May 17, 2010.

Putnam, Robert D. *Bowling Alone: The collapse and revival of American community*. New York: Simon & Schuster, 2000.

Putnam, Robert D., and David E. Campbell. *American Grace: How religion divides and unites us*. New York: Simon & Schuster, 2010.

Reeskens, Tim, and Wim van Oorschot. "Disentangling the 'New Liberal Dilemma': On the relation between general welfare redistribution preferences and welfare chauvinism." *International Journal of Comparative Sociology* 53, no. 2 (2012)120–39.

Ryan, Bernard. "Integration requirements: A new model in migration law." *Journal of Immigration, Asylum and Nationality Law* 22, no. 4 (2008): 303–16.

Rydgren, Jens. "Explaining the emergence of radical right-wing populist parties: The case of Denmark." *West European Politics* 27, no. 3 (2004): 474–502.

Sainsbury, Diane. *Welfare States and Immigrant Rights: The politics of inclusion and exclusion*. Oxford: Oxford University Press, 2012.

Sartori, Giovanni. "Concept misformation in comparative politics." *American Political Science Review* 64, no. 4 (1970): 1033–53.

Sawyer, Caroline. "The United Kingdom." *EUDO Citizenship Country Reports*. Florence: EUDO Citizenship, Robert Schuman Centre for Advanced Studies, EUI, 2010.

Schain, Martin A. "The extreme-right and immigration policy-making: Measuring direct and indirect effects." *West European Politics* 29, no. 2 (2006): 270–89.

"The state strikes back: Immigration policy in the European Union." *European Journal of International Law* 20, no. 1 (2009): 93–109.

Scheffer, Paul. *Immigrant Nations*. Cambridge, UK; Malden, MA: Polity, 2011.

Schierup, Carl-Ulrik, Peo Hansen, and Stephen Castles. *Migration, Citizenship, and the European Welfare State: A European dilemma*. Oxford: Oxford University Press, 2006.

Schnapper, Dominique. *Community of Citizens: On the modern idea of nationality*. New Brunswick, NJ: Transaction Publishers, 1998.

Scholten, P. W. A., Han Entzinger, Eleonore Kofman, Christina Hollomey, and Claudia Lechner. "Integration from Abroad? Perception and Impacts of Pre-Entry Tests for Third Country Nationals." In *Promoting Sustainable Policies for Integration (PROSINT)*, edited by ICMPD, 2012.

Scholten, Peter, and Ronald Holzhacker. "Bonding, bridging and ethnic minorities in the Netherlands: Changing discourses in a changing nation." *Nations and Nationalism* 15, no. 1 (2009): 81–100.

Schönwälder, Karen, and Triadafilos Triadafilopoulos. "A bridge or barrier to incorporation? Germany's 1999 citizenship reform in critical perspective." *German Politics & Society* 30, no. 1 (2012): 52–70.

Schuster, Liza. "Asylum seekers: Sangatte and the tunnel." *Parliamentary Affairs* 56, no. 3 (2003): 506–22.

Seawright, Jason, and John Gerring. "Case selection techniques in case study research: a menu of qualitative and quantitative options." *Political Research Quarterly* 61, no. 2 (2008): 294–308.

Seveker, Marina, and Anne Walter. "Country Report Germany." In *The INTEC Project: Integration and naturalisation tests: The new way to European citizenship*. Nijmegen, the Netherlands: Centre for Migration Law, Radboud University, 2010.

Shachar, Ayelet. *The Birthright Lottery: Citizenship and global inequality*. Cambridge, MA: Harvard University Press, 2009.

Significant. "Evaluation report integration in the Netherlands *(Evaluatierapport Inburgering in Nederland)*." Barneveld, the Netherlands: Significant, 2010.

"Monitoring the integration from abroad exam (*Monitor Inburgeringsexamen Buitenland*)." Barneveld, the Netherlands: Ministerie van Sociale Zaken en Werkgelegenheid, 2012.

Simon, Patrick. "French national identity and integration: Who belongs to the national community?" Washington, DC: Migration Policy Institute, 2012.

Smith, Anthony D. *National Identity*. Reno: University of Nevada Press, 1991.

Smith, Rogers M. "The "American creed" and American identity: The limits of liberal citizenship in the United States." *Western Political Quarterly* 41, no. 2 (1988): 225–51.

Civic Ideals: Conflicting visions of citizenship in US History. New Haven, CT: Yale University Press, 1999.

"Citizenship and the politics of people-building." *Citizenship Studies* 5, no. 1 (2001): 73–96.

"Citizenship: political." In *International Encyclopedia of the Social & Behavioral Sciences*, edited by Neil J. Smelser and Paul Baltes, 1857–60. New York: Pergamon, 2001.

Stories of Peoplehood: The politics and morals of political membership. Cambridge, UK: Cambridge University Press, 2003.

Somerville, Will, and Sara Wallace Goodman. "The role of networks in the development of UK migration policy." *Political Studies* 58, no. 5 (2010): 951–70.

Soysal, Yasemin. *Limits of Citizenship: Migrants and postnational membership in Europe*. Chicago: University of Chicago Press, 1994.

Spiro, Peter J. *Beyond Citizenship: American identity after globalization*. Oxford; New York: Oxford University Press, 2008.

Stasi, Bernard. "Rapport au President de la republique. Rapport de la commission de reflexion sur l'application du principe de laïcité dans la republique." Paris: La Documentation française, 2003.

Stern, Joachim, and Gerd Valchars. "Naturalisation procedures for immigrants: Austria." In *EUDO Citizenship Observatory Naturalisation Procedures Reports*. Florence: EUDO Citizenship, Robert Schuman Centre for Advanced Studies, EUI, 2013.

Stouten, J., and M. Bring. "Doorstroom Praktijkexamen Inburgering." Amsterdam: Regioplan, 2010.

Strik, Tineke, Anita Böcker, Maaike Luiten, and Ricky van Oers. "Synthesis report." In *The INTEC Project: Integration and naturalisation tests: The new way to European citizenship*. Nijmegen, the Netherlands: Centre for Migration Law, Radboud University, 2010.

Strik, Tineke, Maaike Luiten, and Ricky van Oers. "Country Report the Netherlands." In *The INTEC Project: Integration and naturalisation tests: The new way to European citizenship*. Nijmegen, the Netherlands: Centre for Migration Law, Radboud University, 2010.

Tarrow, Sidney. "The strategy of paired comparison: Toward a theory of practice." *Comparative Political Studies* 43, no. 2 (2010): 230–59.

Thelen, Kathleen. "How institutions evolve: Insights from comparative historical analysis." In *Comparative Historical Analysis in the Social Sciences*, edited by James Mahoney and Dietrich Rueschemeyer, 208–40. Cambridge, UK: Cambridge University Press, 2003.

Thelen, Kathleen Ann, and Sven Steinmo. "Historical institutionalism in comparative politics." In *Structuring Politics: Historical institutionalism in comparative analysis*, edited by Sven Steinmo, Kathleen Ann Thelen, and Frank Longstreth, 1–32. Cambridge, UK: Cambridge University Press, 1992.

Tilly, Charles. *The Formation of National States in Western Europe*. Princeton, NJ: Princeton University Press, 1975.

"Introduction." In *Citizenship, Identity and Social History*, edited by Charles Tilly, 1–17. Cambridge: Cambridge University Press, 1996.

"The emergence of citizenship in France and elsewhere." In *Citizenship, Identity and Social History*, edited by Charles Tilly, 223–36. Cambridge; New York: Cambridge University Press, 1996.

Torpey, John. *The Invention of the Passport: Surveillance, citizenship, and the state*. Cambridge, UK: Cambridge University Press, 2000.

Triadafilopoulos, Phil. "Illiberal means to liberal ends? Understanding recent immigrant integration policies in Europe." *Journal of Ethnic and Migration Studies* 37, no. 6 (2011): 861–80.

Uberoi, Varun, and Tariq Modood. "Inclusive Britishness: A multiculturalist advance." *Political Studies* 61, no.1 (2012): 23–41.

UK Border Agency. "Impact assessment of pre-application English language requirements." London: Home Office, 2009.

"Impact assessment: English language requirement for spouses." London: Home Office, 2010.

van der Zwan, Arie, and Han B. Entzinger. *Beleidsopvolging Minderhedendebat*. Den Haag: Ministerie van Binnenlandse Zaken, 1994.

van Heerden, Sjoerdje, Sarah L. de Lange, Wouter van der Brug, and Meindert Fennema. "The immigration and integration debate in the Netherlands: Discursive and programmatic reactions to the rise of anti-immigration parties." *Journal of Ethnic and Migration Studies* 40, no. 1 (2014): 119–36.

van Kersbergen, Kees, and André Krouwel. "A double-edged sword! The Dutch centre-right and the 'foreigners issue'." *Journal of European Public Policy* 15, no. 3 (2008): 398–414.

van Oers, Ricky. "Citizenship tests in the Netherlands, Germany and the UK." In *A Re-Definition of Belonging? Language and integration tests in Europe*, edited by Ricky van Oers, Eva Ersbøll, and Theodora Kostakopoulou, 51–106. Leiden; Boston: Martinus Nijhoff, 2010.

Deserving Citizenship: Citizenship tests in Germany, the Netherlands and the United Kingdom. Leiden; Boston: Martinus Nijhoff Publishers, 2013.

van Oers, Ricky, Betty de Hart, and Kees Groenendijk. "The Netherlands." In *EUDO Citizenship Observatory Country Reports*. Florence: EUDO Citizenship, Robert Schuman Centre for Advanced Studies, EUI, 2013.

van Oers, Ricky, Eva Ersbøll, and Theodora Kostakopoulou. *A Re-Definition of Belonging?: Language and integration tests in Europe*. Leiden; Boston: Martinus Nijhoff Publishers, 2010.

van Reekum, Rogier. "As nation, people and public collide: Enacting Dutchness in public discourse." *Nations and Nationalism* 18, no. 4 (2012): 583–602.

Varshney, Ashutosh. "Discovering the 'state-nation'." *Journal of Democracy* 23, no. 2 (2012): 162–66.

Vasta, Ellie. "From ethnic minorities to ethnic majority policy: Multiculturalism and the shift to assimilationism in the Netherlands." *Ethnic and Racial Studies* 30, no. 5 (2007): 713–40.

Veen, Tim. "Positions and salience in European Union politics: Estimation and validation of a new dataset." *European Union Politics* 12, no. 2 (2011): 267–88.

Vertovec, Steven. "Towards post-multiculturalism? Changing communities, conditions and contexts of diversity." *International Social Science Journal* 61, no. 199 (2010): 83–95.

Vink, Maarten P. "Dutch 'multiculturalism' beyond the pillarisation myth." *Political Studies Review* 5, no. 3 (2007): 337–50.

Vink, Maarten P., and Gerard-Rene de Groot. "Birthright citizenship: Trends and regulations in Europe." In *EUDO Citizenship Comparative Reports*. Florence: EUDO Citizenship, Robert Schuman Centre for Advanced Studies, EUI, 2010.

Waldrauch, Harald, and Christoph Hofinger. "An index to measure the legal obstacles to the integration of migrants." *New Community* 23, no. 2 (1997): 271–85.

Walzer, Michael. *Spheres of Justice: A defense of pluralism and equality*. New York: Basic Books, 1983.

What It Means to Be an American. New York: Marsilio, 1992.

Weber, Eugen. *Peasants into Frenchmen: The modernization of rural France, 1870–1914*. Stanford, CA: Stanford University Press, 1976.

Weil, Patrick, and Catherine Porter. *How to Be French: Nationality in the making since 1789*. Durham, NC: Duke University Press, 2008.

White, Patricia. "Immigrants into citizens." *The Political Quarterly* 79, no. 2 (2008): 221–31.

"Who wants a passport? Minuscule fail rate for German citizenship test." *Spiegel Online*, February 1, 2009.

Wiesbrock, Anja. "Discrimination instead of integration? Integration requirements for immigrants in Denmark and Germany." In *Illiberal Liberal States: Immigration, citizenship and integration in the EU*, edited by Elspeth Guild, Kees Groenendijk, and Sergio Carrera, 299–314. Farnham, Surrey; Burlington, VT: Ashgate, 2009.

Wright, Matthew, and Irene Bloemraad. "Is there a trade-off between multiculturalism and socio-political integration? Policy regimes and immigrant incorporation in comparative perspective." *Perspectives on Politics* 10, no. 1 (2012): 77–95.

Wright, Sue, ed. *Citizenship Tests in a Post-National Era. International Journal on Multicultural Societies*, 10, no. 1 (*UNESCO*, 2008).

Zysman, John. "How institutions create historically rooted trajectories of growth." *Industrial and Corporate Change* 3, no. 1 (1994): 243–83.

Index

active citizenship, 151, 152
Adamo, Silvia, 112, 115
Akkerman, Tjitske, 76
Anderson, Benedict, 15, 229
Australia, 7, 136
Austria
  Alliance for the Future of Austria (BZO), 92, 98, 99
  Austrian People's Party (ÖVP), 92, 94, 95, 97
  CEFR language levels, 61, 97, 99, 100
  Citizenship Act of 2006, 92, 98, 99
  citizenship policy, 28, 93–94, 100
  citizenship policy change, 95–96, 99
  CIVIX scores, 49–50, 53–55
  concept of nationhood, 93–94
  demographic context, 94
  dual citizenship, 93, 95
  entry requirements, 222–223
  Freedom Party (FPÖ), 92, 94, 95, 96, 97, 98, 99
  Green Party, 92, 95, 99
  income requirement, 47, 100
  integration agreement, 61, 96, 98, 99, 101
  language requirements, 61, 96, 99
  Liberal Forum, 95
  naturalization test, 99, 102
  permanent residence, 44, 96–97, 100, 101
  requirements for family members, 39, 102, 223
  Settlement and Residence Act of 2005, 92, 98, 100
  Social Democratic Party (SPÖ), 92, 94, 95, 99, 100

Bale, Tim, 76, 153
Balkenende, Jan Peter, 173, 177, 212
Barriers to Naturalization Index (BNI), 81, 82, 247
Bauböck, Rainer, 93
Belgium, 46, 55, 57, 63, 209
  Flanders, 51
belonging. *See* membership, 17
Ben-Ishai, Elizabeth, 240
Bertossi, Christophe, 187, 191, 199
Blair, Tony, 149, 150
Bleich, Erik, 78
Block, Laura, 209
Blunkett, David, 144, 145, 146, 147, 149, 150
Böcker, Anita, 70
Bonjour, Saskia, 176, 209
Brown, Gordon, 150, 152
Brubaker, Rogers, 22, 27, 28, 78, 121, 142, 190
Brunstetter, Daniel, 190, 193

Cameron, David, 142, 155
Canada, 7, 30, 52
Carens, Joseph, 236
Carrera, Sergio, 186
case study, 8, 119, 228
  case selection, 14
causal asymmetry, 77
causal mechanisms, 8, 14, 88, 161, 228, 234
chain of conditionality, 7, 11, 85, 91, 159, 179
Chirac, Jacques, 189, 190, 192
Çinar, Dilek, 93, 94, 96
citizenization, 3, 53

citizenship, 6
  ceremonies, 26
  concept map, 19
  declaration and registration, 20
  definitions, 6, 10, 12, 17, 18, 21, 28, 71, 78
  distinction with membership, 18–21
  dual citizenship, 10, 20, 26, 78, 79, 82, 232
  empirical distribution of policy, 80–84, *See individual country case studies*
  inherited policy, 77–79
  jus sanguinis, 20
  jus soli, 20, 28
  liberal policy, 6, 7, 82, 84
  naturalization, 20, 26, 77
  policy configurations, 86
  policy legacy. *See inherited policy*
  residency requirements, 28
  restrictive policy, 6, 82, 84
  value, 22
  variable, as a, 79
Citizenship Policy Index (CPI), 39, 81, 83, 105, 248
CITLAW, 56, 82, *See* EUDO Citizenship
civic integration
  citizenship requirements, 45–47
  concept validity, 9–10
  contracts, 45, 47
  definition, 1–2
  demographic context, 70–72
  differentiation, 10–11, 45
  entry. *See civic integration, external*
  entry requirements, 42–43, 205–206
  external, 202–203, 204, 228, *See* entry requirements
  goals, 16
  internal, 14
  settlement requirements, 43–45
  significance, 11–12
  value commitments, 46
  variation in requirement design, 61–62
  variation in requirement scope, 62–63
  variation in requirement sequencing, 63
Civic Integration Policy Index (CIVIX), 13, 37, 87, 227
  change, 55
  comparison to other indexes, 20, 59
  components, 38–40
  data sources, 48
  empirical evidence, 48–55, *See "CIVIX scores" under individual case studies*
  scoring, 13, 40–41, 42–47
  variation beyond scores, 59–63
Cohen, Job, 172, 212
Common Basic Principles, 208
Common European Framework of Reference for Languages (CEFR), 40, 243
conjunctural causation, 67, 76, 120
constitutional patriotism, 31, 46, 130, 235, 238
Crick, Bernard, 34, 145, 146, 148

Dahl, Robert, 22
Davy, Ulrike, 127
demi-citizenship, 6, 66
Denmark
  24-year rule, 110
  Aliens Act, 107
  CEFR language levels, 112, 113
  Circular on Naturalization of 2002, 111
  citizenship policy, 105–106, 111, 112, 115
  citizenship policy change, 106, 109–110, 112
  citizenship test, 34, 112, 115, 116
  CIVIX scores, 49–50, 53–55
  concept of nationhood, 104, 106
  Conservative Party, 107, 108, 109
  Danish People's Party, 104, 105, 107, 108, 109–110, 112, 115, 220
  Danish Progress Party, 107, *See Danish People's Party*
  demographic context, 106–107, 110
  dual citizenship, 106, 108, 111
  immigration exam, 42, 206, 221
  Integration Act Amendment of 2006, 112
  Integration Act of 1999, 108, 110
  integration contract, 31, 110, 112, 114
  integration course, 61, 108, 110
  language requirements, 111, 114
  Liberal Party, 106, 107, 108, 109, 111
  Ministry for Integration, 113
  permanent residence, 44, 108, 109–110, 111, 112, 113
  points-based system, 61, 112, 114
  requirements for family members, 108, 110
  Social Democratic Party, 107, 109, 113
  study guide, 31
Diez, Thomas, 122
diffusion, 15, 38, 211, 219, 223

English Speakers of Other Languages (ESOL), 146
equifinality, 67, 76
Erbøll, Eva, 111, 112
EUDO Citizenship, 47, 56
European Convention of Human Rights, 92

European Union (EU), 15, 22, 41, 53, 56, 82, 112, 201, 203, 207, 208, 210, 211, 220, 221
European Union Directives, 98, 135, 203, 207, 208–211, 228

far-right political parties, 13, 74, 76
Favell, Adrian, 78, 186, 190
Feldblum, Miriam, 188
Finland, 26, 29, 39, 62, 79
Fortuyn, Pim, 173
France
  assimilation, 29, 69, 162, 184, 187
  assimilation requirement, 29, 62, 187, 188, 195, 198
  CEFR language levels, 187, 188, 193
  citizenship policy, 29, 185–186, 198
  citizenship policy change, 188–191
  CIVIX scores, 49–50, 53–55
  cohabitation, 192
  concept of nationhood, 186–188
  demographic context, 188–189
  dual citizenship, 186
  entry requirements, 42, 206, 223
  French identity debate of 2009, 30, 196
  High Council on Integration, 190, 191
  Hortefeux Law of 2008, 223
  information session, 42, 59, 162, 191, 193, 194, 197
  integration contract, 30, 62, 88, 184, 192, 193–194, 195, 196, 223
  laïcité, 187
  language requirements, 184, 192, 193, 194, 197, 198
  Ministry of Immigration, 196
  National Front, 185, 187, 188, 190, 196, 201
  oath, 29
  Pasqua Law of 1986, 189
  permanent residence, 192
  republicanism, 184, 186, 187, 200
  requirements for family members, 194, 196, 223
  Sarkozy Law of 2003, 192, 194, 197
  Sarkozy Law of 2006, 88, 194, 196
  Socialist Party, 88, 189, 191, 195, 197, 210
  Union for a Popular Movement (UMP), 192, 210

Germany
  "ethnic-Germans," 53, 123
  "Muslim test," 134
  Aliens Act of 1990, 53, 123
  Aussiedler, 49, 57, 123, 124, *See "ethnic Germans"*
  Baden-Württemberg, 134
  CEFR language levels, 119, 131, 133, 136, 221
  Christian Democratic Union (CDU/CSU), 120, 126, 128, 130, 134, 221
  Christian Social Union (CSU), 126, 130, *See Christian Democratic Union (CDU/CSU)*
  Citizenship Act of 1999, 83, 120, 122, 124, 128, 133, 139
  citizenship policy, 28, 120, 121–122
  citizenship policy change, 120, 122–123, 126–129, 133–135
  citizenship test, 3, 133–135, 136, 137, 236
  civic orientation course, 43, 61, 131
  CIVIX scores, 49–50, 53–55
  concept of nationhood, 122–124
  demographic context, 124–126
  dual citizenship, 122, 127
  entry requirements, 42, 204, 221–222
  federal system, 120, 132, 134
  Free Democratic Party (FDP), 127
  Green Party, 118, 120, 126
  guest worker scheme, 125
  Hesse, 127, 134
  Immigration Act of 2004, 120, 131, 133
  integration course, 131, 136
  integration funding, 132
  Interior Ministers Conference (IMK), 134
  language requirements, 53, 123, 127, 131, 133
  Leitkultur, 78, 130
  Naturalization Guidelines of 1977, 29, 52, 121
  Optionsmodell, 122, 127
  permanent residence, 43, 123, 131, 137, 138
  positive sanctions, 131–132
  role of courts, 133
  role of opposition, 120, 138
  Social Democratic Party (SPD), 118, 120, 126, 128
  social welfare benefits, suspension of, 132
  Spätaussiedler, 124
  Süssmuth Commission, 129, 130
  test content, 1, 31, 135
  value commitments, 29, 128, 134
Goethe Institute, 42, 221
Goodman, Sara Wallace, 74, 248
Gravesen, Laura, 112
Greece, 3, 44, 45, 46, 48, 53, 54, 55, 59, 61, 62, 63, 79
  integration exam, 60

Greece (cont.)
  naturalization requirements, 29
  oaths, 29
Green, Simon, 121, 125, 126, 127
Groenendijk, Kees, 176, 209
guest worker "myth," 125
Guiraudon, Virginie, 192, 207

Habermas, Jürgen, 31, 235
Haider, Jörg, 92, 95
Hailbronner, Kay, 126, 137
Hajjat, Abellali, 187, 191, 199
Hall, Peter, 86
Hampshire, James, 153
Hansen, Randall, 33, 78, 142
Hartnell, Helen, 127
Headscarf Affair, 184
Hollande, Françoise, 197
Howard, Marc Morjé, 39, 56, 74, 81, 126, 165, 189
Howard, Michael, 150
Human Rights Watch, 62, 214, 219

ideological orientation of governments, 75, 85
  left, 72, 74, 85
  right, 72, 74, 85
illiberal liberalism, 2, 10, 235
Independent Commission on Migration. *See Süssmuth Commission*
Indicators for Citizenship Rights of Immigrants (ICRI), 56, 81, 244, 247
  comparison to CIVIX, 56–58
inherited policy, 78, 80
INTEC, 26, 110, 171, 177, 194, 220
Ireland, 46, 55, 141, 227
Islam, 15, 169, 173, 229, 242
Israel, 19, 21, 28
Italy, 3, 20, 26, 44, 45, 46, 53, 61, 62, 63, 79, 236, 250
  oath, 29
  points-based system, 61
  Security Act of 2009, 46

Janoski, Thomas, 56, 74, 81
Joint Council for the Welfare of Immigrants (JCWI), 147
Joppke, Christian, xi, 4, 12, 19, 20, 28, 54, 68, 72, 141, 226, 234, 237, 238
Jospin, Lionel, 190, 191

kingmaker, 75, *See coalition governments*
Kiwan, Dina, 146
Klaver, Jeanine, 181
König, Karin, 95
Koopmans, Ruud, 56, 57, 81
Kostakopoulou, Dora, 12, 239, 240
Krzyzanowski, Michal, 97
Kymlicka, Will, 25, 235

Le Pen, Jean-Marie, 147, 190, 191
liberalism, 3, 4, 12, 15, 25, 32, 33, 34, 70, 104, 106, 229, 231, 235, 236, 238, 239, 240
  values, 31, 32
"logic of sameness," 17, 27, 29, 30, 32, 35
"logic of togetherness," 17, 32, 34, 184, 230
London Bombings, 149
Luxembourg, 26, 45, 46, 47, 49, 53, 55, 62, 63, 79

Marshall, T. H., 20
McGhee, Derek, 150
medium-N analysis, 8
membership
  anchoring citizenship, 232–234
  concept map, 19
  definition, 12, 17, 18
  distinction with citizenship, 18–21
  loyalty, 25–26
  requirements, 18, *See civic integration requirements*
  value, 23–26, 230
Merkel, Angela, 120
Merz, Friedrich, 130
Migrant Integration Policy Index (MIPEX), 56, 57, 105, 166, 245
  comparison to CIVIX, 57–60
Miller, David, 25
Milward, Alan, 231
Modood, Tariq, 155, 158
Morocco, 167, 215
Mouritsen, Per, xi, 5, 106, 107, 111
Müller, Jan-Werner, 235
multiculturalism, 68, 107, 141
  failure of, 68–70

national identity, 2, 3, 8, 16, 17, 21, 26, 27, 28, 47, 94, 130, 166, 229, 230, 234, 235, 242
  as requirements, 28–30
  definition, 27–30
nationalism, 2, 17, 18, 27, 52, 93, 106, 235, 238
nationality, 28, *See citizenship*
nation-building, 2, 5, 9, 18, 25, 35, 226, 230, 232, 234, 242
  thick versus thin, 25

nation-state, 7, 16, 18, 29, 35, 226, 234, 238, 242
Netherlands, the
  Aliens Act of 2000, 212
  CEFR language levels, 172, 175, 182, 217
  ceremonies, 172
  Christian Democratic Appeal (CDA), 75, 118, 165, 168, 170, 171, 173, 174, 212
  citizenship policy, 165–166
  citizenship policy change, 170–172
  Civic Integration Abroad Act of 2005, 208, 213, 216
  Civic Integration Act of 2007, 172, 174–177
  CIVIX scores, 49–50, 53–55
  concept of nationhood, 166–168
  Deltaplan of 2007, 177
  demographic context, 167
  dual citizenship, 165, 171
  Dutch Nationality Act of 1985, 168
  Dutch Nationality Act of 2003, 170, 172
  financing, 61, 178
  Freedom Party (PVV), 178
  inburgering, 3, 163
  income requirement, 180
  integration course, 170
  integration exam, 1, 44, 172, 175–176, 178, 180
  Integration from Abroad exam, 42, 205, 213
  Labour Party (PvdA), 75, 165, 169, 172, 177, 212, 216
  language requirement, 41, 170, 171, 172, 178
  Liberal Party (VVD), 75, 169, 171, 174, 212
  Minorities Policy, 165, 168
  model for other states, 96, 129, 162, 170, 204, 219, 220, 228
  multiculturalism, 162, 168, 169, 172–173
  naturalization ceremony, 61
  naturalization test, 172, 179
  Newcomers Civic Integration Act of 1998, 3, 23, 48, 162, 170
  permanent residence, 175, 176, 180
  pillarization, 167–168
  Pim Fortuyn List (LPF), 173, 174, 201, 212
  requirements for family members, 213, 216
  role of the far-right, 173–174, 178
  Scientific Council for Government Policy (WRR), 168
  Social Democrats (D66), 75, 169, 174, 212
  test content, 31
  test preparation, 33, 61

oath, 25, 29, 33, 47, 56, 142, 189
Ode, Arend, 181
Oldfield, Adrian, 236
Olsen, Tore Vincents, 106, 107, 111
Orgad, Liav, 31
Osborne, George, 154

Pascouau, Yves, 199
path dependence, 13
Pautz, Hartwig, 130
Pearce, Nick, 144
Perchinig, Bernhard, 44, 95, 96, 99, 103
permanent residence, 79, 85, 91
Permoser, Julia Mourão, 97
policy drift, 69
policy learning, 11, 38, 63, 204, 219
policy transfer, 204
populism, 13, 95
Portugal, 39, 55, 62
postnationalism, 7, 77

repressive liberalism, 2, 235
retrenchment, 91, 92, 105
Ryan, Bernard, 152
Rydgren, Jens, 107, 110

Sarkozy, Nicolas, 69, 192, 193, 196, 223
Sawyer, Caroline, 142, 143
Schain, Martin, 207
Scheffer, Paul, 173
Schily, Otto, 130
Simon, Patrick, 195
Simonsen, Torkild, 108
Skocpol, Theda, 241
Smith, Anthony, 27
Smith, Rogers, 18, 24, 34, 230
social cohesion, 17, 21, 23–24, 144, *see membership value*
  definition, 23
Soysal, Yasemin, 18
Spain, 45, 47, 48, 55, 59, 62, 250
  draft bill for integration test, 38
Spencer, Sarah, 145
Spiro, Peter, 28
Squire, Vicki, 122
state identity, 2, 3, 8, 15, 16, 17, 26, 27, 30, 34, 91, 118, 159, 184, 229, 230, 239
  conflicts with liberalism, 32–33
  definition, 30
  differentiation with national identity, 2–3
  requirements of, 30–31, 32, *See civic integration requirements*
status, 79, *See* citizenship
Strike, Tineke, 70

supranationalism, 7
Süssmuth, Rita, 130
Sweden, 26, 41, 46, 55, 209, 227, 252, 254

Tilly, Charles, 21, 28, 71
Torpey, John, 22
transnationalism, 7
Turkey, 94, 125, 167, 215

United Kingdom, 69
  "cricket test," 154
  "two-path" approach, 44, 146, 153, 156
  active citizenship, 34, 236
  Borders, Citizenship and Immigration Act (BCIA) of 2009, 139, 151
  British National Party, 147, 150
  British Nationality Act (BNA) of 1948, 142
  British Nationality Act (BNA) of 1981, 141, 142
  Britishness, 79, 141, 143, 148, 155, *See concept of nationhood*
  Cantle Report, 144
  CEFR language levels, 153
  citizenship acquisition rates, 156
  citizenship ceremony, 29, 146, 149
  citizenship curriculum for schools, 145–146
  citizenship policy, 141
  citizenship policy change, 149, 151
  citizenship test change, 154–155
  CIVIX scores, 49–50, 53–55
  coalition government, 34, 151, 152, 154, 158
  concept of nationhood, 139, 141–143
  Conservative Party, 139, 150, 151, 154, 159
  Council for Racial Equality, 145
  demographic context, 143
  Department for Communities and Local Government, 145
  dual citizenship, 141
  entry requirements, 42, 205, 222
  Home Office, 144, 145, 149
  Labour Party, 75, 118, 139, 143, 144, 145, 151, 152, 154, 160
  language requirements, 141, 146, 153
  Liberal Democratic Party, 153
  Life in the UK Advisory group, 148
  Life in the UK Handbook, 30, 157
  Life in the UK test, 1, 34, 44, 46, 146, 148, 151, 153, 154, 155–156
  London Bombings, 151
  multiculturalism, 143, 144
  Nationality, Immigration and Asylum Act (NIA) of 2002, 146
  Northern Riots, 144
  permanent residence, 149, 151, 152
  probationary citizenship, 151
  role of public opinion, 147, 151
  subjecthood, 142
  The New and the Old, 17
  United Kingdom Independence Party, 155, 159
United States, 3, 7, 21, 26, 30, 34, 52, 136, 236, 237
  oath, 29

Van Gogh, Theo, 212
van Oers, Ricky, 182
van Reekum, Rogier, 166, 167
Verdonk, Rita, 177, 208, 212
Vink, Maarten, 163

Weber, Max, 27
Weil, Patrick, 191, 198
welfare chauvinism, 71
welfare state, 70
Wiesbrock, Anja, 114
Wilders, Geert, 178
Wodak, Ruth, 97

www.ingramcontent.com/pod-product-compliance
Ingram Content Group UK Ltd.
Pitfield, Milton Keynes, MK11 3LW, UK
UKHW021829030125
452957UK00015B/70

9 781107 635852